CW01429134

The Badminton Library

OF

SPORTS AND PASTIMES

EDITED BY

HIS GRACE THE DUKE OF BEAUFORT, K.G.

ASSISTED BY ALFRED E. T. WATSON

CRICKET

CAUGHT AND BOWLED

CRICKET

BY

A. G. STEEL

AND THE

HON. R. H. LYTTELTON

WITH CONTRIBUTIONS BY

A. LANG, W. G. GRACE, R. A. H. MITCHELL, AND F. GALE

WITH NUMEROUS ENGRAVINGS AFTER LUCIEN DAVIS
AND FROM PHOTOGRAPHS

ASHFORD PRESS PUBLISHING
SOUTHAMPTON
1987

Published by   ASHFORD PRESS PUBLISHING 1987
                 1 CHURCH ROAD
                 SHEDFIELD
                 HAMPSHIRE SO3 2HW

First published in 1888
Republished 1987

Introductory Note © 11th Duke of Beaufort 1985

British Library Cataloguing in Publication Data

Steel, A.G.
    Cricket.—(The Badminton library of sports and pastimes).
    1. Cricket
    I. Title   II. Lyttelton, R.H.   III. Series
    796.35'8   GV917

    ISBN 1-85253-014-6

Printed and bound in Great Britain

Introductory Note

My great great-grandfather, the 8th Duke of Beaufort, was always proud to say that he had been instrumental in bringing about one of the great sporting achievements of this century. In 1882, he and his great friend, Alfred Watson, set about compiling The Badminton Library, a series of books that would attempt to highlight, examine and explain all of the many great sports that this nation enjoys. The aim was simple; the Library was to become an encyclopaedia of sport that would supply basic information to all amateur sportsmen.

As a result of their work some 23 volumes were published that covered all sorts of activities: Hunting, of course, a subject always very close to my family's heart; Fishing; Racing and Steeplechasing; Lawn Tennis; Shooting; Driving; Athletics; Football, and even Cycling and Motor Driving. For each volume the most influential specialists were asked to impart their particular expertise, and indeed many of these are still remembered today for their sporting achievements. I think particularly of Lord Brassey on Yachting, Lord Walsingham on Shooting and the 8th Duke of Beaufort himself on Driving and Hunting – but the list of names is endless and each has a claim to our attention.

The finest illustrators were also eager to add their contribution: Archibald Thorburn and A.C. Sealy are notable examples. And so a magnificent sporting library was born, created from the greatest talents and with the immense tradition of Badminton firmly behind it. As might have been expected, the Library was a huge success. During the years it has gained great respect and instant recognition all over the world, and the books, although somewhat rare now, are still very much sought-after.

My great great-grandfather was more than the notional editorial figure-head that some might wrongly imagine. He worked enthusiastically to cull the best talents available and to edit them into a series of readable, entertaining volumes. He was rightly very proud of his part in commissioning and compiling the Library: it has remained one of his greatest achievements.

The reissue of the Library is long overdue; it could not have come at a better time. Far from losing its popularity, sport is now once again at its height. Television has had a major impact and modern day lifestyles have enabled many more people to participate in and enjoy sport at both amateur and professional levels.

At the same time, sport in its truest sense is threatened today by many evils that my great great-grandfather would never have imagined – hooliganism, financial influences, drugs, politics, and even terrorism. Let us hope that the best of sport will survive and that the reissue of the Badminton Library will remind us of at least some of what is best in sport.

The Badminton Library offers lifetimes of experience gained by a host of illustrious sportsmen, and provides a fascinating insight into the traditions and rites of the sports as they were enjoyed so many years ago.

It has now fallen to me to follow in the family tradition, and I take great pleasure in being able to help re-launch the Badminton Library. In introducing it I hope I have managed to convey just a fraction of the enthusiasm with which my family has always regarded these volumes.

I commend the Badminton Library to a new generation of sportsmen and women; hopefully they will gain as much pleasure from reading these volumes as I have; and undoubtedly they will increase their abilities by listening to the great mass of advice and anecdotes offered by such an esteemed selection of our great sporting forebears.

The 11th Duke of Beaufort
June 1985

DEDICATION

TO

H.R.H. THE PRINCE OF WALES.

———◆◇◆———

BADMINTON : *June*, 1888.

HAVING received permission to dedicate these volumes, the BADMINTON LIBRARY of SPORTS and PASTIMES, to HIS ROYAL HIGHNESS THE PRINCE OF WALES, I do so feeling that I am dedicating them to one of the best and keenest sportsmen of our time. I can say, from personal observation, that there is no man who can extricate himself from a bustling and pushing crowd of horsemen, when a fox breaks covert, more dexterously and quickly than His Royal Highness ; and that when hounds run hard over a big country, no man can take a line of his own and live with them better. Also, when the wind has been blowing hard, often have I seen His Royal Highness knocking over driven grouse and partridges and high-rocketing pheasants in first-rate workmanlike style. He is held to be a good yachtsman, and as Commodore of the Royal Yacht Squadron is looked up to by those who love that pleasant and exhilarating pastime. His encouragement of racing is well known, and his attendance at the University, Public School, and other important Matches testifies to his being, like most English gentlemen, fond of all manly sports. I consider it a great privilege to be allowed to dedicate these volumes to so eminent a sportsman as His Royal Highness the Prince of Wales, and I do so with sincere feelings of respect and esteem and loyal devotion.

BEAUFORT.

PREFACE.

A FEW LINES only are necessary to explain the object
with which these volumes are put forth. There is no
modern encyclopædia to which the inexperienced man,
who seeks guidance in the practice of the various British
Sports and Pastimes, can turn for information. Some
books there are on Hunting, some on Racing, some
on Lawn Tennis, some on Fishing, and so on ; but one
Library, or succession of volumes, which treats of the
Sports and Pastimes indulged in by Englishmen—and
women—is wanting. The Badminton Library is offered
to supply the want. Of the imperfections which must
be found in the execution of such a design we are
conscious. Experts often differ. But this we may say,
that those who are seeking for knowledge on any of the
subjects dealt with will find the results of many years'
experience written by men who are in every case adepts
at the Sport or Pastime of which they write. It is to

point the way to success to those who are ignorant of the sciences they aspire to master, and who have no friend to help or coach them, that these volumes are written.

To those who have worked hard to place simply and clearly before the reader that which he will find within, the best thanks of the Editor are due. That it has been no slight labour to supervise all that has been written he must acknowledge ; but it has been a labour of love, and very much lightened by the courtesy of the Publisher, by the unflinching, indefatigable assistance of the Sub-Editor, and by the intelligent and able arrangement of each subject by the various writers, who are so thoroughly masters of the subjects of which they treat. The reward we all hope to reap is that our work may prove useful to this and future generations.

THE EDITOR.

CONTENTS.

ILLUSTRATIONS.

(ENGRAVED BY J. D. COOPER AND R. B. LODGE, AFTER DRAWINGS
BY LUCIEN DAVIS, AND PHOTOGRAPHS BY G. MITCHELL, MARTIN
& TYLER, AND MEDRINGTON & CO.)

———◆———

FULL-PAGE ILLUSTRATIONS.

WOODCUTS IN TEXT.

A YOUNG CRICKETER

(From a Picture ascribed to Gainsborough belonging to the M.C.C.)

CRICKET.

———◆———

CHAPTER I.

THE HISTORY OF CRICKET.

(BY ANDREW LANG.)

Archæology of the Game.

HUNDREDS of pages have been written on the origin and early history of Cricket. The Egyptian monuments and Holy Scriptures, the illuminated books of the Middle Ages, and the terra-cottas and vases of Greece have been studied, to no practical purpose, by historians of the game. Outside of England,[1] and before the fortieth year of the reign of Elizabeth, there are no documents for the existence of cricket. Doubtless in rudimentary and embryonic forms, it may have existed. Of those forms we still possess a few, as 'rounders' and 'stool-ball,' and we can also study degraded shapes of cricket, which naturally revert to the early germs of the pastime as degenerate human types throw back to the monkey. There is a sport known at some schools as stump-cricket,' 'snob-cricket,' or (mysteriously and locally) as ' Dex,'[2] which is a degenerate shape of the game, and which is probably very like the rudimentary shapes. These degradations are reversals or returns to primitive forms.

[1] Outside of England Mrs. Piozzi found ' a game called *Pallamajo*, something like our cricket.' If she meant *Pallone*, she merely proved herself no cricketer. Mr. Arthur Evans has noticed, in Dalmatia, a kind of trap-bat, a ' cat' being used in place of a ball, and the length of hits being measured by the stick that serves as bat.

[2] The learned have debated as to the origin of the local term 'Dex.' Let it suffice to say that it is not what they suppose.

A ball, more or less light and soft, is bowled or tossed at any fixed object, which, in turn, is defended by a player armed with a stick, stump, hair-brush, or other instrument. The player counts as many points as he can run backwards and forwards, after hitting the ball, between the object he defends and some more or less distant goal, before the ball is returned. He loses his position when the object he defends is struck by the ball, or when the ball is caught, after he has hit it, before touching the ground. Such is the degraded form of cricket, and such, apparently, was its earliest shape. Ancient surviving forms in which a similar principle exists are ' rounders ' and ' stool-ball.' The former has been developed in America into the scientific game of ' base-ball,' the name being Old English, while the scientific perfection is American. It is impossible to trace cricket farther back than games in which points are scored in proportion to the amount of ground that the hitter can cover before the return of the struck ball. Now other forms of ball-play, as tennis, in different guises, can be found even among the ancient Aztecs,[1] while the Red Indians practised the form which is hockey among us, and the French and Walloons have sports very closely corresponding to golf ; but games with the slightest analogy to cricket are very rare. Stool-ball is the most important foreshadowing of cricket. As early as 1614, Chapman, in his translation of the sixth book of the ' Odyssey,' makes Nausicaa and her girls play stool-ball. Chapman gives certain technical terms, which, of course, have nothing corresponding to them in Homer, but which are valuable illustrations of the English game.

Nausicaa seems to have received a trial ball—

> Nausicaa, with the wrists of ivory,
> The *liking-stroke* struck.

Again,

> The Queen now, for the upstroke, struck the ball
> Quite *wide* of th' other maids, and made it fall
> Amidst the whirlpools.

[1] See M. de Charnay's *Ancient Cities of the New World*, p. 96. London, 1887.

thereby, doubtless, scoring a lost ball. He describes this as 'a stool-ball chance.' Chapman does not say whether the ball was bowled to Nausicaa. Everything shows that Dr. Johnson was writing at random when he described stool-ball as a game 'in which a ball is driven from stool to stool.' Chapman conceives Nausicaa as making a 'boundary hit.' There would be no need of such hitting if balls were only 'driven from stool to stool.'

Strutt's remarks on stool-ball merely show that he did not appreciate the importance of the game as an early form of cricket. 'I have been informed,' he says, 'that a pastime called stool-ball is practised to this day in the northern parts of England, which consists simply in setting a stool upon the ground, and one of the players takes his place before it, while his antagonist, standing at a distance, tosses a ball with the intention of striking the stool, and this it is the business of the former to prevent by beating it away with his hand, reckoning one to the game for every stroke of the ball,' apparently without running. 'If, on the contrary, it should be missed by the hand and strike the stool, the players change places.' Strutt adds, in a note, that he believes the player may be caught out. He describes another game in which stools are set as 'bases' in a kind of base-ball. He makes the usual quotations from Durfey about 'a match for kisses at stool-ball to play.' [1]

Brand's notes on stool-ball do no more than show that men and women played for small wagers, as in Herrick,

> At stool-ball, Lucia, let us play
> For sugar, cakes, and wine. [2]

It is plain enough that stool-ball was a game for girls, or for boys and girls, and Herrick and Lucia. As at present played stool-ball is a woman's game ; but no stool is used : what

[1] Strutt's *Sports and Pastimes*, 1810, pp. 89, 90 ; cf. Durfey's *Pills to Purge Melancholy*, i. 91.

[2] *Popular Antiquities*, i. 153, *note*. London, 1813. The lines are quoted by Brand from *A Pleasant Grove of New Fancies*, p. 74. London, 1657. He might have gone straight to Herrick, *Hesperides* (1648), p. 280.

answers to the wicket is a square board at a certain height on a pole, much as if one bowled at the telegraph instead of the stumps.   Consequently, as at base-ball, only full pitches can be tossed.   However, in stool-ball we recognise the unconscious beginnings of better things.   As much may be said for 'cat-and-dog.'   This may be regarded either as a degraded attempt at early cricket, played by economists who could not afford a ball, or as a natural *volks-kriket*, dating from a period of culture in which balls had not yet been invented.   The archæologist will prefer the latter explanation, but we would not pedantically insist on either alternative.   In Jamieson's 'Scotch Dictionary,'[1] cat-and-dog is described as a game for three.[2]   Two holes are cut at a distance of thirteen yards.   At each hole stands a player with a club, called a 'dog.'   A piece of wood,[3] four inches long by one in circumference, is tossed, in place of a ball, to one of the dogsmen.   His object is to keep the cat out of the hole.   'If the cat be struck, he who strikes it changes places with the person who holds the other club, and as often as the positions are changed one is counted as won in the game by the two who hold the clubs.'   Jamieson says this is an 'ancient sport in Angus and Lauder.'   A man was bowled when the cat got into the hole he defended.   We hear nothing of 'caught and bowled.'[4]

Cat-and-dog, or, more briefly, cat, was a favourite game with John Bunyan.   He was playing when a voice from heaven (as he imagined) suddenly darted into his soul, with some warning remarks, as he was 'about to strike the cat from the hole.'   The cat, here, seems to have been quiescent. 'Leaving my cat on the ground, I looked up to Heaven,' and beheld a vision.   Let it be remembered that Bunyan was playing on Sunday.   The game of cat, as known to him, was,

---

[1] Edinburgh, 1841.

[2] In married life, two are quite enough to play 'cat and dog.'

[3] Compare *Loggat.* See *Hamlet*, v. 1, and *Nares' Glossary*, s. v.

[4] Brand, ii. 287, quotes a reference to 'cat and doug' from the *Life of the Scotch Rogue.* London, 1722.   The Scotch Rogue says nothing about cricket.

apparently, rather a rude variety of knurr and spell than of cricket. This form is mentioned by Strutt.[1] Both stool-ball and cat-and-dog have closer affinities with cricket than club-ball as represented in Strutt's authorities.[2] Perhaps we may say that wherever stool-ball was played, or cat-and-dog, there cricket was potentially present. As to the derivation of the word 'cricket,' philologists differ as much as usual. Certainly 'cricket' is an old word for a stool, though in this sense it does not occur in Skeat.[3] In Todd's 'Johnson,' we find, 'Cricket: a low seat or stool, from German *kriechen*, to creep.' In Scotland we talk of a 'creepy-stool.'

> It's a wise wife that kens her weird,
> What though ye mount the creepy !

says Allan Ramsay, meaning the stool of repentance. If, then, stool-ball be the origin of cricket, and if a cricket be a stool, 'cricket' may be merely a synonym for stool-ball. Todd's 'Johnson,' with ignominious ignorance, styles cricket 'a sport in which the contenders drive a ball with sticks or bats in opposition to each other.' Johnson must have known better. In the 'Rambler,' No. 30, he writes, 'Sometimes an unlucky boy will drive his cricket-ball full in my face.' Observe, he says 'drive,' not 'cut,' nor 'hit to leg.'

Professor Skeat says nothing of this derivation of 'cricket' from cricket, a stool. He thinks 'et' may be a diminutive, added to the Anglo-Saxon *cricc*, a staff. If that be so, cricket will mean club-play rather than stool-ball. In any case, Professor Skeat has a valuable quotation of 'cricket' from the French and English Dictionary compiled in 1611, by Mr. Randle

[1] P. 101.

[2] The miniature in which a woman bowls to a back-handed player with no wicket is dated 1344. Bodl., 264. But the evidence of art is never very trustworthy. The painter may have been a woman, or a monk, or an uneducated person. Many of the pictures in modern books give a misleading view of cricket.

[3] *Etymological Dictionary*, 1882. The writer here owes a great deal to Dr. Murray, of the *English Dictionary*, who kindly lent him the 'slips' (short, of course) on Cricket, as far as they have been collected.—A. L.

Cotgrave. He translates the French *crosse*, 'a crosier, or bishop's staffe, also a *cricket staffe*, or the crooked staffe wherewith boies play at cricket.' Now the name of the club used in French Flanders at the local kind of golf is *la crosse*. It is a heavy, barbaric kind of golf-club.[1]

Thanks to Cotgrave, then, we know that in 1611 cricket was a boy's game, played with a crooked staff. The club, bat, or staff continued to be crooked or curved at the blade till the middle of the eighteenth century or later ; and till nearly 1720 cricket was mainly a game for boys. We may now examine the authorities for the earliest mentions of cricket.

People have often regarded Florio's expression in his Italian Dictionary (1598) *cricket-a-wicket* as the first mention of the noble game. It were strange indeed if this great word first dropped from the pen of an Italian ! The quotation is ' *sgrittare*, to make a noise as a cricket ; *to play cricket-a-wicket*, and be merry.' I have no doubt myself that this is a mere coincidence of sound. The cricket (on the hearth) is a merry little beast, or has that reputation. The term ' cricket-a-wicket ' is a mere rhyming reduplication of sounds like ' hob-nob ' or ' tooral-ooral,' or the older ' Torelore,' the name of a mythical country in a French romance of the twelfth century. It is an odd coincidence, no doubt, that the rhyming reduplication should associate wicket with cricket. But, for all that, ' cricket-a-wicket ' must pair off with ' helter-skelter,' ' higgledy-piggledy,' and *Tarabara* to which Florio gives cricket-a-wicket as an equivalent.[2]

Yet cricket was played in England, by boys at least, in Florio's time. The proof of this exists, or existed, in the ' Constitution Book of Guildford,' a manuscript collection of records once in the possession of that town. In the ' History of Guildford,' an anonymous compilation, published by Russell in the

---

[1] See M. Charles Deulin's tale, ' Le Grand Choleur,' in *Contes du Roi Gambrinus*. There is a good deal of information in *Germinal*, by M. Zola. The balls are egg-shaped, and of boxwood. The game is a kind of golf, played across country.

[2] Cotgrave's *French Dictionary*, ' Crosse,' 1611.

Surrey town, and by Longmans in London (1801), there are ex-
tracts from the 'Constitution Book.' They begin with a grant
anno li. Ed. III. For our purpose the only important passages
are pp. 201, 202. In the thirty-fifth year of Elizabeth one William

'Miss Wicket.' (From an old print, 1770.)

Wyntersmoll withheld a piece of common land, to the extent of
one acre, from the town. Forty years before, John Parvishe had
obtained leave to make a temporary enclosure there, and the
enclosure had never been removed. In the fortieth year of

Elizabeth this acre was still in dispute, when John Derrick, gent, aged fifty-nine, one of the Queen's Coroners for the county, gave evidence that he 'knew it fifty years ago or more. It lay waste and was used and occupied by the inhabitants of Guildeford to saw timber in and for saw-pitts. . . . When he was a scholler in the free school of Guildeford he and several of his fellowes did run and play there at crickett and other plaies.'

This is the oldest certain authority for cricket with which I am acquainted. Clearly it was a boy's game in the early years of Elizabeth. Nor was it a very scientific game if it could be played on a wicket agreeably diversified by 'saw-pitts.' William Page may have played cricket at Eton and learned to bat as well as 'to hick and hack, which they will do fast enough of themselves, and to cry *horum.*' It has already been shown that, in 1611, 'boyes played at crickett,' with a crooked bat or 'cricket-staffe.'

In 1676 we get a view of a summer day at Aleppo, and of British sailors busy at the national game.

Henry Teonge, Chaplain on board H.M.S. ships 'Assistance,' 'Bristol,' and 'Royal Oak,' Anno 1675 to 1679, writes:—

[At Aleppo].

6.—This morning early (as it is the custom all summer longe) at the least 40 of the English, with his worship the Consull, rod out of the cytty about 4 miles to the Greene Platt, a fine vally by a river syde, to recreate them selves. Where a princely tent was pitched ; and wee had severall pastimes and sports, as duck-hunting, fishing, shooting, handball, krickett, scrofilo ; and then a noble dinner brought thither, with greate plenty of all sorts of wine, punch, and lemonads ; and at 6 wee returne all home in good order, but soundly tyred and weary.[1]

When once the eighteenth century is reached cricket begins to find mention in literature. Clearly the game was rising in the world and was being taken up, like the poets of the period, by patrons. Lord Chesterfield, whom Dr. Johnson found a

[1] *Diary,* p. 159 ; May, 1676.

patron so insufficient, talked about cricket in a very proper
spirit in 1740.[1] 'If you have a right ambition you will desire
to excell all boys of your age at cricket . . . as well as in
learning.' That is the right style of fatherly counsel; but
Philip Chesterfield never came to 'European reputation as
mid-wicket-on,' like a hero of Mr. James Payn's. Lord Chesterfield also alludes to 'your various occupations of Greek
and cricket, Latin and pitch-farthing,' very justly coupling the
nobler language with the nobler game. Already in the fourth
book of the 'Dunciad,' line 592, Mr. Alexander Pope had
sneered at cricket.[2] At what did Mr. Pope not sneer? The
fair the wise, the manly,—Mrs. Arabella Fermor, Lady Mary
Wortley Montagu, Mr. Colley Cibber, and a delightful pastime,
—he turns up his nose at them and at everyone and everything !

> *O le grand homme, rien ne lui peut plaire !*

See, he cries to Dulness, see—

> The judge to dance his brother serjeant call,
> The senator at cricket urge the ball.

Cricket was played at Eton early. Gray, writing to West,
says, 'There is my Lords Sandwich and Halifax—they are
statesmen—do you not remember them dirty boys playing at
cricket?'[3] In 1736 Walpole writes, 'I can't say I am sorry I
was never quite a school-boy: an expedition against barge-
men, or a match at cricket may be very pretty things to recollect; but, thank my stars, I can remember things very near as
pretty.'[4] The bargee might have found an interview with Miss

---

[1] i. p. 197. Letter xxi.

[2] The bibliography of the *Dunciad* is not a subject to be rushed into
rashly, nor in a note; but this must have been written between 1726-1735, there
or thereabouts. The Scholiasts recognise Lord John Sackville as the Senator,
and quote a familiar passage from Horace Walpole (June 8, 1747) about
Cricketalia, instituted in his honour. We may, perhaps, regard Lord John
as one of the early patrons of the game.

[3] Gray's *Works*, 1807, ii. p. 2. See also 'urge the flying ball,' which
must refer, I think, to cricket. That ode was first published in 1747. Johnson
carelessly paraphrases 'drives the hoop, or *tosses* the ball !'—C. W.

[4] To George Montagu, May 6, 1726.

Horace pretty to recollect, but when Horace pretends that he might have been in the Eleven if he liked, the absurdity becomes too glaring. We are reminded of Charles Lamb's 'Here is Wordsworth saying he might have written "Hamlet" if he had had the "mind."' Cowper pretends (in 1781) that 'as a boy I excelled at cricket and football,' but he adds, with perfect truth, 'the fame I acquired by achievements that way is long since forgotten.' The author of the 'Task,' and of a good many hymns, was no Mynn nor Grace. We shall find but few of the English poets distinguished as cricketers, or fond of tuning the lyre to sing Pindaric strains of batters and bowlers. Byron tells a friend how they 'together joined in cricket's manly toil' (1807). Another noble exception is George Huddesford,[1] author of 'Salmagundi' (1791, p. 66)—

> But come, thou genial son of spring
> Whitsuntide, and with thee bring
> *Cricket*, nimble boy and light,
> In slippers red and drawers white,
> Who o'er the nicely measured land
> Ranges around his comely band,
> Alert to intercept each blow,
> Each motion of the wary foe.

This passage gives us the costume—white drawers and red slippers. The contemporary works of art, whereof see a little gallery on the walls of the pavilion at Lord's, show that men when they played also wore a kind of jockey cap. In a sketch of the Arms of Shrewsbury School, little boys are playing ; the bat is a kind of hockey-stick as in the preceding century. There are only two stumps, nor more in Hayman's well-known picture engraved 1755. The fields are well set for the bowling, and are represented with their hands ready for a catch. There

[1] See also his *Wiccamical Chaplet,* 1804, where there is an excellent 'Cricket Song' (p. 131 to 133) for the Hambledon Club, Hants, 1767, in the course of which the following names of cricketers occur : Nyren, Small, Buck, Curry, Hogsflesh, Barber Rich ('whose swiftness in bowling was never equalled yet'), 'Little George, the longstop, and Tom Suter, the Stumper,' Sackville, Manns, Boyton, Lanns, Mincing, Miller, Lumpy, Francis.—C. W.

are umpires in their usual places ; the scores are kept by men who cut notches in tally-sticks. Such 'notches' were 'got' by ' Miss Wicket,' a sportive young lady in a somewhat later caricature (p. 7). The ball (1770) has heavy cross-seams. But a silver ball, about a hundred years old, used as a snuff-box by the Vine Club at Sevenoaks, is marked with seams like those of to-day. Miss Wicket, also, carries a curved bat, but it has developed beyond the rustic crooked stick, and more nearly resembles some of the old curved bats at Lord's, with which a strong man must have hit prodigious skyers. We may doubt if bats were ever such ' three-man beetles ' as the players in an undated but contemporary picture at Lord's do fillip withal. The fields, in this curious piece, are all in a line at square-leg, and disappear in a distance unconscious of perspective.

Cricket had even before this date reached that height of prosperity which provokes the attention of moralists. ' Here is a fine morning : let us go and put down some form of enjoyment,' says the moralist. In 1743 a writer in the ' Gentleman's Magazine ' was moved to allege that 'the exercise may be strained too far. . . . Cricket is certainly a very good and wholesome exercise, yet it may be abused if either great or little people make it their business.' The chief complaint is that great and little people play together—butchers and baronets. Cricket ' propagates a spirit of idleness at the very time when, with the utmost industry, our debts, taxes, and decay of trade will scarcely allow us to get bread.' The Lydians, according to Herodotus, invented games to make them forget the scarcity of bread. But the gentleman in the magazine is much more austere than Herodotus. ' The advertisements most impudently recite that great sums are laid ' ; and it was, indeed, customary to announce a match for 500*l.* or 1,000*l.* Whether these sums were not drawn on Fancy's exchequer, at least in many cases, we may reasonably doubt. In his ' English Game of Cricket' (p. 138) the learned Mr. Box quotes a tale of betting in 1711, from a document which he does not describe. It appears that in 1711 the county of Kent played All England,

and money was lost and won, and there was a law-suit to recover. The court said, 'Cricket is, to be sure, a manly game and
not bad in itself, but it is the ill-use that is made of it by betting
above 10*l.* on it that is bad.' To a humble fiver on the University match this court would have had no kind of objection
to make. The history of betting at cricket is given by Mr.
Pycroft in the 'Cricket Field' (chap. vi.). A most interesting
chapter it is.

The earliest laws of the game, or at least the earliest which
have reached us, are of the year 1774. A committee of noble-
men and gentlemen (including Sir Horace Mann, the Duke of
Dorset, and Lord Tankerville) drew them up at the 'Star and
Garter' in Pall Mall. 'The pitching of the first wicket is to be
determined by the toss of a piece of money.' Does this mean
that the sides tossed for which was to pitch the wicket? As
Nyren shows, much turned on the pitching of the wicket.
Lumpy (Stevens) 'would invariably choose the ground where
his balls would shoot.'[1] In the rules of 1774, the distance
between the stumps is the same as at present. The crease is
cut, not painted.[2] The stumps are twenty-two inches in height;
there is only one bail, of six inches in length. 'No ball,' as
far as crossing the crease goes, is just like 'no ball' to-day.
Indeed, the game was essentially the game of to-day, except
that if a ball were hit 'the other player may place his body
anywhere within the swing of his bat, so as to hinder the
bowler from catching her, but he must neither strike at her nor
touch her with his hands.'

At this moment of legislation, when the dim heroic age of
cricket begins to broaden into the boundless day of history,
Mr. James Love, comedian, appeared as the epic poet of the
sport.[3] His quarto is dedicated to the Richmond Club, and is

---

[1] *The Cricketer's Guide,* fourth edition, *s. a.,* p. 58.

[2] The Bishop of St. Andrews can remember when the creases were cut,
before chalk was used.

[3] *Cricket,* An Heroic Poem, illustrated with the critical observations of
Scriblerus Maximus. By James Love, Comedian, London. Printed for the
Author, MDCCLXX. (Price, One Shilling.)

After a Picture by Hayman, R.A., belonging to the M.C.C.

inspired ' by a recollection of many Particulars at a time when
the Game was cultivated with the utmost Assiduity, and
patronised by the personal Appearance [1] and Management of
some of the most capital People in the Kingdom.' Mr. Love,
in his enthusiasm, publishes an exhortation to Britain, to leave
all meaner sports, and cultivate cricket only.

> Hail CRICKET, glorious, manly, *British* game,
> First of all sports, be first alike in fame,

sings Love, as he warms to his work. He denounces ' puny
Billiards,' played by ' Beaus, dressed in the quintessence of the
fashion. The robust *Cricketer* plays in his shirt, the Rev. Mr.
W——d, particularly, appears almost naked.'

One line of Mr. Love's,

> *Where fainting vice calls folly to her aid,*

appears to him so excellent that he thinks it must be plagiarised,
and, in a note, invites the learned reader to find out where he
stole it from. To this a critic, Britannicus Severus, answers that
' Gentlemen who have CRICKET in their heads cannot afford to
pore over a parcel of musty Authors.' Indeed, your cricketer
is rarely a bookworm.

> ' Leave the dissolving song, the baby dance,
> To soothe the slaves of Italy and France,

and play up,' cries this English bard.

In the second book, the poet comes to business—Kent *v.*
All England. The poet, after the custom of his age, gives
dashes after an initial, in place of names. In notes he inter-
prets his dashes, and introduces us to Newland, of Slendon, in
Sussex, a farmer, and a famous batsman ; Bryan, of London,
bricklayer; Rumney, gardener to the Duke of Dorset; Smith,

---

[1] Talking of appearances, there is just one story of a ghost at a cricket
match. He took great interest in the game, and went home in a dog-cart as
it seemed to the spectators, though he (the real man, not the wraith) was on
his death-bed at a considerable distance. The spectral dog-cart is the puzzle
of the Psychical Society. The scene of the apparition was the cricket ground
of a public school.

keeper of the artillery ground ; Hodswell, the bowling tanner of Dartford; Mills, of Bromley; Robin, commonly called Long Robin ; Mills, Sawyer, Cutbush, Bartrum, Kips, and Danes ; Cuddy, the tailor ; Derigate, of Reigate ; Weymark, the miller, with Newland, Green, two Harrises, and Smith made up the teams. The match is summed up in the Argument of the Third Book.

The Game.—Five on the side of the Counties are out for three Notches. The Odds run high on the side of Kent. Bryan and Newland go in ; they help the Game greatly. Bryan is unfortunately put out by Kips. Kent, the First Innings, is Thirteen ahead. The Counties go in again, and get Fifty-seven ahead. Kent, in the Second Innings, is very near losing, the two last Men being in. Weymark unhappily misses a Catch, and by that means Kent is victorious.

It was a splendid close match—but let us pity Weymark, immortal butter-fingers. In the first innings the wicket-keeping of Kips to the fast bowling of Hodswell was reckoned fine.

If Love was the Homer of cricket, the minstrel who won from forgetfulness the glories of the dim Heroic Age, Nyren, was the delightful Herodotus of the early Historic Period. John Nyren dedicated his 'Cricketer's Guide and Recollections of the Cricketers of my Time,' to the great Mr. William Ward, in 1833. He speaks of cricket as 'an elegant relaxation,' and congratulates Mr. Ward on 'having gained the *longest hands* of any player upon record.' This famed score was made on July 24, 25, 1820, on the M.C.C. ground. The number was 278, '108 more than any player ever gained ;' Aylward's 167 had previously been the longest score I know. Mr. Ward's feat, moreover, was 'after the increase of the stumps in 1817.' Old Nyren was charmed in his declining hours by a deed like this, yet grieved by the modern bowlers, and their habit 'of throwing the ball.' The history of that innovation will presently be sketched.

Nyren was born at Hambledon, in Hampshire, on December 15, 1764, and was therefore a small boy when Love sang. He died at Bromley, June 28, 1837. Like most very great men, he was possibly of Scottish blood. He was a Catholic and believed that the true spelling of the family name was Nairne, and that they came south after being 'out in the '15 or '45.' Mr. Charles Cowden Clarke describes him as a thoroughly good and amiable man, and as much may be guessed from his writings.

Mr. Clarke agreed with him in his dislike of round-hand bowling, save when Lillywhite was pitted against Fuller Pilch— a beautiful thing to see, as the Bishop of St. Andrews testifies, 'speaking,' like Dares Phrygius of the heroes at Troy, 'as he that saw them.' In Nyren's youth—say 1780—Hambledon was the centre of cricket. The boy had a cricketing education. He learned a little Latin of a worthy old Jesuit, but was a better hand at the fiddle. In that musical old England, where John Small, the noted bat, once charmed an infuriated bull by his minstrelsy, Nyren performed a moral miracle. He played to the gipsies, and so won their hearts that they always passed by his hen-roost when they robbed the neighbours. Music and cricket were the Hambledon man's delight. His father, Richard Nyren, was, with Thomas Brett, one of the chief bowlers. Brett was 'the fastest as well as straightest bowler that was ever known' ; no *jerker*, but with a very high delivery. The height of the delivery was not *à la Spofforth*, but was got by sending the ball out from under the armpit. How this manœuvre could be combined with pace is a great mystery. Richard Nyren had this art, 'always to the length.' Brett's bowling is described as 'tremendous,' yet Tom Sueter could stump off it—Tom of the honourable heart, and the voice so sweet, pure and powerful. Yet on those wickets Tom needed a long-stop to Brett— George Lear. The Bishop has seen three long-stops on to Brown ; 'but he *was* a jerker.' At that date the long-stop commonly dropped on one knee as he received the ball. An old Eton boy, G. B., who was at school between 1805 and 1814, says, in a letter to the *Standard* (dated September 21, 1886), that 'a pocket-handkerchief was allowed round the dropping knee of long-stop.' A bowler with a low delivery was Lambert, 'the little farmer.' 'His ball would twist from the off stump into the leg. *He was the first I remember who introduced this deceitful and teasing way of delivering the ball.'* Cricket was indeed rudimentary when a break from the off was a new thing. 'The Kent and Surrey men could not tell what to make of that cursed twist of his.' Lambert acquired the art as Daphnis learned his minstrelsy, while he tended his father's sheep. He would set up hurdles instead of a net and bowl for hours. But it needed old Nyren to teach him to bowl outside the off stump, so little alert was the mind of this innovator. Among outsiders, Lumpy, the Surrey man, was the most accurate 'to a length,' and he was much faster than Lord Frederick Beauclerk. In these days the home bowlers pitched the wickets to suit themselves. Thus they had all the advantage of rough wickets on a slope ; yet, even so, a yokel with pluck and 'an arm as long as a hop-pole,' has been known to slash Lumpy all over the field. But this could only have done at single wicket. A curious bowler of this age was Noah Mann, the fleetest runner of his time, and a skilled horseman. He was a left-handed bowler, and, as will be seen, he anticipated the magical 'pitching' of experts at base-ball. How he did this without throwing or jerking is hard to be understood. 'His merit consisted in giving a curve to the ball the whole way. In itself it was not the first-rate style of bowling, but so very deceptive that the chief end was frequently attained. They who remember the dexterous manner with which the Indian jugglers communicated the curve to the balls they spun round their heads by a twist of the wrist or hand will at once comprehend Noah's curious feat in bowling.' He once made a hit for ten at Windmill-down, to which the club moved from the bleakness of Broadhalfpenny.

We have followed Nyren's comments on bowlers for the purpose of elucidating the evolution of their ingenious art. All the bowlers, so far, have been under-hand, but now we hear of 'these anointed clod-stumpers' the Walkers. They were not of Broadhalfpenny, but joined the club at Windmill-down, when the move there was made on the suggestion of the Duke of

Dorset. 'About a couple of years after Walker had been with us' (probably about 1790), 'he began the system of throwing instead of bowling, now so much the fashion.' He was no-balled, after a council of the Hambledon Club, called for the purpose. This disposes of the priority of Mr. Willes (1807), and incidentally casts doubt on the myth that a lady invented round-hand bowling. Nyren says, 'The first I recollect seeing *revive* the custom was Wills, a Sussex man.'

From the heresiarch, Tom Walker, we come to the classic model of a bowler in the under-hand school—that excellent man, christian and cricketer, David Harris.

It would be difficult, perhaps impossible, to convey in writing an accurate idea of the grand effect of Harris's bowling ; they only who have played against him can fully appreciate it. His attitude, when preparing for his run previously to delivering the ball, would have made a beautiful study for the sculptor. Phidias would certainly have taken him for a model. First of all, he stood erect like a soldier at drill ; then, with a graceful curve of the arm, he raised the ball to his forehead, and drawing back his right foot, started off with his left. The calm look and general air of the man were uncommonly striking, and from this series of preparations he never deviated. I am sure that from this simple account of his manner, all my countrymen who were acquainted with his play will recall him to their minds. His mode of delivering the ball was very singular. He would bring it from under the arm by a twist, and nearly as high as his arm-pit, and with this action *push* it, as it were, from him. How it was that the balls acquired the velocity they did by this mode of delivery, I never could comprehend.

When first he joined the Hambledon Club, he was quite a raw countryman at cricket, and had very little to recommend him but his noble delivery. He was also very apt to give tosses. I have seen old Nyren scratch his head, and say,—' Harris would make the best bowler in England if he did not toss.' By continual practice, however, and following the advice of the old Hambledon players, he became as steady as could be wished ; and in the prime of his playing very rarely indeed gave a toss, although his balls were pitched the full length. In bowling, he never stooped in the least in his delivery, but kept himself upright all the time.

His balls were very little beholden to the ground when pitched ; it was but a touch, and up again ; and woe be to the man who did not get in to block them, for they had such a peculiar curl that they would grind his fingers against the bat ; many a time have I seen the blood drawn in this way from a batter who was not up to the trick : old Tom Walker was the only exception—I have before classed him among the bloodless animals.

Harris's bowling was the finest of all tests for a hitter, and hence the great beauty, as I observed before, of seeing Beldham in, with this man against him ; for unless a batter were of the very first class, and accustomed to the first style of stopping, he could do little or nothing with Harris. If the thing had been possible, I should have liked to have seen such a player as Budd (fine hitter as he was) standing against him. My own opinion is, that he could not have stopped his balls, and this will be a criterion, by which those who have seen some of that gentleman's brilliant hits, may judge of the extraordinary merit of this man's bowling. He was considerably faster than Lambert, and so superior in style and finish, that I can draw no comparison between them. Lord Frederic Beauclerc has been heard to say that Harris's bowling was one of the grandest things of the kind he had ever seen ; but his lordship could not have known him in his prime ; he never saw him play till after he had had many fits of the gout, and had become slow and feeble.

To Harris's fine bowling I attribute the great improvement that was made in hitting, and above all in stopping ; for it was utterly impossible to remain at the crease, when the ball was tossed to a fine length ; you were obliged to get in, or it would be about your hands, or the handle of your bat ; and every player knows where its next place would be.

This long extract is not too long, for it contains a dignified study of the bowler.

> This is the perfect Trundler, this is he,
> That every man who bowls should wish to be.

Harris was admired for ' the sweetness of his disposition and his manly contempt of every action that bore the character of meanness,' and he chiefly bowled for catches, as did Lord Frederick Beauclerk. Nyren is no great hand at orthography, and he soon comes to speak of a Sussex bowler named Wells.

This is apparently the Wills, or Willes, who has more credit than perhaps he deserves for bringing in round-hand. ' He was the first I had seen of the new school, after the Walkers had attempted to introduce the system in the Hambledon Club.' Willes had a twist from leg, and Nyren thinks Freemantle showed astonishing knowledge of the game because he went in front of his wicket and hit Willes, and 'although before the wicket, he would not have been out, because the ball had been pitched at the outside of the stump.' A man might play hours on that system ' by *Shrewsbury* clock,' but I doubt if David Harris would have approved of Freemantle's behaviour.

The student of the evolution of round-hand and over-hand bowling now turns to the early exploits of William Lillywhite (*b.* June 13, 1792). Whatever Mr. Willes may have done, whatever Tom Walker may have dreamed, William Lillywhite and Jem Broadbridge are practically the parents of modern bowling. When Lillywhite came out, the law was that in bowling the hand must be below the elbow. Following the example of Mr. G. Knight, of the M.C.C., or rather going beyond it, Lillywhite raised the hand *above* the shoulder, though scarcely perceptible. Lillywhite's performances in 1827 caused much discussion among cricketers and in the 'Sporting Magazine.' Letters on this subject are reprinted by Mr. W. Denison, in ' Sketches of the Players,' London, 1846.[1]

The last great match of 1827 was between Sussex and Kent, with Saunders and Searle given. Mr. Denison, reviewing the match at the time, predicted that if round-hand were allowed, there would be no driving and no cutting to point or slip. This of course is part of Unfulfilled Prophecy. ' Broadbridge and others will shew that they cannot be faced on hard ground without the most imminent peril.' As a compromise, Mr. Denison was for allowing straight-armed bowling, ' so that

---

[1] The edition of Nyren's *Cricketer's Guide,* used here, is the fourth, London, *s. a.* I owe it to Mr. Gerald Fitzgerald. Any cricketer who has borrowed my own copy of the Editio Princeps will oblige me by returning it. —A. L.

the back of the hand be kept under when the ball is delivered.'
Mr. Steel's chapter on bowling shows what the effect of that
rule must have been.

In February, 1828, Mr. Knight published his letters in
defence of round-hand bowling. There had been, in the origin
of cricket, no law to restrain the bowlers. About 1804,
the batting acquired such mastery, and forward play with
running-in (as Nyren knew) became so vigorous, that Willes
and Tom Walker tried round-hand. This round-hand was
' straight armed, and for a time (1818–28) did very well, till
bowlers took to raising the hand, even above the head.' M.C.C.
then proclaimed an edict against all round-hand bowling.
Mr. Knight proposed to admit straight-armed bowling, which
could not be called 'throwing.' To define a throw was as
hard then as now—a man knows it when he sees it ; it is like
the trot in horses. Mr. Knight's proposed law ran, ' The ball
shall be bowled ; if it be thrown or jerked, or if any part of the
hand or arm be *above* the *shoulder* at the time of delivery, the
umpire shall call *No Ball.*'

In one of the trial matches (Sept. 1827) it is said that Mr.
Knight, Broadbridge, and Lillywhite, all bowled high over the
shoulder. There are no wides in the score. When a man was
caught, the bowler's name was not given. Lillywhite has thus
no wicket to his name.

Mr. Knight's law was discussed at Lord's (May 19, 1828),
and the word *elbow* substituted for *shoulder.* But Lillywhite
and Broadbridge bowled as before, and found many followers,
till the M.C.C. passed the law proposed by Mr. Knight. But
the hand was soon raised, and the extraordinary pace of Mr.
Mynn (born 1807) was striven for by men who had not his
weight and strength. These excesses caused a re-enactment of
the over-the-shoulder law in 1845.

Lillywhite was now recognised as the reviver of cricket.
His analysis in 1844 and 1845 gives about $6\frac{7}{8}$ runs for each
wicket. Round-hand, with a practical license for over-hand, was
now established ; but, as late as 1860, a high delivery was a

rarity. The troublesome case of Willsher ended in permitting any height of delivery, and the greatest of all bowlers, Mr. Spofforth, sends in the ball from the utmost altitude.

This is a brief account of the evolution of round and over-hand bowling. As to slow and fast bowling, Lord Frederick Beauclerk and one of the Walkers were very slow bowlers in old days. William Clarke (*b.* Dec. 24, 1798) was the classical slow bowler. Clarke was not a regular lob bowler, but, like Lambert, delivered 'about midway between the height of the elbow and the strict under-hand, accompanied by a singular peculiarity of action with the hand and wrist just as the ball is about to be discharged.[1]' He had a tremendous twist, and great spin and ingenuity. Perhaps his success was partly due to the rarity of slow bowling in his time. Men imitated Mr. Mynn, who was as big a man as Mr. W. G. Grace, and a very fast bowler. In old underhand times, Brett had a 'steam-engine pace,' and later, Browne of Brighton was prodigiously fast. The Bishop of St. Andrews remembers seeing a ball of Browne's strike the stumps with such force and at such a point that both bails flew *back* as far as the bowler's wicket. That was at Brighton. He also remembers how at Lord's, when Browne bowled, all the field were placed *behind* the wicket, or nearly so, that is at slip, leg, and long-stop, till Ward went in, who, playing with an upright bat, contrived to poke the ball to the off, and Browne himself (a tall, heavy man) had to go after it. But this having happened more than once, a single field was placed in front. Yet Beldham, as Mr. Pycroft tells, quite mastered Browne, and made 76 off him in a match. Beldham was then fifty-four. Browne's pace was reckoned superior to that of Mr. Osbaldistone. It is not easy to decide who has been the fastest of fast bowlers. In our own day, I think that Mr. Cecil Boyle, when he bowled for Oxford (1874), was the swiftest I have seen, except a bowler unknown south of the Tweed, Mr. Barclay, now a clergyman in Canada. Mr. Barclay was faster with under-hand than with round-hand. Beldham and his comrades played Browne with-

[1] *Sketches of the Players*, p. 23.

out pads ; I have seen this tried against Mr. Barclay—the results were damaging. Famous names of fast bowlers are Mynn, Marcon, Fellowes, Tarrant, Jackson, Freeman, Hope Grant, Powys, and Robert Lang.

The history of bowling precedes that of batting, because the batsman must necessarily adapt his style to the bowling, not *vice versâ*. He must also adapt it to the state of the wickets. There are times when a purely rural style of play, a succession of 'agrarian outrages,' is the best policy. Given an untrustworthy wicket, good bowling, fielding ground in heavy grass, a stone wall on one side, and another wall, with a nice flooded burn beyond, on another side, and a batsman will be well advised if he lifts the ball over the boundaries and into the brook. Perhaps Mr. Steel will recognise the conditions described, and remember Dalbeattie. In the origin of cricket, when the stumps were low, and the bat a crooked club, hitting hard, high, and often must have been the rule. A strong man with good sight must have been the pride of the village. When David Harris, Tom Walker, Lumpy, Brett, and other heroes brought in accuracy, spin, twist, and pace, with taller wickets to defend, this batting was elaborated by Beldham and Sueter and others into an art. Tom Sueter, first, fathered the heresy of leaving the crease, and going in to the pitch or half-volley.[1] Sir Horace Mann's bailiff, Aylward, was the Shrewsbury of an elder age. 'He once stayed in two whole days, and got the highest number of runs that had ever been gained by any member— *one hundred and sixty-seven.*' Tom Walker was a great stick.. Lord Frederick was bowling to him at Lord's. Every ball he dropped down just before his bat. Off went his lordship's white, broad-brimmed hat, dash upon the ground (his constant action when disappointed), calling him at the same time 'a confounded old beast.' 'I doan't care what ee zays,' said Tom, whose conduct showed a good deal more of courtesy and self-control than Lord Frederick's. Perhaps the master-bat of old times was William Beldham from Farnham. He comes into

[1] Nyren, *op. cit.* p. 50.

Bentley's 'Cricket Scores' as early as 1787. The players called him 'Silver Billy.' He was coached by Harry Hall, the ginger-bread baker of Farnham. Hall's great maxim was 'the left elbow well up.'

From Nyren I extract a description of Beldham's batting :—

BELDHAM was quite a young man when he joined the Hambledon Club ; and even in that stage of his playing, I hardly ever saw a man with a finer command of his bat ; but, with the instruction and advice of the old heads superadded, he rapidly attained to the extraordinary accomplishment of being the finest player that has appeared within the latitude of more than half a century. There can be no exception against his batting, or the severity of his hitting. He would get in at the balls, and hit them away in a gallant style ; yet, in this single feat, I think I have known him excelled ; but when he could cut them at the point of the bat, he was in his glory ; and upon my life, their speed was as the speed of thought. One of the most beautiful sights that can be imagined, and which would have delighted an artist, was to see him make himself up to hit a ball. It was the *beau idéal* of grace, animation, and concentrated energy. In this peculiar exhibition of elegance with vigour, the nearest approach to him I think was Lord Frederick Beauclerc. Upon one occasion at Mary-le-bone, I remember these two admirable batters being in together, and though Beldham was then verging towards his climacteric, yet both were excited to a competition, and the display of talent that was exhibited between them that day was the most interesting sight of its kind I ever witnessed. I should not forget, among his other excellencies, to mention that Beldham was one of the best judges of a short run I ever knew ; add to which, that he possessed a generally good knowledge of the game.

In 1838 Beldham used to gossip with Mr. Pycroft. That learned writer gives Fennex great credit for introducing the modern style of forward play about 1800 ; this on the evidence of Fennex himself (1760–1839). But probably accurate bowling, with a fast rise, on fairly good wickets, must have taught forward play naturally to Fennex, Lambert, Fuller Pilch, and others. It is not my purpose to compile a minute chronicle of cricket, to mark each match and catch, nor to chant

the illustrious deeds of all famous men. The great name of
Mr. Ward has been already mentioned. The Bishop of St.
Andrews, when a Harrow boy, played against Mr. Ward, and
lowered his illustrious wicket for three runs.[1] Thus, with Mr.
Ward, we come within the memory of living cricketers. Much
more is this the case with Mr. Budd, Fuller Pilch, Alfred Mynn,
Hayward and Carpenter, Humphrey and Jupp. Mr. Mynn
was the son of a gentleman farmer at Bearstead, near Maidstone.
His extraordinary pace actually took wickets by storm ; men
were bowled before they knew where they were. The assiduous
diligence of Mr. Ward was a match for him. When about to
meet Mynn, he would practise with the fastest of the ground
bowlers at Lord's, at eighteen or nineteen yards' rise, so to
speak. Mr. Ward's great reach also stood him in good stead.
Mr. Mynn's pace, and the excesses committed by his imitators,
for some time demoralised batting. Few balls were straight
(among the *imitatores, servum pecus*), and men went in to hit
what they could reach. The joy of getting hold of a leg-ball
from a very fast bowler, or of driving him, overpowered caution,
and these violent delights might have had violent ends if
accuracy had not returned to bowling. In 1843 Mr. Mynn's
analysis gave $5\frac{2}{3}$ a wicket. His average was but 17 an innings.
Scores were shorter fifty years ago.[2]

My attempt has been to trace the streams of tendency in
cricket rather than to produce a chronicle—a work which would
require a volume to itself. Nothing has been said about fielding ; because, however the ball is bowled, and however hit, the
tasks of catching it, stopping it, and returning it with speed
have always been the same. True, different styles of batting

[1] It was three or five—I forget which. I know it was the *lowest score* he
had that year !—C.W.

[2] Was this so? The long scores caused the introduction of round-hand
bowling. From among my brother's papers (late Bishop of Lincoln) a letter
has lately been returned to me which contains the following :—' Christ Church,
Oxford : May 24, 1831.—Cricket, I suppose, does not interest you ; but you
may like to know that in three following innings, on three following days last
week, I got 328 runs. Christ Church has been playing—and beating—the
University.'—C. W.

and bowling require alterations in the position of the fielders.[1] But the principles of their conduct and the nature of their duty remain unaltered. One change may be noted. In 'Juvenile Sports,' by Master Michel Angelo,[2] the author speaks of *byes* and *overthrows* as 'a new mode,' 'an innovation with which I am by no means pleased. It is indeed true that this places the seekers out continually on their guard, and obliges them to be more mindful of their play ; but then it diminishes the credit of the player, in whose hands the bat is, as a game may be won by a very bad batsman owing to the inability of the wicket-man, or the inattention of the seekers-out.'

The fallacy of this argument does not need to be exposed.

M.C.C.

No sketch of the history of cricket would be complete without a note on the fortunes of the Marylebone Club. This is the Parliament of cricket, and includes almost all the amateurs of merit. There is nothing very formal in its construction ; and any clubs which please may doubtless arrange among themselves to play *not* according to M.C.C. rules. But nobody so pleases ; and Marylebone legislates practically for countries that were not even known to exist when wickets were pitched at Guildford in the reign of Henry VIII. Marylebone is the *Omphalos*, the Delos of cricket.

The club may be said to have sprung from the ashes of the White Conduit Club, dissolved in 1787. One Thomas Lord, by the aid of some members of the older association, made a ground in the space which is now Dorset Square. This was the first 'Lord's.' As to Lord, he is dubiously said (like the ancestors of Nyren) to have been a Scot and a Jacobite, or mixed up, at least, in some way with the '45. Lord was obliged to move to North Bank, and finally, in 1814, to the

---

[1] My experience, in one respect, is, I suppose, unique. Hitting a leg-ball, I alarmed the umpire, who turned round, and I was caught by the wicket-keeper off his back ! Naturally enough—but yet—justly ? he gave me out !—C. W.

[2] London, 1776, p. 76.

present ground. The famous Mr. Ward had played at Lord's before this migration ; his first match here was in 1810, and he played, more or less, till 1847, being then sixty years of age. His bats are said to have weighed four pounds. Mr. Ward bought the lease of the ground from Lord in 1825, 'at a most exorbitant rate ;' and, in 1830, Dark bought the remainder of the lease from him. The first match on our present Lord's, or the first recorded, was M.C.C. *v.* Hertfordshire, June 22, 1814. In 1825 the pavilion was burned, after a Winchester and Harrow match. The burning of the Alexandrian Library may be compared to the wholesale destruction of cricket records on this melancholy occasion. In 1816 the Club reviewed the Laws : the result will be found in Lillywhite's ' Scores,' i. 385. ' No more than two balls to be allowed at practice when a fresh bowler takes the ball before he proceeds.' A great deal too much time is now wasted over these practice balls. ' The ball must be delivered underhanded, not thrown or jerked, with the hand below the elbow at the time of delivering the ball.' The umpire is to call ' no ball,' 'if the back of the hand be uppermost.' As to l.b.w., the batter is out 'if with his foot or leg he stop the ball which the bowler, in the opinion of the umpire, shall have pitched in a straight line to the wicket, and would have hit it.'

The names of the Presidents are only on record after the fire. Ponsonby, Grimston, Darnley, Coventry are among the most notable. The renowned Mr. Aislabie was secretary till his death in 1842 ; in the pavilion his bust commemorates him. Mr. Kynaston and Mr. Fitzgerald, of ' Jerks In from Short Leg,' are other celebrated secretaries. In 1868 the Club purchased a lease of 99 years, at the cost of 11,000*l.* There have been recent additions to the area, and to that celebrated monument, the pavilion.

Lord's is, as all the world knows, the scene, not only of Club and of Middlesex matches, but of Eton and Harrow, Oxford and Cambridge, and Gentlemen and Players, which is also contested at the Oval. Winchester used moreover to play

The Royal Academy Club in Marylebone Fields. (After Hayman, R.A. The property of the Club.)

Eton here, but the head-masters have long preferred a home and home affair. In other chapters these great matches will be chronicled and criticised.

The various epochs in the history of the game may now be briefly enumerated by way of summary. First we have the prehistoric age, when cricket was dimly struggling to evolve itself out of the rudimentary forms of cat-and-dog, and stool-ball. This preceded 154–, when we find an authentic mention of the name of CRICKET. Just about the end of the seventeenth century it was mainly a boys' game. With the Augustan age it began to be taken up by statesmen, and satirised by that ideal whippersnapper, the ingenious but in all respects un-sportsmanlike, Mr. Pope. By 1750 the game was matter of heavy bets, and scores began to be recorded. The old Hambledon Club gave it dignity, and the veterans endured till quite modern times dawn with Mr. Ward. Then came the prosperous heresy of round-hand bowling, which battled for existence till about 1845, when it became a recognised institution. The wandering clubs, chiefly I. Z. and the Free Foresters at first, carried good examples into the remoter gardens of our country. The migratory professional teams, the United and All England Elevens at least, showed the yokels what style meant, and taught them that Jackson and Tinley were their masters. But the lesson lasted too long. Nothing was less exhilarating than the spectacle of twenty provincial players, with Hodgson and Slinn, making many duck's eggs, and fielding in a mob. 'The first 'ad me on the knee, the next on the wrist, the next blacked my eye, and the fourth bowled me,' says the Pride of the Village, in 'Punch,' after enjoying 'a hover from Jackson.' Such violent delights had violent ends. The old travelling elevens are extinct, but railways have 'turned large England to a little' field, so to speak, and clubs may now meet which of old scarcely knew each other by name. The Australian elevens have in recent days given a great impulse to patriotic exertions.

Scotch cricket is a thing of this century. Football and golf are the native pastimes of my countrymen, as hurling is of Ireland. The Old Grange Club is the M.C.C. of the North. The West of Scotland and Drumpellier are other clubs of standing. That ever-flourishing veteran, Major Dickens, still upholds the honour of Kelso. The Moncrieffs have been the Wards and Budds of Edinburgh, nor will a touching patriotism allow me here to omit the name of George Charles Hamilton Dunlop. For some reasons Scotland has not been productive of bowlers. Professionals are seldom reared there, nor have amateurs devoted themselves to the more scientific and less popular part of the game. Mr. Barclay has already been commemorated for his speed ; a few only will remember Mr. Sinclair and Mr. Glassford, who died young, and very much regretted. Few men have done more for Scotch cricket than Mr. H. H. Almond, head-master of Loretto School, which has contributed several players to the Oxford eleven. An old 'pewter' may here congratulate Mr. Almond on the energy with which he kept his boys to the mark, and on the undaunted example which he set by always going in first. The names of Arthur Cheyne, Jack Mackenzie, Edward Henderson, Chalmers, Hay Brown, Leslie Balfour, and Tom Marshall are only a few that crowd on the memory of the elderly Caledonian cricketer. In the Border district, of which more hereafter, the houses of Buccleuch and Roxburgh have been great friends of the game, and that was a proud day for ' the Rough Clan ' when Lord George Scott scored over 160 in the University match of 1887. Abbotsford, too, has been well to the front, thanks to the Hon. J. Maxwell Scott, and, for some reason, Scotland has been occasionally represented by Mr. A. G. Steel, and the Hon. Ivo Bligh, known to the local press as ' the Titled Batsman.' But these are alien glories *et non sua poma.*

Three things are prejudicial to Scotch cricket. First, there is the climate, about which more words were superfluous. Next, boys leave school earlier than in England, for professions or for college. Lastly, the University session' is in the winter months, and the University clubs are therefore at a great disadvantage. I shall never forget the miraculous wickets we tried to pitch on the old College Green at Glasgow, and the courage displayed by divinity students in standing up to Mr. Barclay there. As for St. Andrews, golf is too much with us on that friendly shore, and will brook no rival.

*** The author of the historical introduction is much indebted to the Bishop of St. Andrews, a veteran of the first University Match, for his kindness in revising proofs, and adding notes. He has also to thank the Viscountess Wolseley for the loan of her picture of ' Miss Wicket '; and Mr. Charles Mills, M.P., for a sight of the silver ball of the Vine Club. It was filled with snuff, and tossed from hand to hand after dinner ; he who dropped it being fined in claret, or some other liquor.

CHAPTER II.

BATTING.

(By the Hon. R. H. Lyttelton.)

FIG. 1.—The champion.

T H E great and supreme art of batting constitutes to the large majority of cricketers the most enjoyable part of the game. There are three especially delightful moments in life connected with games, and only those who have experienced all three can realise what these moments are. They are (1) the cut stroke at tennis, when the striker wins chase one and two on the floor ; (2) the successful drive at golf, when the globe is despatched on a journey of 200 yards ; (3) a crack to square-leg off a half-volley just outside the legs. When once the sensation has been realised by any happy mortal, he is almost entitled to chant in a minor key a 'Nunc Dimittis,' to feel that the supreme moment has come, and that he has, indeed, not lived in vain.

After what has been said in the foregoing chapter we shall here only touch upon the cricket of the past in so far as seems necessary to make this dissertation on batting tolerably complete, and shall then proceed to discuss the principles and science of the art as it now exists.

The shape of the bat in the year 1746—which may be taken as a beginning, for it was in that year that the first score of a match was printed and handed down to posterity, at any rate in Lillywhite's 'Scores and Biographies'—resembled a thick crooked stick more than a modern bat.

From the shape of the bat, obviously adapted to meet the ball when moving along the ground, one may infer that the bowlers habitually delivered a style of ball we now call a 'sneak.' How long this system of bowling remained in vogue cannot exactly be told. The famous William Beldham, who was born in 1766, and lived for nearly one hundred years, is reported by Nyren to have said that when he was a boy nearly all bowling was fast and along the ground. As long as this was the case it is probable that the bat was nothing but a club, for if the ball never left the ground the operative part of the bat would naturally be at the very bottom, as is usual in clubs. The renowned Tom Walker was the earliest lob bowler ; he probably took to the style late in life, or about the year 1800, and several bowlers, notably the great E. H. Budd, raised the arm slightly; but it is believed that the first genuine round-arm bowlers were William Lillywhite and James Broadbridge, both of Sussex, who first bowled the new style in 1827. That year was from this cause a year of revolution in cricket, and the shape of the modern bat dates from that period. As a rule, up to the year 1800 the style of batting was back. William Fennex is supposed to have been the inventor of forward play, and Beldham reports a saying of one Squire Paulett, who was watching Fennex play : ' You do frighten me there, jumping out of your ground.' The great batsmen of the early era of cricket were Lord Frederick Beauclerk, Mr. Budd, Beldham, Bentley, Osbaldeston, William Ward, Beagley, William Lambert, Jem Broadbridge, W. Hooker, Saunders, and Searle. The great skill of these players when opposed to under-hand bowling was what determined the Sussex players to alter the style of bowling, and indeed it is generally the fact that too great abundance of runs raises questions as to the desirability of altering rules.

After the year 1827 the shape of the bat became very like what it is now, but it was much heavier in the blade and thinner in the handle, which seems to indicate that the play was mostly of the forward driving style, and the great exponent of this method of play was the renowned Fuller Pilch. Anyone who has the opportunity of handling a bat of this period will find that its weight renders it inconvenient for cutting, but suitable for forward play. The change from under-hand bowling to round-arm having been effected by slow developments makes it probable that the style of play was generally forward until the under-hand bowling was altogether superseded by round-arm. Some bowlers followed the new order of things by changing from under to round-arm. Round-arm bowling was at first less accurate than under-hand, and consequently all-round hitting greatly developed ; and we find Felix, the father of cutting, who began play in 1828, chiefly renowned for this hit. Scoring greatly diminished when round-arm bowling was thoroughly established, and increased again as grounds got better.

Judging from the scores of that day, the best bat in England from 1827 to 1850 was Fuller Pilch, and his scoring would compare favourably with that of nearly all modern players, with the exception of W. G. Grace. He was a tall man, and used to smother the ball by playing right out forward.

The principle on which his whole play was founded was evidently to get at the pitch and take care of the ball before breaks, bumps, and shooters had time to work their devilries. In order to carry out this method, he used frequently to leave his ground, and consequently the famous Wm. Clarke always found Pilch a harder nut to crack than any of his other contemporaries.

Clarke's slow balls, tolerably well up, were met by Pilch, who left his ground and drove him forward with a straight bat. His master appears to have been the great Sam Redgate, who was fast and ripping, and who on one occasion got him out for a pair of spectacles, while, on the other hand, twice in his life he got over 100 runs against Wm. Lillywhite's bowling, considered in those days to be an extraordinary feat. After Pilch, Joseph Guy, of Nottingham, and E. G. Wenman, of Kent, were considered the best ; but several—C. G. Taylor, Mynn, Felix, and Marsden, for example—scored largely, and they all passed through a golden age of bowling, namely, about 1839, when Lillywhite, Redgate, Mynn, Cobbett, and Hillyer all flourished, to say nothing of Sir F. Bathurst, Tom Barker, and others.

From the year 1855, when Fuller Pilch left off play, to the year 1868, when W. G. Grace burst on the world with a lustre that no previous batsman had ever approached, there was nevertheless a grand array of batsmen—among professionals, Hayward, Carpenter, Parr, Daft, Caffyn, Mortlock, and Julius Cæsar ; and among amateurs, Hankey, F. H. Norman, C. G. Lane, C. G. Lyttelton, Mitchell, Lubbock, Buller, V. E. Walker, and Maitland. These are a few of the great names. They are, however, surrounded by several almost as renowned, such as Stephenson, T. Humphrey, Hearne, Cooper, Burbidge, Griffith, and others, who, we think, made this era of the game productive of more exciting cricket than has been known since. It may seem odd, but the overpowering genius of W. G. Grace after this time somewhat spoilt the excitement of the game. His side was never beaten. Crowds thronged to see him play, all bowling was alike to him, and the record of Gloucestershire cricket, champion county for some time through his efforts, is the only instance of one man practically making an eleven for several years. The other Gloucestershire players will be the first to acknowledge the truth of this. Gloucestershire rose with a bound into the highest rank among counties when W. G. Grace attained his position amongst batsmen, a head and shoulders above any other cricketer. It rose and flourished with him, and at the present time shows symptoms of falling with him. To return to the period between 1855 and 1868 : the greater equality of players made the matches more exciting and established a keener because more evenly balanced rivalry. The grounds were not so true as those of to-day, and the matches were not so numerous ; consequently cricketers were not so frequently worn out by the wear and tear of long fielding and days and nights of travel as they are now. The long individual scores having been less in number and at longer intervals, the few great innings were more vividly stamped on the memory, and it is doubtful if even the modern 200 runs per innings will survive as historical facts longer than Hankey's famous innings of 70 against the Players on Lord's, Daft's 118 in North v. South on the same ground, and Hayward's 112 against Gentlemen also on Lord's.

The bowling during this period was generally fast or medium, varied by lobs, but of genuine slow round, like that of Peate, Buchanan, and Alfred Shaw, there was hardly any in first-class matches. To fast bowling runs come quicker than they do to slow ; consequently the game was of more interest to the ordinary spectator, and there was none of that painful slowness, in consequence of the extraordinary accuracy of modern slow bowling, that is so common now, and helps to produce so many drawn matches. The professionals had literally only two genuine slow-round-arm bowlers in those days—George Bennett, of Kent, and Buttress, of Cambridgeshire—and of course this fact accounted largely for the batting style of the period. Wickets being often rough, the most paying length for fast bowling was naturally that length which gave the ground most chance, and prevented the smothering style of play—a little shorter than the blind spot, compelling back play over the crease, instead of forward play. The best batsmen were great masters of this style of play, with which the name of Carpenter is strongly identified. To modern players the sight of Carpenter or Daft dropping down on a dead shooter from a bowler of the pace of George Freeman or Jackson was a wonderful one; but it is rapidly becoming a memory only, for in these days a fast shooter is very rarely seen, and when it does come it nearly always gets a wicket. The reader must always bear in mind that fast bowling cannot be so accurate as slow; it is therefore a certainty that all-round hitting in the fast-bowling days was more common than it is now, in first-class matches. There is one hit in particular that in these days is very seldom seen—that is, the smite to long-leg with a horizontal bat, and much nearer the ground than a square-leg hit. During the entire progress of a match nowadays, between Notts and Lancashire, or Yorkshire and Notts, the unhappy batsman will hardly get a single ball outside his legs to hit. So great is the accuracy of the bowling, that over after over will go by, and not even a ball on his legs will soothe his careworn and anxious brain. This accurate bowling has caused another change in the way of batting. As no ball is bowled on the leg side at all, so it consequently follows there is no fieldsman on the on side except a forward short-leg and a deep field. There is not much to be gained by continually cracking the ball straight to a row of safe fieldsmen on the off side. What, then, does the modern batsman do on a smooth wicket? He waits till the bowler slightly overtosses a ball—whether pitched outside the off stump or on the wicket he cares not; he sweeps it round to square leg, where no fieldsman stands, and he makes four runs by the hit. In other words, he deliberately 'pulls' it. Twenty years ago, on seeing such a hit, the famous Bob Grimston would have shown his emphatic disapproval in a characteristic manner. But the match must be won by runs; to attain this object the ball must be hit where there is no field, and it is useless to waste energy by hitting the ball to every fieldsman on the off side. W. W. Read, H. V. Page, and A. J. Webbe, are all masters of this stroke, which revives the drooping attention of the crowd and relieves the monotony of the scorers. We do not wish the reader to infer from these remarks that we think the batsmen of to-day are a whit inferior in hitting power to their predecessors. If the welcome sight of a fast bowler being put on is seen now, the hitting becomes at once a joy to behold. But there is little doubt that batsmen of the real 'sticking' type are now more numerous, because the bowling is much straighter, and therefore far fewer balls are bowled that are easy to hit.

Bowling having been in former days generally fast, the cut was a hit largely in vogue, and the perfection to which some players arrived with regard to this stroke has never been surpassed by later batsmen. It is, of course, as will be explained later on, much easier to cut fast bowling than slow, and the heroes of the cut in those days were numerous. The champion cutter of his period, by universal testimony, was C. G. Lyttelton, whose hits in the direction of point are remembered by spectators to this day. Tom Humphrey, of Surrey, was another great cutter; and there was a player, not of the first rank, who was famous for this hit—namely, E. P. Ash, of the Cambridge University Eleven, 1865 and 1866. The four champion bats of this era—1855 to 1868—were, in the opinion of the writer, Hayward, Carpenter, Parr and Daft, and the first two, both from the town of Cambridge, were a little superior to the others. The scoring of Hayward and Carpenter between 1860 and 1864 was very large; both excelled on rough wickets, and it is on these wickets that genius exhibits itself.

In all times of cricket, until the appearance of W. G. Grace, there has been a large predominance of skill amongst the professionals as compared with the amateurs. We are talking now of batting; in bowling the difference has been still more to the advantage of the professionals. The Gentlemen won a match now and then, but their inferiority was very great.

W. G. Grace altered all this ; and from 1868 to 1880 the Gentlemen had a run of success which will probably never be seen again. It was entirely owing to him, though the Players were astonishingly weak in batting from 1870 to 1876 ; but nothing could stop the crack, and his scoring in the two annual contests was simply miraculous.

We will now attempt to lay before our readers a more detailed exposition of the principles which ought to govern sound batting, and a careful observance of which is found in the method of every sound player. The first consideration is the choice of a bat, and as to this each individual must determine for himself what is the most suitable. It is probable that a strong man will prefer a heavier bat than a batsman of less muscular calibre. In any case the style of play is an important consideration.

At the beginning of this century, when the bowling was fast under-hand, the bat used was of a style suitable for meeting such balls—namely, a heavy blade with great weight at the bottom ; for, as already mentioned, the bowling being straight and frequently on the ground, driving was the common stroke, and for this a heavy blade is best adapted. So now, if a player finds that his is not a wrist style of play, but a forward driving game, he will probably choose a heavier bat than the wrist-player; for a forward drive is more of a body stroke—that is, the whole muscular strength of the shoulders and back is brought into use, and the ball, being fully met, gives more resistance to the bat than a ball which is cut. This, perhaps, needs a little explanation. Just consider for a moment, and realise the fact that a tolerably fast ball, well up and quite straight, has been delivered. Such a ball is just the ball that ought to be driven. The batsman lunges forward and meets it with very nearly the centre of his bat, just after the ball has landed on the ground, at the time, therefore, when, if there is any spin on it, it is going at its fastest pace. Obviously, therefore, when the pace and weight of the ball are taken into consideration, there is great resistance given to the lunge forward of the bat. The heavier the blade of the bat the better is it able to withstand and resist the contrary motion of the ball. As a rule, players are not equally good both at the forward driving and the wrist-playing games. Some few excel in both, but usually batsmen have preferences. Now let us examine the cut—of course we are now discussing a ball on the off side of the wicket. A wrist-player will cut a ball that the exponent of the driving style would drive, and therefore meet with the full, or nearly full, bat. The cutter does not meet the ball, for the ball has gone past him before he hits it. Take a common long-hop on the off side. The driver meets it with a more or less horizontal bat, and hits it forward between cover-point and mid-off, or cover-point and point, thereby resisting the ball and sending it almost in an opposite direction to its natural course. He hits the ball some time before it arrives on a level with his body, while the cutter, on the other hand, does not hit the ball so soon ; in fact, he hits it when it is about a foot in front of the line of the wicket, sometimes almost on a level with the wicket. He then, with his wrist, hits it in the direction of third man. He does not meet the ball at all, but he takes advantage of the natural pace of the ball and, as it were, steers it from the normal course towards long-stop, in the direction of third man. The whole essence of the distinction lies in this fact, that in driving the ball is met directly by the bat ; in cutting this is not so ; but the ball is, as it were, helped on, only in a different direction. The faster the bowling, the harder, therefore, will be the cut. The reader will at once see from this that the wrist-player will probably prefer a lighter bat than the driving batsman, and a bat that comes up well, as it is called, or is more evenly balanced.

We will now suppose a batsman properly equipped in pads and two gloves (both of which we consider quite essential) and with a bat to his taste ; our next inquiry must be as to his position at the wicket. He must remember that, after having chosen one position—the most natural and convenient to him— he ought to adopt that position invariably ; not alter it from day to day. You never see any material alteration in the position of any great player, and if anyone takes the very necessary trouble to find out the easiest position, he will be a foolish man who varies it, as any change must be for the worse. There is an old engraving, often seen, of a match between Surrey and Kent about the year 1840. Old William Lillywhite is about to bowl, and Fuller Pilch is about to play. The attitude and position of Pilch were taken by the author of 'The Cricket Field' as a model; and there is no objection to be raised to the position: it is a fair assumption that it was the natural and most convenient position for Fuller Pilch himself. The author, however, goes on to say that this is substantially the attitude of every good batsman. To this we can only rejoin, that out of the thousands of batsmen who have played cricket, it would be difficult to find two who stand exactly alike. To begin with, some stand with their feet close together, others have them apart; some indeed so far apart that it almost seems as if they were trying to solve the problem of how much length of ground can be covered between the two feet. Some stand with the right foot just on the leg side of a straight line drawn between the leg-stump of the batsman's wicket and the off stump of the opposite wicket; others stand with the right foot twelve inches or thereabouts from the leg-stump in the direction of short-leg. Players who adopt this position run a risk of being bowled off their legs, one would think; but they ought to know best; we should not, however, advise a beginner to adopt this attitude. W. G. Grace faces the ball, and there is no intervening space between his hands whilst holding the bat and his legs. If you look at the position of Pilch, you will see a considerable interval of distance from the back of his left hand and the right leg. There were three notable batsmen— namely, A. N. Hornby, W. Yardley, and F. E. R. Fryer—who used to throw their left leg right across the wicket so as almost to hide it from the view of the bowler.

Mr. A. J. Webbe stoops very much in his position, while some players stand almost at full height; notably is this the case with W. G. Grace. There are, as far as we know, only three rules which must be observed in taking up a position. The first is—(1) stand so that no part of the right foot is in front of the wicket or outside the crease ; (2) stand in the attitude most natural and convenient to yourself ; (3) do not place the toes of the right foot nearer the wicket than the heel. The first rule is essential, for the good player never ought to move his right foot to fast bowling. If, therefore, any part is in front of the wicket, he runs a risk of being leg before wicket when the ball beats the bat ; if his foot is outside the crease, he is in danger of being stumped ; and if the toes of the right foot are nearer the wicket than the heel, he will find himself in a very awkward position—unable to get over the ball. Subject to these rules, the batsman takes any position he pleases. The bat should be held firmly with the right hand and loosely, or comparatively loosely, with the left ; neither hand should be tightly clenched.

FIG. 2.—W. G. Grace ready to receive the ball.

The late Mr. Wm. Ward spoke the truth when he told a sculptor who had made a statue of a batsman at guard that he was no cricketer—the wrists were too rigid and hands too much clenched. It seems that most players lift their bat from the block-hole while the bowler is running prior to delivering the ball, and fig. 2 shows W. G. Grace standing just before the ball leaves the bowler's hand. His whole position is changed from what it was a few seconds before. His first position, before the bowler has begun his run, is given in the

sketch at the head of the chapter. The figure here shows
him to be standing almost at his full height, his bat suspended
in the air, and his weight if anything thrown rather on his
right foot. Most players, however, take up a position and stick
to it, except that they raise the bat slightly just before the ball
leaves the bowler's hand. Nature is the best guide. Let every
player therefore find out the easiest attitude and always adopt it.

We will now consider the manner in which the bat should
be held by the hands. This varies in a few trifling particulars
with different players : but in very rare instances is there
any substantial difference. The muscles ought not to be in a
state of rigidity, and whilst the batsman is standing in position
waiting for the ball the bat should be held firmly, but not
by any means tightly. The batsman cannot depend on any
particular ball coming to him ; consequently, while the ball is in
the air, his mind has to be made up ; he has then to set himself for a stroke determined absolutely by the pace, length, and
direction of the ball, and there are only a few seconds for him
both to make up his mind and make the stroke. There is, no
doubt, a scientific, anatomical reason why quickness of hand
and muscles is incompatible with rigidity of muscle, but quite
practicable when the muscles and sinews' are in a natural and
easy state of elasticity ; but any man will find this out for himself if he begins to play. Hold the bat, then, loosely with the left
hand, nearly at the top of the handle, with the back of the hand
turned full towards the bowler, the fingers folded round the
handle, and the thumb lying easily between the first and second
fingers. The right hand is fixed exactly contrary to the left as
far as the back and fingers are concerned, for the back is turned
away from the bowler and the fingers are turned towards him. The
thumb lies across and rests on the top of the first finger, touching
the finger about a quarter of an inch from the top on the inside.
When any sort of hit or block is made the bat at that instant is
held tightly, and both thumbs are slightly shifted so as to lie on
and clutch, not the fingers that hold the handle, but the handle
itself. Whether the hands are high up on the handle or low

down near the blade depends very much on the style of the player. There is no rule on the subject, but we think the old motto, ' In medio tutissimus ibis,' is good to observe, and the middle of the handle is, on the whole, the safest. Some players, however—notably Mr. Frank Penn, in his day a tremendous off-hitter and altogether a grand bat—hold the bat with the knuckle of the first finger of the right hand almost touching the top of the blade ; and big hitters, rather of the slogging order, as a rule hold the bat higher up, with the left hand almost on the top ; in fact, they adopt what may be called the ' long-handled style.' In holding the bat, however, follow the precept given before— namely, ascertain the most natural method, and cling to it for your cricketing life.

The actual position at the wicket is the same for both slow bowling and fast, with perhaps this trifling difference, that the batsman ought not to stand so firmly on the right foot to slow as he would to fast. The reason of this will be explained hereafter, when we consider the right method of playing slow bowling. At present we will confine our attention to playing fast bowling, and let us assume that the batsman has taken his natural position with his right toe clear of the wicket and that a fast right-handed bowler is bowling with hand raised above the shoulder and over the wicket. This is the method of bowling most in vogue in these days ; in fact, the strict round-arm bowling round the wicket, with a curl from leg, is for some inscrutable reason now comparatively rare. Why this is so nobody can tell, and we believe that some of the present gigantic scoring is partly owing to the absence of this sort of bowling.

However, the popular method will be the first we shall try and instruct the batsman to meet successfully, and we will suppose that the wicket is fast and true. We will begin with laying down one or two rules that must rigorously be observed by every player if he wishes to become a first-rate cricketer. (1) *Never move the right foot when playing fast bowling except to cut.* Nobody will ever become a first-rate player if he does not strictly observe this rule. The spot of ground on which the

right foot rests is the vantage-point from which every batsman
has to judge of the direction of the ball, and if he shifts away
from this, all sorts of faults will crop up, chief of which will be
an inability to play with a straight or perpendicular bat. He
will also, if he moves his right foot towards short-leg—which is
the commonest form this vice takes—find that he will drive balls
with a crooked bat, when from a proper position he would have
hit them to leg. He will also find himself further removed from
the off side, and quite unable, therefore, to play with a straight
bat on the off stump. These are a few of the faults that come
from not keeping the right foot still. All coaches know that
this habit of moving the right leg is the fault most commonly
found in young players, and it is most difficult to remove.
This arises from the fact that the ball is a hard substance ;
the beginner naturally dislikes being hit anywhere on the body,
and his first and most powerful instinct is therefore to run
away. But many instincts are base in their nature, and the
young cricketer must realise in this, as in other cases, that
the old Adam must be put away and the new man put on.
He will find, as he improves, that in these days of true
wickets he will not often get hit ; the bat will, as a rule, protect
him, and if he is hit anywhere on or below the knee the pads
will perform a similar function. If he does get hit, well, he
must grin and bear it, and try to emulate the heroism of some
giants of old in ante-pad-and-glove days, of one of whom, the
famous Tom Robinson, we read that he used to rub his bleeding fingers in the dust, after the Tarrant of those days had
performed a tattoo on his fingers. (2) Never pull a straight
fast ball to leg. If you miss it, you are either bowled out or else
you run a great chance of being given out leg before wicket.
This also is a common fault, and the fact that often on good,
true wickets it comes off is no justification of the practice;
for it is a bad hit, and even a ball that would not actually hit
the wicket, but just miss the leg-stump, should be driven
past the bowler and mid-on, not hit to leg. The bowling of
the present day is so accurate that in a first-class match we

seldom see a long or deep square-leg, and batsmen often get impatient and go for a pull. But it is a bad stroke, and cricketers ought not to attempt to make four runs by such a hit, but content themselves with a safe drive forward for one or more runs. (3) Never slog wildly at a ball well outside the off stump, but of a good length. This hit also may occasionally come off, but there is no trap more frequently laid by modern bowlers. Attewell, for example, bowls it so frequently, that 'the Attewell trap' is becoming a stock phrase, and a little consideration will show how dangerous a stroke it is. A good length ball is one that it is impossible to smother at the pitch, and if it is outside the off stump it has to be played with a more or less horizontal bat, if the slog is attempted. What must be the consequence ? The ball is not smothered, consequently any break, hang, or rise that the bowler or the ground may impart to the ball must almost inevitably produce a bad stroke, frequently terminating in a catch somewhere on the off side. The proper way to play such a ball will be discussed later on, but under no circumstances must the ball be hit at wildly at the pitch. (4) Keep the left shoulder and elbow well forward when playing the ball. It is more important in back play than forward, because in forward play the ball is, or ought to be, smothered at the pitch, and the value of the left shoulder being forward is that you are much more master of the ball if it should happen to bump or shoot ; besides which, the bat cannot easily be held straight unless this rule is observed, neither can the full face of the bat be presented to the ball. In the case of the shooter, or ball which keeps low after the pitch, the movement of the left shoulder towards the left or leg side will inevitably make it more difficult to ground or lower the bottom of the bat.

The art of defence—which is the style of play adapted to stop the ball, as distinguished from the offensive method, where the object is to hit the ball so as to obtain runs—may be roughly divided into forward play and back play. The object of all forward play is to smother the ball at its pitch ; that is to say, the contact of the bat with the ball must be almost simultaneous with the contact of the ball with the ground. The player must reach out with a straight bat as near to the pitch of the ball as is possible. It stands to reason that a tall man will reach out much further than a short man, and a bowler, if he is wise, will bowl shorter-pitched balls to a tall man than he will to a short. Let anybody take a bat and reach forward as far as he can, keeping the bat, when it touches the ground at the end of the stroke, slanting so that the top of the handle is nearer to the bowler than the bottom of the blade. There comes a distance when this slant cannot be maintained, and the bat has either to be held in a perpendicular position or with the handle sloping behind the blade and pointing towards the wicket-keeper. Here, then, we come to an invariable rule, viz. never play forward to a ball so that you are unable to keep the bat at the proper slant, with the handle of the bat further forward than the blade. Also, let every player remember that the left foot must be placed as far forward as the bottom of the bat, and all play, whether forward or back, is really between the two feet, or, more strictly speaking, in forward play the bat must not be put further forward than the left foot, and in back play not further back than the level of the right foot.

Some old players may very likely not agree with this precept, and players of the date of Fuller Pilch constantly had their bat a great deal further out than the left foot, which used not to be thrown out so far. Mr. C. F. Buller, again, in his day a magnificent bat, used to play forward in the same style. But let anyone take a bat and throw out his left foot to the fullest extent ; he will find that the bat ought not to go any further if the proper slant be maintained, and he will find also that he has greater command over the ball in this position than in Fuller Pilch's. Look at the position in fig. 3, and you will see that the bat has come down strictly on a level with the left foot. That a greater command is obtained by this method cannot be proved in writing, but anyone who tries the old and the new style will find that the new is preferable as far as command of the ball is concerned. We are not implying that the great

players of the old style were bad players because they played
in the contrary way, for great players rise above rules and play
by the force of their greatness ; but we are chiefly concerned
with the ordinary mortal, and our advice is, throw the left leg
right out and play to the level of the left foot. Some good
players maintain that, as the shooter comes so seldom nowadays, it is wasting power to ground the bat when playing forward, it being sufficient if it is placed according to circumstances,

FIG. 3.—Forward play.

varying with the state of the ground. It is certain that shooters
are far less frequent than they were ; still, unless a man's bat
be grounded, a shooter will inevitably bowl him, so he raises
his bat at his own risk. Fig. 3 illustrates grounding the bat
in forward play, and fig. 14, at the end of this chapter, illustrates
playing forward without grounding.

The ball which is too short for the player to play forward
to with his bat at the proper slant must be played back and

not forward. To be a good judge of a ball's length is a source of strength in any player, and a strictly accurate player seldom makes the mistake of playing forward when he ought to play back, and *vice versâ*. In cricket, however, poor human nature is apt to err oftener perhaps than in most walks of life, and the question may now be asked, What is the batsman to do when he finds himself playing forward, but unable to smother the ball at the pitch? He has made a mistake ; how is he to get out of the difficulty? Let it be remembered that we are at present only concerned with a fast and true wicket, the play on a slow tricky wicket being so different that it will be noticed separately.

Let us assume, then, that the batsman is forward in the position here shown, but that he finds he cannot reach far enough to smother the ball at the pitch. On a fast wicket there is no time to rectify the error by getting back and playing the ball in the orthodox manner; and yet the batsman must do something or he will be bowled out. There are three courses open to him. (1) He may trust to Providence and a good eye, and take a slog, or adopt what a humorous cricketer once called 'the closed-eye blow,' in which case, if hit at all, the ball will probably be propelled into the air, but perhaps out of harm's way, or, as is quite as likely, into a fielder's hands. The famous E. M. Grace, who is blessed with as good an eye as any cricketer, frequently plays this stroke with success. (2) He may adopt what lawyers would call the cy-près doctrine ; in other words, though he ought to play forward and smother a ball, he may at the same time play forward and not smother the ball, which may hit the bat nevertheless. The dangers of this play are obvious to every cricketer, for it leaves him at the mercy of the ball that bumps, hangs, or turns. Modern grounds are so good that this stroke is far safer than it used to be ; for in the majority of instances the ball comes straight on, and only the experienced observer sees that the batsman comes off with flying colours owing to the excellence of the ground rather than to his skill. (3) He may, after he has got

forward and perceived his error, effect a compromise and perform what is sometimes called a 'half-cock stroke.' This stroke
does not require a violent shuffling about of the legs and feet,
which are placed as they would be while playing forward,
but, instead of the arms and hands reaching forward, they are
brought back so as to hold the bat quite straight over, or a
little in front of, the popping crease. This position and style
of play may be observed in fig. 4, and it is worth a careful
examination ; for, in our opinion, it is the proper way for
a man to extricate himself out of the difficulty he has been led
into by misjudging the length of the ball. Nobody can play
a ball in this way more skilfully than W. G. Grace,
and the figure shows him in the act of thus playing
to a ball which is on the blind spot—that is, either
adapted for forward or back play, and therefore
eminently qualified for over the crease play, a
compromise between the two. The merit of this
style of play is that it gives the batsman time to watch
the ball, and if it should bump or turn he may alter
his tactics to meet it,

FIG. 4.—' Half-cock ' or over the crease play.

whereas by the second method his play is fixed and cannot be
altered, and the awkward hanging, bumping, or twisting ball
beats him. Practise by all means this half-cock stroke ; on fast
grounds it may be found more useful than even the orthodox
back play; for in back play, unless the ball is very short, the
pace of the ground may beat a man, especially when he first
goes in and has not got accustomed to the pace. The golden
rules to guide the beginner in playing forward may be very

briefly stated. (1) Play forward when the ball is fairly well pitched up, but remember that the faster the bowling and the faster the wicket the more frequently will forward play be the safer style of play. (2) Keep the bat quite straight and the left shoulder and elbow well forward. (3) Get as near to the pitch of the ball as possible. (4) Do not put the bat further forward than the level of the left foot, which ought to be thrown right forward.

It is often a doubtful question whether a straight drive forward is what is technically a drive or hit, or mere forward play. Of course, when the batsman is well set, he may hit as hard as he can to a straight half-volley ; but there are many players whose forward play is so powerful that it practically amounts to a drive. Alfred Lyttelton's forward play frequently makes mid-off tremble, and the same may be said of Bates, Ulyett, and several other players.

But to the beginner again: until you are well set, do not let all your strength go out to any straight ball ; if you do, you will lose more than you gain. On Lord's, for instance, a hit over the ropes can only realise four, the same as a hit under the ropes; you will very likely, therefore, score as many for a straight hard bit of forward play as you will for a regular swipe.

When the art of back play to fast bowling is discussed, the converse of what has been said about forward play is true, viz. that as the faster the ground the more balls ought to be played forward, so under the same circumstances will fewer balls be played back. As a general rule, it may be observed that strong-wristed players play more back than batsmen who play chiefly with their arms and shoulders. A weak-wristed player playing back on a very fast wicket will frequently be late, and either miss the ball altogether or else half-stop it, in which latter case it may dribble into the wicket. The value of a strong wrist is that the batsman can dab down on a ball and do the feat in a far shorter space of time than a shoulder-and-arm player. The difference between a strong wrist and a weak wrist in playing back is a little similar to what is observed in an altogether different line. Look at a great underbred cart-horse with a leg like a weaver's beam, and then look at the real thoroughbred with its slim proportions; at first sight it appears that a kick from the cart-horse will inflict much greater damage than a kick from the thoroughbred. People who are learned in horses, however, inform us that the contrary is the case, and the greater weight of the leg of the cart-horse is more than counterbalanced by the far more rapid and sudden movement of the thoroughbred. The bat wielded by a player with a strong wrist goes through the air like lightning, and comes down on the ball far quicker and harder than a ponderous stroke from the arms and shoulders of the batsman with no wrist action. Perhaps the champion back-player of the century was Robert Carpenter, of Cambridgeshire and United All England renown, whose back play on Lord's to the terrific fast bowling of Jackson and Tarrant will never be forgotten by those who beheld it.

A back style of play does not smother the ball at the pitch, but plays at the ball when its course after contact with the ground is finally determined, and a careful watching of the ball is therefore of the highest importance. It is bad ever to assume that, because a ball has pitched on a line with the off stump, therefore you are safe if you protect the off stump only, on the assumption that the ball is going on straight. The ball may break back, and in order to ascertain that it has done so, and to shift your bat to guard the middle and leg stumps, you must carefully watch the ball. Apart from breaking or curling, the ball may shoot or bump; in either case the batsman has only his eye to guide him, and the wrist has to obey the eye. Fig. 5 represents 'back play' to a bumping ball. Sometimes a ball may be so short that if the batsman has got his eye well in, and is thoroughly accustomed to the pace of the ground, he may by a turn of the wrist, keeping the left shoulder and elbow well forward, steer the ball through the slips. The beginner, however, must be careful to attempt nothing but

the orthodox forms of play ; he is not W. G. Grace or Shrewsbury and such-like, who, in their turn, do not attempt exceptional
feats until they are well set. The ball ought to be met with the

FIG. 5.—' Back play ' to a bumping ball.

full face of the bat, and under no circumstances ought the ball
to be allowed to hit the bat, which must be the propeller, not
the propelled. Mind to respect and carefully follow out the
two great commandments—never to move the right foot, and

to keep the left shoulder forward and left elbow up. The
number of hours that a youngster has to be bowled at before
that fatal right foot can be relied upon to keep still is prodigious ; but the bat cannot be straight if the body is gravitating
towards the direction of short leg while the ball is in the air.
To a very short ball different methods of play may be adopted.
The one alluded to above, the steering of the ball through the
slips, is not often attempted, and a safer method would be to
try and come heavily down on the ball and force it past the
fields for two or three runs.   This is a safe stroke, much safer
to adopt than the other.   The bat must be straight, and it is
wise not to let your whole strength go out, for one or two contingencies may arise for which the player ought to be prepared.
In the first place, the ball may shoot, and the crisis must be
met accordingly.   Now, if the whole of the strength and all the
faculties of a batsman are bent towards the carrying out of
one particular stroke, there will be no reserve left to provide
for any other contingency, for the muscles will be wholly set
for one stroke, and one stroke only, and the player will infallibly
be late if the ball should shoot or even keep a little low.   Of
course, on a great many grounds in these days the chances
of such contingencies are reduced almost to a minimum on
account of the excellence of modern wickets; but still we have
to inform the reader what *may* happen, not only what happens
commonly.   Some few players rise superior to grounds, and
though of course they can get many more runs on easy wickets,
still they show good cricket when the wicket is in favour of the
bowler.

The prevalence of easy wickets is not, in our opinion, an un-
mixed blessing. You may go and watch a match when the ground
is as hard as iron and as true as truth, and see a magnificent
innings played by some batsman. The same player on a bowler's
wicket is not less uncomfortable than the proverbial fish out
of water.   A man may be a lion on a lawn, but a mere pigmy
when the ground is not a lawn.   There are a great many of
these lions on lawns in these days, and to hear them all with

one consent begin to make excuse when they have been bowled
out on a crumbling wicket is very amusing. The ball hung,
or it kept low, or 'broke back a foot, I assure you, dear boy.
W. G. in his best days wouldn't have been near it.' In his
best days, and almost in his worst, Mr. Grace would have often
played it, and so would Steel, Shrewsbury, and one or two others
—planets among the stars, to watch whom getting thirty runs
out of a total of eighty on a difficult wicket is far more enjoyable to a skilled spectator than to see the hundreds got on A B C
wickets. But this is a digression, and we will return to our
subject. The chances that on a hard smooth wicket the very
short ball will do anything abnormal is, nowadays, reduced to
a minimum. But still it may happen, and it is therefore wise
to have in reserve a little strength and a little elasticity. You
can play very hard, nevertheless, and for this hard forcing stroke
off a short straight ball W. Yardley, the late B. Pauncefote,
and H. C. Maul, who still plays for Warwickshire, have never
been surpassed.

The ball most to be dreaded for the forcing stroke is the
hanging ball, which stops and does not come on evenly and
fast to the bat. The batsman will fail to time the ball, with
the almost certain consequence that the bat will go on and the
ball will be hit from underneath, and up it will go. The advice
that has been given to keep a slight reserve of strength to provide against such contingencies as the hanging ball has the
same force now. If you have not altogether let the whole
force go out, you will have a better chance of doing the correct
thing to a ball of this description—namely, to drop the bat and
allow the ball to hit it, the exact opposite of your original intention. This is an exception to the general rule that the bat
should hit the ball, and not the ball the bat.

In all cases a quick and correct eye will enable its owner
to come out of the difficulty with flying colours, and any rules
that may be laid down will be utterly useless to him who puts
his bat just where the ball is *not*, but where his inaccurate eye
thinks it is. If a youth with the best intentions, but with a

false and crooked eye, after reading and thoroughly compre-
hending every rule directing how every ball ought to be played,
stands up and tries to play cricket, what will be the result?
He may even have courageously learnt to pin his right foot
firmly to the ground; but, notwithstanding this, the result of his
efforts will be that, though all proper and necessary postures
may be assumed, he will be bowled out, for the bat, except
by a lucky chance, will always be in the wrong place, though
held quite straight. If cricket could be played with no ball,
the careful eyeless cricketer would shine ; but the introduction of that disturbing element dashes all his hopes to the
ground.

There is a ball that in these days more frequently than any
other succeeds in bowling people out, and that is the familiar
'tice' or 'yorker.' This is nothing else than a ball right up, that
pitches in fact near the block-hole, but is not a full pitch.
This ball ought to be met by the bat just when it touches the
ground, and the bat ought to come down very heavily on the
ball. It is a little difficult to understand why this ball is so
frequently fatal, as it comes straight up and only requires a
straight bat and correct timing. Probably most batsmen hope
that the eagerly-looked-for half-volley has at length come ; this
induces them to lay themselves out for a smite, and when they
see their mistake it is too late to alter the tactics. Others, on
the contrary, think that a full-pitch is coming, and advance
their bat to meet it ; the result is, the ball gets underneath it.
In fact, the length of the ball is not correctly judged, and the
batsman is caught in two minds. A bowler who is in the habit
of sending down yorkers is fond of doing so the first ball after
a new batsman comes in, and if a batsman is known to be of a
nervous temperament there is no better ball to give in the
first over. It may be here said, however, that it is next door to
impossible to bowl a ' yorker ' to some batsmen. W. G. Grace,
for instance, seems always to be able to make a full-pitch of this
ball, and a fourer often results. It is obvious that if a ball pitches
near or on a level with the block-hole when the batsman is

standing still, it ought to be easy to make it a full-pitch by stepping out to meet it. Mr. Grace does this even to fast bowling.

Having endeavoured to the best of our ability to enunciate a few principles as to defensive tactics, we will now try and discuss offensive tactics, or hitting. A curious feature of the present day is that new hits have come into existence. These have not sprung up because they were not occasionally brought off in earlier days, but formerly when they were the batsman used to apologise to the bowler for having wounded his feelings, and a sort of groan used to be heard all round, as if there had been some gross violation of a cricket commandment. The grounds have improved to such an extent that bowlers have had to resort to new tactics to effect the grand object of all bowlers—namely, to get wickets.

They cannot bowl the first-class batsmen out, so they must place the field accurately and bowl for catches. In order to do this with success the bowling must be accurate to a degree, or rather the bowler must learn to pitch the ball to a nicety on some given spot. He must carry out a predetermined plan likely in his judgment to tempt the batsman to a false hit, having previously arranged his field also in accordance with the same plan. But this extreme accuracy is only compatible with slow bowling, and it is owing to this fact that fast bowling is now at a discount. It is because of the smoothness of the modern wickets, and for no other reason. On rough wickets a wise captain will put on his fast bowlers, if he has got them—not by any means always the case—for they will get wickets at a less cost ; the rough ground makes the ball bump, and a fast bumping ball frightens the batsman. He cannot run out to fast bowling ; therefore balls of a certain length are never smothered at the pitch as slow bowling sometimes is; consequently the bump, shoot and turn may come, and frequently do come. On such wickets, at the present day, Barnes is the best bowler in England ; and Lohmann and Barnes, if they happened to be on the same side, would begin the attack.

But on smooth wickets you would see Peel at one end, and perhaps Bates at the other, with eight fields on the off side, and three balls out of four pitched on the off side with good length. The result would very likely be that the unwary batsman would send a catch to the field, or at any rate that his labour would be in vain, and the good hits would only be stopped. Obviously the best chance of making runs is to hit the ball where there are no fields. Nearly the whole of the on side is open, and if one of the off balls is suitable, either by being bowled a little short or too far up, the batsman will sweep it round without a moment's hesitation. Unorthodox this may be, but he will have accomplished five great and useful feats— he will have delighted himself, added to his score, disconcerted the fields, enraged the bowler, and set the opposite captain thinking. At the same time it is not a graceful stroke, but is one of the many instances of deterioration of style, regarded from a purely æsthetic point of view, which, we find, has taken place in comparing modern cricket with that of bygone days. So great must be the caution used in playing this extraordinarily accurate slow bowling almost entirely on the off stump, or on the off side of the wicket when seven or eight fields are on the off side, that it is becoming quite a common feature of the game to see balls of a dangerous length on the off side entirely ignored by the batsman, as far as the bat is concerned, while both legs are placed entirely in the front of the wicket in case the ball should break. This is safety play with a vengeance. At the same time the spectators may reasonably be excused if they find looking on at cricket a little dull. When the bowling is fast the general result is wickets or runs, and that was the case twenty years ago. We hear that the Australian spectators in their own country loudly expressed their disapproval when, in a great match, two batsmen were batting two hours, during which time they produced the magnificent result of forty-five runs and wore out the patience of bowlers, field, and gallery. The full discussion of the vexed question of l.b.w. will be found in the chapter on Cricket Reform.

Of all hits, the most fascinating to the intelligent spectator is the cut. This requires a very strong use of the wrist, and, like all wrist strokes, charms the spectator by accomplishing great results at the expense of apparently little effort. Cricket reporters of the present day are very apt to call any hit that goes in any direction between cover-point and long-slip a cut, and thereby make the term include both snicks and off drives. This is a mistake, as nearly every cricketer can sometimes make an off drive, and all can snick the ball, even the worst ; indeed, with some it is the only stroke they seem to possess, but there are many who have hardly ever made a genuine cut in their lives. The real genuine cut goes to the left side of point—assuming that point stands on a line with the wicket —it is made with the right leg thrown over, and its severity depends largely on the perfectly correct timing of the ball. The ball is hit when it has reached a point almost on a line with the

FIG. 6.—Gunn cutting.

wicket, and the length of the ball is rather short ; if far up, it is a ball to drive and not to cut. The bat should hit the ball slightly on the top, and the most correct cutting makes the ball bound before it gets more than six yards from the player. Figs. 6 and 7 show Gunn and Shrewsbury in the position proper for cutting. It is a mistake to suppose that the right leg should be thrown over a long way; it is sufficient if the foot be put in front of the off stump. When the player is well in and has thoroughly got the pace of the ground, he very often makes what may be called a clean cut ; that is to say, he hits with a bat quite horizontal to the ball, and not over it. This produces a harder hit, as the force is wholly directed towards sending the ball in the proper direction, and not hard on the ground. It is not so safe, because, if the ball should bump, the bat, not being over the ball, may hit its lower side and send it up. Therefore be careful to hit over, and sacrifice some of the severity, if you wish to play a safe game.

FIG. 7.—Shrewsbury cutting.

Some careful players would hit over the ball even after they have scored one hundred runs, and we have never seen Shrewsbury, for instance, cut in any other way. In the figure the ball must be presumed to lie rather low, for it is certain that he is following his invariable custom of getting over the ball. In any case we should never recommend the clean cut to any but the best players, and that only on a perfect wicket and when they are well set. If you are in the position to cut and the ball should bump, it is wise to leave it alone, for the danger of being caught at third man is very great. We have seen lusty hitters get right under a bumping off ball and send it high over third man's head, but it is a perilous stroke, and is not correct cricket. If the ball, on the other hand, keeps a bit low after the pitch, it is a most effective stroke to come heavily down on it ; if the force is put on the ball at the right moment it will go very hard, and may be called a 'chop.' Mr. K. J. Key, who is a strong player from every point of view, excels at this stroke, and he hits the ground at the same time as the ball with a great power of wrist. It is useless for anybody to hope to cut well unless he has both a strong wrist and also a quick eye to judge the correct second wherein to hit the ball—in other words, a power of timing the ball ; the latter no book can teach, and the former cannot even be acquired by practice, which the second in some instances can.

The question now arises, What is the player with a weak wrist to do with a ball that a strong-wristed man cuts? Some would say that if he cannot cut in the orthodox vigorous way he ought at any rate to go as near to it as he can, and if he cannot make a clean cut for four, at least he should content himself with two. We think, however, there is for such players a more excellent way. In the cut we have been describing the right foot is shifted across : suppose the player now moves his left foot, not across, but simply straight forward to a ball that is in every way suitable to cut ; let him then wait till the ball has gone just past his body, and then hit it with the full force of his arms and shoulders and with as much wrist as he has got. The ball will naturally go in the same direction as the orthodox cut, and quite as hard. The player must stand upright, and must especially be careful not to hit the ball before it has passed his body. If he does this off a fast long hop, he will bring off a vulgar sort of stroke, which cannot go so hard as the ball hit later, because there is greater resistance to the bat ; in the correct way the bat hits the ball partly behind it and, as it were, helps it on in its natural course, whereas at the incorrect moment the ball has to be thumped in order to send it in an exactly opposite direction from that in which it is going before meeting the bat.

In our judgment coaches ought to teach all beginners this stroke wherever they find weakness of wrist. The body is put in such a way as to compensate for a weak wrist, and if anyone takes up this position with a bat in his hand he will find that the stroke partakes of the qualities of a drive more than of a cut. Young players are generally rather impatient, and very apt to hit the ball before it reaches the level of the body, and this fault must be removed.

Let us now discuss the leg hit—most glorious of hits—where every muscle of the body may safely be exerted ; for if you miss it the ball is not straight, so you cannot be bowled, and the harder the hit the less chance is there of being caught, at any rate in first-class matches in these days of boundaries. Bowling having become slow, or slow medium as the rule, and therefore far straighter and more accurate, there is not half so much leg hitting now as there used to be, and in the present day you hardly ever hear of a batsman known for his leg hitting as George Parr was formerly, as also Mr. R. A. H. Mitchell, and several others.

There are plenty of men who can hit to leg, but in these days they do not often get a chance, and it is a rare event nowadays to see any fieldsman standing at the old-fashioned position of long-leg. There

FIG. 8.—Old-fashioned sweep to leg. (Gunn.)

is generally a field, stationed against the ropes to save four byes when a fast bowler is on, who can also stop leg snicks from going to the ropes; but, to carry the illustration farther, as in leg hitting there is no George Parr, so in fielding at long leg there is no Jack Smith of Cambridge. It is rapidly dying out. In a match which we ourselves saw at Sheffield in 1887, between Notts and Yorkshire, for a whole day and a half there was not one genuine leg smack except off lobs, and at

no time was a field placed there. This is hard for the batsman, but it is even harder for the spectators who love to see
a grand square-leg hit. George Parr's leg hit, for which he
was unrivalled, was the sweep to long-leg off a shortish ball
that many modern players would lie back to and play off
their legs. George Parr would extend his left leg straight forward, and sweeping round with a horizontal bat, send the ball
very hard, and frequently along the ground. This hit has really
almost totally disappeared in these days ; why, it is difficult to
explain entirely, though, no doubt, it is partly caused by bowling being so much over the wicket and over-hand and so very
straight. When George Parr played he used to punish terrifically
bowlers like Martingell, of Surrey and Kent, who relied on a
curl from leg and bowled round the wicket—a most effective
style, naturally producing, however, many leg balls. It is all
the other way now, and it may be taken for certain that for
every leg ball you see now in first-class matches you saw ten
or twenty in former days. However, young players in schools
are certain to get plenty of convenient balls to hit, so they must
remember to throw out the left leg and hit as near to the pitch
as possible and as hard as they can. The ball may start in the
direction of square-leg, but its natural bias after it has gone a
certain distance will be towards long-leg or behind the wicket,
and the fieldsman must remember this, or he will find the ball
fly away behind him on his right side. Be very careful never to
try this stroke to balls that are on the wicket, or even nearer the
wicket than four inches at least. If it is within that distance it
is a ball to drive, and not to hit to leg. Fig. 8 shows Gunn
carrying out this stroke, and the batsman may put his left leg
in front of the wicket if he is certain the ball did not pitch
straight. This hit ought only to be attempted when the ball
is short of a half-volley. If the ball is a half-volley or at any
rate well up, the proper hit is in front of the wicket or to
square-leg, and with a vertical, not a horizontal bat. In this hit,
how far to throw out the left leg depends on the length of the
ball ; the batsman may even sometimes have to draw it back a

little and stand upright and face the ball if it is well up. There is no hit that can be made harder than this to square-leg, and there have been many records of gigantic square-leg hits. Some hitters have sent the ball as far by the lofty smack straight over the bowler's head, but more batsmen can generally hit farther to square-leg, and only a short time ago Mr. Key sent a ball right out of the Oval. In years gone by Lord Lyttelton and R. A. H. Mitchell were renowned for their square-leg hitting, as was Carpenter also. There is no very special rule to be observed for this hit, except that the ball must be on the legs or just outside them, and not straight, or within

FIG. 9.—Square-leg hit. (W. G. Grace.)

four or five inches of the leg stump. If the ball is tolerably wide on the leg the bat will be more horizontal as it hits the ball, which will in consequence go sharper, and *vice versâ*, if the ball is just crooked enough to hit; it will, when hit, go more straight, and be called by the cricket reporters an 'on drive,' though it is a square-leg hit. Fig. 9 is supposed to represent W. G. Grace hitting to square-leg, and the reader must assume that the fieldsman is running to field the ball going on a line or in front of the wicket, and not behind it.

Some players there are who never seem to hit at any ball, but push it all along the ground, and for this purpose they get farther over the ball, and simply utilise the weight of the body, using the arms and shoulders but little.

This is an eminently safe game, but to these players we would only observe that they deprive themselves of the glorious sensation, alluded to at the beginning of this chapter, which comes when a ball is hit with all the force that nature can supply and a fine driving bat can supplement. Cricket is a game ; the primary object of games is to give pleasure to the players, and it is quite impossible that the same amount of keen gratification can await the stick who never hits as is realised by the man who, though he may only be at the wickets half the time, yet in that time makes at least ten great hits that will realise forty runs. There is, however, a good length ball on the legs to which this push can be usefully applied if the batsman is one of the numerous class of cricketers who cannot make use of the sweep to leg. This stroke is made by slightly moving out of the ground, or rather, the whole weight of the body being inclined forward the right foot is dragged forward also. This may seem to violate a cardinal rule laid down before—that the right foot should never be moved. It must be remembered that the reasons why the right foot should not be moved mainly apply when the foot is moved in front of the wicket or towards short-leg. It is invariably wrong to go out of your ground when the fast ball is straight or on the off side, for in both these instances, if you miss the ball, even if it does not hit the wicket, you are under the risk of being stumped. But to move out of your ground to a fast ball on your legs practically lays you open to no danger of being stumped, for if you should miss the ball you will stop it with your legs. Now imagine yourself utterly unable to sweep the ball to leg as George Parr used to do, and receiving a ball that you cannot reach at the pitch so as to hit with a straight bat—in other words, rather a short ball—what are you to do? If the ball is very short you will probably get back, bring your left foot on a line with, and close to, the right, and try either to make the ball glide off your bat to long-leg or play it with a full face for a single in front of short-leg.

Fig. 10 shows W. G. Grace attempting the glide, and apparently he has hardly moved either leg ; presumably, therefore, the ball is not very short, but only just too short to hit. This is a stroke in which W. G. Grace excels, as indeed he does in most others ; but it is a dangerous one unless the left elbow is kept well up, for otherwise, if the ball bumps, you will find your bat sloping backwards and the ball will go up.

We must now think of the proper way to play a ball on the legs that is not short enough for the batsman to play back to in this way, though, on the other hand, it cannot be hit to square-leg with a straight bat. The batsman also, on account of some natural disabililily, has always been unable to learn the secret of the George Parr sweep. This sort of ball must be played forward, and, if necessary, the batsman may even leave his ground and push it in front of short leg. As has been said before, if he should miss the ball his legs will save him from being stumped. The ball must be smothered as far as possible and pushed on in front of short-leg, and the reason why it is not hit harder is simply because you cannot quite get at the pitch, and if, therefore, you hit hard at it, you

FIG. 10.—' The glide.' (W. G. Grace.)

would probably sky the ball. The bat must be kept at the proper slope: as the body is lunging forward a great deal of impetus will be given to the hit by the mere weight of the body, and the ball will frequently find its way to the ropes. This play is most useful when opposed to left-handed bowlers, for then the ball is apt to follow the arm and come straight in the direction of the batsman's left hip. The famous trio of Uppingham cricketers, Messrs. Patterson, Lucas, and D. Q. Steel, were very strong in this stroke, and in an innings of over a hundred which Mr. Patterson played at Lord's in 1876 against Oxford a large proportion of his runs were made in this way. In ancient days many balls on the leg side used to be played by a now practically obsolete stroke called the 'draw,' which consisted of an ugly lifting up of the left leg and letting the ball glide off the bat between the legs towards long-leg. It was as much part of the *répertoire* of a player of the old style as a cut or a drive, but it has utterly gone out of fashion as a stroke to be learnt, simply because it had no further effect than the glide off the bat as now practised ; the modern style has also the additional advantage of being more elegant, and there is less chance of the ball hitting the foot. The famous Jemmy Grundy used frequently to play this stroke, and his mantle appears to have descended on some younger Nottingham players, for at the present day they sometimes use it. It used to be brought off occasionally by the famous Richard Daft, and was in fact the only stroke of this graceful and most correct player that was not elegant. As we have now got on the subject of the draw, we may as well describe the other sort of obsolete draw, which was performed by just touching the ball with the bat quite straight, but with its left side turned towards the wicket-keeper, or what soldiers would call left half-face, held some way behind the body. Tom Hearne used to be great at this sort of draw, but it is even more entirely gone out of fashion as a stroke than the other style. The same effect is produced by what is frequently seen—namely, a batsman only just snicking a ball off the leg stump, or just touching it, leaving the spectator uncertain whether the ball has been played or has hit the wicket. Tom Hearne, who was the last player who used to practise this stroke methodically, was in the habit of jumping with both feet towards short-leg, and leaving the bat in the correct position for the draw ; and not unfrequently he was caught at the wicket owing to the ball not being turned sufficiently ; sometimes, though not often, if the bound towards short-leg happened to be a little too much in front, he used to be stumped. This stroke necessitated moving the right leg towards short-leg, and it is on this ground mainly that we contend that it is not sound cricket ; but, as has

before been stated, it is now quite obsolete, and to imagine it
you must also imagine yourself in the days of tall hats, pads
under the trousers, and braces holding up a curious type of
pantaloon, such as the late Mr. Burgoyne, treasurer of the
M.C.C., used to wear up to the day of his death. The play
shown in fig. 11 is made by drawing back the left foot, coming
hard on to the ball, and forcing it in the direction of short-leg.
In our judgment, this is the right play for all short balls on the
legs, for the ball is near to the body and consequently to the
eye ; you have therefore
great facility in placing it,
and you have also the bat
at a proper angle. It is
more correct than the stroke
shown in fig. 10, for there if
the ball should bump it will
run up the shoulder of the
bat, and possibly get caught
by the wicket-keeper, short-
slip, or even point and
short-leg, and we have seen
several instances of the ball
hitting the bat, not in the
front but at the side of
the bat. In the former play
the ball has to hit the bat,
in the latter the bat hits the ball, and, according to the fancy
of the batsman, can either be hit in front of short-leg or be
suffered to glide towards very sharp long-leg. The figure, however, does not quite convey the impression that the ball is
being hit hard. The bat may have descended from over the
batsman's head, especially if the ball is very short, while the
figure only shows the end of the stroke.

FIG. 11.—Forcing stroke off the legs.

　　The off drive in the direction of cover-point and to the right
hand of point is a favourite hit with many players. Barnes
of Nottingham plays it to perfection. The ball to hit in this

CAUGHT AT THE WICKET

way is one well up on the off side, though it need not be a half-volley. The left foot is thrown across, the ball is hit with a nearly perpendicular bat, and the stronger the wrist the cleaner and harder will be the hit. In this and every other hit correct timing is most important, and whatever the beginner may try, do not let him attempt to hit wildly at the pitch of the ball. Let the left foot be put across, and be careful to hit over the ball in order to keep it down, for if you do not, and the ball bumps, it will inevitably go up. The ball should be a foot or so wide of the wicket ; the batsman at the moment of striking the ball will be facing cover-point, and will have his left shoulder well forward, as in fig. 12. The bat is well over the shoulder, and is coming down nearly perpendicularly on the ball, which is not a half-volley ; if it were, the bat would be straighter and the ball would be driven straighter. But the ball is hit after it has gone about a foot from the pitch. If the ball is a foot or two wide of the wicket and well up it would be hit in a similar position, for the bat cannot be held straight to hit a ball at this distance from the wicket ; if it should go straight it would be a pull and not a clean hit, and the further the ball from the wicket the further ought the left foot to be moved across. Whatever you do, refrain from hitting a ball when there is reasonable expectation of the umpire calling 'Wide.' You may hit it for two or three runs ; you are more likely only just to touch it with the end of the bat and get caught by third man or point ; you are still more likely to cover it and not score off it, thereby losing a run for your side.

So completely has the modern method of bowling on the off side for catches established itself, that cautious players like Hall, Shrewsbury, and Scotton have got into the habit of leaving off balls altogether alone. Granted that the bowling is accurate and the fields well placed, county clubs will very soon find out that, if this course is pursued much further, cricket will become a very dull game to watch, and a match will probably seldom lead to a decisive result. It may be done to a good length ball outside the off stump when you first go in, and have neither got

a good sight of the ball nor the pace of the ground ; but that
batsmen should habitually watch the wicket-keeper take the
ball while they stand right in front of the wicket, with their
bats behind them, is carrying caution so far that some people
would call it not a virtue but a vice.   We actually saw a

FIG. 12.—Off drive.

cautious player receive four consecutive off balls and not
make an attempt to hit one.   What pleasure can there be
in batting if these tactics are adopted?   And let such players
please think of the unhappy spectators and of the coffers of
the county club.   The ball can be hit if you will only get your
left foot well across and get well over the ball, and even if

your energies are chiefly directed towards hitting the ball on the ground, the ball will be hit, and the field may make a mistake ; at any rate you have made an effort, and not given up in despair. It is like a timid man running away from danger instead of facing it, as he should, and it is better to try and to fail than not to try at all. Never mind your average; you cannot win a match by such tactics, though you may make a draw of it.

The off drive by cover-point must be always made by putting the left leg across, and not the right ; and the old principle never to be departed from, namely, to keep the left shoulder and elbow well forward, must be again emphasised. When you have once got into position you are master of the situation : you are right over the ball, and you may leave it alone if it should bump ; or you may wait till the ball has passed you, and then make the cut with left leg over in the way described before. You are not in the most favourable attitude for the cut, because your left leg is too much over, but it can be brought off ; and if only a great deal of practice is given to this off drive there will be no necessity for leaving balls alone.

There are several players to whom is denied the ability and capacity to make these off strokes, who are defective in wrist and careful timing of the ball, but who are fully capable of taking quite proper care of a half-volley or balls well up. Such players are under a great disadvantage when they get balls on the off side that are shorter than the half-volley, for they certainly cannot take the same advantage of them. But they have a great many courses open to them, and if they will get the left leg over, and hit over the ball, they will run no risk of getting out, and a casual ball will be well timed and hit accordingly. But they have also the waiting stroke open to them, and this consists of letting the ball get past them, and simply letting it glide off the bat in the direction of long-slip. The faster the bowling the more runs will result from this stroke, as the ball is hit at a longer time after it has pitched than it is when the batsman meets it by the more effective method ;

there is more time to observe its pace and direction ; and if such a player is only careful to get over the ball, he will get a lot of runs in this way.

Lastly, there is the hard drive, which partakes largely of forward play, but yet is a hit to which you can open your shoulders. It is made with a straight bat either on the off side, on side, or straight over the bowler's head.

To fast bowling the difficulty arises of distinguishing this stroke from forward play, for so many balls from fast bowlers on hard wickets are played forward that are not by any means half-volleys and yet go very hard. In fact, there are occasions when fast grounds and fast bowling combine to make batting very easy—when, as a well-known Yorkshire fast bowler said, ' If you poke at her she goes for four.' There is no real necessity for ever having a regular smack at straight balls from a very fast bowler ; it is practically as effective to play them forward, with the weight of the body thrown on the left foot and the arms and shoulders kept free and loose. But by all means hit as hard as you possibly can at a half-volley outside the off stump ; the ball will either make mid-off tremble, or else go straight to the ropes between mid-off and cover-point. You move the left foot slightly forward a little in front of the wicket and you hit at the ball with a straight bat and get well over it to keep it along the ground. Hold your bat tight, for if it should turn in your hands there will be a miss-hit and you will be caught at cover-point or elsewhere. You can hit your hardest at the half-volley just off the wicket, for the simple reason that if you do miss the ball you cannot be bowled, and there is no more chance of missing if you put out your whole strength to it than if you simply drive it forward with a straight bat. So keep a little reserve of strength in all straight balls, but to a crooked half-volley put your whole force into the blow and hit as though you wished to do the ball an injury.

About the half-volley on the on side very little need be said. We have observed before that the ball just outside the leg stump, to within two or three inches of it, is a ball to drive and not hit to leg. It should be hit towards mid-on or between the bowler and mid-on ; and to apply what has been said before, hit it as hard as you can, as if you do miss it you will not be bowled. Keep the right leg still and lunge forward on to your left foot, which should be a little thrown forward, and hold the bat tight.

We have now sufficiently discussed the principles that ought to guide the young player in playing fast bowling on a good fast wicket, and if he observes what has been said he will find that he plays a good safe game, assuming that his eye is straight and that he is able to put his bat in the place where his eye shows him it ought to go. The play to fast bowling on slow tricky wickets brings out the batsman's real talent, and he will discover that what was easy on a hard wicket is full of difficulty on a soft. There are no decisive rules to guide the player on such wickets ; he must trust to his eye and capacity for watching the ball. The player that can watch the ball carefully is the man who will succeed on slow difficult wickets ; and anybody who has seen Grace, Shrewsbury, and A. G. Steel bat under these circumstances will understand what this watching the ball means. If the ground is very fast there is hardly any time for a careful watching of the ball ; the player must play largely by instinct, which will tell him where the ball is going, and as the wickets nowadays are so very true the ball will nearly always take a natural course, that is, straight from the pitch. The left-handed bowler round the wicket will come with the bowler's arm slightly from off to leg, the right-handed bowler also round the wicket from leg to off, but these are both the natural courses the ball ought to take. On slow wickets, however, the ball will come slower ; it will take all sorts of fantastical turns and twists, it will get up straight, and sometimes hang or stop a little. It will generally be found that very fast bowlers do not shine on slow soft wickets, for they have great difficulty in getting a good foothold. It is the medium and slow bowlers who revel on such ground, as Peate, Barlow, and

Lohmann can tell you. The batsman will find that he is bound to play more back and less forward, for it is little good to play forward unless the ball can be smothered, owing to the extraordinary pranks the ball will indulge in after it has pitched. He will therefore be found playing more on his right leg, and the runs will inevitably come much slower. It has been ascertained by experience that hitters are of more value on these difficult wickets than sticks ; for the latter, though they may stay in for an hour, will perhaps not get a dozen runs during that period. The hitter, however, if he brings off four hits, does more execution in a quarter of an hour than the stick will do in thrice that time.

The value of three or four hitters in an eleven was never more distinctly shown than in the case of the Australian Elevens of 1882 and 1884. The 1882 eleven had four big hitters— McDonnell, Bonnor, Giffen, and Massie. In the great international match at the Oval in 1882, Massie got the fifty-five runs in Australia's second innings that practically won the match, and to say he hit at every ball is scarcely an exaggeration. There was also a match against Yorkshire at Holbeck, where McDonnell's scores of over thirty in one innings and over forty in the other certainly won for his side. In 1886 Surrey had to go in to get eighty-seven runs to win. Abel was playing for an hour and three-quarters, while Garrett and Evans were bowling, every ball dead on the wicket, and during that time laboriously compiled thirteen runs. The result of the match was really very doubtful after the fall of the seventh wicket, but Jones, a courageous cricketer, seeing what was the right game, went out and hit Palmer over the ropes for four, and the value of this hit cannot be exaggerated. As a rule it may be taken for granted that steady and slow play, useful and good as it is in its way, will not win matches on slow difficult wickets unless there is a sprinkling of three or four hitters in the eleven. By the doctrine of chances you will find that one of the number will come off, and one innings like Massie's may win the match. To the player who has any hit in him we therefore advise the playing of a freer game on slow difficult wickets than on easy ones. In the latter case runs are bound to come if only you stop there, but they will not in the former. You may leave your ground even to fast bowling on slow wickets if you think you can bring off a hit by so doing, and generally hold the bat nearer the top and give her the long handle. The defensive player, if he cannot do this, must play generally back with the weight on the right leg, watch the ball very carefully, take advantage of any loose ball that may be bowled, and try and place the ball for singles to short-leg, or in the slips. The bowlers find it more easy to put on break or curl on soft wickets, so whereas on hard wickets you may almost assume that the ball will play no pranks but come on straight, on soft you may almost assume the contrary. The ball that hangs or stops a bit after pitching instead of coming on is perhaps the most fatal ball that is bowled. If the batsman plays forward to such a ball he will very likely find that he has done playing before the ball has reached his bat; this means that the bottom of the bat goes on and gets under the ball, and he is caught and bowled. So frequently does this ball come that it is well not to play hard on soft wickets, for if the ball hangs at all it must go up on being hit. For defensive play, we think the bat ought not to be held at all tightly, but rather slackly, for you cannot get a run by hard forward play or hard back play on such wickets.

The general characteristics of play to slow bowling such as that of Peate, Watson, Bates, Peel, Flowers and others are so very different that we must make a few special remarks on them. The great amount of slow bowling is a development of modern times; not that slow round-arm bowling did not formerly exist, but it certainly did not to anything like the extent it does now. In the days which we all of us have heard talked about by old cricketers at Lord's, when Mynn, Redgate, Hillyer and Lillywhite flourished, there were some lob bowlers notably the famous Wm. Clarke, but there were few genuine slow round-arm bowlers, and Wm. Lillywhite had a long stop even when the renowned Tom Box was keeping wicket, as may be seen in the well-known engraving of the match between Kent and Sussex played about the year 1840. Coming to later times, from 1860 to 1868, there were, as far as we can gather, but two real professional slow round-arm bowlers, namely, Buttress and George Bennett, and the first had a very short career. In these days every batsman must be prepared to meet more slow bowlers than fast, and the only style among amateurs now appears to be every variety of slow ball, the good ones hardly furnishing a very large proportion.

From a theoretical point of view, to real slow bowling all forward play ought to be banished. If the ball is short, play back to it; if it is tolerably well up there ought to be time to go out and meet it, and drive it at the pitch. There are some quick-footed players who carry this theory into practice, but generally, if you observe first-class cricket, you will find that there are plenty of players who never leave their ground, even to slow bowling, unless they are really well set. This partly comes from the great caution which is undoubtedly exercised more now than it was twenty or thirty years ago, and partly from the fact that the bowling, though some of it very slow, is not tossed up so high in the air as it was by Bennett and earlier bowlers. Peate, for instance, in his prime the best length bowler for the last twenty years, did not toss the ball at all high in the air, nor did the renowned Alfred Shaw, the most accurate bowler that ever lived. But we still think that more running in might be practised, for there is nothing that more completely demoralises a bowler than a player who comes out and drives when the ball is at all over-pitched. We have seen slow bowlers who do not possess much head completely demoralised by a quick-footed player like Mr. A. G. Steel. They preserve their dignity by bowling so short, that though maiden overs might abound wickets certainly would not fall. Let the cricketer, when playing to slow bowling, stand a little easier, in order that, when he has made up his mind to meet the ball, his right foot will not be rooted to the ground, as it ought to be when playing to fast bowling on fast wickets. Fig. 13 shows Shrewsbury going out to drive, but he is evidently only at the beginning of his jump, and by the time the bat has got over the ball he will be a couple of yards outside the crease. Remember, if you are to be stumped, you may as well be hanged for a sheep as for a lamb. You are equally out if you are an inch or ten yards out of your ground, so never hesitate to go out as far as you can in order to make the hit a certainty, and if you can hit the ball full-pitch by all means do so, as you ought never to miss a full-pitch. You can also pull a full-pitch to leg or anywhere on the on side where fields-men are scarce, and it is a sign that for that parti-cular occasion the bowler is defeated if the batsman has not permitted the ball to touch the ground.

If you find, on going out to hit a ball, that it is too short, and you cannot get at the pitch of it, you have several courses open to you. If you are a very big hitter, and the field is not very far out, it is worth while to try the experi-ment of hitting as hard as you can ; the ball must go

FIG. 13.—Running out to drive. (Shrewsbury.)

high, and may go over the ropes or out of harm's way ; indeed, some great hitters seem to prefer a ball that is not quite a half-volley. Mr. C. I. Thornton, the biggest hitter the world has ever beheld, with the one exception of G. J. Bonnor, has made his longest hits off such balls as these ; while Bonnor, who possesses a prodigious reach, seldom leaves his ground at all, and constantly sends the ball out of the ground by hitting short of the actual pitch. If the ball is smothered it cannot go up in the air, and though it is more correct cricket to get over the ball and drive it forward, as Shrewsbury and A. G. Steel do, it .is probable that the great hitters would lose more than they gained by playing the orthodox game. There is a golden rule to be carefully remembered in playing slows, and that is, never to run out to a ball that is well outside the off stump. We do not mean to bar the player from running out to a ball which is absurdly over-pitched, and which he is certain to get full-pitch if he goes out ; but he should not leave his ground to the half-volley unless it is nearly straight. There is more than one reason for this. In the first place, if you miss the ball, it is the easiest sort for the wicket-keeper to take, and any moderately decent wicket-keeper will certainly have you out. In the second place, an off ball is one that it is impossible to hit or play with a straight bat, and if you run out to slows you ought always to hit thus ; and this rule is sound even when you run out to a ball on your legs, for that is generally hit to long-on with a straight bat, and not to leg. It is generally true that you should never leave your ground to any ball that may be called crooked, whether it is to leg or to the off, for in either case you run a serious risk of being stumped ; it is only straight or nearly straight balls that you ought to meet by going out of your ground. The modern slow bowler is so very accurate that he very rarely bowls on the leg side at all, and the old-fashioned lobber who used to bowl on the leg side with a twist from leg and have four or five fields on the leg side is gradually disappearing. The ball that in nineteen cases out of twenty you have to meet by going out of your ground is, therefore, the straight ball.

As far as lobs are concerned, you can play them by stopping in your ground ; but the really good player to lobs runs out to a certainty when the ball is overpitched, and the famous Wm. Clarke used to say that Pilch played him best, as he used to wait his opportunity and meet him and run him down with a straight bat. If you come to reason out the theory of batting to slows, and think how you can best defend your wicket and best score off such bowling, you will easily satisfy yourself that by playing back and gently forward you may ensure safety for a considerable period, but you cannot score even moderately fast. The ball does not come up to the bat fast off the ground as in fast bowling, and if you play forward hard you run the enormous risk of being caught and bowled or caught at mid off. In other words, while to fast bowling you play forward to get runs, to slow bowling you play forward to defend your wicket. If, therefore, you play the extra-cautious game and stick in your ground, or from some cause or another are unable ever to 'give her the rush,' you will not be able to score except by casual singles, unless you wait and fully avail yourself of a full pitch or an outrageous long hop, relished, and often obtained, when amateurs are bowling, but very seldom delivered in first-class matches, and practically never by professional players.

This is the state of things that largely accounts for the tedious character of so much of the modern play : slow bowlers deliver ball after ball dead on the wicket or on the off side with good length, there are seven or eight mousetraps in the shape of fieldsmen on the off side on the watch to entrap the unwary, and batsmen, whether from extreme caution or otherwise matters not, are unable to leave their ground and hit or drive. What can the result be but twenty runs an hour ? It is difficult to know what to do with the good length off ball. It is much harder to cut slow bowling than fast : greater strength of wrist is wanted, and there are many players who are unable to do more than merely pat the ball towards third man for a single or two runs. Slow bowlers have a great fancy for bowling without a field at third man, and this is to the advantage of the batsman ; but even if there is a third man, at any rate he cannot cover more than a certain amount of ground, and you will find that many a run may be got by the pat. Mind and get over the ball, and you cannot then come to grief by being caught at third man or short-slip, and very rarely by the wicket-keeper. The bumping ball ought to be left alone ; this sort of ball is the only one in meeting which prudence is the better part of valour, and no attempt ought to be made to hit at all. The old Adam within them forces a great many players to try and hit, but it is almost a certainty that if the ball is hit it must be from underneath, and up in the air it will consequently go. On a soft slow wicket any run getting to good slow bowling is extremely difficult, but even on such wickets you will lose nothing and gain the casual single by the pat.

The good length ball on the off side is the modern batsman's bugbear, but it is far easier to play when the bowling is fast than when it is slow. It is easier to cut in the first instance, and there are seldom so many fields on the off side to the fast bowler. But the slow ball can be and ought to be driven along the ground if the batsman gets well over it, times it correctly, and throws the left leg across in the same way as we explained in describing the proper method of making this stroke off fast bowling. It is more difficult to time good slow bowling, when the bowler is continually altering his pace, than fast, and herein lies the difficulty of hitting these off balls. Bear in mind, however, that by keeping well over the ball you practically run no risk of being caught anywhere ; sooner or later you will get your eye in, and when that desirable consummation is accomplished, you will be astonished to find how safely you will hit many balls that when you are looking on it seems impossible to hit without incurring considerable danger. But nothing can be gained by leaving balls alone; you run the minimum of risk by hitting at them, if only you observe the two rules which ought to be hung in your bedroom and branded into your brain, ' Put the left leg over,' and ' Get on the top of the ball.' Above all things do not play for a draw.

From what has been said on the principles which govern the proper playing of fast and slow bowling, the reader may be led to think that slow bowling is far more difficult to play successfully than fast. *Chacun à son goût* is true, no doubt, but we are inclined to think that, to the majority of players in the prime of their play, slow bowling is on the whole more diffi-

cult to play, especially on hard wickets. Take the case of
W. G. Grace. It was almost a waste of time on hard wickets to
put on fast bowlers when Mr. Grace was at his best. The sole
advantage to be derived from so doing arose from the fact that
it was advisable to distract his eye, and for this purpose a fast
bowler was useful. By this we mean that, when slow bowlers
were on at both ends, his eye would become more accustomed
to the pace of the ground, and in a shorter time than it would
have been if a fast bowler had been on at one end. But the
fast bowler was on mainly to enable the slow bowler to get him
out, and if the reader looks at Mr. Grace's enormous scores of
a few years back he will find that Shaw, Southerton, Peate, and
Lillywhite got him out a dozen times to the fast bowlers' once.
And the runs that came from bowlers like Martin McIntyre
were astonishing ; anywhere, cuts, pushes through any number
of short-legs, big drives and colossal leg hits—all were alike to
the great batsman.

On soft wickets, though many think otherwise, we believe
that fast or medium-paced bowling is more difficult. This must
be assumed only in the case of those fast bowlers who have
power to keep their precision and pace on slow wickets. The
variety of wickets, as is shown in the chapter on Bowling,
is very great, and on the real mud, farmyard sort of wicket
it is generally safe to presume that fast bowlers cannot act.
When there is a slight drizzling rain, which keeps the ball
and surface of the ground wet, fast bowlers flounder about
like porpoises, and the only bowlers who can act at all are the
slow, though they are very much handicapped. But on the real
bowler's wicket, soft, yet gradually hardening by the effect of
the sun, *cæteris paribus*, the fast or fast medium bowler will, as
a rule, be the most deadly. The year 1879 was, on the whole,
the wettest year for cricket that the present generation has seen,
and it is instructive to turn to the result of the season's bowling
for the County of Nottingham. This county possessed in Alfred
Shaw and Morley the two best bowlers in England—one slow,
the other fast. Here is the analysis of each for Nottingham :—

	Overs	Maidens	Runs	Wickets	Average
Morley. . .	725	349	867	89	9˙66
Shaw . . .	794	453	651	62	11˙31

It will be seen from this pair of analyses that Morley's is slightly better all round than Shaw, with the exception of the number of maiden overs. But maiden overs are not the final goal of the bowler's ambition. They are only means to an end. The true bowler's one idea is to get wickets. The reader will note that Morley, the fast bowler, got no fewer than twenty-seven wickets more than Shaw, which more than makes up for the latter's greater success in bowling maidens. The year 1879 was doubtless a great year for bowlers, but none the less we doubt whether, taking a whole season's work for a county, this record has ever been surpassed by any *pair* of bowlers at any time, and it is as good an illustration of the truth of our theory that in wet years slow bowlers are not likely to succeed so well as fast or medium-pace.

It has always appeared to us that the reason why real slow bowling is slightly less deadly than fast or medium on slow wickets is simply that the batsman is more at the mercy of the eccentricities of the ground when playing to the latter class of bowling than when playing to the former. He always has the power, if he would only exercise it, of leaving his ground to balls of a certain length from the slow bowler, and smothering them. And again let the beginner lay this axiom to heart : the ground can commit no devilry if the ball is smothered at the pitch. On slow wickets, therefore, to slow bowling leave your ground with even less hesitation than on fast, and argue in this way, that as life against these bowlers and on this wicket is certain to be a short one, therefore it had better be a merry one for the sake of the score.

There are and have been a few great men with the bat who obey no law, but possess that strange indefinable gift called genius, which rises superior to any difficulty of ground or bowling ; these batting luminaries may play their ordinary game on slow difficult wickets, and their genius enables them

to do what ordinary mortals cannot. But let the ordinary
player, who has acquired a certain amount of skill in batting,
remember that cricket on hard and fast wickets and cricket
on slow are two quite different things, and that he must alter
his game to suit the circumstances. The very fast-footed,
bookish sort of player is the one who is most at sea on soft
wickets; and this last bit of advice we respectfully urge upon
him —that one hit for four and out next ball will probably be
of more value to his side than twenty minutes' careful defence
and no run. It is not on soft wickets that drawn games are
played, unless there is rain after the match has begun; it is on
dry wickets, with boundaries close in, that the plethora of runs
makes the game dull to all except the ignorant spectator and
the voracious batsman. Of course, if there is only a short time
left before the drawing of stumps and conclusion of the match,
say an hour and a half or two hours, it may be of importance
to play for a draw; then the twenty-minutes-without-a-run
batsman may be the means of salvation for his side, as Louis
Hall has proved to be more than once for Yorkshire ; but,
except under such circumstances, the hitter who runs a certain
risk for the sake of a hit is the more valuable man.

A few words now on running. A man is out if run out as
decisively as if his middle stump is knocked down ; but being
run out is more annoying than being bowled, so everybody
ought to learn how to run. Some fieldsmen are so renowned for
their throwing and rapidity of movement that when such a man
is going for the ball the batsman will not venture on a run
which, under ordinary circumstances, he might safely make.
In any event do not run if you feel any doubt of its safety.
The first invariable rule is that the striker calls the run if the
ball is hit in front of the wicket. This is simple to remember,
and there is no exception. It is also true that the striker should
call runs when the ball is hit to third man under certain circumstances. These circumstances refer to the fieldsman himself.
If the third man knows his business and throws to the bowler,
the striker has to run the risk ; therefore he ought to call. If

the third man is a player of tradition and always throws to the wicket-keeper, the non-striker is in danger, and he ought then to call. Remember also that the non-striker is backing up, and therefore has start of the other, who is not in a position to start quickly. All hits behind the wicket—except in certain cases as above mentioned—must be called by the non-striker, and the striker must not look at the ball after he has hit it, but at the non-striker. The man who has not to judge the run must have a simple childlike faith in the judgment of his partner, and if he gets run out he may remonstrate gently with him afterwards with good reason. The man who is receiving the ball can easily get into the habit of watching it after it has passed him on its way to the long-stop or if he has hit it to long-slip ; but this is a bad habit, and if indulged in will result in the two batsmen holding different ideas as to whether a run can be got or not, on which subject there must be no difference of opinion. If the batsman to whom rightly belongs the call shouts 'run,' and his colleague shouts 'no,' unless one gives way promptly there may be a crisis at hand. Never do batsmen look so foolish as when they affectionately meet at the same wicket, and nothing is so maddening to the supporters of a side as to see a good batsman well set deliberately lose his wicket by the folly of either his colleague or himself. If batsmen will only remember that the decision of the run must rest with one man, and that his call must be obeyed at once, there will not be many runs out. When, say, the third run is being made, and the question whether a fourth can be success-fully attempted arises, that batsman who has to run to the wicket nearest the ball ought to call. The reason of this is, that as the ball is a considerable way from the nearest wicket it is almost certain to be thrown there, and the batsman who calls ought to be he who runs the risk. We will give the following rules to be remembered by every cricketer with regard to run-ning. (1) The striker must call every time when the ball is hit in front of the wicket. (2) The non-striker must call every run when the ball is hit behind the wicket, except in the case of hits to third man as mentioned above. (3) Whoever has to shout, let him shout loudly ; there is no penalty attaching to a yell, and it is comforting to a man when he knows his colleague's intention without any doubt. (4) If a bye is being run, the striker must run straight down the wicket, as he may be saved from being run out by the ball hitting his head instead of the wicket, for which mercy he ought to be duly thankful. (5) On all other occasions run wide of the wicket so as not to cut it up. (6) Always run for a catch if sent reasonably high into the air ; if it is caught no harm is done to you, and to be missed and to secure a run in one and the same hit is a veritable triumph. (7) Run the first run as hard as you can, and turn quickly after grounding your bat within the popping crease, for the fieldsman may bungle even the easiest ball, and it is never safe to assume that there can be no second run.

We hope that we have now explained the true principles of batting to guide the youthful player in his path. One other word of caution. A young cricketer may go to Lord's and watch a great match ; he may see the giants of the game perform—W. G. Grace, Shrewsbury, A. G. Steel, and Barnes. He will wonder and admire, but let him beware of imitation, which may lead him into innumerable quagmires. In another walk of life, literature, you will find facetious writers who are fond of imitating the style of famous authors, and very amusing the attempts sometimes are ; but it is easily seen that the points they successfully imitate are the roughnesses and eccentricities which are frequently characteristic of great authors. An imitator of Carlyle, for instance, revels in the brusque eccentricities of the great man's style, but he never succeeds in portraying his noble qualities. It is much the same in cricket : genius defies imitation, and is only by poor struggling humanity to be admired. In the prime of his play nothing in cricket was grander than the sight of W. G. Grace scoring two runs off a ball that any other cricketer would have been only too happy to stop. No school coach that understood his business would tell a youth to play certain balls as they are played by Mr. A. G. Steel, who sometimes adopts the most daring methods, and it is not safe to infer that anybody else in the world can play in a like manner. It is so with hitting. Bonnor or Ulyett can hit many balls which the great majority of other cricketers would only venture to play gently forward. Some critics who are great at criticism, but great at nothing else, have been known to shake their heads at some of the methods of great players ; but we can assure these gentlemen that real genius admits no more of criticism than it does of imitation. The four never-to-be-violated rules previously mentioned need not trouble the genius at all; no human law need concern him : he is a law to himself, and looks down from a lofty eminence on his weaker brethren. What is the good of telling A. G. Steel not to move out of his ground to fast bowling, seeing that he does so constantly, and gets four runs by a fine hit when he 'gives her the rush'? He will not heed you; and why should he?

Apart altogether from the natural accuracy and quickness of hand and eye, without a proper allowance of which labour will be in vain, a great deal depends on the temperament of each player. Whether failure is owing to health, to inability to recover elasticity of spirits after a few defeats, or to some other cause, it is impossible to say. But let the good player who goes through a whole month, or perhaps even a season, with very bad luck, and comes out in the end with a bad average, comfort himself with this reflection, that not only have good players had these reverses, but even the very best. Mr. W. G. Grace must be accustomed to hear and see his name referred to, but even he has had spells of bad luck, and he will, we are sure, excuse us if we put in full the following figures of innings which were played when he was in his prime :—

June 15 and 16, 1871.—Gloucestershire v. *Surrey.*
    c. R. Humphrey, b. Street I

June 19 and 20, 1871.—M.C.C. v. *Cambridge University.*
    c. Ward, b. Bray 4
    c. Thornton, b. Bray 4

June 22 and 23, 1871.—M.C.C. v. Oxford University.
 c. and b. Butler 15
June 29 and 30, 1871.—Gentlemen of South v. Players of South.
 c. Lillywhite, b. Southerton   4
 b. Lillywhite   11

These figures show how the mighty do sometimes fall, and this certainly ought to console those in the humbler walks of the cricket world. Some players have shot up like rockets, played for a season or so, and then have been heard of no more; but the county that plays a series of county matches will act unwisely if it shunts a player who has shown that he possesses real batting ability. Of course there are limits to the patience of every club committee, but all committees would be wise if they were to err on the side of leniency in this matter.

It is of very little avail writing any sort of homily on nervousness, which is in the constitution, and cannot be got rid of by much or any reading. It is common to all, in greater or less degree, and if any man tells you that he does not know what nervousness in cricket is, do not believe him. To say that there is no sensation other than a distinctly pleasant one in walking to the wickets is absurd. It is true that nervousness does not appear to affect the play of some batsmen, who on first going in seem to be playing their ordinary game. But the sensation is there, and these are the fortunate men whose play suffers but little in consequence.

Nervous players must try and reason to the effect that they are sometimes in the habit of making runs, and that therefore there is no great presumption on their part if they assume that the chances are they will do so again. They must also remember that, after all, cricket is but a game, and no moral disgrace will attach to them if they fail. These are but poor consolations at the best, but the game is a glorious one, and, as we have before remarked, it is better to try and to fail than never try at all.

It has always been assumed that the crack English Eleven that failed to make the necessary seventy-nine runs against the

Australians in 1882 were nervous because they did not succeed in making them. We are not sure that they all were, or that there was more nervousness than usual ; but the wicket was difficult, the Australians' fielding superb, and their bowling extraordinarily good. Certainly two or three of the Englishmen were nervous, and no eleven could be got together anywhere to play such an important match without this being the case. But the longer anyone plays the less nervous will he become, and the fortunate men in cricket are those, like the famous Tom Emmett of Yorkshire, who can, as he modestly said, ' bowl a bit sometimes.' The player who plays only because he is a good bat, and never bowls after he has laid his duck egg, has no opportunity of retrieving his character by getting four or five wickets with the ball. The unhappy batsman makes one bad stroke and his wicket is lost, and he has possibly no further chance in the match. But though the bowler may bowl a wide one ball he may take a wicket the next, and we believe that these all-round players find more enjoyment in cricket than the man who only bats. To their credit be it said that at no previous period have the professionals combined the two so much as they do at the time of writing, and we congratulate Ulyett, Bates, Peel, Barnes, Flowers, Barlow, Briggs, Lohmann, George Hearne, Jesse Hide, and Abel accordingly.

The obvious advice to give to players whose success depends mainly on health is to implore them to look after and pay great respect to the laws by which health is regulated. Not to eat and drink too much, great though the temptation may be to do both, is a rule that ought to be observed by cricketers ; but there is another, not so obvious, but of great importance, and that is, avoid sitting up late at night. There is such a lot of play in these days that some amateurs and a great many professionals play six days in the week. There is the corresponding amount of travelling to be got through, and a lot of fatigue to be undergone ; sleep, therefore, must not be neglected, and long hours devoted to convivial evenings not only entail loss of health but loss of runs also. It is a curious

and unwholesome feature of the present day that it is judged
expedient to have enormous meals in the middle of the day,
with salmon, forced meats, creams, jellies, champagne, and
everything calculated to disturb digestion and pervert the sight.
This meal is not only the cause of much indigestion, but also
of a gross waste of time. Instead of half an hour being taken
up by the legitimate luncheon, a precious hour is stolen from
the middle of the day. It must be confessed that on the
principal public grounds there is no reason to complain of the
luncheons : excess is more the custom on private grounds.

As we have in this chapter implored captains of elevens to
be merciful to good players who may happen to be out of luck,
so now, in justice to the other side of the question, let us beg
the batsman not to be superstitious.

Superstitions abound in most games, but we have no
objection to examples of the weakness which cause inconvenience to nobody except the possessor. We have heard, for
instance, of a really great player who never goes in to bat in
a match with anything new about him, not even a shoe-lace ;
but such superstitions are harmless. There is, however, the
man who has got it into his head, or possibly has dreamt, that
it is quite impossible for him to score if he goes in first or fifth,
or in some particular place ; consequently the unhappy captain,
after he has written out, with great care, an order of going in,
is bothered and worried by men who begin to make excuse.
One is certain that he cannot score if he goes in first, another
thinks he ought not to be put so low down as eighth, and so on.
Our advice to the captain is to care for none of these things ;
let him use his own judgment and not consider the absurd whims
and eccentricities of nervous batsmen. The responsibility of
managing a match is quite enough anxiety and trouble for him
without being bothered by a mutinous eleven, and we entreat
batsmen to obey without murmuring their captain's orders, and
go in without grumbling.

The rules of cricket are imperfectly understood even by
some reputedly famous umpires ; it may be well, therefore, to

remind batsmen how many ways there are of getting out. They know what it is to be bowled out, caught out, stumped, run out, to get out leg before wicket, or to hit wicket; and a great many think that nothing else will get them out. This is a mistake, and it was a comical sight to see, as we saw some years ago, a first-rate professional diddled out in another way. It is against the rules to wilfully hit the ball twice. It is essential, in order to lose your wicket, that you do it in a wilful manner; if you refrain from this, there is no rule, as far as we know, to prevent the ball being hit a hundred times. In the case alluded to, Barlow was batting in a North and South match at Lord's. He hit the ball twice, and, unfortunately for him, started to run. This starting to run proved the more or less wilful nature of the act. There was a roar of 'How's that?' from the colossal throat of W. G. Grace, standing at point; it was a case of 'You'll have to go, Barlow,' and naturally, in a somewhat moody manner, Barlow went to the pavilion. It is absurd to say that there was anything unfair in this; he violated a distinct rule of cricket. A lot of players think that the ball must not be hit twice under any circumstances, and they would as soon think of touching a red-hot coal as hitting the ball a second time. If there is no wicket-keeper and the ball is played dead against the foot, it may save a few seconds of time if the batsman shove the ball back to the bowler with his bat and stand still, thus saving point the trouble of picking the ball up and returning it. The ball while 'in play' must never be picked up by the hand, for handling the ball wilfully loses a wicket as much as having two stumps knocked down. It is an easy rule to remember, and is very rarely broken, but still it is a rule that must be observed. Obstructing the field is another violation of rule for which the extreme penalty is exacted. Of course a witness may tell an untruth in the witness-box, but unless it is spoken wilfully it is not perjury. So it is with obstructing the field. Many hundreds of times has a batsman standing in his ground prevented a wicket-keeper from catching him out; the mere fact that the player's body, being in a certain position, forces the wicket-keeper to run round him instead of straight at the ball will make an uppish ball as unreachable as the sun. The fieldsman is obstructed, but not wilfully, so no penalty is incurred. But if the batsman were to hit up a ball to point, for instance, and either strike at the ball with his bat or wilfully baulk the fieldsman in any way, he would be out, and deservedly so. In this, as in other like matters, the umpire must be the sole judge, and it ought to be pretty plain and easy for him to give a right decision. About twenty years ago the well-known Cambridge University cricketer, Mr. C. A. Absalom, playing for his University against Surrey, was running a bye, and whilst running to the opposite wicket the ball hit his bat, possibly preventing him from being run out. The umpire gave him out ; but the umpire was wrong, for the ball came from behind him, and as it was never alleged that he looked to see the course the ball was taking and then interposed his bat, it was obviously impossible that he could have wilfully obstructed the ball : it merely chanced that while running in towards the wicket the ball by accident hit his bat. We do not mean to imply that the batsman ought to run wide of the wicket to a short run in order to give the fieldsman every chance of running him out ; on the contrary, if a short bye is to be run, we advise the batsman to run straight down the wicket, for then, as pointed out elsewhere, the ball will very likely hit him and prevent him being run out. But he must not deliberately get in the way of the ball or in any way contribute to the fact of the ball hitting him. A case of wilful obstruction ought easily to be detected by any decent umpire.

It is amusing to ask experienced cricketers in how many ways it is possible for a man to be got out at cricket, and it is astonishing to find many who give most absurd answers. There are nine distinct ways of getting out—(1) bowled ; (2) caught ; (3) stumped ; (4) leg before wicket ; (5) hit wicket ; (6) run out ; (7) handling the ball ; (8) obstructing the field ; (9) hitting ball twice. It is well to know these facts, for the batsman who gets out in an untoward and unusual way feels himself to be a fool, and generally looks like one. Mr. Alfred Lyttelton, when playing some years ago for Cambridge University Eleven against M.C.C. at Lord's, got back to a slow long hop and with his foot just touched the leg stump, the bail of which did not at once fall off. Oblivious of this fact, and only conscious that he had caught the ball in the middle of the bat and sent it far away, off he started for his runs with radiancy on his face and a mocking smile on his lips. No less than five runs were run, and not until then did anyone except the wicket-keeper notice that the leg bail, after hanging on a frail basis for a few seconds, had fallen off. The appeal was made and the facts examined, the deadly verdict was given, and it was a case of a return to the pavilion. The batsman on such occasions as these may look pleasant ; but that is only one of the beneficent results of civilisation, for, as a matter of fact, he feels extremely bitter, and there are innumerable swords in his heart. In the case mentioned the unhappy batsman felt hot and out of breath after his exertions in running the five runs, and there was a sad reversal of the pleasant feelings that attend a successful hit—the applause of the crowd was all wasted, the expected increase to the score was not realised, all had vanished, and a melancholy man walked drearily to the dressing-room.

Batting may be called the most enjoyable feature of the great and glorious game of cricket. A man even in full training invariably feels the effect of fatigue after bowling sixty or seventy overs, and fieldsmen go through the same experience during a long outing. But it may with truth be said that the keen pleasure which is realised by every cricketer worthy of the name, while he is actually at the wickets, prevents him from feeling fatigue as an inconvenience until the innings is over. We do not believe, though with bated breath let it be said, that the fine rider on a fine horse in a good position and over a grass country with a burning scent can feel so supremely content with the world and its glorious surroundings while galloping and jumping close to hounds, as does a batsman who feels himself master of the bowling on a good wicket in a first-class match, with a fine day and a large crowd keenly anxious for his well-doing. He is conscious that his side is gaining a glorious victory by his efforts, and life can give him no prouder moments. To the young cricketer let us therefore say, in conclusion, that, as the pleasure is so intense and the excitement so keen, he should strive to attain proficiency by care, practice, and the advice of great masters. Above all, he must cultivate the moral qualities that of necessity must have a place in such a great, glorious, and unsurpassable game as cricket.

FIG. 14.—Gunn playing forward.

CHAPTER III.

'The demon bowler.'

VERYONE who knows anything at all about cricket will at once admit that bowling is, to say the least, as important a feature of the game as batting. The same share of fame has always been conferred on a really good bowler as on an expert at the other great branch of the game ; but, though this has been so from the very earliest days of cricket, there is no doubt that the number of good bowlers whose names figure in the chronicles of the game is much smaller than the number of good batsmen. This would seem to show that the art of bowling is more difficult of attainment than its sister accomplishment, and in face of this supposition, it seems strange that the energy devoted to practising bowling by all beginners at the game should be so greatly exceeded by that devoted to batting. The reason for this may easily be found in the fact that the pleasure derived from making a long score, and the indescribable feelings of delight experienced by every keen cricketer when he has a bat in his hand, seem to offer greater attractions than the more sober, less flashy, and apparently more mechanical duties of a bowler. It is a great pity, in the interests of the game, that at our large public schools and universities more care is not taken to coach beginners in bowling. Hours upon hours are devoted to the teaching of batting, but it is very, very seldom any professional ever thinks of endeavouring to instil into his pupils any of the most elementary rules of bowling.

A question which cannot fail to present itself to the minds of all cricketers, and especially those who recollect some of the heroes of bygone days, is whether the bowling of to-day is as good as it used to be. This particular question—so often put, and answered so differently—seems to me to be one which it is impossible to decide, as the whole nature of the game has altered so much in the last few years. This alteration is due, firstly, to the great improvement in the condition of the grounds; secondly, to the corresponding improvement in batting, for ' the better the grounds the better the batsmen,' is generally a correct saying. Formerly bowlers were greatly assisted by the unevenness of the grounds; whereas now, on our billiard-table-like wickets, even our very best bowlers know well that their chance of getting rid of a strong batting side for anything under 300 runs is extremely remote. It is impossible to compare the tall-hatted old heroes of the ball with bowlers of the present day. In olden days the badness of the grounds caused the best batsman's wicket to be in frequent jeopardy, and fast erratic bowlers were well aware that there would be ample compensation for any accuracy which might be wanting in their delivery in the far from infrequent shooters and abruptly rising balls which so often either levelled the stumps or compelled the retirement of the batsman by a catch in the slips. Nowadays a bowler is nothing unless he is accurate ; batting is so good and grounds are so level that the slightest inaccuracy of pitch or direction almost invariably meets with condign punishment. Consequently our best bowlers—and these consist almost exclusively of the professional class—seem to aim not so much at getting rid of a batsman as at keeping down the runs by bowling a good even straight length, and trusting to chance or the impatience of the batsman for his dismissal. As, however, this subject is one which will best be treated later on, and about which there is a good deal to be said, we will leave it for the present, and turn our attention to a short retrospect of bowling from the earliest days.

Round-arm bowling seems to have come into vogue in 1825. It has been generally supposed that Mr. Willes was the first to start it, and the following story is told of the way in which that gentleman found out the advantages of the round-arm delivery. Mr. Willes, being a most enthusiastic cricketer, and not content with the summer months for his favourite sport, used in the winter daily to repair to his barn, and there measure out the proper distance, pitch the stumps, and, with his sister (also an enthusiast) as bowler, enjoy a good practice. Now everyone who has seen ladies attempting to throw a stone or cricket ball will remember that they invariably have a half-round, half-under sort of delivery, and this Miss Willes, in common with the majority of ladies, seems to have possessed. Her brother, accustomed to play against what in those days was the only known style of bowling, viz. under-arm, was somewhat perplexed and worried with this unknown feminine species of ball, which doubtless he found difficult to tackle. How amusing it would have been to have watched this keen cricketer, probably not unconscious of his own merits as a batsman, entirely puzzled by the deliveries of a lady! We are not told whether his feelings of shame at being thus defeated, or of delight at discovering this new style of bowling, predominated, but we *are* told that shortly afterwards he made his *début* as a round-arm bowler, and met with (until he was stopped by the conservatism of the crowd) the greatest success.

From the year 1825 down to the present, round-arm bowling has been universal, and it is now quite an exceptional occurrence to come across a fast under-arm bowler of the old style. This is not much to be regretted, as every attribute of good bowling which was obtainable by the fast under-arm delivery is much more easy of attainment by the round or over-arm style; and many accomplishments pertaining to the bowler's art are possible to the round-arm which, from the very nature of the action, are impossible to the fast under-arm bowler. Break, spin, and quickness from the pitch are common to both styles, but certainly the two latter are made easier of acquirement by the round-arm style; and with regard to break— an easier matter for the under-arm bowler—the ball that breaks or twists the most is not as a rule the ball that gets the most wickets. To a fast under-arm bowler the variations in flight and pace, so well known to the best round-arm bowlers, are unknown. Slow under-arm bowling, of course, must be excepted from these remarks; later on in this chapter I shall have something to say on the subject of this most useful style, which unfortunately in later years seems almost to have died out.

Nowadays all the bowling, i.e. the good bowling, of England is in the hands of professionals, a fact which is greatly to be regretted for several reasons. It is also noticeable that to-day we have barely got one first-class amateur bowler. The falling off in the quality and quantity of amateur bowlers is owing to the great demand there has been in the last few years for professional bowlers at schools. Thirty years ago there was not one professional bowler to every twenty there are now. The large public schools in those days had, as a rule, one professional bowler, who took charge of the ground, coached the boys, and made himself generally useful in various capacities. Consequently, each boy at practice had to bowl. The professional could only bowl to one boy at a time, and so everyone did his very best at practice to bowl straight and well, as a batsman would not care to practise to bowling that was slack and crooked. The outcome of this system resulted in every cricketer becoming more or less of a bowler, and many boys from constant practice grew fairly proficient who otherwise would never have been heard of, and consequently would never have been able to take part in the most fascinating part of the game. To-day our large schools, as a rule, boast perhaps three or four professional bowlers ; the boys who have the privilege of being coached by them daily get their half-hour's batting practice from their straight accurate bowling, and then usually their lesson is finished. Perhaps a boy may take a ball and bowl for a short time to a companion at the same net as the professional, but it is generally done, if done at all, in a careless, haphazard sort of fashion, there not being the same inducement to bowl straight and well as there used to be when professional bowlers were more scarce.

What a pity it is that even a tenth part of the care and attention devoted to teaching batting is not expended on bowling ! A few words of instruction or encouragement to a beginner might have the effect of awakening in him the interest and keenness about bowling which would eventually cause his development into a good bowler, or at any rate a fairish one. Who has not seen over and over again a boy come up to a net where a companion is practising, and picking up a ball, which as likely as not is about half as large again as a match ball, proceed to hammer away at the batsman for about ten minutes or more in all directions, with all pitches, and, what is worse than every-thing, with different lengths of run ? Then, perhaps, getting a little tired, as any bowler will who bowls for long without a rest (which he would get in a match at the end of each over), he exclaims, ' Now I'll give you some of Spofforth's patents ! ' and then, with a long run and a kangaroo-like bound (but, probably, altogether unlike the famous Australian bowler), he proceeds to hurl the ball wider and in a more erratic style than ever. Then, perhaps, he will say, ' Would you like some of W. G.'s ? ' and immediately assuming the well-known and somewhat inartistic pose of the English champion, proceed to toss the ball lifeless up in the air. Now this is not the way to learn how to bowl.

Bowling, like everything else worth doing, takes a lot of careful practice before it can be expected to meet with success.

There can be no doubt that were boys carefully trained at school in the art of bowling, as they are in that of batting, our universities, from which the ranks of our first-class cricketers are usually replenished, would be continually sending up men who could take the position as leading bowlers now occupied by professionals. But, it may be asked, if we have a supply of fairly good bowlers, what does it matter whether they are professionals or amateurs? There are two answers to this question : first, that the Gentlemen every year play the Players, and are naturally always anxious to beat them ; and, secondly, that the more cricket gets into the hands of professional players, the worse it will be for the game and its reputation. Now we wish most positively to state that, while laying down this second proposition, we do not wish or intend to say one word against the personal character of the English professional cricketer ; on the contrary, our opinion is that the great majority of this class are honest, hard-working, and sober men. We only say that it is not in the interests of cricket that any branch of the game should be left entirely in their hands. Let us just take a glance at our professional as we have usually found him. As a rule, he is the son of a small tradesman, or person in that rank of life, and has been born in a neighbourhood where the greatest interest is taken in sport of all kinds, cricket during the summer months being sedulously played. These neighbourhoods are far more frequent in the northern than the southern counties ; the sporting tendencies of the people of Lancashire, Yorkshire, and Nottingham being developed to a much greater extent than in the more southern shires. These three counties, and especially Notts, turn out large quantities of young professionals yearly.

A boy who has been born in one of these cricketing districts is sure to devote a fair share of his time to watching the victories and defeats of his village club, and consequently to imbibing that feeling of 'pleasing madness' connected with the game which attacks every cricket enthusiast. The height of his ambition is to bowl a ball or two to the village champion batsman, and when the opportunity arises to gratify his wish you will see him, hardly higher than the stumps, bowling with an action exactly similar to the crack village bowler, and scorning to encroach so much as an inch over the line of the bowling stump. And, oh ! what sleepless nights ensue from the anticipation of actually seeing with his own eyes on the following Saturday one of the real cracks of England—one who has positively played in Gentlemen *v.* Players, or represented England against Australia ! No wonder the boy becomes imbued with keenness for the game, when everyone in the village, from the parson to the old lady who keeps the sweetshop, is continually talking about cricket. As the boy grows older he begins to make his mark in the village club, and when he is eighteen or nineteen, to the delight of his father, mother, sisters, and himself, he is selected to make one of the twenty-two colts of his county that are chosen to play against the county team. After having played in public, and perhaps tasted the pleasures of success, the father finds that his son is restless and disturbed in his trade, and wishes to give it up and become a professional cricketer. So it happens that his name is sent up to the county secretary as wanting a situation, and the young fellow finds himself launched into the world on his own account as a cricket professional.

With regard to the young man's prospect of success on starting in his new life, we are bound to say that, assuming he has only the average cricket ability of the ordinary professional, his chances of even making a livelihood are not particularly bright. He may, and no doubt will, earn as much as 2*l.* a week, or even more, during the summer months ; but at the end of August or beginning of September he will find himself with very little money in his pocket, and seven of the coldest and worst months of the year to face. He *may* get employment in the winter months—many professionals do, either as colliers or as porters, or some other work. We have known them to do clerk's work for railways in the winter ; but all work for men only willing to stick to it for a few months is extremely uncertain, and there can be no doubt that many cricket professionals have a bad time in the winter.

There are, of course, prizes in his profession as there are in every other, but these are only open to a man of conspicuous cricket ability. Even if a young man obtain a regular place in his county team, he can only reckon on earning about 80*l.* in the summer months, out of which he has to pay his own expenses ; as a county will play about fourteen or fifteen matches in the season, giving 5*l.* a head to the professionals, and 1*l.* extra if the team wins. There is also a possibility for a man to earn what is called his 'talent-money,' viz. 1*l.* extra by making fifty runs or over. After a professional cricketer has rendered conspicuous services to his county for a number of years, and generally just before his retirement, he receives what is called a 'benefit,' i.e. the proceeds from the gate, collected at some important contest on his own county ground ; and if the man is a favourite with the crowd, it means a good round sum in his pocket, sufficient to keep him to the end of his days, or else set him up in a small way of business. Men have got as much as 1,200*l.* from their 'benefit,' but, as a rule, a well-known man in a good county will only secure from 500*l.* to 600*l.* Should a professional show great merit in his county matches, either as bowler or batsman, he is chosen to play in the great matches, such as Gentlemen and Players ; and then, should he establish his reputation as a really first-class player, he will earn almost 10*l.* a week for the months June, July, and August, there being very few weeks during that time that he does not play two matches at 5*l.* and the usual extras. The very best players, however, cannot ensure anything like a certainty, as they know there will come a time, and that not far distant, when their limbs will grow stiff and their eyes less keen. Cricket is a game which requires quickness of eye and of limb, and, as a rule, after thirty-four or thirty-five, either one of the two—the former or the latter, and perhaps both—must begin to fail. Then the professional cricketer is going downhill, and shortly will have to retire and see his place filled by younger and more active men. Lucky for him if he has been an economical man during his years of success, or if he gets some good position, such as custodian of a cricket ground, which, with his benefit money, will suffice to keep him. There are numerous instances of men retaining their place in first-class cricket up to the age of forty, or even more. The evergreen Tom Emmett, of Yorkshire, who probably never bowled better in his life than in 1886, is considerably over that age, and W. G. Grace, at the time of writing, is close on forty ; but, as a rule, there is considerable labour and sorrow connected with a veteran (at cricket) of thirty-eight or forty who fights against nature to retain his place in first-class cricket. The sinews in the calf and the thigh keep going ; the shoulder gets stiffer and stiffer for throwing, or even jerking ; there is generally more to carry between the chest and the legs, which prevents the alacrity in stooping for which the fieldsman was once so famous ; though perhaps (if a batsman), with a warm day, a good wicket, and every condition in his favour, he will still show his former powers by playing an unexceptionable innings.

The preceding remarks about professionals will show that it is a very dangerous profession for a young man to embark upon, unless his merit is so great that his success in first-class cricket is almost a certainty. We should never recommend any young cricketer who came to us for advice on the subject to enter on the precarious life of a professional unless he had absolutely nothing else to turn his hand to, or appeared to be of the most exceptional merit.

The first-class professional cricketer is usually a well-made, strong-looking man, ranging from two or three and twenty to thirty-five, with agreeable, quiet manners with his superiors on the cricket field, the result, no doubt, of being so constantly in their society. He is generally dressed, we are bound to say, in rather dirty white flannels, and always in the hottest weather wears thick woollen drawers, half an inch of which is generally visible above the waistband of his trousers. He is a great favourite with the crowd, and when his side is in may be seen walking round the ground surrounded by a body of admirers, any one of whom is ready and willing at any moment to treat his ideal hero to a glass of anything he may wish for. It is greatly to the player's credit that in the face of this temptation to insobriety he is such a sober, temperate man. I have never seen on a cricket field a first-class professional player the worse for drink, and I have only on one occasion heard the slightest whisper against the sobriety of such a man during the progress of a match. I believe that, as a class, and considering the thirsty nature of their occupation and the opportunities that offer themselves for drinking, there is no more sober body of men than cricket professionals.

Having attempted to give a short, and it is hoped impartial, description of the cricket professional, let us, before resuming the subject of bowling, return to the assertion that the more cricket gets into the hands of professional players the worse it will be for the game and its reputation. At present cricket is perhaps the most popular of all our national recreations ; it is certainly the most popular *game*, and is rightly considered to be the manliest and the freest from all mischievous influences. What these latter are, and what a pernicious and enervating influence they exercise on other branches of our national sports, is known to everyone. I allude to the betting and book-making element which from the earliest days has been the curse of sport. What is the worst feature about horse-racing ? To what do English lovers of true sport owe the fact that every racecourse is the rendezvous of the biggest blackguards and knaves in the kingdom ? Is it not betting, and the pecuniary inducement it offers to every kind of dirty, shabby practice ? The sullying influence has spread to the running-path, and even, if report says true, to the river. Happily there is never the slightest whisper of suspicion against the straightness of our cricket players, and this is entirely owing to the absence of the betting element in connection with the game. It is an unfortunate fact that the tendency of first-class cricket nowadays is to swamp the amateur by the professional. Some of our best county teams are almost wholly composed of the latter class. The time taken up in big matches is so great, owing to their being drawn out by a late start and early finish each day, that the amateur is beginning to realise his inability to give up from his business or profession so much of this valuable commodity. What has happened in consequence? Cricket—i.e. first-class cricket—is becoming a regular monetary speculation. Thousands upon thousands troop almost daily to see the big matches, flooding the coffers of the county or club, which does its very best to spin out the match for the sake of the money. If this continue, our best matches will become nothing better than gate-money contests, to the detriment of the true interests of the game and its lovers.

Bowling is as much worthy of the name of an art as any other branch of sport. The skill, science, and practice which are necessary before a man can throw a good salmon fly, or before he can reckon on bringing down a good average of high rocketing pheasants, are equally necessary for one who wishes to become an adept at bowling. Perhaps bowling does not require the same oneness of hand and eye as batting, but it demands, if possible, more practice and experience, and to a far greater extent the exercise of mental qualities. The object of the bowler is to outmanœuvre the batsman; he has either to hit the stumps or draw him into some incautiousness or hesitation of play, which will result in the ball being caught from the bat or in the batsman being stumped out by the wicket-keeper. This is a wide field, and suggests at once that to become proficient a bowler must think—and think deeply too—not once or twice every few minutes, but before each ball, for none should ever be delivered without a particular object. Every ball must be part and parcel of a scheme which the bowler has in his mind for getting rid of the batsman. The object of every bowler, whether fast or slow, is always to bowl what is called a 'good length'—i.e. to pitch the ball so close to the batsman that he cannot play it on the 'bounce,' or, in cricket parlance, 'on the long-hop,' and yet so far that he cannot play it just as it touches the ground or immediately on the rise—i.e. on the 'half-volley.' There can be no precise measurement of the exact spot on which the 'good-length' ball must pitch, as it is constantly varying according to the state of the ground and the size and style of the batsman. When the ground is 'slow' and 'sticky' from recent rain, the good-length ball will have to be pitched considerably farther than when it is 'hard' and 'fast,' as, of course, the ball will come faster off the ground when it is in the latter state than when in the former. The reason why the bowling of this particular ball is always the object of every bowler is because it compels the batsman to meet the ball with the bat by forward play, and because in so doing he often loses sight of the ball from the moment it touches the ground till it strikes the bat. No one can be called a good bowler until he has the power at will of bowling ball after ball of this sort. It often happens when two batsmen are well set, and every wile and 'dodge' of the bowlers has been tried without avail, that two bowlers will have to go on to bowl, or try to bowl, nothing else but good-length balls, in the hopes of keeping down the runs. If this can be done effectually, a batsman is bound through impatience to make a mistake which in time may cost him his wicket.

Every ball that leaves the bowler's hand has, in addition to the propelling power imparted by the bowler, one of four different motions. The ball as it travels is either spinning from right to left; or from left to right; or with a downward vertical motion; or an upward vertical motion. It is a fact that it is well-nigh an impossibility for a ball to leave the hand of the veriest beginner without having one of these four motions to a certain extent imparted to it.

On these four rotary motions depends how much and in what direction the ball will twist or deviate from its course, and also the speed and height it will assume after touching the ground. One of the arts of a bowler is to cheat the batsman by making the ball pitch in one spot and, after the pitch, suddenly take a different direction ; another is to make the ball rise quicker off the ground than a batsman would be led to expect from the ordinary rules of reflection. These arts are accomplished by different movements of the fingers and hand at the moment of delivering the ball ; for the reason why every ball has a certain amount of spin on it is because the fingers, being in contact with the ball as it leaves the hand, cause it to rotate (though perhaps so infinitesimally as not to be noticeable) on its journey to the ground.

The spin, or rotary motion, from right to left is gained by grasping the ball chiefly with the thumb and first and second fingers, the third and fourth fingers being placed together round the other side of the ball. The moment the ball leaves the hand the latter is turned quickly over from right to left, and at the same time the first and second finger and thumb, coming over with the hand, impart a powerful twist to the ball, which leaves the hand when the latter is turned palm downwards. There is also at the time of delivery an outward and upward movement of the elbow which gives the arm the shape of a curve, or almost a semicircle. The ball goes on its way spinning rapidly from right to left, and the moment it touches the ground twists very sharply towards the off side of the batsman. This ball, termed in cricket parlance the ' leg-break,' when well bowled is perhaps one of the most deadly of all balls, but it is also the most difficult for a bowler to master. It is always a slow ball, as to bowl it fast with any accuracy of pitch is an impossibility—at any rate, it may be assumed to be so, as no bowler has ever yet appeared who could bowl it otherwise than slow. Palmer, the Australian bowler, was about the fastest ever known at this ball, but his faster ones were very inaccurate in pitch, and he could only bowl them, strange to say, very occasionally. The author, although he has played innings after innings against this bowler, never remembers receiving a single fast leg-break from him. The fact of the hand having to turn over from right to left, and of the ball being delivered underneath the hand, so to speak, causes it to be extremely difficult to attain accuracy of pitch and direction. There are many men who can bowl this ball in practice at the nets, but who never dare attempt it in a match, having no confidence whatever in their ability to bowl it straight, or even fairly straight. It is no uncommon occurrence to see this ball, bowled by one who has tried it in practice, travelling somewhere near to where point is standing. There are some slow bowlers who have become fairly proficient at it, and who have enjoyed at various times, and especially against batsmen they have never met before, a certain amount of success ; but it is a style of bowling which should only be encouraged to the extent of enabling every bowler to use it occasionally. If nothing but this ball is bowled over after over, by constant repetition it loses its sting. The batsman gets wary, and when the ball is pitched on his leg side gets before his stumps to protect them, and hangs his bat in front of him, thereby rendering the loss of his wicket extremely improbable ; and when it is pitched straight for the middle stump or on the off side, knowing the danger of a hit at the pitch of this ball, he will simply satisfy himself with protecting his stumps with his legs, and with letting the ball pass the off stump without further protest. The trap laid for the batsman in this style of bowling is the danger he incurs by hitting unless he is actually on the pitch of the ball ; if he falls into the snare, the ball is perfectly certain to go up in the air, and generally in the direction of cover-point or mid-off. This, of course, is owing to the twist of the ball causing it to hit the side and not the centre of the bat. Should the batsman in the act of hitting miss the ball altogether, as is not infrequently the case, he pays the penalty of being stumped unless he happens to be a fast-footed hitter. Now, of course, these two traps are well known to every good batsman, and consequently it is, as a rule, useless to bowl ball after ball of this nature to him — one might just as well whistle for grouse at the end of November to come and be shot.

This ball, therefore, should only be bowled at intervals, and when according to the bowler's judgment it may have a fair prospect of success. Usually this happens on two occasions. The first is when a batsman has just begun his innings, and is playing nervously and without confidence ; a twisting ball then from the leg side is extremely apt to fluster and annoy him, and a catch in the slips or at point, or a catch and bowl, is not infrequently the result. The second is when a hitter is in, and is hitting to all parts of the field. Then the ball may be bowled with a great chance of success, especially if the man is anxious and impatient to hit every ball. He is extremely likely to hit a little short of the pitch, with the above-mentioned result. It is not a good thing for the bowler to worry the batsman with this ball if the latter seems not to like it or to play it nervously ; it should at most be used not more than twice in an over. Let the bowler always remember that too much of one particular ball, even if distasteful to the batsman, will frighten and steady him, and perhaps in the end teach him to play it correctly. There are some batsmen, and good batsmen too, who never seem to be at home to this ball, although they may have played it scores of times, and I remember once seeing an amusing incident at a match in which a bowler who had adopted it was playing sad havoc with the other side. The first three batsmen had all rushed out to try and hit the leg-break ball, and, failing to do so, paid the inevitable penalty of being stumped. Their captain was furious at their rashness, especially as they were all three good players ; he explained, and rightly, that the proper way to play the ball was either by hitting it on the full volley—i.e. before it touched the ground—or else remaining inside the crease ·and playing it quietly. He went in himself, intending to illustrate this principle, and, lo and behold! was stumped the very first ball he received. He scraped forward a long way to meet the ball, missed it, and remained in a most elegant Fuller Pilch-like attitude, fondly imagining the toe of his boot was inside the crease. It was, as a matter of fact, a good inch outside it. In that match there were five stumped each innings off the same bowler, and the captain was one of them both times.

On another occasion a batsman with rather thin and weedy looking legs kept jumping in front of his stumps every time this ball was delivered. Finally the ball, discovering the weak spot in this gentleman's physical proportions, managed to find (just above the knees) an opening large enough for it to pass through and dislodge the bails. Great was his astonishment and disgust, and as he retired crestfallen to the pavilion he said to the writer, who was one of the fielding side on that occasion, 'It was not the ball or the bowler that did that ; it was all owing to my confoundedly skinny legs!' A dodge well worth trying with this ball is to bowl a good length about two feet to the leg of the batsman ; he is nearly sure to have a hit, and there is a great chance of the spin on the ball causing it to be a miss-hit, which may go straight up in the air, for the wicket-keeper, point, or bowler to secure; even if it is a clean hit to leg it is nearly bound to be in the air, and long-leg may possibly have a chance. If this scheme is to be practised it will be generally a good thing for the bowler to have his long-leg perfectly square, and bring his long field on round till he is almost in the position of a forward long-leg. This should be done by quietly waving the hand in such a manner as to attract the attention of the batsman as little as possible. It is impossible to lay down any rule for the way in which the fieldsmen should be placed for this style of bowling, as this depends so much upon the play of each particular batsman. A long-leg is, however, nearly always necessary, and very often an extra man out on the leg side, as mentioned already. Two men out in the field for the average batsman cannot be dispensed with. The bowler himself, as a rule, will know how to place his field for each batsman, but on no occasion should he ever omit to have a short-slip. This is such a very likely place to get a batsman snapped up that it should never be dispensed with to any style of bowling, except perhaps to slow under-arm, and not always then. A slow bowler who intends to use the leg-break, let us say, once an over, or even once in two overs, and who relies on this ball as most likely to secure wickets, may on ordinary occasions place his men thus, but, as we said before, they must be changed to suit the circumstances.

If the ground is hard and fast, as a rule a third man cannot be dispensed with; but if inclined to be slow, he may be brought forward to extra cover-point, between cover-point and mid-off, or else put deep in the field on the on side. The bowler may, however, see that the batsman is wide enough awake to restrain himself from hitting blindly at the pitch of this ball when straight or on the off stump; it will then be advisable to try him entirely on the leg side—a man may refuse the bait on one side but take it on the other. In these circumstances extra cover-point, and sometimes even cover-point as well, may be brought across the wicket and placed for half-hits wide on the on—i.e. about half the distance from the batsman that a deep field would stand. If the batsman assumes a poky style of play, it is often advantageous, both for saving runs and getting wickets, to have a short-leg a little nearer the stumps than the umpire, and the mid-on as near to the batsman as he can venture consistently with safety. In this, as in every other style of bowling, it is a sovereign rule to make the batsman play to the ball—i.e. to keep it well pitched up, and compel him either to hit or play forward.

A very novel style of this kind of bowling was seen on English cricket grounds in the summer of 1884, when the Australian team of that year included W. H. Cooper, so well known to all our cricketers who have visited the colonies. He bowled round the wicket, and nearly every ball almost a wide to leg. There was more spin and twist on the ball than had ever been seen in this country before (excepting, perhaps, in the bowling of Mr. Stratford, who played for a year or two for Middlesex, but who never made his mark in first-class cricket). The ball seemed to be twisted or screwed out of the side of his hand in the way a billiard-marker will screw a billiard-ball along the table to a certain spot, and then bring it back to him. But, unfortunately for him, he was unable to combine any pace with this tremendous twist. The ball was extraordinarily slow in the air, but directly it pitched it would spin off the ground comparatively quickly, twisting into the batsman on the faster wickets, sometimes as much as a yard or more. All his men except two were on the on side, and he expected his wickets to be obtained by the impatience of the batsman causing him to rush out, miss, and get stumped, or else by wide hitting at the pitch of the ball on the leg side, where there were seven fielders with seven pretty sure pairs of hands waiting for it. In Australia he had met with a fair share of success, especially against some of the English elevens which had been over there. It was this latter consideration which induced the Australian authorities to believe that he would be a useful addition to their team. His bowling was most unsuccessful in this country. Whether this was due to an accident to his hand on the voyage to England, or from the light here being not so glaring and bright for our English eyes as it is in Australia, cannot be said for certain, but I have a strong opinion from my own experience that the reason of his success in Melbourne against Englishmen was owing to the dreadful glare on that ground.

One peculiarity of the leg-twisting ball is that when the ground is soft and sticky it is comparatively of no avail. The ball then, of course, twists to a greater extent than when the ground is hard, but it leaves the pitch so very slowly that the batsman can either wait for it on the long-hop or hit it on the full or half-volley. The leg-break ball on a soft ground, if bowled at all, must be bowled faster than on hard, in order to counteract the deadness of the turf. The best states of the ground for this bowling, as indeed for most, are when the ground has been hard and fast, and has since become crumbly and covered with loose bits of grass and worn turf, and when there has been heavy rain to saturate the ground which is being rapidly dried and caked by a hot sun. In the former state the ball takes plenty of twist, and also leaves the ground very quickly, in addition to sometimes getting up uncomfortably high for the batsman. In the caked state the ball takes lots of twist, and puzzles the batsman by the varied and uneven paces at which it leaves the ground, sometimes coming sharply and high, at others stopping on the ground and, in batsman's parlance, 'getting up and looking at you.'

The 'leg break' ball is usually bowled from round the wicket,

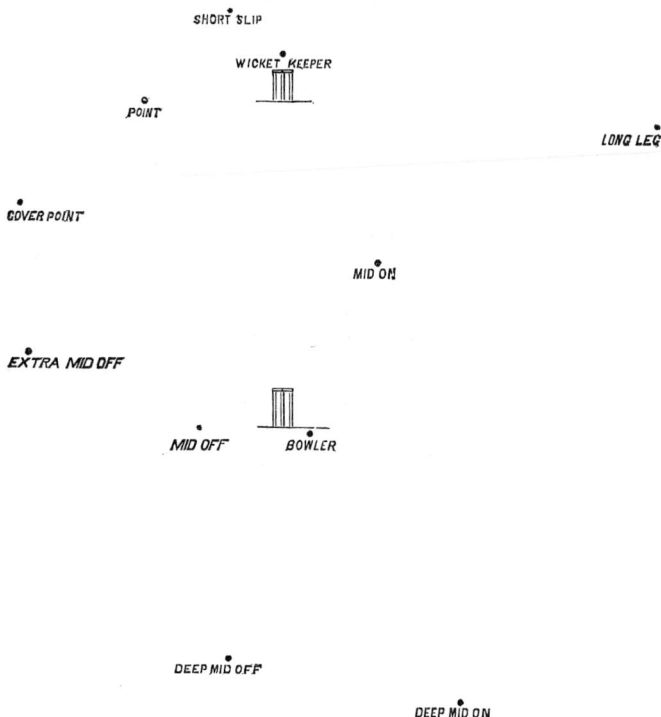

SHORT SLIP

WICKET KEEPER

POINT

LONG LEG

COVER POINT

MID ON

EXTRA MID OFF

MID OFF   BOWLER

DEEP MID OFF

DEEP MID ON

The leg-break diagram.

These positions of the fieldsmen will suit under-arm bowling, except that, perhaps, extra mid-off may be put out on the on side.

as from this side there is more scope for the bowler to make the ball twist. It is doubtless the best side of the stumps to choose for the delivery of this ball, but every bowler should remember that it is very nearly as good as a change of bowling to change from ' round ' to ' over ' the wicket, and this is especially

so with leg-break balls   The ball delivered from round the
wicket generally leaves the hand a good foot outside the ex-
tremity of the bowling crease ; this means that it starts about
4 feet 4 inches from the middle stump of the bowler's wicket,
and in its journey through the air, even if pitched in a line with

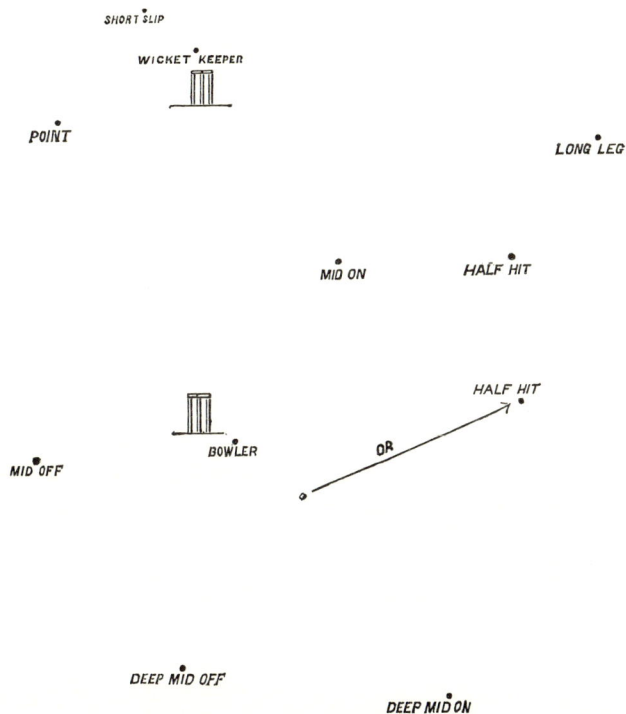

SHORT SLIP

WICKET KEEPER

POINT

LONG LEG

MID ON   HALF HIT

HALF HIT

BOWLER   OR

MID OFF

DEEP MID OFF

DEEP MID ON

Position of field if bowling on leg side.

the leg stump of the batsman's wicket, it has to make considerable way from the leg side of the wicket.   This, of course, makes
the ball go across the wicket more from the pitch, and, as a rule,
means that a leg-stump leg-break ball round the wicket misses
the wicket on the off side.   A batsman, if the ball is pitched off
his wicket, may defend it, as the rule of leg before wicket now

stands, with his legs, and consequently the bowler has not much chance of hitting it. When bowled from over the wicket the leg-break ball, being delivered in a direct line with the batsman's wicket, will naturally, if pitched on the leg-stump or between the legs and the wicket, not twist so much, thus making it more likely to hit the wicket if missed by the batsman. There is also a direct advantage to be gained by bowling over the wicket if the batsman is inclined to get in front of his stumps, as there is always a better chance for the bowler to get an appeal for leg before wicket answered in his favour than when bowling from the other side.

Although, as previously mentioned, there has never been any instance of the leg-break ball being bowled by a fast bowler, some of the best bowlers of the past generation of cricketers used to bowl with a considerable bias from the leg side, and were also of well over medium pace. Martingell and Silcock were bowlers of this class. This old style was very effective, and it is greatly to be regretted that it has almost entirely disappeared from the game at the present day. It differed from the slow ball that has been discussed only in the amount of spin ; and as there was so much less power expended in spinning or twisting, the pace of the ball was greatly in excess of that which can be got on to the slow leg-break. The ball was delivered round the wicket, at the very extent of the crease, in order to make the angle from the hand to an imaginary straight line between the two middle stumps as great as possible. The hand was very little higher than the hip when the ball was delivered, and instead of the hand and wrist being completely turned over at the moment of delivery, as in the slow leg-break, the fingers imparted a right to left spin to the ball. The ball, coming from a great distance round the wicket and with a considerable amount of leg spin, would be gradually working away to the batsman's off side every inch of its journey, both before and after pitching. Catches in the slips and on the off side were numerous from this style of bowling, and it required the batsman's greatest care and caution to guard himself against playing inside the balls. It is a great pity we do not see more of this bowling now.

The next spin or twist on the ball which we will discuss is the rotary motion from left to right. This, in cricket phraseology, is termed the ' off ' break, and is far more universal than that from the ' leg.' In fact, so common is it, and so easy to learn,

The leg-break.

that nearly everyone who has ever bowled in a match knows more or less how to put this spin on the ball. It is, of course, always easier to get spin on to a slow ball than on to a fast one.

When the ball to be delivered is a slow one, the fingers and hand may be twisted into almost any shape, as so little power is required actually to deliver the ball ; all the strength of hand,

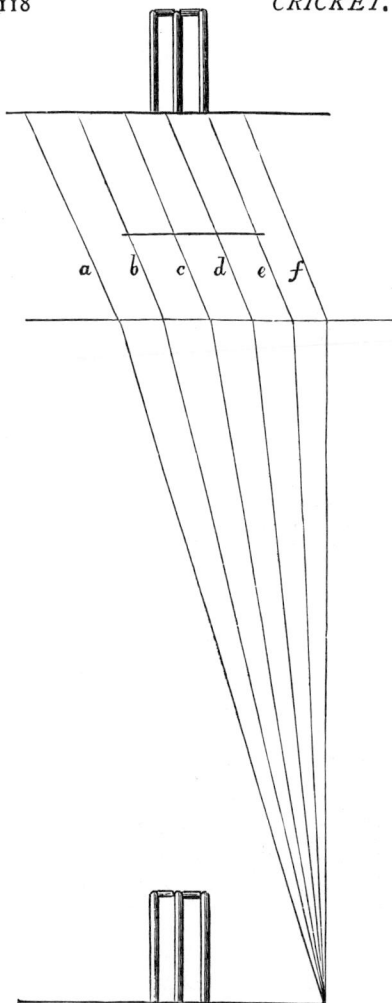

Likely balls; and what may become of them if
not correctly played.

a, a likely one for a wild hitter to get himself out on
the off side; *b* and *c,* likely for a stump, or, if hit
with straight bat, a catch to deep field-off; *d* and *e,*
likely for 'catch and bowl;' *f,* long-leg and half-hit
chances—short-slip and wicket-keeper often get an
easy chance of this ball.

of wrist, and of the fingers may be utilised for the purposes of spin alone. When the ball has to be a fast one, the power necessary to propel the ball at the required pace prevents so much of the power of fingers, &c., being expended on spin. A slow ball always takes the spin, after leaving the ground, to a greater extent than a fast one, because it is longer on the ground when it pitches, and the spinning has more time to take effect on the turf.

The natural spin on every ball which is bowled is from left to right—i.e. the off break. Even when a fielder throws in a ball from a distance it almost invariably has this spin on it. If you watch the smallest boy in the street throwing a stone, you will find, nine times out of ten, the stone has acquired this spin. It is then no wonder that almost every right-handed bowler relies upon this twist as his principal artifice. The twist depends rather more on the power of the fingers than on the hand and wrist, as in the 'leg-break.' The ball is usually, by a slow bowler, grasped firmly with all the fingers resting on the seam, as this gives more purchase and resistance for the fingers to operate. The latter at the moment of delivery spin the ball, almost in the same way as they would spin a top, and instead of an upward and outward motion of the elbow, as in the 'leg-break,' there is an inward motion towards the side of the bowler. The hand is turned over outwards when the ball is delivered, and, if properly bowled and pitched just outside the off stump, and under good conditions of ground, the ball, after the pitch, will change its course abruptly towards the batsman and the wicket.

Differing from the 'leg-break,' this ball can with practice be accompanied by a great accuracy of pitch—an accuracy which has been attained almost to perfection by some of our best known bowlers. The late James Southerton, the famous Surrey bowler, could bowl in this style for hours with only a very occasional variation from a perfect 'good length.' Alfred Shaw, of Nottingham, though a little *passé* now, was perhaps the greatest exponent of accuracy of pitch combined with the slow 'off break,' or what is generally termed 'break-back.' This ball should be bowled a good length, and generally about two or three inches outside the off stump.

Of course the amount of twist the ball will take depends on the state of the ground, and this should at once be apparent to the bowler. The danger most to be apprehended by the batsman from the off break is that in playing forward, if not quite on the pitch of the ball, he is very apt, owing to the twist, to play outside, and allow it to pass between his bat and right leg to the wicket. It is never a wise thing for the bowler to use the 'off break' every ball, although there are many who do so. Even if he is devoid of all other artifice, and has no command over the arts of 'change of pace,' 'flight,' or the 'leg-break,' he should often vary his style by a ball without any twist at all, and this should not always be straight. If a batsman has been playing over after over nothing but good-length 'off break,' a ball pitched about the same spot, two or three inches outside the off stump, and without any off break at all, will very often be found to go to hand in the slips, because the batsman is expecting the break and plays inside the ball.

The off break.

The fast 'off break' is a most deadly ball; but, owing to the difficulty, as before mentioned, of imparting any great amount of spin to a fast ball, it is but rarely that a bowler can deliver it with any degree of certainty, except when the conditions of the ground are extremely favourable. A slight slope in the ground from the off side is always a great advan-

tage to fast bowlers who try the 'break-back.' This comparatively rare ball, when it does come, is sure to try the very best
batsman. Its difficulty arises from the fact that the ball is of
such a pace as to necessitate quick forward play, when the
sudden turn after the pitch causes it to be missed. For playing
'off breaks' of all paces, it is a great and
golden rule for batsmen to remember : *Never
allow space between the bat and the left leg
for the ball to pass through.* This rule, which
insures the left leg of the batsman being
placed well across the wicket when playing
forward, if followed, will render it almost
impossible for him to be bowled out with an
'off break.' It is an astounding fact that this
simple rule, which should be patent to everyone, seems unknown to all our best batsmen
with one or two notable exceptions. W. G.
Grace has always played with his leg up to
his bat, thereby preventing the ball from
finding an opening between the two. W. W.
Read, of Surrey, is another who plays thus.
We do not express any opinion here as to
the bearing of this rule on the leg-before-
wicket question. It is sufficient for a batsman at present, as the rule now stands, that
so long as the ball does not pitch between
the two wickets he cannot be given out
'l.b.w.'

'Off breaks.'

A, B, C, all good ones ;
D, if the batsman stands
with his legs some way
from the leg stump, this
is likely to bowl him
off his legs ; but it is a
beauty to hit on the on
side.

The two 'spins,' from the leg and the
off, are the chief and most important for all
practical purposes. If a bowler by constant practice has acquired the power of
twisting the ball from off or leg at will, and can at the same
time bowl a 'good length,' he has laid a tolerable foundation
for future success. We say tolerable, because, in bowling, twist,
as we shall see later on, is not everything ; it is an essential

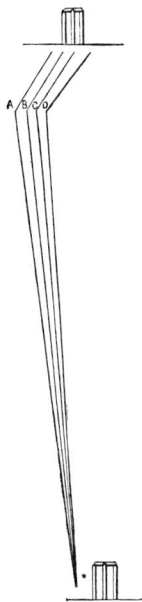

element in good bowling, but it is only one of several, all of which must combine together before anyone can earn the reputation of a first-class bowler.

The two other spins which can be put on the ball are what have been called the 'upward vertical' and the 'downward vertical.' By the 'upward vertical,' I mean when the ball spins in its way to the ground vertically, and upwards with regard to the bowler. It may be compared to the spin imparted to the billiard ball in the screw stroke. This is effected by striking the ball low down, which makes it revolve in its course upwards. The effect this upward revolution has is seen when the striker's ball meets the object ball, the former having a decided inclination to stop and return to the striker. In the same way a cricket ball, when made to revolve upwards, has a tendency to stop and go slower off the pitch than it went before it reached the ground.

This twist, as a matter of fact, is never practised ; and it is a great pity that more attention has not been paid to it. Of course it is very much more difficult to make the ball revolve in this manner than in either the leg or the off break, but it is quite within the powers of the possessor of a fairly strong set of fingers. The lower half only of the ball should be held, so that the upper half protrudes above the hand and fingers, and at the moment of delivery, which must be from the level of the shoulder or lower, the fingers and hand must impart as much upward spin as possible.

The downward vertical spin is the reverse of this, and is caused by the upper half of the ball being grasped instead of the lower, as in the upward. This spin imparts to the ball a tendency to come quicker from the pitch than the pace in the air would seem to suggest, and is analogous to the 'following up' stroke at billiards. The latter is made by striking the ball at the top, making it revolve downwards and vertically from the striker. Very many bowlers possess this downward spin in their bowling without being at all aware of the fact. They know, as also do those who play against them, that every now and then one of their balls will, in cricket slang, 'make haste from the pitch.' The batsman finds he has mistaken the pace of the ball, which flies past him before he is anything like ready to play it, and when his stumps lie prostrate, as often as not he will come back to the pavilion with the old, old story, 'Bowled with a shooter ;' whereas, in fact, the ball has hit the middle or even upper part of his stumps. He has entirely lost the ball from the pitch owing to his misjudgment of its pace, and concludes erroneously that it has shot underneath his bat.

We have now considered the four kinds of spin which can be put on to a cricket ball. Of course there may be combinations of two kinds, as, for instance, the ball may be spinning from right to left or left to right, and at the same time be revolving to a certain extent vertically downwards or upwards ; but it would be impossible to discuss the result of every such combination.

The ball may break from ' leg,' and at the same time show by its acceleration in speed after the pitch that it has been revolving downwards as well, and the same may happen with the break from the ' off ;' but such variations are beyond the reach of any practical discussion.

Let us now turn to another element of good bowling— change of pace. It does not require any great amount of technical cricket knowledge to understand that, if a bowler delivers every ball at the same uniform pace, his bowling is easier for a batsman to judge and play than when he is continually altering and changing the pace. If a batsman mis-judges the pace of the ball he often loses his wicket. If he plays too slow for a fast ball, or too fast for a slow one, he generally makes a fatal mistake. As it is necessary for a shooter to accurately judge the pace of a driven grouse before pulling the trigger, so is it equally necessary for a batsman to judge the pace of the ball before he plays to it. This power of judging pace only comes after long experience ; but when it does exist it seems to be exercised almost intuitively, and without any conscious thought—indeed there is often no time for thought.

Perhaps the one thing which made Mr. Spofforth, the famous Australian bowler, superior at his best to all others, and has earned him the reputation of being the best bowler that has ever lived, was his wonderful power of changing the pace of the ball without making it perceptible to the batsman. In his bowling the same run, action, and exertion were apparently used for delivering a slow or medium paced ball as for a fast one. Many a time, especially on his first arrival in England, when this bowling was strange to our batsmen, the ball seemed to dislodge the bails long after the bat had completed the stroke, and was perhaps high in the air. Change of pace, to be effective, must not mean change of action ; and the first thing a bowler who wishes to practise this art must understand, is that the slightest variation in style or action for a slower or faster ball will at once put the batsman on the *qui vive*, and destroy the effect of the device.

When a slow or medium-pace bowler wishes to deceive the batsman by a change of pace, he has, of course, two courses open to him—either to accelerate the speed of the ball or diminish it. When he wishes to bowl a faster ball than usual, he must remember that the object of the experiment is to make the batsman play slower to the ball than he has been doing, and that this result will be far more easily accomplished by pitching a good-length—if anything, a little further than a good-length—ball, than by a short one. If the latter is bowled, the batsman, although deceived in the pace up to the pitch, has time to discover his mistake before the ball reaches him, and consequently has his bat ready in time to stop it. If a ball is, however, pitched a good length, or a trifle beyond it, and up to the pitch is successful in deceiving the batsman, he will not have much chance of stopping it afterwards.

Palmer, another of the famous Australians, sends down the best fast ball that has been seen from a medium-pace bowler. There is no change of action to warn the batsman, no longer or faster run, but the ball comes with lightning rapidity, generally pitched well up, and very often in the block-hole, making that most deadly ball a 'fast yorker,' about which something will be said farther on. The change from slow or medium-pace bowling to quite slow is much more frequently practised than the change to fast, and consequently we may presume it is more easy of accomplishment. There are few slow or medium-pace bowlers who do not try occasionally to deceive the batsman by making the high slow ball pitch a little shorter than the rest have been doing. But although there are many bowlers who endeavour thus to deceive, there are but few who are really skilful in the art.

It is an extremely difficult thing to reduce the pace on the ball without altering the action. Mr. Spofforth, the Australian, as we have observed, excelled in this, as also did Alfred Shaw, of Nottingham, when at his best. For many years Shaw had the reputation of being the best slow bowler in England, and justly so. His most deadly device was, after he had bowled three or four of his ordinary paced ones, to toss the ball a little higher, a little slower, and a little shorter. Unless the batsman detected the alteration in speed at the moment of delivery, he made what was often a fatal mistake. If he hit, the ball would go high in the air, generally in the direction of deep field-on ; if he played forward, a catch and bowl was the very likely result. If this ball is bowled without deceiving the batsman, it generally meets with a very heavy penalty, as, if rightly judged at first, it can generally be either waited for and hit almost to any part of the field on the 'long-hop' or bound, or run down and driven past the bowler ; but the latter feat can only be accomplished by batsmen who are very quick on their legs.

Some of the best exponents of this ball appear, just prior to delivery, to greatly exert their bodies, and go through their whole customary action, while the arm, dragged slower than usual through the air, delivers the ball when the body is comparatively at rest. This, no doubt, gives the batsman the idea that the ball is going to be delivered before it really does leave the bowler's hand. But it would be quite beyond the capabilities of the writer to furnish any intelligible hints as to how to bowl this ball ; every bowler will with practice find this out for himself.

As a rule, good bowlers of the present day bowl with their arms above the shoulder, and it is a rudiment in the art that the action of delivery should be as high as possible. The high delivery is certainly the most successful where the ground is hard, fast, and true, as then little or no twist can be put on to the ball, and the higher it is made to bound the more chance there is of the batsman making an uppish stroke. In addition to this advantage which the high has over the low delivery, the higher the arm is raised above the shoulder, the more difficult it is for a batsman to judge the pitch and flight of the ball.

With regard to the amount of success that slow and fast bowling meet with, at the present time there cannot be much doubt that slows as a rule are most successful. In saying this not one single word is said against fast bowling ; it is indeed very greatly to be regretted that there are not more fast bowlers. They are a race of cricketers that, especially amongst amateurs, seems to be dying out—a fact which must cause the greatest anxiety to all who play the game, when it is recollected that no side, however strong in batting, fielding and bowling, is really complete without a thoroughly good fast bowler. But still slow bowling is generally found to be the most successful. It may be that this is partly the result of the numerous wet grounds which slow bowlers have to assist them during the cricket season, or of there being more slow bowlers than fast. But it is also true that slow bowling is more difficult to play than fast. The advantages that it possesses over fast are as follows :—

First.—The slowly delivered ball describes a curved line in the air both before it pitches, and afterwards to the bat ; and balls coming in a curved line are far more difficult to play accurately than those which come quick and straight from the pitch. If the batsman properly judged the fast ball, by simply putting his bat straight forward he would always meet and stop it. It is not quite so with the slower ball. The ball, coming on to the ground in a curve, will leave it in a curve, and may consequently go over the shoulder of the bat. Besides, the quicker the ball is, the shorter time the batsman has to play it ; his mode of playing must be decided on instantaneously, so he has no time to get into two minds on the subject.

Secondly.—In slow bowling there is always more actual hitting than in fast, and the more hitting the greater chance there is of the ball going up in the air. Fast bowling may perhaps be driven more—that is to say, it may be pushed hard by good for-

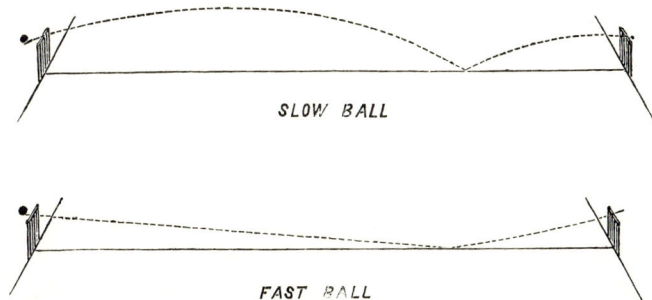

SLOW BALL

FAST BALL

ward play in front of the wicket in all directions ; but it is not often with this style of bowling that the bat is lifted high in the air, and the shoulders, arms, and whole body combine together for a big hit or 'slog,' as it is sometimes called, whereas slows often tempt the best of batsmen to hit without quite getting on to the pitch of the ball, the consequence being that the ball goes up in the air somewhere.

It is a very common occurrence to see a slow bowler who is bowling really well, and with tolerable success, taken off at once on the advent of some batsman who has earned a reputation for big hitting. He himself may be nervous about the fearful smashing the batsman may give him, and suggest to his captain to put on some fast bowler in his place, or else the captain may make the change himself. What is the usual result? The fast bowler compels the hitter to play a steady game, and then, when the latter has just got his eye well set and fit for hitting, on go the slows again, with the probable result of being utterly knocked to pieces in a few overs. If the slows had been allowed a chance at first, when the batsman's eye had not got settled down to the light, and he himself was still suffering from the nervousness inevitable to every man on first going in, what a different tale might have been told! It is always the best thing to put on slows to a big hitter when he first comes in. His anxiety to begin to hit at once is fostered by the slow, easy-looking balls that give him such time to lift his bat and put his whole strength into the stroke; this anxiety is often helped, too, by his nervousness, which in many instances produces a tendency to hit.

On a certain occasion one of the biggest hitters our cricket grounds have ever seen made about eighty runs without having a single slow ball bowled to him. The captain at last put on a slow bowler out of sheer desperation. As the slow bowler walked up to the wicket to bowl, the big hitter turned to him and said, 'What, are *you* going to bowl your donkey-drops? I'll hit them all out of the ground.' 'If you *keep on* doing it I shall have to go off,' was the modest reply. The third ball of the over there was a terrific slog; the bat fairly whistled with the speed it went through the air, and the ball, touching the shoulder, landed in short-slip's hands.

There are only two exceptions to the golden rule to put on slows when a hitter first comes in: the first is when there is something peculiar connected with the condition of the ground which is making a fast bowler at that particular time especially deadly; and the second, when the condition of the game renders it imperatively necessary to keep down the runs at all costs. In the latter case a slow bowler may prove too expensive, as even the miss-hits of a strong hitter are apt to go to the boundary.

Thirdly (to resume the consideration of the advantages of slow bowling, interrupted by the anecdote and the statement of the rule and its exceptions).—Slow bowling offers more opportunity to the wicket-keeper for stumping than fast. It is so tempting for a batsman to rush in and drive the slow tossed-up ball that often he chooses the wrong one, misses it, and is left standing still a yard or two out of his ground. Chances to the wicket-keeper are also much easier off slows than fast, and consequently a great many more wickets are taken.

Fourthly.—The very slowness of the ball induces liberties of all sorts to be taken, besides that of hitting mentioned above. The batsman, when his eye is well in, often tries to score by placing balls to a particular spot, which their pitch does not justify. A favourite error that even the best batsmen fall into is that of trying to hit the leg-stump half-volleys too much to the on side, and sometimes absolutely to leg, a stroke which would never enter his head were a fast bowler bowling.

Fifthly.—A slow bowler has much greater command of pitch, pace, and spin than a fast one. The power which is expended by the latter on the pace of the ball is available by the former for these more subtle devices. There is consequently a much wider field for experiment open to the slow bowler. Usually a fast bowler bowls away ball after ball in the hopes of breaking down the batsman's defence by a good-length ball or a 'yorker;' if he fails to do this he retires in favour of the next change. A slow bowler has many devices, of which actually bowling the batsman out is perhaps very seldom resorted to. He should be able to pitch the ball within a few inches of the spot he wishes, and thus, when he has ascertained any particular weakness the batsman seems to possess, he is able to take advantage of it. There are very few batsmen who have not certain favourite strokes; some may have a partiality for cutting, others for playing on the on side for ones and twos, others for off driving; but whatever the particular *penchant* may be, a slow bowler's business is to make himself acquainted with it and then take the greatest possible advantage of it. Suppose a batsman shows by his play that he is always on the look-out for a cut, and even goes so far as to cut balls which should be driven or played forward to, on the off side, a slow bowler by his command of pitch and pace may do much execution. A ball pitched a trifle further up than usual on the off side and a trifle faster may, and often does, induce the batsman to try his favourite stroke, at the imminent peril of placing the ball in the hands of point or third man, or of being caught at the wicket. A slower and higher ball than usual pitched on the leg-stump will often induce a batsman to try a favourite 'on side' stroke, at the risk of playing with a cross bat and being bowled or out leg before wicket. In fact, every fault that it is possible for a batsman to possess may be taken advantage of by a slow bowler to a much greater extent than by one of great pace. How often one sees a batsman who has given great trouble dismissed by a slow bowler who seems to have absolutely no merit whatever ! The ball is tossed high in the air, with apparently no spin of any sort, and so slow as hardly to reach the wicket, and yet the well-set batsman falls a prey to his over-anxiety to play the ball where the pitch of it does not warrant.

Sixthly.—A slow bowler has the advantage over a fast one of having what is equivalent to an extra man in the field, viz. himself. After the ball is bowled he is firm on his legs, ready to run in for a catch and bowl, or to dart to the on or the off side as the batsman shapes to play the ball. No matter how hard the ball is returned from the bat, he has always ample time to get down with the right hand or the left or to jump high in the air ; when the batsmen are running he is always able to get behind his wickets ready to receive the ball when returned by the fielder, a golden rule for every bowler which is too often neglected. A fast bowler is generally unsteady on his legs after the ball is delivered ; the pace with which he runs up to the wicket carries him on a few paces after the delivery, and he is thus generally unable to exhibit the same activity and sharpness in fielding his own bowling as a slow bowler does. In days gone by, when grounds were bad and rough, slow bowling was not so successful as fast, but the general improvement in the ground has altered this.

And now, having seen some of the advantages slow bowling possesses over fast, and before discussing the latter's merits, let us see on what principles a slow bowler should endeavour to

A hot return.

bowl, and what rules he should follow in order to attain success. Whilst speaking of slow bowling we shall refer to any pace under that of medium, as the rules and principles of medium are included in what is said on fast bowling. Perhaps the most important thing that every bowler, whether fast, medium, or slow, should realise is, as we have said before, to keep the ball well pitched up when a batsman first comes in.

The importance of this rule is manifest, as a short-pitched ball requires no play, whereas one pitched a good length, or even farther, requires steadiness and accuracy of eye to play ; because there is a moment after its pitch when it is lost to the vision, and consequently if the eye lacks accuracy the ball will be missed or bungled. An old professional cricketer, one who has made his mark in times gone by both with bat and ball, once observed to the author, 'Anything rather than straight long-hops, sir, when a man first comes in ; wides and full-pitches are better,' and he was right ; straight long-hops, which, alas ! many of our professional bowlers bowl only too often, in order to prevent runs being made off them, do more to get in the eyes of batsmen than any other sort of ball. Often and often one sees a bowler, and perhaps one who has the name of being first-class, send down to a new batsman straight long-hops one after the other—balls which it is impossible, or nearly so, to score off, and then at the end of each over walk to his place with a thoroughly satisfied air, as if adding one more maiden over to his analysis had really helped his side on to the ultimate goal of victory. It is always better for a bowler to see a fresh batsman make half a dozen runs from well-pitched balls or half-volleys his first over than to see him stop four straight long-hops.

On the fall of a wicket the bowler should always remember that the new batsman is entirely unaccustomed to the light and not yet warm to his work, and that consequently the pet devices which may have been clearly seen through and mercilessly punished by the retiring batsman are for the present quite fresh for the new one. He should consequently begin by doing all he can to get rid of him at once before he gets 'set.' He should in the first two or three overs try every effective ball he knows—and certainly in the first over he should try a 'yorker.' This ball, called in days gone by a 'tice,' an abbreviation of 'entice,' is certainly one of the most deadly balls that can be bowled, if not absolutely the most deadly. We believe that, if statistics could be kept of how every wicket fell during the course of a season, more would be found victims to the 'yorker' than to any other ball. We can find no derivation for the word 'yorker,' but are told that it came from the Yorkshiremen, who were fonder of bowling this ball than any other. A story is told of a famous old Yorkshire professional who, on being asked whether he knew why this ball was called a 'yorker,' replied, 'Of course I do.' 'Well?' said his questioner. 'Why, what else could you call it?' was the answer, with a puzzled look and a scratch on the top of his head. The ordinary definition of a 'yorker' is a ball that pitches inside the crease, and this, no doubt, is correct so far as it goes, but it does not go far enough. It really should be, any ball that pitches directly underneath the bat. It is quite possible for a man to be bowled out with a 'yorker' when he is two or three yards out of his ground, if he misjudges the ball, and allows it to pitch directly beneath his bat, although the ball pitches as far from the crease as he is standing. The most deadly sort of 'yorker,' however, is the one that pitches about three or four inches inside the crease. One mistake which the batsman makes with this ball is that he imagines it is going to pitch shorter for a half-volley, and gets ready to hit, when he finds the ball coming farther than he expected, and is then too late to stop it. Another grave error which many batsmen fall into is that of lifting their bats up, after judging the pace and pitch of the 'yorker,' intending to come down on it as it touches the ground, which really is at the very last moment. It seems an easy thing to stop a 'yorker' in this way, but it really requires the greatest nicety in timing, and a moment late means that the ball has passed and the stumps are down. Whenever a batsman is playing 'yorkers' by chopping down on them inside his crease, it is as certain as can be that he is not at all at home with them, and the bowler may hope for success with every one he tries. Even if the bat does come down on a 'yorker' in the crease at the last moment, it often dribbles on with the spin, and just dislodges the bails. The only proper, workmanlike way to deal with 'yorkers' is to play them forward. The bat should be thrust forward directly the ball is seen to be right up to the batsman, and then it cannot fail to be stopped. One great peculiarity of 'yorkers' is that it is impossible to bowl such a ball to some batsmen. W. G. Grace hardly ever gets one ; directly the ball leaves the bowler's hand he sees its destination, viz. an inch inside the crease ; he puts the bat out to meet the ball, and makes it one of the easiest possible, viz. a full-pitch. If there were no such thing as misjudgment on the part of a batsman, there would be no such thing as a 'yorker.' It depends for its very existence on being taken for something else. If every batsman were perfectly accurate in his sight and judgment of pitch, every so-called 'yorker' would be neither more nor less than a 'full-pitch.' However, as every batsman, we are thankful to say, is liable to err in judging the pitch, and as nearly every batsman when first going in is more liable to err with a 'yorker' than any other ball, the bowler should most decidedly try it. A slow bowler should first try a medium-paced 'yorker,' somewhat faster than his usual pace, and then a slower one. It is astonishing how many wickets fall to slow 'yorkers ;' the ball is mistaken for everything but what it really is, viz. a full-pitch— for every ball pitching inside the crease must be playable as a full-pitch.

When a bowler is put on to bowl by his captain, it is his duty to do everything in his power to dislodge the batsman. It is really quite a secondary consideration for him whether many or few runs are being made off his bowling. It is the duty of the captain to tell the bowler when he wants the pace in the run-getting to be diminished, and then, and not till then, must the bowler begin to bowl straight and short with that object. But until certain instructions are given, the bowler must never stop for an instant in his endeavour to get the batsman's wicket. If he has experimented with every one of his arts and is unsuccessful, or even if he becomes too expensive in run-getting before he has done this, the captain's duty is to take him off.

.It is a common sight enough to see a bowler put on in a

match who simply dare not try the experiments which he has practised with success, for fear of being hit for a four or two and taken off. He is quite content to see ball after ball played full in the middle of the bat straight back to him, knowing well that with such bowling he has not the remotest chance of getting a wicket. In the hopes of getting a wicket a slow bowler should often try leg half-volleys ; they are, of course, delightful balls for a batsman to hit, but, at the present day, when the old George Parr leg hit is comparatively unknown—viz. to fine long-leg all along the ground well behind the wicket—and the leg hitting off slows is generally high and square, they often result in a long-leg catch, and sometimes one at the wicket, through the batsman hitting too quick at the ball. A bowler who has been sending down ball after ball with the off break on should often try pitching one on the same spot but without the break ; the batsman is very apt to play inside this ball, and place it in short-slip's hands. In addition to the change of pace which we have above commented on, it is a most excellent thing occasionally to lower and heighten the action. Alfred Shaw used continually, by lowering his action, to send in a ball which skimmed, so to speak, from the pitch at a great pace, and much faster than his ordinary balls. The raising of the arm higher than usual makes the ball bound higher, which is very often an advantage, especially on rough cut-up grounds. The good-length ball outside the off stump, pitched perhaps eight inches to a foot wide of it, and without any break on at all, is often a most telling ball, especially to eager, excitable batsmen. The ball, not being straight, cannot be met with the full face of the bat, and consequently, unless the batsman puts his left leg right across the wicket, he must, in playing it, lift it up in the air, when it is probably captured by cover-point or mid-off. If this ball can be made to go ever so little from the leg side after it has pitched it becomes more deadly, as then there is a much greater chance of the batsman being unable to get over the ball sufficiently to keep it along the ground.

There has grown up in late years a most deplorable practice amongst batsmen of leaving balls on the off side alone, for fear of risking their wickets. In every match, big and little, one may see batsmen jump in front of their wickets time after time to off balls, allowing the ball to go by unplayed at, or if it twists to hit their legs. We call this a most deplorable practice, because it is not real cricket. The true object of the batsman is to defend his wicket with his bat ; let him use his legs as well if he likes, but his bat he should certainly use, and when he holds the bat high in the air and guards his wicket with his legs, and legs alone, in our opinion he goes beyond the limit of legitimate batting. A batsman is perfectly right in refusing to hit or play at wide balls on the off side, but when he remains passive to balls a few inches only outside the off stump, he not only acknowledges his want of confidence in himself, but also degrades the dignity of a cricket bat by substituting in its place his own usually nervous legs. We remember seeing, some years back, a batsman who had completed his hundred refusing, on a perfectly good wicket, to play ball after ball on the off side. The famous old bowler David Buchanan was bowling at one end, and could not understand how some of his most lovely half-volleys were allowed to pass by unlooked at and despised. The batsman, however, was thoroughly well roasted by his own side and the other for his tame play ; and it was satisfactory afterwards to learn that he had given up his weakness for seeing long-hops and half-volleys pass on the off without being first heavily taxed for the good of his side. It is rather a difficult thing for a slow bowler to know what to do when he has to bowl to a batsman of this sort. He might, of course, go on bowling on the off side, and try to tire the batsman out and make him play; but this, in these present days of good wickets and lengthy matches, would take far too long. The best course for a bowler to take is continually to alter his pace, and endeavour by pitching a ball sharper from the pitch and quicker than usual on the off stump to get the batsman out leg before wicket. Just the very slightest degree outside the off stump is also a good place for this class of player ; he gets undecided whether to adopt his mawkish style of play or not, and in his indecision is apt to make mistakes.

A favourite scheme for a slow bowler to get rid of a batsman is by bowling him off his legs. This is always more easy of accomplishment when the batsman's legs stand some distance from the leg-stump and his bat. When this is going to be tried an extra man should be put out on the on side between long-leg and deep field-on, as the ball which is to be bowled will, if hit by the batsman, generally go in that direction. If the bowler can dispense with a long-leg, it is advantageous to have a short-leg, perhaps a yard or two in front of the umpire, and also a mid-wicket on as near to the batsman as he can with safety venture. The ball should then be bowled with as much off break and as good a length as possible, in a line with the leg-stump ; if played at and missed on account of the twist it hits the legs, and so cannons into the wicket. If it is met with the bat there is always a chance of the twist taking it into the hands of short-leg or mid-on. The place on which the ball pitches must depend on the state of the ground and the amount of twist that can be put on to the ball.

Spofforth, the Australian, was a bowler who used this ball very successfully, as indeed he did most others. When he had the ground in a suitable state—i.e. when it was sticky or else crumbled and loose—he used to place a short-leg close in to the batsman about two yards behind the wicket ; he would also have another short-leg or mid-on close in to the batsman and fairly straight. He would then bowl about medium pace, pitching ball after ball a good length on the leg-stump, and with as much off break as he could get on, which, of course, would vary with the state of the ground. The result of this manœuvre was to make the batsman's chance of remaining at the wickets for long extremely doubtful. The pace (medium) would compel him to play forward to all good-length balls ; the break-back and abrupt rise or kick then made it very probable that he would either place the ball in the hands of one of the expectant short-legs or else be bowled off his bat or legs. The author recollects on one occasion having to play against the redoubtable Spofforth under the above circumstances. After receiving a few balls he came to the conclusion that it was absolutely impossible to prevent being captured by one of the short-legs, who were both standing ridiculously close, and every ball was rising uncomfortably high. He determined to take the liberty of pulling, and did so once or twice with success, till he paid the usual penalty of the practice on a kicking wicket by being badly cut over. He then tried jumping in front of his wicket and trying to slide the breaking balls off his bat to very fine long-leg. Spofforth, however, was too much for him, and almost immediately bowled a straight middle stump ball without any break on it and rather faster than the others ; it kept low, hit the shin, and there was as dead a case of 'l.b.w.' as any bowler could wish for.

A favourite trick of some slow bowlers is to bowl from different distances. Sometimes the bowler will have one leg behind the wickets and the other in front, and sometimes both behind ; we have even seen some bowl occasionally with the front leg as much as two yards behind the wicket. The object of this is to deceive the batsman as to the pitch of the ball by changing the distance the ball has to travel. This is doubtless an excellent theory, but in our opinion it is not of much worth in actual practice. We have seen bowlers of all sorts repeatedly try this experiment, but in our experience it never meets with any appreciable success. This is perhaps owing to the fact that the batsman can always see very clearly when the bowler does not come up the whole way to the wicket, and is accordingly on the alert for a shorter pitched ball than usual. The only practiser of this trick who ever seems to turn it to good account is Tom Emmett, the left-handed Yorkshire veteran ; he usually bowls his slow wides from some distance behind the crease, and certainly obtains a fair share of wickets with these balls ; but even in his case we think that it is generally not so much the difference in the distance that

the ball has to travel which causes disaster to the batsman, as
the latter's anxiety and impatience to score from slow wide off
balls, which look so easy and are really so deadly.   However,
though our opinion of this bowler's 'dodge' is not particularly
high, we still think it is worthy of trial at times by every slow
bowler.   A slow bowler should try every wile that can possibly be attempted ; by adopting slow bowling he has under-
taken to use the 'wisdom of the serpent' in the guise of the
'harmlessness of the dove,' and has sacrificed pace to cunning
and thought. No slow bowler is worth his salt who merely tosses
the ball into the air and trusts to chance for success, even if it
has a little spin on it ; he must continually think and diagnose
every particular case which comes before him, and then adopt the
measures necessary for each one.   With this object it is the duty
of every slow bowler to take advantage of any local peculiarity
which the size and situation of the ground may afford.   He
should almost always have the choice of ends, except on occasions when the captain of the side considers that for some
reason his fast bowler is more likely to get rid of the batting side
for a small score than the slow, and then, of course, the fast
must have the choice.

For example, in the University matches from 1878 to 1881,
Oxford was so overmatched by Cambridge that in each of
these years before the play began it was considered by the
outside public as a foregone conclusion for the latter.   The
really knowing ones, however, who thoroughly understood the
game, were aware that there was one man on the Oxford side
who might any day get rid of the best side in England for a
very small score.   That man was Mr. Evans, the famous fast
bowler.   He was the only man on the side who, humanly
speaking, seemed capable of turning the chances of the game.
He consequently chose his own particular end—the one he
thought most suited to his style, quite irrespective of any
mediocre slow bowler that was on his side ; and the havoc he
played amongst the Cambridge wickets for those four years
may be seen from the old scores.   It is, however, an exception

when a side depends almost entirely on its fast bowling, and it is only when this exception arises that a slow bowler (assuming him to be one who is competent to judge) must not have his choice of ends. Of course we mean his choice of ends at the commencement of an innings, as after that it is the captain's duty to put any bowler on at either end, and it is the duty of every bowler to obey his captain cheerfully.

As already remarked, every slow bowler should take advantage of every local peculiarity that may offer itself. For instance, there may be a ground where a high tree is behind one of the wickets ; the slow bowler, if he thinks this tree will help him at all, should take his measures acordingly. We hope none will think we are advocating anything at all unfair in the game, or anything that is even on the line between fairness and 'not quite straight.' As a rifle-shooter takes advantage of a lull in the wind to pull his trigger, as a deerstalker of every rock and unevenness of ground to approach his game—in short, just as in every kind of sport natural facilities may be utilised —so in bowling every peculiarity of time and place should be enlisted on the side of the bowler in his (in these days of good wickets and good batting) by no means easy task of getting rid of the batsman. If a bowler, who, we will say, usually bowls over the wicket, perceive that by bowling round the wicket he may make his bowling more difficult to see, and consequently more effective, on account of a tree, house, or hedge that is directly behind that side of the wicket, he should most certainly change and make the most of that advantage. An injudicious and talkative batsman often materially assists a bowler by such remarks as, 'I can't see your bowling a little bit. When tossed high in the air that beastly tree is right behind ;' or, 'When you bowl over the wicket the ball gets right in a line with the dark windows of the pavilion, and I can't see it at all.' Can anyone imagine for a moment that a bowler will not do his very best instantly to make the most of the dark branches of the tree or the windows of the pavilion? The sun, too, often materially assists a slow bowler, especially during the last hour or hour and a half of the day's play. If there are any trees round the ground, the shadows, beginning to lengthen, will often lie right across the pitch, and if there is one anywhere near where a good-length ball should pitch, it is advisable to try pitching one occasionally on it. If the sun is behind the bowler's wicket and getting a little low, the bowler should try by bowling high slow ones to get it in the line of the batsman's vision. Every possible advantage within the limits and spirit of fair play may be considered legitimate for a bowler. Local advantages of ground and weather are certainly within these limits, but any peculiarity of dress or tricks of manner, which are in themselves calculated to baulk or annoy a batsman, is not.

For example, bowling with a long loose and flapping sleeve in order to distract the batsman's attention from the ball, a habit which of late has been seen on our English grounds, is in itself intrinsically unfair and unworthy of any true cricketer. And again, waving the arms behind the ball after it has been delivered, or any other trick adopted in order to worry or harass the batsman, is manifestly unfair. Some batsmen are extremely fastidious, and are distracted by the merest trifle. The writer remembers on one occasion taking part in a match when a batsman objected to a bowler on the ground that he was wearing a stud made of some bright material or stone, which glistened so in the sun that it diverted his attention from the ball. This, of course, sounded absurd, but the bowler at once removed the glittering nuisance, and rightly too.

A slow bowler must bear in mind what has before been mentioned, viz. that it is often almost as good as a change of bowling to change from over to round the wicket, or *vice versâ*, quite apart from the advantage he may gain from any local obstruction to good light. Supposing a slow bowler has been ' on ' for some time over the wicket, as a rule the great majority of his balls have been pitched a few inches outside the off stump and breaking in to the middle or middle and leg. The batsman has got thoroughly into the way of playing this particular ball and does not show any signs of making a mistake. The bowler goes round the wicket, and although he still continues to pitch a little outside the off stump, the ball is quite different now from what it was from over the wicket.   It is, of course, impossible to get as much 'break-back' spin on to the ball when bowling round as over the wicket, because the ball is delivered several feet from a straight line between the two wickets, but in most conditions of the ground it is possible to get a certain amount on.   The change in the direction of the ball, or rather in the spot from which it is delivered, combined with the diminution in the amount of break, makes it often a most effective change and one well worth the trial.   In addition there is always from round the wicket the chance of a batsman playing inside a ball which, delivered without any spin at all, keeps going across the wicket, as it is technically called, 'with the arm.'

We cannot omit, when enumerating the different balls of which a slow bowler may avail himself, one which is by no means used as often as it should be, viz. the full-pitch.   In slow bowling there are three different kinds of full-pitches—the high-dropping full-pitch, which will pitch either on the top of the wicket or a few inches before it; the ordinary slow full-pitch, which reaches the batsman about the height of his knees ; and the medium-paced full-pitch, which will hit the stumps nearly at the top.   The high-dropping full-pitch is a ball that is seldom used, the reason for its rarity probably being the extreme difficulty of bowling it accurately and the certain punishment it will meet with if it falls at all short either in height or length of what it should be.   It should be delivered as high as possible ; there is no limit to the height this ball may go in the air, as the higher it ascends the more difficult it is to play.   It should be bowled so that it reaches its highest point when it is almost directly over the head of the batsman, and should pitch on the very top of the stumps.   It is strange that this ball is not more often practised by slow bowlers, as, especially to the pokey, nervous style of batsmen, it is fraught with considerable uneasiness and requires some skill to play properly. To really first-class punishing batsmen it is a ball which has comparatively no terrors, and on which not much reliance can be placed, though it should always, in our opinion, be tried at least once to every batsman who is getting 'well set.' But to the poker, the man who refuses to do anything

A pokey batsman dealing with a high-dropping full-pitch.

but stick his bat in front of the wicket, who lets half-volleys, full-pitches, and long-hops pass unscathed and unplayed on both sides of him—to him who considers he is doing his side good service by wasting three hours of valuable time for a dozen runs on his side of the balance, and three hours' wear and tear of the wicket on the other—to him who helps so greatly to fill up the records of drawn matches, the high-dropping full-pitch is an excellent ball. He does not know what to do with it ; he is afraid to step back to play it for fear of hitting his wicket, and he hardly likes to be so bold as to try to cut or hit it on the on side. One of the most amusing sights we have ever seen at cricket was one of these batsmen having ball after ball of this sort bowled to him ; it was not till after he had nearly lost his wicket a dozen times, only keeping it by exceptional good luck, and had afforded the greatest merriment to players and spectators alike, that he burst out from sheer desperation into wild and furious hitting—a line of conduct which had the immediate effect of compelling the bowler to desist from his lofty attacks.

The second kind of full-pitch—the one reaching the batsman about the height of his knees—is the most usual of full-pitches, and enjoys the distinction of being considered the easiest of all balls to hit. A good batsman can hit this ball from a slow bowler to almost any part of the field ; consequently, though it often happens in the chapter of accidents that a wicket falls to this ball—a catch in the country perhaps, or a hard catch and bowl—it is of all balls the very worst for a slow bowler to deliver.

The third kind—the medium-paced full-pitch straight to the top of the stumps—is occasionally, for a slow bowler, a very useful ball. In the first place, it is not quite so easy to hit as it appears to the batsman ; the change in pace from slow to medium often causes him to hit a trifle slower than he should do, when the ball, coming on faster than expected, hits the top or splice of the bat, and goes straight up in the air. This ball is generally more successful with players who have a partiality for on-side hitting than with others, as it is never a difficult one to play quietly ; it is only when the batsman tries to hit that it becomes likely to get a wicket. It is also useful when a hitter, by running out and hitting every ball, is demoralising bowler, fielders, and the whole side. If the bowler sees the intention of the hitter to run out before the ball is delivered—and he is often able to do this—he can do nothing better than bowl a good medium-paced full-pitch straight at the top of the middle stump ; if the batsman goes on with his intention of running out, he is not only apt to overrun this faster than usual ball, and let it pass over the top of his bat, but if he does hit it he is likely to send it high in the air, from the above-mentioned cause of catching it with the top or splice of the bat. There is, however, nothing so flurrying to a bowler as a batsman who runs out to every ball, and who evinces his intention of doing so before the ball is delivered. The writer has often talked with old cricketers on this subject, and they have remarked how well the old bowlers of their early days used to keep their heads under these trying circumstances. Doubtless they deserve the very greatest credit for doing so, for there is nothing so trying to a bowler ; it spoils his pitch, and is rather apt to do the same to his temper. The regular attendant at matches may have seen almost every bowler of reputation in England so thoroughly flurried and upset by a batsman doing this, that, in spite of all efforts to keep cool, the bowling was simply paralysed and rendered useless to the side for the time being. The best courses for a slow bowler to pursue on these occasions is, 1st, to bowl the sort of full-pitch just discussed ; and, 2nd, to increase his pace a little, and bowl a little short of a good length, about a foot or more outside the legs of the batsman. There is nothing a rushing-out batsman finds so hard to hit as a ball well outside his legs.

Widish off balls are also useful, as a batsman going down the wicket is not only apt to miss, but also, if he can reach, to sky them. A high full-pitch into the hands of the wicket-keeper is likewise sometimes successful ; but, though we may lay down certain rules and suggestions as to what is best for a bowler to do at this very trying time, we are afraid that, unless he is able to keep exceptionally cool, they will be of no practical assistance.

The variableness of the English climate plays a very important part in the success or otherwise of slow bowlers. A

shower of rain in the night often has the effect of making particularly deadly a slow bowler who, the day before, on a hard
and fast ground, was comparatively harmless and ineffective.
Up to 1884 the disadvantage of a rainfall in the night to a
side that had begun but not finished its innings was increased
by the rule forbidding the ground to be rolled except before
the commencement of each innings. Rain in the night not
only softens the ground, but brings up to the surface numbers
of worms, which cover the pitch with little heaps of earth
mould. These little heaps, in the absence of any rolling,
made the ground bumpy and treacherous, and consequently
entailed serious discomfiture to the batting side. The only
plausible argument ever advanced for this injustice was that it
might happen to either side, and was one of the chances of the
game. However, the M.C.C. wisely decided, though not till
quite recently, that this rule should be abolished, the reason
for the decision being that the side which won the toss had a
great advantage as it was, from having the first and best of the
wicket, and that, as the other side was usually batting at the
end of the day, it gave the men an extra and unfair disadvantage in having the wicket spoilt by rain and worms without the
chance of having it rolled. No rule, however, can affect the
drawback under which a batting side is placed whose wicket
is softened by a heavy rainfall in the night. The roller may level
the worm moulds, but it cannot alter the slow, sticky state of
the ground ; in fact, it often brings up more water, and makes
the pitch still more sticky and slow. It is on occasions such
as these that slow bowlers meet with their greatest success. So
frequently during the course of the season do these soft wickets
occur, even in what are called our hot summers, that it is part
of the science of bowling to know how to turn such grounds
to the best advantage. The different states of the ground
caused by the weather may be roughly, and for all practical
purposes, divided into five : 1st, the hard and dry state ; 2nd,
the hard state, with the grass wet ; 3rd, the very soft and slow
state, (*a*) with the grass dry, (*b*) with the grass wet ; 4th, the

drying state, when it has been very slow and soft, but is gradually drying under the influence of a hot sun or wind ; 5th, the
hard and crumbled state. The hard and dry state calls for no
comment, as everything written on the subject of bowling, unless otherwise specified, refers to the ground in this condition.
The hard state, with the grass wet, is perhaps the most trying
time for a slow bowler. He has to bowl with a wet ball, which
he has great difficulty in holding ; he cannot get on the slightest
degree of twist, as the wet ball slips off the wet grass directly
it pitches, allowing no time for the ball to 'bite' the ground
and take the twist. A good batsman on these wickets knows
that all he has to do is to play forward with a straight bat
when the ball is anything like a good one, and he is bound to
meet it. The slippery ball flies off the bat like lightning, and
travels, if the grass is short and not too thick, over the hard
ground faster than it does when the grass is dry. Every now
and then a ball may be inclined to keep low or shoot ; but a
shooter does not possess the same terrors on a wet as on a dry
ground, because in almost every instance it can be played
forward to, and a good batsman in playing forward always
keeps his bat low enough to stop shooters (especially on wet
wickets) until he actually sees the ball rise.

The only course for a slow bowler to adopt on these wickets
is to bowl as good a length as he can, and as straight as
possible. He should also bear in mind that the ball leaves the
ground far more quickly than usual in its wet, slippery state,
and that, consequently, the most likely place in the field to
capture a batsman is short-slip. Easy as the ground is for a
batsman when once he gets the pace of it, it often happens
that at first he is surprised at the great pace from the pitch,
plays back instead of forward, and places the ball in the slips.
It is a golden rule for every bowler, slow and fast, on these
wickets to have short-slip 'finer' than on ordinary occasions,
and a trifle further back. It is often advisable to have an
extra man standing about three yards squarer than the regular
short-slip, but no farther from the wicket. Two quick active

men, who are capable at times of bringing off smart one-hand catches, should be chosen for these places. They are by far the most likely men in the field to dismiss good batsmen on wet hard wickets ; in fact, it is often difficult to see how two such batsmen are to be separated on these occasions except by a catch at one of these places, or at the wicket. A bowler should with this object keep bowling a good length on the off stump and just outside it, recollecting that good-length balls must pitch considerably shorter than usual on these very quick wickets.

The very soft and slow state is the result of heavy rain which has left the surface of the pitch dry, but the ground itself thoroughly sodden. This condition of the ground is popularly supposed to favour a slow bowler. How often, on coming on to the ground to inspect the wicket after a night's rain, is he accosted something in this style : 'Well, Jack, this ought to suit you ; those twisters of yours will want some watching to-day !' Jack, after looking at the pitch, which is as soft and sodden as a piece of dough, knows full well that it will be a long time before the ground gets back enough of its half-drowned life to help him in the slightest degree. There is no poorer fun for a slow bowler than having to bowl on these utterly lifeless wickets. On a hard true ground, though it may be favourable to the batsman, he has good sport in trying every dodge he can think of ; he fishes and feeds and angles as warily as Izaak Walton himself ; the ground and ball are full of life and go, and very often, unfortunately for the bowler, the batsman too. On wet hard wickets, when he can get no twist on, there is still life and pace in the ground ; but in the sodden dead state, directly the ball touches the ground it sinks in, loses all life and pace, and comes on to the batsman like what a Yorkshire professional was once heard to call a 'diseased lawn-tennis ball.' There is no greater fallacy at cricket than to suppose that a sodden wicket is an advantage to a slow bowler. The time when it begins to assist him is when the surface is 'caking' under the influence of the sun or a drying

wind ; and then it is that, as we said above, the greatest suc-
cesses of slow bowlers are met with. A slow bowler having to
bowl on a sodden wicket perceives at once that it is extremely
difficult for him to bowl to a good batsman a 'good-length'
ball for the following reasons :—

What is called a 'good-length' ball on ordinary occasions
remains on the ground so long and comes off the pitch so slow
that a batsman, if he is so minded, can with ease play it back
—i.e. he can see it coming on from the pitch in time for him
to get back and play it as a simple 'long-hop.' Anything short
of this will all the more be capable of being played as a 'long-
hop.' If the ball is pitched farther than a good length, it
becomes at once—certainly to batsmen quick on their legs—
a half-volley. Thus, if a batsman really gets the time of the
ground, he has only to play these two simplest of balls. No
amount of spin will help the bowler ; the ball in the soft ground
may twist at right angles, but it does it so slowly that the batsman has ample time to defend his wicket. In these circumstances there is only one thing for a slow bowler to do, and
that is to bowl faster and endeavour, by giving extra pace to
the ball, to make it come off the ground quicker. There are
some batsmen whom, on these sodden wickets, it is almost impossible to get rid of. They remain for hours, perfectly con-
tented if a whole day is taken up with their innings and forty
runs added to the total, the chances of a draw being thereby
greatly augmented. A famous professional stick, on one occasion, remained at the wickets when the ground was sodden for
one hour and fifty minutes before troubling the scorer ; he was
then so flustered by the jeering of the mob that he rushed out,
hit a catch, was missed, and, amidst as much cheering as if he
had wanted one run to complete his hundred, broke his duck's-
egg. Louis Hall, of Yorkshire, is a desperate man to bowl to
on these grounds ; every ball that is bowled he either plays
back or smothers. Nothing in cricket can be more dull or
dismal than bowling to this batsman on a sodden wicket at
Bramall Lane Ground in a real Sheffield fog.

Although, as has been said, slow bowlers are not assisted by the ground when in this condition, and it is extremely difficult to bowl anything approaching a good ball to a good batsman, there are some batsmen, and real good ones too on a hard true ground, who are utterly unable to adapt their style of play to a slow ground, or rather never can realise that a ball pitched into a lump of dough will leave it much slower than when pitched on to a stone. These batsmen, if they kept their keenness of eye and activity till they were a hundred, would still be seen playing a quick forward stroke on the sodden ground, sending the ball up in the air in every direction. A batsman who persists in playing forward on a dead wicket and finishing his stroke as he would do on a fast wicket is certain not to last long. It is very curious to notice how sometimes nearly a whole batting side will make a mistake about the condition of the wicket. The first batsmen see the ground slow and the ball twisting a good deal, and begin playing as they would do on a faster wicket, viz. playing forward to the pitch instead of waiting and playing a back game. Four or five batsmen will follow, play in the same style, and lose their wickets, generally bowled, or caught and bowled. Some batsman will then come in who at once finds out what the slow bowlers have long since known—that it is a slow easy wicket he has to bat on, and not a 'caked,' 'kicky' one. What happens? He plays every ball back except those that he hits, and he hits everything except a long-hop, because he can get to the pitch of anything else. The slow bowlers who have been doing the mischief are soon knocked off, and his side, in spite of the failure of its four or five most competent batsmen, makes a good score. On one occasion in a first-class match the first seven wickets fell for fifty runs, the wicket being deadly slow and dull ; the eighth man came in, and, by dint of playing back and hitting and a little luck, made over a hundred in about an hour and a half, being fortunate enough to have some one to stick in with him at the other end.

When the ground is very soft and the grass wet, the bowler

is in about the same position as when the grass is wet on a
hard wicket ; he has to bowl with a wet slippery ball, and cannot get any twist at all upon it. This is called the 'cutting
through' state, which means that, the ball being slippery and
the ground and grass wet, it cuts through the surface of the
pitch, taking with it a small piece of wet sticky turf. As in
the hard state with wet grass, short-slip is an important place
and likely to get chances. Although the ground when in this
condition is in favour of the batsman, cricket is miserable under
such circumstances, and is enjoyed neither by batsman, bowler,
nor fielders. The batsman cannot stand on the slippery mud ;
the bowler, with wet dirty hands, and boots and trousers
bespattered with slush, is utterly unable to do anything with
the slimy ball ; and the fieldsmen can neither hold nor stop it.
The ground is covered with sawdust, without the use of which
it would be impossible for the bowler to grasp the ball firmly,
and altogether the whole scene is so unlike cricket, essentially
a fine-weather game, that it always seems a pity under such
conditions to go on playing.

The drying state, when the ground has been very soft and
sodden, but is gradually drying and caking on the surface
under the influence of a hot sun or wind, is the time when slow
bowlers have it all their own way. It is on this condition of
ground that bowlers like Alfred Shaw, and Peate, of Yorkshire,
have so often astonished the cricket community with wonderful
analyses. When the ground has got into this state, it will often
remain so for several hours. At Lord's, when the ground after
being soft has become caked on the top, it is no unusual occurrence to see thirty good wickets or more fall in the course of
the day. When a side, no matter how many really good batsmen it may number, has to go in on 'caked' wickets against
good bowling, they may think themselves lucky if they get 100
runs. The ball takes almost as much twist as a bowler wants
to put on ; it comes off the ground at different paces, one part
of the pitch being a trifle drier and harder than another. The
first ball of the over will perhaps get up almost straight and

very quickly from the pitch as a batsman is playing it; the next pitches a trifle shorter, may stop in the ground, and 'get up and look at you,' as it is called, making correct play an impossibility. Or perhaps one ball will get up very quickly and high, and hit the batsman on the arm or side, and the next, pitched in almost the same spot, will leave the pitch equally quickly, but never rise more than an inch from the ground. It is no recommendation to a bowler to be able to get wickets on such grounds as these; any bad bowler might bowl a good batting side out for a small score with such assistance. The only way a batsman can reasonably hope to add any notches to the score of his side is to grasp the situation at once, throw careful correct play to the winds, and hit, pull, and slog in every direction where he thinks he can get rid of the teasing ball. The Australian eleven of 1882 were particularly good on this class of wicket; they had four men—Giffen, Bonnor, McDonnell, Massie—who, rarely needing much inducement to hit, used to launch out most vigorously and successfully on these occasions, often cracking up twenty or thirty runs in about half the number of minutes, and securing victory for their side.

Although very badly caked wickets are not uncommon, perhaps the best for bowling and the worst for batting in modern experience was at the Oval during the last innings of the England *v.* Australia match at the Oval, 1882. It is the only disastrous match for England in the whole list of national fixtures that have been played in this country. It may be remembered that England, having only a few runs to get to win, nearly made them for the first two wickets, Grace and Ulyett both making about twenty. The ground at this time was drying and becoming every minute more difficult, and the way in which our English wickets were mowed down by Spofforth is now a matter of cricket history, too well known to repeat. Spofforth was bowling rather more than medium pace, bringing the ball back a foot or more very quickly from the pitch, sometimes kicking to the height of the batsman's head and at others shooting. Some of our cricket reporters talked in an airy manner about the 'funk' of the English team on that occasion, but the charge was wholly without foundation. A batsman's consciousness that twenty thousand spectators were watching each ball with breathless interest, and that on his own individual efforts depended the reputation of English cricket, that the bowling was about as good and the ground as bad as any cricketer had ever seen, might, and probably did, cause a feeling of intense anxiety in the minds of each of the English players who failed in his efforts to win victory for his side ; but to say that their efforts were paralysed, or that any one of them was unnerved by what is popularly called 'funk,' is certainly unjust to the well-tried cricketers who did battle for England on that memorable and disastrous occasion.

The hard and crumbled wicket is perhaps almost more difficult for batsmen than when it is caked. The ball will twist a great deal on this class of wicket, and does it very quickly. It is also inclined both to 'pop' and keep low. Spofforth, Giffen, Peate, Barlow, and Barnes are all most deadly bowlers on such a wicket as this.

Some of our most successful slow bowlers have been left-handed. The peculiarity and difficulty about left-hand bowling is that the natural spin imparted to the ball by a left-handed bowler is the off-spin, which, of course, makes the ball after the pitch twist from the leg side of the right-handed batsman to the off. This, as we have mentioned above, is the most difficult twist for a batsman to play, as an off break is more easy to watch after the pitch than a leg-break. The leg-break which a bats-man has to meet from a right-handed bowler is not so difficult to play as that from a left-hander ; because, first, the latter is usually faster than the former, and, secondly, it is much more disguised. The right-hand leg-break is impossible without getting the ball in the centre of the hand and screwing the hand round just as if it were twisting a corkscrew the reverse way—an action which at once prepares the batsman for the leg-twist. Thirdly, because it usually twists very much less than the right-hand leg-break. It is not the ball which twists the most that gets the wickets ; it is the ball that just twists enough to beat the bat.

The mode of attack generally adopted by a slow left-hander is to place all his men, with the exception of a short-leg and a deep mid-on, on the off side. He then proceeds to bowl on the off stump and outside it, making the ball go away from the batsman to the off as much as possible after the pitch. Great care has to be taken by the batsman, as the slightest mistake in hitting or forward play will give a catch to one of the numerous traps laid all round on the off side. It is the object of the bowler to get the batsman either to hit at a ball which is not quite far enough to be smothered, or to reach out and play forward at one which is a little beyond his reach. A favourite device of the left-handed bowler is to get the batsman to hit at widish ones on the off side, a stroke that must cause an uppish hit somewhere, as it is impossible for a batsman to smother a ball that is a trifle out of his reach. It is often a good thing for a left-handed bowler to send down a ball without any twist on it at all, especially if he is bowling on a wicket where he is able to 'do' a good deal. The ball without any spin on it should pitch on the middle and off stumps ; and if the bowler is bowling from round the wicket, as left-handers usually do, it will then come on in a line with the pitch and the hand at the moment of delivery, and if not stopped by the bat, take the leg-stump. This slow ball that comes with the arm in the middle of others going the other way is very successful. Slow left-handed bowlers often have their tempers sorely tried by a class of batsmen that were discussed in a previous portion of this chapter, namely, those who are so frightened of getting out that they will never play at an off ball, long hop, half-volley, or good-length. There are many enticing balls bowled by left-handed bowlers that ought to be left alone by every batsman, notably those that pitch too wide to enable them to be played forward and smothered. There is no greater or more successful trap for wild young players than these widish off balls. But it is indeed a trying time for the bowler when he keeps pitching just outside the off stump, and is not even played at by the batsman. Bowlers should, in these circumstances, bowl ball after ball on the off stump and just outside it. It is by no means an uncommon occurrence to see these punishing batsmen taken in by a ball that comes in a little with the arm, and removes the bail while they are striking an attitude, bat over shoulder.

We have had some excellent left handed-bowlers in England, and there can be no doubt that every team should possess one of this sort if possible. Peate for some years enjoyed the reputation of being the best left-hander in England, and rightly so. He was an exceptional good length, difficult to see, and had a lot of work on. Some of his performances against the Australians are truly wonderful. When Peate first began to play cricket he was a very fast, high-actioned bowler, and the writer remembers thirteen or fourteen years ago finding him on the slow sticky wicket of the Carlisle ground very nasty to play. He subsequently altered his pace to slow, and it is a remarkable fact that, though a fast bowler once, and still a young man, he has now lost the power of sending down a really fast ball. Another of our great slow left-handed bowlers was David Buchanan, and, strangely enough, he too was in his early days a fast bowler. As one of the slow school he is best known, and we have no doubt that he at the present moment has taken nearly twice as many wickets in the course of his career as any other living cricketer. His bowling was celebrated for the great amount of work he got on to the ball ; unless the batsman was on the pitch of it, a mistake was certain. The only team that ever seemed to enjoy Buchanan's bowling was the Rugby boys, and constant practice had robbed it of all terrors for them.

The best left-handed medium-paced bowler we have in England now in the writer's opinion is Briggs, the Lancashire professional. He possesses a marvellous strength of wrist and fingers, which give him great power of twist and pace. His very fast ball is nearly as good as that of Palmer, the Australian. One of his best performances was in England *v.* Australia at Lord's in 1886. None of the English bowlers on this occasion could do much with the ball except Briggs. There is one Australian left-handed bowler who we regret has never been seen on English cricket grounds—Tom Kendall. In 1878, when the first colonial team visited this country, great accounts of Kendall's prowess with the ball had reached us. His name was included in the list of the players whom we were led to expect, but for some reason or other, though he did actually start with the team, he left it at Adelaide or at some other port at which the ship touched. The writer saw him and played against him in 1882 in Tasmania, and, though getting on in years and rather on the big side for bowling, he was about as nasty a left-hander as any batsman could wish to play. He had a high action, changed his pace well, from slow to medium, and then to very fast, had lots of work both ways on his slow and medium balls, and the very fast ones went with the arm. When the writer saw him his length was not as good as it might have been, or, from all accounts, as it once was. His action reminded us rather of that excellent bowler J. C. Shaw, in his day the best left-hander in England.

In the first Australian team that visited this country, in 1878 there was another left-handed slow bowler named Allan, about whom the Australians themselves spread most extraordinary statements. It was said that Allan, 'the bowler of the century,' as he was called in Australia, possessed some of the most remarkable qualities. Rumour declared his spin off the ground was so great that the slowest ball came off up to the bat at ten times greater speed than it had travelled to the pitch ; that he could twist either way, to almost any degree, at will, and that his bowling had a most remarkable curve in the air, which rendered it most deadly. This left-handed bowler is mentioned because, though his powers of bowling had, of course, been greatly exaggerated, it was certainly most puzzling. He met with some considerable success at the outset of the tour; but subsequently his health gave way before the wearing work of cricket every day, and he was unable to bowl at all. His bowling had a considerable amount of spin, but what was the most extraordinary thing connected with it was the inward curl in the air towards the body of the batsman, and then, after the pitch, the outward twist of the ball. A ball that goes one way in the air, and another after the pitch, is calculated to try the mettle of the best batsman. It is a subject for regret that Allan, through increasing years and his consequent inability to stand hard work, has not accompanied any of the later teams, as his bowling was so very different from anything we have ever seen at home.

Does bowling curl or twist in the air? is a question we have often been asked, and we have frequently heard disputes, by men who possessed some considerable knowledge of the game, as to whether it was possible for balls to travel thus or not. It seems almost incredible that men who have over and over again handled the bat should doubt the tendency of some kinds of bowling to twist or curl in the air. Nearly all leg-break slow bowlers curl inwards towards the batsman before the pitch, and no one who has ever played against W. G. Grace's bowling can doubt that the real secret of his success as a bowler has been in the peculiar flight his action gives the ball, causing it to curl before it pitches.

However, the question as to balls turning in the air has been definitely settled by the American base-ball players. In this game the pitcher throws one full-pitch after another to the batsman, and even if the latter happen to be one of the best and most experienced in the game he misses a considerable proportion of these full-pitches. And why? because of the twist or curl in the air which the pitcher imparts to the ball. A very interesting account is given by Mr. R. A. Proctor in 'Longman's Magazine' for June 1887 of a well-known English cricketer's failure to strike the full-pitches of one of the best American pitchers. Time after time the bat struck the air and nothing else; and this was simply owing to the curl the pitcher put on the ball. Mr. Proctor scientifically explains the curl in the air, and it may be of interest to insert a short extract from his article :—

Where a ball (or in fact any missile) is advancing rapidly through the air, there is formed in front of it a small aggregation of compressed air. (In passing we may remark that the compressed air in front of an advancing cannon ball has been rendered discernible—we can hardly say visible—by instantaneous photography.) In shape the cushion of air is conical or rather conoidal, if the ball is advancing without spin ; and therefore it resists the progress of the ball equally on all sides, and only affects the ball's velocity. The same is the case if the ball is spinning on an axis lying along its course. But in the case we have to consider, where the ball is spinning on an axis square to its course, the cushion of compressed air formed by the advancing ball has no longer the symmetrical shape. On the advancing side of the spinning surface the air cannot escape so readily as it would if there were no spin ; on the other side it escapes more readily than it would but for the spin. Hence the cushion of air is thrown towards the side of the ball where the spin is forwards and removed from the other side. The same thing then must happen as where a ball encounters a cushion aslant. A ball driven squarely against a very soft cushion plunges straight into it, turning neither to the right nor to the left, or if deflected at all (as against the billiard cushion) comes straight back on its course ; but if driven aslant against the cushion, it is deflected from the region of resistance. So with the base ball. As the cushion of air against which it is not advancing is opposed squarely to it, but is stronger on one side than on the other, the ball is deflected from the region of greatest resistance.

There is one style of slow bowling that has of late years almost completely vanished from first-class cricket : we refer to under-hand slows. As under-hand was at one time the only bowling that was allowed by the rules of cricket, and as it met with a great amount of success, even after the raising of the arm was permitted, it will be as well to refer to the cause that has brought about its practical abolition. This is owing to the increasing popularity of the game, and the consequent great increase in the number of good batsmen. The greatest under-hand bowler that ever played was probably William Clarke, whose merits have been so often discussed in cricket writings that it is unnecessary to repeat them here. In order to ascertain the style of batsmen Clarke made his great reputation against, we must refer to some one who has seen and known the great bowler and conversed with those who were in the habit of playing against him. We are told that Clarke had perfect accuracy of pitch, a quick rise from the ground, and a good leg twist on his bowling. These attributes in an under-arm bowler, most excellent as they are, would not nowadays, with the present efficient state of batting, justify the name of the possessor being placed in the first rank, because we consider no amount of accuracy of pitch, twist, or anything else can ever secure this coveted distinction to a bowler of this kind. Mr. Pycroft gives us the information we require on the subject of batting against Clarke's bowling. He says with regard to Pilch, at that time the best batsman of the day, 'He played him back all day if he bowled short, and hit him hard all along the ground whenever he over-pitched ; and sometimes he would go in to Clarke's bowling, not to make a furious swipe, but to "run him down" with a straight bat.'

Now this description of the play of a man who was able to meet Clarke's bowling is interesting to us, because it shows us that the way in which the great bowler was played by one of the few who could oppose him successfully is exactly the same method in which every good batsman of the present time *does* play under-hand bowling. If any man of to-day, chosen to take part in the Gentlemen *v.* Players match as a batsman, were to endeavour to play under-hand bowling in any other manner, he would be laughed at as being devoid of the most elementary rules of the game. Mr. Pycroft goes on to tell us the way which many did adopt in playing Clarke. He says, 'This going in to Clarke's bowling some persons thought necessary for every ball, forgetting that discretion is the better part of cricket ; the consequence was that *many wickets fell* from positive long-hops.' This description shows that a great number of those who fell victims to Clarke's bowling were absolutely uninitiated in the first principles of playing slows, viz. never to hit except on the volley, or just as the ball pitches. Nowadays every batsman—at any rate all who play in first-class cricket—knows the danger of playing wildly at under-hand 'lobs,' as they are called. Occasional mistakes are made, no doubt, when an unexpected lob bowler appears, but more from wildness and anxiety to score than from any ignorance as to the mode of playing such balls. The way to play lobs is exactly the method Mr. Pycroft tells us was adopted by the great Fuller Pilch.

Slow lobs have therefore in first-class cricket died a natural death, and although we may expect to find a lob bowler occasionally cropping up here and there, we do not think there is much prospect of seeing an exemplar of this style who will ever attain the rank of a first-class bowler such as that acquired by Clarke, Mr. V. E. Walker and Tinley. Mr. A. W. Ridley was the last well-known under-arm bowler who made a mark in first-class cricket. His performance against Cambridge in the now famous University match is too well known to need record here. Humphreys of Sussex has occasionally been successful with this style of bowling, and will be again, no doubt, to wild batsmen. Although we have stated that lob bowling has died a natural death, and cannot ever be expected to cope with the present state of batting, still under-hand slows are occasionally such an excellent change that we are sorry they are not more practised. It is not, however, wonderful that there are so few lob bowlers who can go on at a pinch for a change, when we consider what has been already said about batting having mastered the art of under-hand ; men will not practise any art unless they have some fair prospect of being ultimately successful, and knowing that lobs will only be useful very occasionally and cannot attain to great success, they will not practise them. It is a pity they do not, as over and over again we see instances of a good wicket falling to a poorish lob bowler when everything else has failed. The previous remarks about under-hands refer to first-class cricket ; against schools and against second-class batsmen lobs have been and always will be particularly deadly. There is something so tempting to an inexperienced player in seeing a ball chucked up in the air slowly and simply, it looks so very easy to hit, so peculiarly guileless, that a wild slog is frequently the result, too often followed by disastrous consequences.

For this reason the captain of every school eleven should insist on one of his team devoting himself to lob bowling ; a little practice will enable any one to get a fairly accurate pitch, and twist from the leg side any boy can manage. Lob bowling thus acquired at school will often be useful in after days as a change, even in first-class cricket. There are one or two simple rules connected with lob bowling which everyone who attempts this style should master.

First.—Do not bowl too slow ; if the ball is thrown high and slow in the air, a good batsman, quick on his legs, will have time to reach and hit it before it pitches. Old Clarke used to say, 'It wants a certain amount of pace to make a good-length ball with proper rise and twist.' The ball should be sent at such speed as will oblige the batsman to play forward to it.

Secondly.—A good long run should be taken, as this gets way and 'fire' on to the ball, and is always more likely than a short run to deceive the batsman as to the pitch.

Thirdly.—Generally bowl round the wicket.

Most of the remarks that we have made on slow round-arm leg-break bowling apply to slow lobs.

Having devoted a number of pages to the subject of slow bowling, let us now turn to the consideration of what is almost equally important : fast bowling ; indeed, it may be said that the co-operation of a good fast bowler is absolutely essential if a team wants to rank amongst the best, particularly as, if there be one of each sort bowling at either end, the change in pace is more likely to embarrass the batsman than if he had to play two bowlers of the same pace. There has been for several years a great dearth of good fast bowlers, a fact which is greatly to be regretted by all lovers of the game. We have scores of slow bowlers turned out year after year from our universities and public schools, but scarcely ever a fast one worthy of the name of 'bowler.' Few men care to be at the trouble and exertion of bowling fast when they find that inferior batsmen, by dint of playing straight and assisted by a perfect wicket, can successfully defy all efforts to dislodge them. When a man has become fairly proficient with the bat there is no easier bowling to play, if the wicket be a really good one, than fast. Men will not be at the great trouble of practising fast bowling and trying to get accuracy of pitch and direction when they see the best fast bowlers in England occasionally treated by second-class batsmen with the utmost disrespect.

Although fast balls are easy to play on good wickets, however, it is but seldom that a wicket which is good at the beginning of a match remains so to the close. The ground wears and cuts up with the continual pitching of the ball and the tramp of feet, and fast bowling on such occasions often becomes most deadly. Then, again, a fast quick delivery to a new-comer, even though the best of batsmen, may deceive him in the pace, and, before the eye gets accustomed to the light and the hand becomes steady, cheat him into playing back at a ball which ought to have been met with forward play. Often have crack batsmen been dismissed summarily by the first or second ball coming quicker than they expected off the pitch. Murdoch, the famous Australian batsman, was particularly apt to mistime fast bowling on first going in, and several times has the author seen his stumps shattered immediately by an ordinary straight fast ball without any 'work' at all on it. The tail end of a team are usually victims to a good straight fast bowler, as, unless a fast bowler is met by straight fearless forward play, he is bound to be dangerous, and it very rarely happens that the tail end of an ordinary team, even a county team, is capable of this. A great deal has been said and written about young fast bowlers bowling too fast for their strength, thus overtaxing their powers and over-bowling themselves. It is doubtless a fact that many young promising fast bowlers have been rendered useless by this anxiety to get more pace on the ball than their strength warranted; and there can be no better advice to a young aspirant for the honours of a fast bowler than that so often given, viz. 'Bowl within your strength, or else you will over-bowl yourself.' Although the wisdom and truth of this warning are generally ascertained by personal experience pretty early in the career of most fast bowlers, it is seldom, we are sorry to say, remembered in actual practice—which remissness, we are bound to add, does not in the least surprise us. It may possibly sound like heresy to many old cricketers to say that in fast bowling pace is nearly everything; but such is our opinion. Assume that a man can bowl straight and a good length—i.e. has a good command over the ball—and then it may be said that the faster he bowls the more likely he is to get wickets. And this is generally discovered by young bowlers who have an aptitude for fast bowling, with the result that many 'over-bowl' themselves, strain muscles, rick shoulders, and render themselves useless.

The object of fast bowling is to beat the batsman by the pace of the ball, and if this object be accomplished the ball will either be missed or a bad stroke will be made by the batsman. The faster the bowling the more likely it is that a batsman will be beaten both before and after the ball leaves the ground. Should the ball 'shoot' or 'get up,' the chances of its being played accurately are rendered much less when the ball leaves the ground with lightning-like speed and is almost invisible to the eye than when it leaves it with less speed, and gives the batsman an opportunity of seeing what is going to happen for an appreciable moment before it reaches him. Besides, the faster the bowling the more scope there is for the bowler to change his pace should he be one of the few fast bowlers who have the power of so doing with advantage. While saying that pace is everything in a fast bowler, we do not wish for a moment to cry down or disparage the advantages of medium-paced bowling. This style has its own characteristics, which are more closely allied to slow bowling than to fast; but at the same time there are many moderately good medium-paced bowlers now bowling with some success in first-class matches who would be much more deadly and successful could they add about half as much speed again to their bowling. There are, of course, men who, on the other hand, spoil a good style by trying to bowl too fast—men who depend for their success on peculiarity in flight and the work on the ball. Every man must judge for himself; if he possess great powers of twist combined with accuracy, and anything peculiar or difficult to see in his action, then let him devote himself to slow or medium-paced bowling.

It is strange that English first-class cricket is so devoid of really fast bowling. Ulyett, of Yorkshire, now that Allan Hill, of the same county, has retired (and good luck go with him for as honest and cheery a cricketer as ever bowled a ball), is with one exception the only quite fast bowler playing at the present time. There have been brilliant comets for a season or so, who have shone brightly and then quickly disappeared. Harrison, of Yorkshire, seemed likely to make his mark, but after a brilliant beginning vanished from the scene of first-class cricket. Crossland, of Lancashire, for a brief period, mowed down the County Palatine's opponents like ninepins, but he has now likewise retired—a victim to the just cry against unfair bowling. Ulyett's only companion in first-class cricket as a fast bowler is Bowley, of Surrey. We have heard a great diversity of opinion with regard to this bowler. The writer has seen and played against him on several occasions, and thinks he is at the time of writing the best fast bowler in England; but he is the best of a bad lot. Bowley certainly is very fast, and has the additional advantage of being much faster than he looks. If he could raise his arm a few inches and still maintain the same pace, he would be a fine bowler. The amateur fast bowlers of the last few years who have taken part in big matches are Rotherham, Christopherson, Whitby, and Toppin. Rotherham, at the beginning of his career, his last year at Uppingham and the year following, was doubtless a very deadly bowler. He had a good slow ball and a splendid yorker ; but he only lasted a very short time. Christopherson was a fairly good fast bowler at one time, but he took a great deal out of himself with his action, and soon lost the fire and life that are necessary to make a first-class bowler. This absence of fast bowlers (temporary it may be hoped) is one of the most remarkable facts connected with first-class cricket. It is only a few years ago that most of the best bowlers were fast : the list included Tarrant, Jackson, and Freeman, whose bowling used, it was said, to hum in the air ; and, later, what a harvest of fast amateur bowlers there were—Butler, Francis, Powys, Evans, and names far too numerous to mention ! Now we do not possess *one* really good fast bowler. We hope times will mend in this respect, and that the next few years will see some fresh talent developing, to wear worthily the mantle of bygone heroes.

As mentioned above, with reference to slow bowling, the higher the hand and arm are raised at the moment of delivering the ball, the higher the ball will bound after it leaves the pitch. A fast bowler should always bear this in mind, and keep his hand as high as possible. It is simply a matter of ordinary common sense that a ball which rises up high from the pitch is more difficult for a batsman to get over and smother than one that comes on low and skimming. A fast ball when it is anything like a good length, must be met with the bat, i.e. it must be played with the forward stroke ; consequently a ball that rises quickly from the pitch, and is still rising when it meets the bat, is extremely likely to rise higher still after it leaves it, unless it is played with great care and caution.

The low skimming fast bowler is generally an easy man to play ; the batsman, when the ground is true, can play hard forward to almost any length of ball ; there is no abrupt rise to render an uppish stroke probable, even if he does slightly misjudge the pace and length of the ball. There is, of course, in fast bowling, a much greater difficulty in getting any appreciable twist on to the ball than in slow. The ball leaves the ground so quickly that it is hardly in contact with it long enough to

' bite ' the turf, and so avail itself of any spin that may have been imparted to it by the bowler. It is to be remembered, however, that the slightest deviation of a fast ball from its course after it has pitched is, if a good length, most likely to deceive the batsman. The latter is bound to play to the pitch of the ball, as it leaves the ground so quickly as to render it impossible for him to follow it with the eye in its course from the ground. He plays forward with a straight bat to meet it ; should it turn an inch or two he will most likely miss it.

The off break is the one most usually attempted by fast bowlers ; the ball is grasped firmly, generally by the seam, to give the hand a firmer grip, and is delivered in the same way as described for the· slow off break. There have been but few really fast bowlers who have been able consistently to make their balls come ' back.' Every now and then, however, for some unaccountable reason, a fast bowler finds that he is making the ball do a lot from the off side. Perhaps his grasp is firmer and his wrist and fingers are more powerful than on ordinary occasions, or the ground may have more turf on it, or, for some other reason, his bowling twists in from the pitch with most fatal results to the batsmen.

If a fast bowler happen to be a man of strong physique, which is usually the case, a fairly long run up to the wickets before delivering the ball is an advantage to his bowling. This gives more impetus to the ball, and what is popularly known as ' devil.' Spofforth, the Australian bowler, when bowling fast, takes a much longer run than when bowling medium pace. It is also an advantage to keep the batsman waiting for the delivery of the ball, which happens when the bowler runs several yards up to the wicket. For a fast bowler who intends to change his pace from very fast to medium slow, a long run is of great advantage, as the sight of the bowler coming up to the wicket before the delivery of a slow ball as fast as before the delivery of a fast one, is extremely likely to take in the batsman with regard to the pace. There are not so many tricks and dodges in the art of bowling fast as there are in bowling slow ; the chief object to be sought is to bowl straight and good length, and to make the ball bound. A fast bowler, when first being put on, should remember that his muscles are probably stiff, and that he may not at first be able to bowl as accurately and as fast as he will be when thoroughly warmed to his work. For this reason it is always well to bowl two or three balls to one side of the wicket before beginning. These should be not quite at full speed, for fear of straining or ricking a muscle not yet in full swing, but a good medium pace. It is always best for a fast bowler to try a ball or two before beginning, excepting in circumstances when he is called upon to bowl to some one he has never bowled to before, and especially so to some one who has never seen him bowl. How often when batting have we silently chuckled with joy at seeing a man quite unknown to us rapidly loosening his arms with two or three balls before beginning to bowl ! It is a great thing to have an unknown bowler on one's side, but he loses half his value if his style and action are revealed to the batsman before he receives the ball. In 1886 the writer was playing in a match against the Australians, when, although things had been going very well for the English side, the team was beginning to get tied up into a knot owing to the steady careful way in which Scott, the colonial captain, was defying all the efforts of our bowlers to dislodge him. A fast bowler, who had never seen Scott in his life before, was deputed to bowl, and was proceeding to get ready for 'two or three down' to loosen his arm, when he was told not to mind his arm being stiff, but to bowl the first over as fast as ever he could. The first ball sent Scott's leg-stump flying ; it was quite a simple ball, never turned a hair's breadth either way, but the action and pace of the bowler took him in, and this would have been very unlikely to happen had he had an opportunity of seeing the bowler's style.

A fast bowler must be straight to be good. This is not the art of one skilled in the dodges of slows ; he has to bowl straight, and a good length too, or else the runs will come at an enormous rate. In the present day it is usual to do with out a long-stop even to the fastest bowlers ; this makes it imperatively necessary for the bowler not to bowl to leg, or, if missed by the batsman, the balls have a good chance of flying past the wicket-keeper to the boundary for four. Whether it is a good principle to do without long-stops, even when the best wicket-keepers are behind the sticks, is a doubtful point. It is not within the province of this chapter to discuss the subject, but an opinion may be briefly expressed to the effect that the absence of long-stops to fast bowling is a mistake, amongst other reasons because it obliges the wicket-keeper to unite in himself the duties of a long-stop and a stumper.

A fast bowler should have such command over the ball as to be able to bowl a 'yorker' whenever he wishes, for the fact may be repeated that a fast 'yorker' is a most deadly ball.

Spofforth and Palmer, the Australians, and Rotherham, the old Uppingham bowler, were about the best fast 'yorker' bowlers of modern times. The ball came from these bowlers as high as the arm would allow, and seemed to fly like an arrow, with lightning-like rapidity, straight to the block-hole, or a few inches inside it. A high-action 'yorker' is more likely to deceive a batsman than a low-action one, as in the former case the starting-point of the ball is above the line of vision, and in the latter on a line with or below it, which naturally makes the course and pace of the ball more easy for the eye to judge. A very common error into which good fast 'yorker' bowlers fall is not being content with trying the ball occasionally to a batsman, and when he first comes on or when they first go on, but persistently trying, over after over, to break down his guard with a ball with which he is evidently quite at home, and which presents no terrors to him. The result of this mistake is that the balls get considerably punished, either by being driven on the full-pitch or else on the half-volley, the latter ball being often the result of a tired-out 'yorker' bowler's persistency. The writer remembers, when playing in a match some years ago, asking W. G. Grace, who was on the same side, what sort of a fast bowler a certain man was who was going on to bowl. 'Oh, I'm never frightened of him ; he is always try- ing to "york" you, and bowls any amount of half-volleys,' was the reply, and this was soon proved to be, like most of the champion cricketer's opinions, perfectly accurate.

A good length just outside the off stump and between the off and middle stump is the direction that may be commended to the bowler who bowls over the wicket, and tries to get a little off spin on the ball. The leg-stump, in olden days, was considered the most deadly spot for a fast bowler to aim at ; but since every first-class batsman now stands up to his wicket, and does not draw away an inch when the ball comes between it and his legs, leg-stump bowling is rather expensive work. By all means let fast bowlers lay siege to the leg-stump of in- ferior batsmen ; but good batsmen, getting over this ball, will play it with an almost perfectly straight bat on the outside, and tax it most unmercifully for the total of their side.

As a rule, it is better for a fast bowler to bowl over the wicket, as by so doing he has more of the wicket to bowl at, and has, consequently, a slightly better chance of hitting it if the ball is missed by the batsman. He has also a greater chance of an appeal for leg before wicket being answered in his favour than if bowling from the other side of the wicket. There are some fast bowlers, however, who must, from the very nature of their action and delivery, bowl from round the wicket, viz. those who have either a natural bias from the on to the off, or who are able by their strength of wrist and fingers to impart such a bias to the ball. A man who bowls from the very extent of the crease outside the wicket, and whose bowling has natu- rally or otherwise this leg side bias—it can hardly be called twist in fast bowling—is a particularly awkward customer for the batsman. There is such a constant tendency and inclination for the ball to keep going farther away to the off side, both be- fore and after its pitch, that the greatest care must be exercised by the batsman to prevent himself playing inside the ball and putting it up either to point, third man, or short-slip. A fast ball that comes in from the leg side is the most difficult ball that has to be played, assuming its good length. There have been very few fast right-handed bowlers who have been able to manage this ball, but there are many instances of left-handed men who have attained to great accuracy with it. The late Fred Morley, of Nottingham, and Emmett, of Yorkshire, are instances.

About thirty years ago there were numerous good fast bowlers, who used to get the leg bias on the ball in the following way : They bowled round the wicket, and delivered the ball from about the height of the hip ; the backs of the fingers were presented to the batsman before and at the moment of delivery ; the result being that the ball had on it a slight amount of what, in slow bowling, we have described as leg-break. This was a useful style, and it is a pity that it has almost altogether died out at the present day.

It is quite impossible to say with any certainty what essentials are necessary in fast bowling before it can be ranked as first-class ; so very much depends on whether the action is easy or difficult for the batsman to see. By the word 'see' is meant whether the pace and pitch of the ball at the moment of delivery can be instantly gauged by the batsman or not. Given equal straightness, pace, and command over the ball in every respect, the bowler who has an action which it is easy to see cannot compare with the man who, from some peculiarity in the movements of his body at the moment of delivery, has an action which is not easy to see. Now, it is a very difficult task to lay down any rules or reasons why some bowlers are easier to see than others; but after a good deal of consideration on this subject the writer has come to the conclusion that the bowlers who do *not* present a square front to the batsman when the ball is delivered, but who stand sideways or half turned, are, as a rule, the most difficult to judge. The hand comes then from behind the body, and is often not plainly seen till the very latest moment before delivery. There may be, and no doubt are, many mannerisms in bowlers which have their effect, but the above suggestion will probably be found to contain a good sound working rule. Take Giffen, the Australian ; almost as much of his back as his front was visible to the batsman when he delivered the ball, and his bowling was most difficult to see—at any rate until the batsman was thoroughly well set.

Low delivery.

Perhaps the best English batsmen have made more bad and utterly mistimed strokes off Giffen than off any other modern bowler. Spofforth may have bowled more men out, but Giffen certainly was the cause of more misjudged and uppish strokes, due, in all probability, to the fact of his bowling being so difficult to see.

The best bit of bowling the writer ever recollects playing against was in the second innings of the Gentlemen of England *v.* Australians, at Lord's in 1884. It was Giffen's day, and a batsman had to have luck on his side if he succeeded in staying in long enough to appreciate the beauty of the bowling. Take Peate and Emmett, the two Yorkshire left-handers, both in their day the best bowlers in England—in fact, the latter delighted his many admirers and friends by topping the list of English bowlers in the season of 1886, a most creditable performance for a man no longer in the first blush of youth. Both these men stand sideways to the batsman when they deliver the ball, and both are most difficult to see. Palmer, the Australian, bowled very nearly quite square ; his bowling was very easy to see and to judge, and the more credit is therefore due to him for being such a successful bowler. There is no doubt a greater difficulty in attaining to perfect length and command over the ball when the body of the bowler is not square at the moment of delivery ; but if these essentials to good bowling are obtained by patience and constant practice, the bowler has this great advantage that his balls are more difficult for the batsman to judge accurately. It seems strange that not one of the numerous published books on cricket has ever suggested the advantage to the bowler which is obtained in this way. In almost every one of these works great stress is laid upon the necessity of the bowler presenting a full face to the opposite wicket at the moment the ball leaves the hand. It is doubtless easier for a beginner to bowl *straight* if he adopts this style of bowling ; but if he can once gain straightness by the other, viz. the sideways style, he has enlisted a great help to success.

W. G. Grace is, however, an exception to this rule. He delivers the ball perfectly square with the batsman ; and yet we suppose that to a batsman who meets him for the first time, his bowling is about as difficult to see and to judge as that of any bowler ever was. It is a fact that his bowling is invariably fatal to men he has not met before. This is owing to the hovering flight that his action imparts to the ball. The first time the writer ever played against W. G. Grace's bowling was at Cambridge in 1878, and on the way to the wickets he was greeted with the cheering cry, 'I'll get you out ; I always get youngsters out !' and surely enough he did, caught and bowled for two or thereabouts. What the champion did next morning showed that he was as generous and kind to young cricketers as he was skilful in the game. He took the writer to the nets prior to the beginning of the second day's play, and saying that youngsters required to know his bowling before being at home with it, he proceeded to bowl for quite twenty minutes to him ; a comprehension of his method was thus gained, and the result was an addition to the Cambridge score of some forty odd in the second innings. Few latter-day cricketers would do this.

Perhaps one of the reasons why W. G. Grace is so deadly to young cricketers is this : the batsman, seeing an enormous man rushing up to the wickets, with both elbows out, great black beard blowing on each side of him, and a huge yellow cap on the top of a dark swarthy face, expects something more than the gentle lobbed-up ball that does come ; he cannot believe that this baby-looking bowling is really the great man's, and gets flustered and loses his wicket. W. G. Grace is certainly enormous, and a year or two ago at Lord's an amusing remark might have been overheard on this subject. The England *v.* Australia match was being played. W. G. walked out into the field side by side with Briggs of Lancashire, the latter, as is well known, being very small, perhaps hardly up to W. G.'s elbow. A small child of about five was in the pavilion with his father, and said, 'Father, who is that big man ?' 'That's Dr. Grace, the champion,' said the papa ; and 'Who is the little one ?' the child continued. 'That is Briggs.' Dead silence for a few moments, and then, 'Papa, is Briggs Dr. Grace's baby ?'

Although power of pace, straightness, and command over the ball are the really essential qualities of good fast bowling—as, indeed, of all sorts—there are many occasions when fortune smiles upon bowling which possesses none of these good attributes. And it is for this reason, we think, that every cricketer should be able to bowl when called upon to do so by his captain. Every man who has played cricket has bowled at a net, and he certainly has an action which is different from everybody else's. As a rule, men who are not considered regular bowlers can send the ball in somehow or other at a fairly fast pace more or less straight, and these unknown, wild, and erratic bowlers often succeed in getting rid of well-set batsmen who have defied all the efforts of the recognised bowlers of the side. There are numerous instances of a side being deeply indebted to a bowler who never before nor afterwards showed the slightest ability to get wickets. In Australia in 1882, when Ivo Bligh's English team was playing combined Australia, on a certain occasion two of the best Australian batsmen—Murdoch and Bannerman—seemed immovable. They had been in for about an hour, and every one of the regular English bowlers had been on and off. A suggestion was made to try C. F. H. Leslie. Now this gentleman, with all his great merits, was never, even in the estimation of his best friends, a great bowler. But on he went with pleasure, as every cricketer should when ordered. The first ball was a very fast one, rather wide, the second ditto, but the third one—'Ah, the third!'—was a head ball, designed after the manner of Spofforth's best; and it pitched on the middle of Murdoch's middle stump! The next comer was Horan, at that time the reputed best player of fast bowling in the Colonies. A very fast long-hop, wide on the off side, was prettily cut straight into Barlow's hands at third man, and Mr. Leslie had secured two wickets for no runs. He continued for another over or two, had Bannerman beautifully stumped by Mr. Tylecote off a fast wide half-volley on the leg side, and then retired in favour of one of the regular bowlers, after having, simply by wild erratic fast delivery, lowered three of the best Australian wickets. We give this as an example of the principle that every cricketer should try to bowl, and if he finds that he cannot attain to any efficiency, even with constant practice, then let him try to 'sling in' as hard as ever he possibly can ; he will often be of use to his side when in a fix.

Before leaving the subject of fast bowling a word must be said about what may be called the great cricket bugbear of the last few years—viz. throwing. It is worthy of notice that when over-arm bowling was first allowed a great outcry arose and there were not wanting those who prophesied that this 'hand over head' style would ultimately result in 'a mere over-hand throw—a kind of pelting, with a little mannerism or flourish to disguise it.' Now it is an astonishing thing that, in a great variety of cases, this is just what actually has happened. Some of the bowling that has been allowed to pass unnoticed by umpires is well described by the phrase quoted ; but although this is so, there are many minor offenders whom all would like to see pulled up short, not out of any ill-will to them personally, but in the interests of the game. Now throwing is most pernicious to cricket, and is calculated, if allowed to increase (as it surely will unless promptly suppressed by the authorities, backed by public opinion), to exercise a most disastrous effect on the game. The subject of throwing is sometimes pooh-poohed by prominent cricketers, who have remarked, 'What does it matter whether a man bowls or throws ?' If it makes no difference, by all means let the M.C.C. at once expunge the rule relating to throwing and jerking. But let us pause for a moment to see if there are any reasons to suppose that it does make a difference. There are, in truth, two very good reasons why throwing should be stopped. First, if it were allowed it would seriously interfere with the art of bowling. The reasons for this proposition are as follows : In throwing there is no scope for dissimilarity of style. All men who throw must, from the very nature of the delivery, send the ball on its course with exactly the same description of spin. It is impossible for a thrower to make the ball go across the wicket from the leg to the on side ; every ball which leaves a thrower's hand has the off-side spin on it, and none other is possible. Any style which tends to cramp bowling, as this does, must be bad. Again, a throwing bowler cannot change his pace as other bowlers do ; he dare not bowl the slow high-dropping ball so successfully used by Spofforth and others, because he knows that when his arm and wrist move slowly the unfair jerk of the wrist and elbow will be more manifest than when it is partially concealed by the usual quick movement of his arm. If throwing tends to cramp bowling, as it does, and render certain essentials for the development of the science impossible, then it must be injurious to the game. Secondly, if throwing were allowed the batsman would be in a position of considerable danger. Many cricketers say, 'Let throwers alone, they are always easy to play ;' and this, no doubt, is so, for the reasons given above, especially when every thrower must, for the sake of appearances, adopt some slight measure of disguise in his action ; but once let it be recognised that throwing is part of the game, and a race of sturdy chuckers will spring up, whose pace will be so terrific that the best and pluckiest batsman will not be able to defend his body, much less his wicket, against their lightning-like deliveries. Imagine what it would be if Bonnor, or Forbes, or Game were to be allowed to throw, all of them having thrown in their best days as much as 120 yards—is it likely that a batsman at a distance of only twenty-one yards could be quick enough with his bat to stop such bowling? Even with an ordinary fast bowler a batsman has sometimes difficulty in preventing himself from being struck by the ball, and with an undisguised thrower the danger would be tenfold.

The question then arises, what can be done to stop the throwing nuisance ? And it is one which every member of the cricket-loving community should ask himself. It is a question of the greatest difficulty, as is evident from the fact that the committee of the M.C.C. have so far found it impossible to legislate with regard to the nuisance. The committee has done everything in its power ; it has instructed the umpires to

watch closely the delivery of every doubtful bowler, and probably the umpires have acted fully up to their instructions ;
but they have stopped here, and absolutely refused to report
to the world the result of their careful observations. It is a
fact that of late years no professional umpire in a first-class
match has no-balled a professional bowler for throwing. This
is not to be wondered at : professional umpires themselves
have been professional bowlers, and they cannot bring themselves to take the bread out of the mouth of one of their own
class by no-balling him, and stigmatising him at once and for
ever as a ' thrower.'

We cannot get amateur umpires to stand : these would, no
doubt, fearlessly no-ball any unfair bowler ; but if we could, we
should probably find that the quantity of bad decisions in the
course of the year would be greatly increased. An umpire wants
practice and experience in keeping his attention and whole mind
fixed impartially on the game, and this can only be acquired by
those who stand day after day in that capacity.

The only way, then, to our mind, to stop throwing, as the
M.C.C. cannot and the umpires will not, is to get public
opinion to step in and sweep it off our cricket grounds. Let
every amateur cricketer, whether he plays for his county or his
village club, set his face resolutely against the evil, and do his
utmost to discourage it. If an ' Anti-Throwing Society ' could
be established amongst cricketers, we firmly believe it would
effect its object. In the North of England, where the game
is ever increasingly popular, there are many ' chuckers ' to
be met with. The clubs who do not possess, to say the least,
a doubtful bowler are, we should say from our experience,
in the minority. Young professional bowlers see the general
laxity that prevails, and adopt the peculiar flick of the wrist
and elbow, hoping thereby to get more twist on the ball, and
this sooner or later develops into a throw. Young bowlers
of this description get drafted from their village clubs into the
county team, and thereby augment the number of ' doubtful '
bowlers in first-class matches. Now if every amateur stood out

against this system, and even went so far as to say, ' I will not be one of a team that wins its matches by such means,' unfair bowling would soon die out.

On the subject of throwing we can learn something from the Australians.   Perhaps it is the only subject connected with the spirit in which the game should be played wherein they are able to give us much assistance, but we ought for that reason to be all the more willing to take any advice which they or their system can afford us.

Now in Australia unfair bowling is absolutely unknown. Directly a bowler begins to develop the slightest tendency to

Doubtful delivery.

throwing he is tabooed. One can traverse the whole of Australia and watch the numerous clubs in all parts of the country without ever seeing a bowler who is even verging on the line of ' throwing.' It is hard to understand why this state of affairs does not exist in the mother country.

It will be well for everyone to realise that, if this question is allowed to drift on from year to year without any serious protest from public opinion, it will become absolutely necessary for the committee of the M.C.C. to do something in the matter.   What this should be is, as we have said, very doubtful, and many and varied would be the opinions of competent judges as to the form of legislation that would meet the evil.   It can almost be taken for granted that it is impossible satisfactorily to define a throw, and even if this were not so the solution of the question would be no nearer, as there would be just the same difficulties in the way of an umpire saying that a bowler came within the defini-tion as there is now in saying that he throws.   What is wanted is to get rid of throwers in small club and village matches, and then we should never get them drafted into first-class cricket.

If the umpire at either end were allowed to no-ball, we believe the system of throwing would receive a serious blow. It often happens that the thrower can only bowl at his own umpire's end ; if he attempted it at the other end he knows what would await him ; and if both umpires had the right to no-ball *for throwing,* this difficulty would be overcome by his not being able to bowl at either end. It is, however, earnestly to be hoped that no change of any sort in the rules will be necessary, but that all true cricketers will unite in discountenancing that which is always a source of wrangling and dispute.

Before leaving the subject of fast bowling a few remarks on the position of the field will not be out of place. Every bowler who is worth his salt knows much better than anyone else how the field should be placed to his bowling. So much depends upon the style and favourite strokes of the batsman to be dislodged and the mode of attack that is going to be brought into requisition, that the general rules we suggest here are more as a guide to young fast bowlers than to those who have gained their experience. To a fast over the wicket round-arm bowler (on a true wicket) the field should be placed as on page 180.

Should the bowler, however, be one who changes his pace to slow and relies occasionally on quite a slow head ball, it will be as well to bring short-leg half-way between the umpire and the bowler, and put mid-on out deep in the field on the on side. On no occasion should short-slip be dispensed with; he should on a fast wicket be fairly fine, and if he is a quick active man with his hands (as he should be for this post), about eight yards from the wicket. The object of short-slip is to pick up snicks which just miss the wicket-keeper, and although he may hold a larger proportion of these quick snap catches when a long way from the wicket, he will get an infinitely greater number when closer in ; consequently, if he is a man of quick sight and tenacious hand, he will actually secure more catches close in, although at the same time he may miss more. The positions of long-leg, third man, short-leg, and mid-on depend to a great extent on the batsman's play. It is a golden rule never to do without a point and cover-point, although in some instances—e.g. when a strong cutting batsman is in on a fast wicket—it is sometimes advisable to place point in front of the wicket and cover-point square. It is,

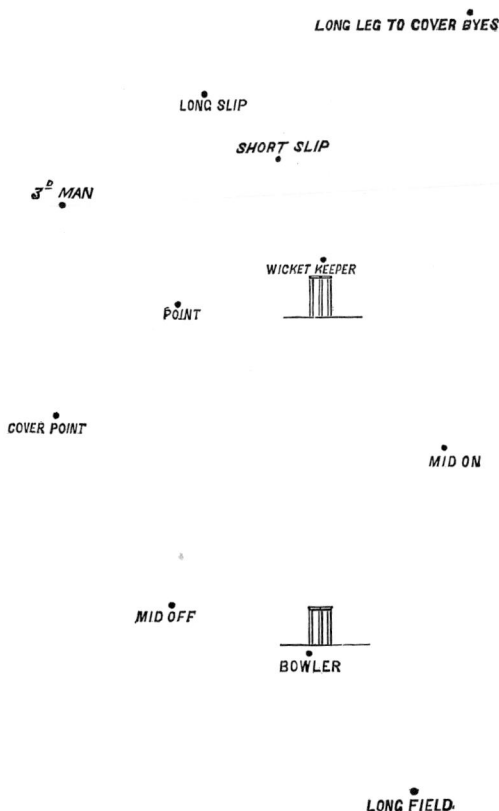

LONG LEG TO COVER BYES

LONG SLIP

SHORT SLIP

3ᵈ MAN

WICKET KEEPER

POINT

COVER POINT

MID ON

MID OFF

BOWLER

LONG FIELD.

The field for a fast right-arm bowler.

however, but seldom that this is necessary, and many cricketers always view the change with some misgiving as to its correctness, because a good active cover-point in the usual place saves a large number of runs and, probably, gets more catches than any other man in the field, with the exception of the wicket-keeper and short-slip. A round the wicket fast bowler requires the field in much the same position. But in his case it is sometimes necessary to have an extra man on the leg side, as these bowlers are very apt to bowl between the legs and the wicket, which means

• *LONG SLIP*

SHORT SLIP

σ² • *MAN*

WICKET KEEPER

•
POINT

•
COVER POINT

•
MID ON

•
EXTRA COVER POINT

MID OFF •

•
BOWLER

•
LONG FIELD OFF

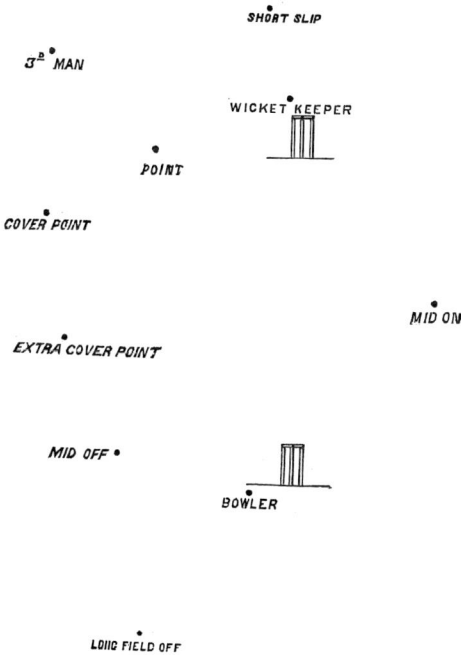

The field for a fast left-arm bowler.

with good batsmen that they get played on to the leg side, between mid-on and short-leg. If this change is necessary long-leg may be sent almost to the boundary, very fine, behind the wicket, and long-stop be brought on to the leg side. A very fine long-leg prevents boundary byes, and generally manages to save the fine long-

leg boundary hits. Unless there is a first-class man behind the
stumps, however, this generally results with first-class bowling in
rather too many extras to justify its continuance. Fast left-hand
bowlers want more men on the off side, as, from the nature of
their bowling, they get more punished in that direction than
anywhere else. If fast left-hand bowling is accurate and straight,
long-leg is usually dispensed with, and, in fact, mid-on as well
is often taken to the other side of the wicket, leaving short-
leg, who is brought forward a few yards, the only man on the leg
side of the wicket. Then there is an unbroken line of fielders
on the off side, which the batsman finds it difficult to break
through if it is composed of active and energetic men. The
way in which fast left-handed bowlers place their field is usually
as on page 181.

There is a class of fast left-hand bowlers who require more
men on the on side—viz. those who give the ball the leg side
bias on delivery, which, to a right-handed batsman, causes the
ball to come in from the off side, or, as it is usually termed,
to come with the arm. It is often necessary with this style of
bowling to have a very fine short-leg, to stop the snicks and leg
byes which are caused by the batsman playing outside the ball.
Then a short-leg by the umpire is necessary, and also a mid-on,
making three on the on side. Mr. Appleby, of Lancashire, is
an example of this style of bowler, as is Barlow, of the same
county, though he hardly comes within the definition of fast
bowling. We have occasionally seen a left-arm bowler, like
Emmett, of Yorkshire—who relies exclusively on the off break,
which, to a right-handed batsman, brings the ball from leg to
off—involuntarily send down a ball that, instead of taking the
bias imparted to it, for some strange and unaccountable reason
went the other way, an accident which places the batsman in a
most awkward fix.

Some bowlers experience great difficulty in bowling to
left-handed batsmen. The necessary alteration in their style
seems to worry them and interfere with their accuracy of pitch.
Usually a slow bowler tries to get a left-handed batsman caught

on the off side. He places most of his men on this side, and
bowls the off break (or, as it would be to a left-handed batsman, the leg-break) with the object of getting the batsman
to play inside the ball, and thus make an upstroke. In short,
he places the men as a left-handed bowler places them when
bowling to a right-handed batsman. Left-handed batsmen
are notoriously strong and powerful in their off hitting, and
consequently in this direction must the bait be laid. As a rule,
left-handed batsmen are apt to be a trifle wild and unable to
restrain their keenness to hit, and consequently they pay the
usual penalty of attempting to hit widish off balls going away
from them. But occasionally a bowler meets a left-hander who
is too wide awake and too good a batsman thus to throw away
his chance of scoring, and then different tactics must be employed. There have been, and are, wonderfully few really good
left-handed batsmen in England, and the chance of a bowler
having to meet one of them is very slight. In England now,
in first-class cricket, there are Scotton of Notts and Peel of
Yorkshire, and that is really about all. The best of this class
was perhaps the late F. M. Lucas, whose recent death in
India has caused such sorrow to his wide circle of friends.
He was really an accomplished batsman, with good sound
defence and great punishing powers. A slow bowler might
bowl for hours on the off side to him, with the sole result
of seeing four after four being despatched all along the ground
to the boundary. Moses of Sydney, who has many times
distinguished himself against our English teams, is another
excellent left-handed batsman. In our opinion, when a really
good left-hander comes in, one who is not likely to get himself
out on the off side by careless hitting, an attack should be made
on his leg-stump. Most left-handers are good leg hitters, but
we have never yet seen one (not excepting the two above
named) who was as good on the leg-stump as a first-class right-
handed batsman. There is an awkwardness apparent in the
left-hander's play to a ball pitching on the leg-stump, or just
inside it, and there is always a great likelihood of a cross bat

being used for a leg hit. Many and many a time has the writer, after trying the off-ball trick unsuccessfully against one of these batsmen, succeeded in dismissing him by bowling over the wicket at the leg-stump and between the legs and leg-stump of the batsman. This manœuvre only entails a couple of men being brought across from the off side to stop the run-getting.

There is one species of ball which we have not discussed, deadly as it is, both in fast and slow bowling. This is the ball which, after the pitch, never rises, but shoots along the surface of the ground, and is commonly called a 'shooter.' The reason why no notice was taken of this when the different kinds of ball which may be bowled were being dealt with is because no amount of practice or skill can enable a bowler to bowl thus. It depends for existence upon inequalities in the ground. There are some grounds which have acquired great reputation for supplying 'shooters' for the benefit of bowlers; but this reputation is unfortunately always accompanied by one for being lumpy and dangerous. Not a great many years ago Lord's used to be celebrated for shooters, owing to its rough condition; and even now, well looked after as it is, shooters are of more frequent occurrence there than on most other good grounds. Although it is not in the power of any man to bowl shooters at will, still there is no doubt that men with a low delivery have a greater chance of being helped by a shooter than men who bowl with a high overhead action. The writer recollects at Cambridge, about 1879 or 1880, being told by a young professional bowler, engaged at the University ground at that time, that he had found out how to bowl shooters. He was a bowler of considerable promise, and had begun to make his mark in county cricket, but it being known that his cricket abilities far exceeded his intellectual powers, the an-nouncement of this wonderful discovery was received with some amount of doubt. However, out he came to bowl, to prove his prowess with the celebrated shooter; but it simply appeared that, instead of bowling with an overhead delivery, which was his wont, he bent his body quite low, and proceeded to bowl in a manner which was hardly removed from genuine under-hand. It is unnecessary to say that there were no shooters. His balls kept low after the pitch because his action was low.

There is one style of bowling sometimes seen in the present day that has not been mentioned, viz. fast under-arm. This is of two kinds : first, that which pitches a good length as with round-arm bowling ; secondly, 'sneaks,' or bowling that pitches near the bowler's hand and travels along the ground till the ball reaches the batsman. The latter can never be of any avail against a good player on a decent wicket, as every ball can be met by the forward stroke and rendered harmless. In country matches it is amusing to see the batsmen holding their bats in the air and trying to pounce down at the very last moment on these balls. This mode of playing such bowling is essentially incorrect, and would even be likely to cause the downfall of a good batsman ; it is as certain as anything can be at cricket that a good forward straight bat cannot miss a 'sneak.' Mr. C. I. Thornton at one time attempted this style of bowling, and was known to get a wicket or two. The good-length fast under-arm, when bowled round the wicket with a good leg twist on, might be made very dangerous. The old style of low round-arm, mentioned a few pages back, was very similar to this style of bowling, and was bowled with the same object as this has in view, viz. catches in the slips and on the off side. We only know of one fast under-arm, leg twist, good-length bowler, and he does not play in first-class cricket. His name is Bunch, an old sergeant of the Black Watch, well known on many military cricket-grounds all over England and India. Some years ago he was decidedly a good bowler, his balls came very fast, pitched good length on the leg-stump, and, having lots of leg stuff on, wanted very careful play.

And now, after having discussed the different styles of bowling known in cricket, let us consider some of the main rules which must guide the action of every bowler in the field. The first and chief principle that a young bowler must master is that he is bowling for his side's success, and not for his own ;

and that, with that object in view, he has voluntarily placed himself under the leadership of his captain. He must, therefore, give in at once, and readily, to every order. A captain is always ready to hear the suggestions of a bowler, and, as a rule, with regard to placing the field, is always willing to adopt them ; but should he not do so, the bowler must accept the decision with the best grace possible. There is nothing more discouraging and demoralising to a side than a sulky bowler— i.e. one who gets angry when spoken to, and subsequently adopts a defiant manner towards his captain. This bowler is usually a very poor stamp of sportsman, but unfortunately he may often be seen, and the marks by which he may be recognised are : First, bowling wildly and much faster than usual. Secondly, getting to his place at the end of his over after everyone else. Thirdly, if he fields a ball, throwing at the wicket, instead of to the wicket-keeper, as hard as he can, generally causing an over-throw. Fourthly, if he misses a ball in the field, standing still and allowing some more remote fielder to run after it, or else running after it himself at about the same pace as if he were just starting on a five-mile race. He is a great nuisance generally in the game. We do not deny that circumstances often arise when one is bowling that tax to the utmost the temper of the mildest man in the world ; it is, to say the least, very irritating to try for half an hour to get a man caught out by a particular stroke off a particular ball, and then at the end see the ball bowled, the stroke made, and the catch missed ; but, as chance enters to a great extent into the game, the bowler ought to do his very utmost to curb his feelings, in the interests of others who are taking part in the game.

A bowler should be ready to take any place in the field when he is not bowling. In these days when slow bowling is frequently on at both ends, there is often a difficulty in getting four men to do the out-fielding. A bowler should not object at all to help his side by doing this out-country work. Although a great specialist in the field, such as an excellent cover-point or point, is always an object of admiration, more admirable still are men good at all places. W. G. Grace, A. N. Hornby, and many others we could mention were at one time equally safe and at home in any position where they were placed.

A bowler should never grumble aloud at catches being missed ; the unfortunate man has done his best and failed, and any censure only makes him more flurried and adds to his discomfiture without doing any good.

A golden rule for every bowler to observe is—after the batsman has played the ball, *get back to the wicket as quickly as possible.* Neglect of this rule loses many a 'run out.' If a bowler does not get back to his wicket, there is no one to take the ball and knock the bails off should the batsmen run and the ball be returned to the bowler's end. When the ball is thrown up, the bowler should not take it till it has just passed the wicket ; he should then seize and sweep the ball into the stumps in one and the same action. Should he stand behind and take the ball before it reaches the wicket, there is great danger of his disarranging the bails before he gets the ball in his hands. Of course there are exceptions to this rule—e.g. when a ball is coming very slowly up to the wicket from a feeble throw or because the ground is sticky and dead; then the bowler must do his best anyhow to get the ball into the stumps before the batsman reaches the crease.

A bowler should never throw the ball at the wicket unless it is the only possible chance of running the batsman out. There is always a chance of the ball slipping out of his hand and missing its aim.

A bowler should take plenty of time between each ball he delivers. If he hurries he will get flurried and out of breath and bowl badly.

It is a mistake for a bowler to appeal unless he has a good chance of getting a favourable decision. Umpires are very peculiar individuals ; once let it enter their heads that a bowler is trying to 'jockey' a decision out of them, up go their backs, and they suddenly become a mechanical toy that glibly answers every appeal with the two words 'Not out,' and those only. A bowler is quite justified in appealing for a leg before wicket even if he is himself doubtful and uncertain as to whether the ball pitched quite straight or would have quite hit the wicket, since he is exceedingly likely not to form a correct impression of its straightness from the fact of his being at the moment of the pitch of the ball a little out of the straight line between the wickets.

Bowlers should always take care before a match that they are shod with good stout shoes with plenty of nails in them. It is a most important thing for a bowler to have shoes which will prevent him from slipping, and this is somewhat difficult when grounds are so constantly changing from hard to soft. For a hard ground nothing is better than big nails or screws; these do not go into the ground, but grip it and give a firm foothold. The left shoe of a right-hand bowler and the right shoe of a left-hand one should be extra well supplied with nails, because in the act of bowling the whole weight of the body comes down upon the left foot with the right-hand bowler and the right with a left-hand one.

For a soft ground the old-fashioned spikes are the best. They can be put in and taken out in a few minutes before the beginning of a match, according to the state of the ground. Every bowler should carry spikes, nails, and screws, a screwdriver and gimlet, in his cricket-bag.

A bowler should do all in his power to prevent cutting up the wicket with his feet in a place where bowling from the other end may pitch. If he finds that he is doing so with either foot he should at once change sides of the wicket, and if he then finds that, do what he will, he cannot help damaging the wicket—which is a most unlikely event—he should at once desist from bowling. If the ground is unduly cut up and made artificially difficult for the batsmen by bowlers' feet, whether it is done intentionally or not, such bowling is unfair and should at once be stopped. Spofforth in some states of the ground used to spoil it terribly, and this although he wore no spikes on the offending foot. The side of this foot, however, came down with great force a few yards in front of his own wicket. No doubt great damage at times was caused to the opposing batsmen by this unfortunate foot, and also to the Australian batsmen themselves, and on one occasion an appeal was made to the umpire as to whether, though caused unintentionally, it was or was not unfair. The umpire declined to give an opinion. But there can be little doubt that a bowler who has unfortunately developed this tendency is transgressing the rules of fair cricket.

A chapter on bowling would not be complete without the addition of some rules for the guidance of those who are beginning to play cricket and who want to learn how to bowl. Success depends so much upon the natural action of the bowler. that the multiplicity of rules so often laid down for the guidance of young bowlers, though followed out to the letter, does not greatly profit the aspirant to bowling honours. There are many straight accurate bowlers who can put as much twist as most men on the ball, and who yet never attain to any eminence in the art. This is due to their action being simple and easy to see, and to their consequent inability to deceive the batsman as to the pace and flight of the ball. There are, however, one or two simple elementary rules which it would be always as well for young bowlers to follow.

First.— Take every opportunity of bowling at imitation cricket with a racquet or fives ball, or any other sort of ball. This teaches you by practical experience the difference in the spins of the ball and what constitutes a good ball. Small cricket with a fives ball and a fives bat is splendid fun, and has initiated many a youngster into the mysteries of break-backs and breaks from leg.

Secondly.—Keep your arm as high as possible.

Thirdly.—If naturally inclined to be a fast bowler, aim at straightness first of all, and take care to bowl well within your strength.

Fourthly.—Always bowl in the same style and action. Bowl every day in practice, but not for more than half an hour. And take a rest of a minute or so after every six balls; remember in a match you have a rest after every four or five. Bowl carefully in practice. If you get tired leave off at once. If you find your bowling is getting worse instead of better, leave off for a few days and have a complete rest.

Fifthly.—Take a good long run, whether you bowl slow or fast ; and if you can, run on a little after delivering the ball. This gives extra ' fire ' to the ball.

Sixthly.—Be sure to practise bowling both sides of the wicket.

Seventhly.—If you want to become a really good bowler, accustom your fingers early to get as much twist as possible on the ball, both ways.

CHAPTER IV.

CAPTAINCY.

(BY A. G. STEEL.)

Going in.

IT IS a strange fact connected with cricket that a good captain is but seldom met with. The game has made such progress in popularity during the last thirty years, and the numbers of those who are proficient in its different branches have increased so enormously, that we should certainly expect to find in our county and other important matches captains who thoroughly understand the duties they are called upon to fulfil. But on looking round we are disappointed to find that the good captains in first-class (including of course county) cricket are extremely few, and these few are amateurs   The cause of this may be that few men are able to take part in first-class cricket after they have served such an apprenticeship as would give them the experience, calmness, and judgment necessary for the difficult post of captain ; or it may be that the qualifications for a good leader in the cricket-field are, from their very nature, seldom met with—in other words, that a captain is born not made, and very seldom born, too. Few professional cricketers (it is a well-known fact) make good captains ; we have hardly ever seen a match played, where a professional cricketer was captain of either side, in which he was not guilty of some very palpable blunders. Take the Gentlemen *v.* Players matches, at Lord's and the Oval, for the last twenty years ; the Players have always been seriously handicapped by the want of a good captain. Bowlers are kept on maiden after maiden without the faintest chance of a wicket, no originality of attack is ever attempted and altogether the captaincy is usually bad.   It must, however, be admitted that ' professional' captains are in a more difficult position than amateurs, inasmuch as they are often exposed to the but thinly concealed murmurings of their fellows, who consider that they have not been treated with the amount of consideration they deserve.   Amateurs always have made, and always will make, the best captains ; and this is only natural. An educated mind, with a logical power of reasoning, will always treat every subject better than one comparatively un-taught.   There are exceptions to every rule, and Alfred Shaw, the best professional captain we ever came across, is the exception here.   The disastrous effects of bad captaincy on the success of a side were never more clearly manifested than by the Australian team that visited England in 1878.   This team contained several good bowlers who, helped by the sticky state of the ground, were very deadly to our best batsmen.   Their batting was rough and rather untutored, but still at times dangerous.   They met with great success until the grounds got hard and firm, when their bowlers were collared.   It is in ad-versity at cricket, as in the more serious walks of life, that the best qualities come to the fore ; and whenever the Australian bowlers were collared, the whole team seemed to go to pieces. Either the captain or the bowlers placed the fielders in the most extraordinary and unheard-of positions, where they had but little chance of saving runs or getting catches. Spofforth during one match at Lord's in that season bowled the greater part of the day to a batsman—the Hon. Edward Lyttelton—who was not dismissed till he had topped his hundred. Ball after ball was neatly cut on the hard true ground to the boundary, past the spot where third man ought to have been but was not. Fancy a fast bowler bowling on a hard ground, while a batsman made a hundred without a third man ; then think that this batsman was one of the finest amateur cutters of his day, and you will wonder what had become of the management of the side ! This was, however, the first year the Australians visited us ; on many subsequent occasions we found out to our cost that they had made good use of their time and experience in England, and had improved, in every branch of the game, to what was to an Englishman's eye an alarming extent. Their captaincy, however, has never been good ; Murdoch, of course, had a thoroughly sound knowledge of the game ; but his better judgment was too frequently hampered by the ceaseless chattering and advice of one or two men who never could grasp the fact that in the cricket-field there can only be one captain.

The chief qualifications for a good captain are a sound knowledge of the game, a calm judgment, and the ability to inspire others with confidence.

Bad captains may be split up into three classes :—

1. Nervous and excitable men.

2. Dull apathetic men.

3. Bowling captains, with an aversion to seeing anybody bowl but themselves.

1. The nervous and excitable class is perhaps the worst of all, and sides which have the misfortune to be led by one of this division are indeed heavily handicapped. The chief

peculiarity of a captain of this sort is that he seems never to be able to keep still for a moment in the field. He is continually rushing about, altering the field every over without any reason, shouting excitedly at the top of his voice whenever a fielder has to stop or throw up the ball, and generally creating a feeling of uneasiness and excitement among players and spectators. He is at one moment tearing his hair distractedly because some unfortunate fielder has let a ball through his legs, and the next shouting and dancing with excitement and joy when some exceptionally good catch or bit of fielding has got rid of a dangerous batsman.

2. A member of the second class may be easily recognised. He walks slowly to his place at the end of each over with his eyes fixed on the ground, as if in deep thought. In reality he is thinking of nothing, or, at any rate, nothing connected with the game. He has put his two best bowlers on, and so long as a wicket falls every thirty or forty runs, what does it matter whether or not time is being wasted by a series of profitless short-pitched maiden overs? It is the bowler's duty, not his, to get the batsmen out, and if the latter put on forty runs without a wicket falling, why it will be time enough then to try someone else, and perhaps later on he himself might have a turn with lobs if things get into a very bad state. It does not take long, with a captain like this, for a side to get thoroughly demoralised and slack.

3. The bowling captains suffer from the very opposite of the feebleness which affects the last class ; over-keenness is their bane. They are generally moderate bowlers, who at times enjoy a fair amount of success, and who are often very valuable to their side as changes. But the power of bowling wherever and for as long as they please is too much for them. Over after over hit to all parts of the field, without the slightest suspicion of a chance of a wicket, only convinces the self-confident captain that something must happen sooner or later—and something generally does after the match has been bowled away. The fascination that bowling has for captains and the danger it often

leads to is a good reason for pausing before selecting as captain anyone who has any pretensions in this branch of the game. It is sometimes, however, impossible for a side to recognise anyone as captain except a bowler. He may be the oldest and most experienced member of the team, or perhaps from his position as a cricketer it may be out of the question to pass him over, and then, of course, the best of a bad job must be made. But a captain who is also a bowler has much heavier responsibilities in the field than one who is not. Even if he happens not to be over-anxious about trundling all day himself, he is apt from shyness and diffidence of his own merits not to put himself on at all—another extreme into which some captains before now have fallen. It would, perhaps, be as well not to mention names of present cricketers in this chapter, but perhaps that well-known and honest player Tom Emmett, of Yorkshire, will not be angry if he is instanced as an example of this modest and retiring class of captains. When he was captain of his county, a post which he probably rejoices to think he does not now hold, it was very seldom that he could be induced to try his hand with the ball. Since his retirement from the onerous duties of captain, he has, perhaps, been the most successful bowler of his side, and still holds his place as one of the best bowlers in England.

The duties of a captain are of two kinds : those out of the field, and those in it, and it is proposed to discuss them in the order named. The first duty of a captain is the choice of his team ; but as it so frequently happens, nowadays, that the team is chosen for him by the committee of his county or his club, this topic may be passed over till we discuss the duties of the captains at the Universities and Public Schools.

When the team is chosen, the captain's first duty is to win the toss ; and assuming that by the aid of his lucky sixpence he has succeeded in so doing, he should at once decide whether he or his opponent is to begin the batting. It is a very old saying that the side that wins the toss should go in, and it is a very true one. No captain who wins the toss and puts the other side in deserves to win the match, unless there are some very exceptional circumstances to be taken into his consideration. There is, perhaps, only one reason to justify a captain putting the other side in first. *If the ground, previously hard, has been softened by a night's rain, and if at the time of beginning it is drying under a hot baking sun, and if the captain is tolerably sure that it is going to be a fine day,* then he will do well to put the other side in. There must be present these three conditions of ground and weather before he *is* justified in refusing to bat. The ground will then for the first hour and a half or two hours make a bowling wicket ; the top soft in the early morning, and gradually getting caked under the hot sun, will in the afternoon, if the weather keeps fine and it has been *hard* before the rain, assume its former hardness and become easy for batting for the last few hours of the day's play If the ground has been soft before the rain and has been made still softer by the rain, it is madness to put the other side in. The first two or three hours will then be easy for batting, as a very slow soft wicket is always against the bowlers, and it will not be till after several hours of hot sun have been on it that it will begin to get caked and difficult for the batsman. Suppose the weather looks uncertain and broken, and the glass has been gradually going down, a captain should never in any state of the ground risk putting his opponents in. Rain is always in favour of the in side ; bowlers cannot stand and cannot hold the ball, which, wet and slippery, cannot be made to take any twist or screw that the bowler may try to give it.

Sometimes in a one-day match it may be advisable to put the other side in under circumstances different from the above, circumstances which are for the captain alone to judge of, and which it is impossible to discuss. Suppose a very strong side is playing against a very much weaker one. It may be that the captain of the former is afraid that if his side once goes to the wickets, so many runs will be made as to preclude all probability of finishing the match ; and he may be content after conference with the members of his team to take the undoubted risk of putting the other side in ; it is, however, a very dangerous thing to do at any time, and his finesse may very possibly end disastrously to his side in the imperfect light of the evening.

There are, however, *some* disadvantages in batting first. In the first place, nearly every cricketer is a better man after luncheon than before. Do not let this be understood for a moment as a hint that the overnight carousals of cricketers (very pleasant though they be) are such as to interfere with correctness of eye and steadiness of hand in the morning. Far be it from me to suggest such a thing. But every man is fitter in the afternoon, his eye is more accustomed to the light, and his digestion is better. And besides, the men that walk to the wickets to bat the first time they go into the field are apt to be more nervous than those who have been playing a few hours and have got accustomed to the light and general surroundings. These are disadvantages certainly, but they are as nothing compared to the advantages gained by batting first. These include getting the best of the light, the best of the wicket, and, last but not least, the incalculable advantage of having in the last innings of the match to save and not get runs on a wicket that has previously stood the wear and tear of three innings. The side that bats second is nearly always in at the close of the first day's play, and the lights and shadows between six and seven often make the ball very difficult to judge accurately ; at Lord's, especially, the light gets bad to- wards the close of the day ; a haze overspreads the ground, making clear and accurate sight extremely difficult. As for the respective difficulties of making and saving runs, a cricketer need only look at his scores and references to see how often the out side at the close of a match has prevented the in side from getting the runs required. The feeling of responsibility which affects the batsmen on these occasions creates an over- anxiety to play steadily and run no risks, and often results in feeble play. Then the bowlers and fielders are nerved to their utmost endeavour to keep the runs down, every fielder runs after the ball at the very top of his speed, half-a-dozen men are backing up to prevent an overthrow, and the bowler not only does all he knows to secure a wicket, but strives hard to avoid the delivery of a punishable ball. Whenever a side goes in for the last innings of the match against a big score and wins, one may feel sure the match has been won by sound and sterling cricket. There are many well-known instances of the fielding side pulling the match out of the fire at the very last moment. In the Oxford and Cambridge match in 1875, Cambridge in their last innings wanted 175 runs to win. Seven wickets fell for 114. The eighth went down at 161. Before this wicket fell it looked any odds on Cambridge, but the eleven were eventually all out for 168, and lost the match by six runs. In England *v.* Australia at the Oval in 1882, England, the last innings, wanted 85 to win, but only made 77. The annals of cricket are full of instances showing that it is better at the end of a match to have to save runs than make them. We remember playing in a match some years ago in Scotland, where the folly of putting in the other side first on a good wicket was clearly shown. It was a two days' match, and the two best batsmen on the side which lost the toss had been travelling all night from England. This, in spite of a good wicket, induced the captain who had been successful in the toss to put the other side in. One of these travel-worn and weary batsmen knocked up over ninety runs, the ground began to cut up, and the side that had refused to bat first came utterly to grief. As the losing captain left the ground, he said, 'One thing this match has taught me—*never* to put the other side in first.' The following year the same match was arranged, and once more the toss was won by the same captain. The ground was very soft indeed, in fact sodden with days of heavy rain. Again, in spite of the former sad experience, the other side were put in first and made over 200 runs. The ground was too soft for bowlers to put any life into the ball, and all bowling was comparatively easy. Next day the ground had got firmer and more solid, and the side that won the toss was again dismissed for two insignificant totals.

With regard to the order in which a captain should send in his men, a good deal depends on the strength of the batting he has at command. With a weakish batting team it is, in our opinion, always better to send in the best batsman first, assuming of course he has no objection to the place. It is of great importance to give the best batsman every possible advantage, and the men who go first to the wickets have a great advantage over the others. They have less waiting for their innings, and consequently less of that restless nervousness from which few men are free ; they have the best of the wicket ; they have often loosish bowling just at first, before the bowlers have warmed to their work ; and, last but certainly not least, they are batting a new ball. Few people realise what a difference a new ball makes to the batsman ; it goes cleaner and firmer off the bat than an old one, and, what is better than all, a hard new ball is much more difficult to twist than one that has had a hundred runs made off it. Let anyone look at an old bowler who has to begin the bowling : his first action is to rub the ball on the ground in the hope of taking off even a little of its slippery newness ; it is not, however, till after its surface has been considerably worn that it begins to take much notice of any twist, at any rate on a hard ground.

With such advantages to be gained by going in first it would be a pity not to give the best batsman the chance of making a good start for his side. A good start gives confidence to the shaky batsman, and shows the bowlers that they are not to have it all their own way. Sometimes the best batsman on a side does not care about going in first ; if so, it is always well to consult his wishes and humour him, but he should *never* go in later than second wicket. With the best batsman should go some steady correct bat, one who plays the game thoroughly and does not take liberties with the bowling. In these days of perfect grounds it is a vast mistake to send in first a regular 'sticker,' one who scores at the rate of eight or ten an hour. The stonewallers of our cricket-fields have a great deal to answer for in the heavy indictment against modern players of leaving so many unfinished matches. An account was lately given in the papers of a man recognised as a first-class county bat who was in on a fast hard wicket in the first innings of a match three hours and forty minutes for thirty-two runs. More shame to him! He did his best to draw the match, and by puddling about for so long only helped to wear out the ground for more capable scorers who were to follow him. Sometimes, when the ground is very bad, it is good to have a sticker, but taken altogether cricket would be very much better off if the whole race of stickers occasionally adopted a somewhat freer style. Nobody objects to slow scoring so long as the batsmen are playing good correct cricket, playing the straight ones with a straight bat and cutting or hitting the crooked ones; but every cricketer objects to seeing ball after ball simply stopped without the slightest attempt to make a run.

Two very fast run-getting batsmen should not be sent in together; they are apt to run each other a bit off their legs. W. G. Grace and A. P. Lucas were the best pair for first that have lately been seen; both played sound correct cricket: the former scored freely, and the latter when the ground was hard quite fast enough.

After the first two have been selected the others must follow generally in order of merit; it is as well not to put in two hard-hitters together if possible, as it often tends to make one hit against the other. First one makes a big hit; the other feels bound to follow suit, quite irrespective of the pitch of the ball, and loses his wicket. It is always an excellent thing to have one or two real good hitters, but they should be kept apart as far as possible in their innings; sixth or seventh wicket down is a very useful place for a hard hitter; the bowling has often begun to get a trifle loose by that time, and good hitting may make a dreadful mess of it in a very short time.

If any of the bowlers on whom the captain relies for his main attack happen to be goodish batsmen and likely to make a few runs, it is just as well to let their innings come off as early as convenient. A bowler who makes forty or fifty runs at the close of an innings never bowls as well after the running about as he would do had he made nothing, and it is consequently best if possible to insure him a rest before he begins his more important duties as bowler. It is exceptional to find a man successful in batting and bowling in the same match. There are a good number of modern cricketers who are very fair all-round men, and shine at times in both branches of the game; but it very rarely happens that success awaits them in both in the same match. Sometimes we find a well-known bowler piling up heaps of runs, but on looking at the other side of the score-sheet we generally perceive that he has done it at the expense of his wickets. Alfred Shaw, the famous Nottingham bowler, used at times to bat with great success, but when he did so he was nearly always unsuccessful with the ball.

When once the captain has arranged the order in which his men are to bat he should stick to it. It is worrying and harassing to the batsmen to be continually shifted up and down. We once saw one of the best batsmen in England put in last but one because the captain thought he looked nervous. His side was beaten by a few runs, and without his having received one single ball. An order made out before the innings begins is more likely to be correct than one hashed and cut about amidst excitement and anxiety. Never should a captain change his order in the second innings; of course a man who is in particularly good form may be given a hoist up a place or so, but the bad bats of the team should not be sent in first so long as there is the remotest possibility of losing; and at cricket this contingency is nearly always on the cards. The good batsmen do not wish to go in if there is only an hour or an hour and a half to play; they may get out and cannot make a really big score, so they fight shy for their average's sake. Captains should put a stop to this and insist on their taking their proper place; first, because the side may otherwise be beaten, and secondly, because those who have the advantage of going in first in favourable circumstances should also take their turn when things are not so bright.

After a captain has written out his order of going in, he should carefully watch the innings from the first to the very last ball. A watchful captain can at times greatly help his side ; a shout of 'steady' when a young batsman appears to be getting rash in his play, or when two players are getting a little abroad as to running, often comes with great effect and authority from a captain, and may prevent such a catastrophe as that represented in the illustration opposite. A word of encouragement to a nervous player as he leaves the pavilion may also often be of service. On no account should a captain ever abuse a batsman, no matter what rash stroke or foolish lack of judgment has cost him his wicket. Nothing is so galling to a batsman when he has made a bad stroke or been guilty of a mistake as being publicly derided or reproved. Afterwards, when the keen sense of vexation has somewhat subsided, a quiet word of advice may be given, and will have much more effect than a noisy public remonstrance. A good cricketer who has made a bad stroke and thereby lost his wicket knows better than any spectator what a mistake he has committed. Pavilion worthies, ye who love cricket for its own sake, ye who sit for hours criticising every ball and every stroke, forbear, we pray you, out-spoken remarks on the arrival of a discomfited batsman. 'What on earth possessed you to try to hit a straight one to leg?' 'You never seemed at home the whole time !' 'You can't keep that leg of yours out of the way !' are all remarks that may be withheld at any rate till the keen sense of failure has diminished.

It may possibly happen that during the course of an innings a point which during the summer of 1887 was considerably discussed, and about which some very extraordinary remarks have been made, may crop up for decision by the captain. Supposing the captain considers that his side has made enough runs to win the match, and that if any more are made there will not be sufficient time to get the other side out. Is he justified or not in giving orders to his men to get out on purpose? A great controversy arose on this point, owing to the captain

LUCIEN · DAVIS ·

Run out.

of one of our leading counties considering that he was entitled to give such orders. If this question be looked at from a cricketer's point of view—and by that is meant from one which is in every way honourable and to the furtherance of the true interests of the game—it will be seen at once that a captain has a perfect right to ask his men to get out whenever he considers enough runs have been made to insure victory.

The true principle of the game is, we take it, that every side should do its utmost honourably to win the match. In days gone by, when grounds were rough and uneven, every match had to be completed in a much shorter time than is now allowed. In these times of improved batting and perfection in grounds, three whole days have been decided on as the time within which every county or club must win, lose, or draw the match. The game is not to lose or to draw; it is to win; and the side that can win most matches in the time allowed is plainly the best side. And should a side make so many runs as to render it impossible to win if they make more, whereas if they get out they must almost inevitably win, and can scarcely lose, we consider it would not be acting up to the true principle of the game if it did not get out. Besides, what sport or individual interest to a batsman is there in making runs after the match is practically finished? A man does not play at cricket for himself so much as for his side; it is not the number of individual notches or wickets that falls to his lot which delights the true cricketer : it is the actual result of 'won or lost.' What pleasure does a member of either of the University elevens derive from making fifty every innings he plays in the inter-University matches if all his matches are lost? There are some who say that directly the principle is recognised that a man has a right to get out on purpose in order to gain victory for his side, it will open the door to all sorts of shady tricks in the game, and there will be no guarantee to the cricket-loving public that a side is trying. We cannot see the relevancy of this argument; if a man sacrifices himself for his side, the more honour is due to him. It is suggested that if the batting side has a right to get out or to forego its right of batting, the fielding side has a right to drop catches purposely and to bowl no balls and wides so as to avoid being beaten. If this latter course were permitted, it would be in direct contradiction to the true principle of the game—viz. the endeavour to win; it would be a dishonest subterfuge to prevent victory from rewarding the side that had played the best; it would be an un-English, dog-in-the-manger policy, and, in our opinion, it would entitle the umpires to say that the game was not being played fairly. There is a vast difference in principle between getting out on purpose in order to win and bowling and fielding badly in order to snatch victory from the best side. A captain is, then, not only perfectly justified, but is bound in the interests of his side, and in the true interests of the game, to order his men to get out if that is the only way to win.

Since the above was written we are pleased to see that the M.C.C. committee have considered this matter, and have made the following recommendation to the general meeting of the club : 'That on the last day of a match, including one-day matches, the in side should at any time be empowered to declare the innings at an end.' At the general meeting, however, it was unanimously decided to postpone for one year any actual legislation upon the subject.

In club and county matches a captain whose side is batting may often have little duties to perform, such as hurrying his men in after the fall of a wicket and allowing no time to be wasted, &c. There is nothing so annoying to a keen cricketer as to see the field waiting three or four minutes whilst some 'local swell' calmly buckles his pads and saunters sleepily to the wicket. A captain should see that the next batsman is always ready to go in directly the preceding one reaches the pavilion ; and a good experienced captain can also give many valuable hints to the younger members of his team as they sit waiting for their innings. 'Play your own game, of course ;' he is the first one to know and realise the truth of the old saying ; but (and there are often many *buts*) 'for goodness sake don't try and hit that curly bowler unless you are on the pitch of him;' 'if you play back to that fast chap you are done; he is out and away faster than he looks;' 'watch that man at cover : he's as quick as lightning with his return.' All these little odds and ends from an old hand are well worth the attention of a young player; they all help to give him more confidence and more knowledge and experience, and consequently make him a better cricketer. And then a captain's eyes must be sharp to detect any slovenliness in the dress of a batsman. What a sorry sight it is to see a man going to the wickets with his pad-straps hanging two or three inches down his legs, his trousers unfolded and sticking out from behind his pads, his shirtsleeves hanging loose, and altogether having a general air of being a slovenly fellow ! A captain must note this ; he knows that there are a good many better ways of getting out than being caught from one's pad-straps or loose trousers that flap gaily in the breeze, or from one's shirtsleeves that float round the forearm with so great an expanse of canvas, looking for all the world like a bishop's sleeve. All these little things are worth knowing; cricket is a game with a great deal of luck in it and full of a great many odd chances, and the sooner a young player realises that he must do all he can to minimise the chances against himself, the better cricketer he will become and the more runs he will make.

The duties of a captain in the field are far more onerous than those out of it. It is here that his good qualities are tested, his knowledge and judgment of the game put to the proof. The most difficult task he has to perform is the management of the bowling. It, of course, occasionally happens that his two best bowlers are put on, and bowl successfully without a chance during the whole of the innings. But this is a very exceptional occurrence, and is but seldom seen in first-class cricket, and then only when the ground is sticky or crumbled. It is in the bowling changes and placing that a captain's skill is principally seen. On a hard fast wicket it is best to begin with fast bowling at one end and slow at the other. A good overhand fast bowler on a hard wicket has more chance of making the ball rise, and getting catches in the slips and at the wickets, than a slow one ; but it is always well to have different-paced bowling on at either end, as in this way the batsman's eye does not get thoroughly accustomed to one pace. The late F. Morley—in his day the best left-hand fast bowler in England— and A. Shaw were always individually more successful when playing together for their county, the fast left hand and slow right being an excellent variation for the eye of the batsman. Poor Morley, what a good bowler he was ! In our opinion he was the best fast bowler we have had in England for a very long time. He was a good pace, had a beautifully easy left-handed delivery, just over his shoulder, and was most wonderfully accurate in his length. He had a good spin and break-back on his bowling, and every now and then sent in one that came with the arm and required a lot of playing. His early death caused a great gap in the ranks of our professionals, and was much lamented by every class of cricketers ; for a more honest and unassuming professional player than Fred Morley never went into the cricket-field. His knowledge of geography was not up to his cricket capabilities ; for after a serious collision in the Indian Ocean, on his voyage to Australia in 1882, a mishap which subsequently ended fatally to him, he said : ' No more ships for me : I'll home again by the overland route ! '

At the beginning of the innings the two bowlers put on should both be asked which end suits them best ; if both want the same, the captain should give the choice to the one on whom, taking into consideration the state of the ground, he relies most. The field should be placed according to the style of the opposing batsman, and in doing this the captain should act with the consent of the bowler. There are many captains who change the field from time to time without ever consulting the bowler, who, if a cricketer, knows better than anyone else where his bowling is likely to be hit.

No rule can be laid down with regard to the frequency of bowling changes, except the more the better. A bowler should never be kept on if he is not getting wickets, and if the batsmen are playing him with ease. It goes no way towards winning a match to bowl ten or a dozen short-pitched consecutive maiden overs. Directly the batsmen seem to have guessed the length and style of bowling it should be changed, if only for a few overs, while some new style is tried for a short time. If a long stand be made, every style of bowling should be quickly tried ; thirty runs should never be allowed without a change of some sort, unless the bowling happens to be particularly puzzling to the batsman, and is being badly played.

As regards the placing of the field, it has already been said that usually the bowler is best able to guess where his own bowling is most likely to be hit ; but there are many things which a captain should recollect, as the suggestions of a captain in whom his bowlers place confidence are always accepted readily. He should keep his eye on short-slip, as this place is, especially on a fast wicket, the most important of all. There are more good batsmen dismissed at short-slip and the wicket, on good wickets, than at any other places. It is an extraordinary fact connected with short-slip that, unless he has had a great deal of experience, he is continually shifting his position ; one over he will be standing fine and deep and the next square and near to the wicket. It is the captain's duty, even more than the bowler's, to see that this does not happen.

On a true hard wicket we never like to see a captain putting his mid-on or short-leg close in to the batsman, to field what is called 'silly' mid-on ; the risk of standing near in on a hard wicket to a batsman who can hit at all is not by any means slight, and we have on several occasions seen men placed in this position get very nasty blows. Boyle, the Australian mid-on, stood about as near in as any man ever did stand; on sticky grounds he made many catches, on fast grounds he missed many which if standing further back he would have caught. He not seldom received nasty injuries, and on one occasion was laid up for several weeks with a broken or injured bone in his hand. A quick active field at mid-on who will run in when he sees the batsman making a quiet forward stroke on the leg side, and when he observes a leg-side ball kick up higher than usual, is all that should be required. In a match at Melbourne, in 1882, we recollect a very amusing little incident in which mid-on played a prominent part. The Australians were batting, and Bates, the Yorkshireman, had just dismissed two of their best bats, McDonnell and Giffen, in two consecutive balls. Bonner, who used to congratulate himself, and not without a certain amount of justification, that he could make mincemeat of our slow bowling, was the next man in. Somebody suggested that, in the faint hope of securing a 'hat' for Bates, we should try a silly mid-on. Bates faithfully promised to bowl a fast shortish ball between the legs and the wicket, and said he was quite certain Bonner would play slowly forward to it. Acting on the faith of this, W. W. Read boldly volunteered to stand silly mid-on for one ball. In came the giant, loud were the shouts of welcome from the larrikins' throats ; now would the ball soar over the green trees even higher than yonder flock of twittering parrots. As Bates began to walk to the wickets to bowl, nearer and nearer crept our brave mid-on ; a slow forward stroke to a fast shortish leg-stump ball landed the ball fairly in his hands not more than six feet from the bat. The crowd would not believe it, and Bonner was simply thunderstruck at mid-on's impertinence ; but Bates had done the hat trick for all that, and what is more, he got a very smart silver tall hat for his pains.

The duties of captains of the University teams and of the Public Schools are far more arduous than those of a captain of a county or a club eleven. At our large Public Schools the captain is responsible for the selection of the team ; he may be assisted to a certain extent by a committee, but the actual filling up of the vacant places in his eleven generally devolves on him alone. An energetic and keen boy captain will usually manage before the close of the summer term to get together a team of fair merit ; even if the stuff he has to work upon is inferior in quality, the great amount of time at his disposal for practice, and the assistance he receives from the

Eton v. Harrow.

school professionals and masters, ought always to ensure a keen captain having a tolerable eleven before the summer holidays begin. It may be taken as true that a bad fielding school eleven denotes a bad and slack captain. Whatever may be the batting and bowling material at his disposal, a boy captain can, if he likes, have a good fielding side; and if in his school matches at Lord's, or elsewhere, he finds that he loses the match by slack fielding, he has none to blame but himself. None of our best county teams can field as boys can if they are properly taught and kept up to the mark. There are few men of thirty taking part in the game who can throw with any effect for more than about thirty or forty yards; their arms and shoulders are stiff, and will not stand it, whereas boys can all throw, and are about twice as active as many of those whose names at the present time figure prominently in our leading fixtures.

A school eleven, as indeed every other, only requires four regular bowlers. ' If you cannot win with four bowlers, you'll never win at all,' is an old and true saying. But this wants a little explanation. The four best available bowlers must be played without regard to their batting powers, and after these four have been selected let the team be filled up with good batsmen and fielders, quite irrespective of whether they can bowl or not. It is an excellent thing for a side that every man should be able to bowl a bit if wanted, and every boy should be able to do so, but it is only necessary in choosing the team to play four men as bowlers only.

Every school eleven should possess a lob-bowler ; if he be a good one so much the better, but one of some sort there must be. Lobs have always been most destructive to boys, and even very indifferent lobs are occasionally very fatal to schools. A little practice will teach any boy to bowl them fairly ; he must take a long and rather a quick run, and bowl just fast enough to prevent the batsman hitting the good-length balls before they pitch. The high slow lob is generally worthless.

The wicket-keeper must also be trained and coached. He should be taught the right and the wrong way to stand, and should practise keeping for a short time every day. And, above all things, the school wicket-keeper should know that for anything over slow and slow medium bowling he is to have a long-stop. The number of good wicket-keepers who have been spoilt by having to perform the office of long-stop as well as their own is legion. There are no first-class keepers nowadays who put out their hands on the leg side and draw the ball to the stumps; they all jump to the leg side in front of the ball to prevent it resulting in a four-bye; and consequently, even if lucky enough to take the ball with their hands, they are so far from the stumps as to make it exceedingly difficult to knock the bails off.

A captain of a University team has not so much to do with training and coaching his team as a school captain. By the time men have reached their University eleven they have generally mastered the elementary principles of the game, and require more practice and experience, keeping up to the mark rather than coaching. A captain's duty is consequently to see that his men engage in constant practice at all parts of the game, and by showing an example of keenness and energy to inspire his team with the same qualities. Some men at the University, and especially those fresh from the restraint of a public school, occasionally require a few words of advice about the mode of life which is necessary for undergoing with success the wear and tear of a University cricket season. A 'Varsity team has about six weeks' hard work, and no man can bear the strain of this if, at the same time, he is keeping late hours and distributing his attentions impartially amongst all the numerous delicacies that adorn the University dinner-tables during the May term. No strict training is required, thank goodness! Cricket does not demand of her votaries the hollow face and attenuated frame, and too often the undermined constitution, that a long term of arduous training occasionally results in, especially to a youth of unmatured strength ; but a cricketer should live a regular life and abstain at table from all things likely to interfere with his digestion and wind. Above all else, smoky rooms should be avoided. A small room, filled with ten or a dozen men smoking as if their very existence depended on the amount of tobacco consumed, soon gets a trifle foggy, and the man who remains there for long will find next morning on waking that his head feels much heavier than usual, and his eyes are reddish and sore. A University captain should never hesitate to speak to any of his team on these matters, should he think warning or rebuke necessary.

The necessity of moderation in drink is happily a thing which few University cricketers require to be reminded of. There are many opinions as to what is the best drink for men when actually playing. By best we mean that which does least harm to the eye. In hot weather something must be drunk, and the question is, What ? Our experience is that beer and stout are both too heady and heavy, gin and ginger beer is too sticky, sweet, &c., to the palate. In our opinion, shandy-gaff, sherry, or claret, and soda are the most thirst-quenching, the lightest, and the cleanest to the palate. The latter consideration is a great one on a hot day at cricket. In a long innings the heat and the dust are apt to make the mouth very dry and parched, and a clean drink is especially desirable.

As a rule a 'Varsity captain has not much difficulty in selecting the first eight or nine of his team—there are usually that number that stand out as far and away better than all the others —but the last two or three places often cause him the greatest difficulty. There may be two or three men of the same merit fighting for the last place, inflicting sleepless nights and anxious thoughts on the captain. He cannot make up his mind, and possibly remains undecided till the very week before the big match. A 'Varsity team owes half its strength to playing so much together. Every man knows and has confidence in the others, and every man's full merits and the use he may be to the side are understood by the captain ; consequently, the sooner the whole team is chosen the better.

Now let us briefly discuss the considerations that should guide the captain in the choice of his team. And perhaps the simplest and best way will be to assume that a captain has to choose the best team in England (our fictitious captain making the twelfth man on the side). The first thing he must do is to choose his bowlers, and, as we have said above, these must be the best four he can get, each one different from the others in style. He wants a fast bowler to begin with ; he has Bowley of Surrey, and Ulyett of Yorkshire, and Pougher of Leicestershire, and that is about all. If he is a wise man he will choose Bowley, as being the fastest, and straightest, and best. This is No. 1. No. 2 must be a good left-hander ; and, now that Peate is not seen as much as he used to be in first-class matches, this is a difficult thing to get. Wootton of Kent is a very good slow bowler, but not quite good enough ; so our captain should fix on Briggs of Lancashire, who is the best of the lot in this particular style of bowling. No. 3—a medium-pace right round-arm bowler—is next wanted. No captain can

doubt who this is to be : Barnes of Nottingham, with his nasty
awkward action, his break-back, and the kicky nature of his
bowling on almost all wickets, is clearly the man.   Some might
say that Lohmann of Surrey should have this No. 3 place.   He
is a very good bowler ; but on a hard true wicket we fancy
Barnes against the *best* batsmen.   No. 4.—Our captain wants
a right-arm slow bowler accurate enough to keep down the
runs (if wanted to) on a hard true wicket, and powerful enough
with the ball to take advantage of crumbled or sticky wickets.
Who is he to take?   Bates of Yorkshire ; Alfred Shaw of Nottingham ; Flowers of the same county; Attewell of ditto, are
all good names.   Bates is not accurate enough, Shaw is not
quite so good as he used to be—but what a good one he was
once !   Perhaps his best performance was in 1875, when for
Notts and the M.C.C. at Lord's he bowled 162 balls for 7 runs
and 7 wickets (bother the maidens : we don't care how many
of them he bowled !), and amongst these seven wickets were
W. G. Grace, Ridley, Buller, and Lord Harris ; in the same
match for the M.C.C. Ridley with his lobs had a good
analysis for the two innings—208 balls, 46 runs, and 10
wickets.   Our captain thinks he could not do better than
Attewell, and we agree with him ; but he has quite made up
his mind to tell this bowler not to bowl for maidens but
wickets.   No. 5.—The wicket-keeper.   There are only two in
it : Pilling and Sherwin.   The best *wicket-keeper* is wanted,
quite irrespective of batting.   They are both very good, but
our captain thinks Pilling is the safest, lets off fewer chances
(all wicket-keepers let off some), has the best hands to stand
fast bowling, and is the quietest behind the sticks.   So
Pilling is chosen as our stumper, and we only hope that his
health will allow him to remain there for many years to come.
No. 6.—Now our captain has got to fill up six places ; he has
up to the present provided for getting rid of the opposite
side : he now turns his attention to providing for his batsmen.
W. G. Grace first, no one disputes.   Does someone suggest
Shrewsbury ?   Well, certainly, in the season of 1887 he had a

wonderful average—78; but for *winning* a match give us
W. G., our first choice. Shrewsbury may be the best to prevent his side being beaten; but we want to win, and if one
man stays in a couple of days for 150 runs there is a great
chance of drawing the game. We like the man who makes
150 in four or five hours, and then gets out and helps to get
the other side out afterwards. So our captain annexes W. G. as
No. 6. No. 7—Arthur Shrewsbury. No. 8—W. W. Read. No. 9
—A. J. Webbe. No. 10.—And now having got nine of his team
our captain must consider what he has and what he has *not* got.

His team at present consists of W. G. Grace, Shrewsbury,
W. W. Read, A. J. Webbe, Pilling, Briggs, Barnes, Attewell,
Bowley. He has therefore five of the very best batsmen in
England—Grace, Shrewsbury, Read, Webbe, and Barnes—
a very good run-getting bat in Briggs, and three comparatively indifferent batsmen in Bowley, Pilling, and Attewell.
He has five bowlers, the four chosen and W. G. Grace, the
best change bowler in England, bar none. Now what has he
in the field? Not quite so good a lot as one would wish the
English side to be. Grace, Shrewsbury, and Read are all
candidates for point; as Shrewsbury is a fairly good point, and
is almost useless anywhere else in the field, owing to his not
being able to throw, he must take this place. Grace and Read
and Barnes must all be in places somewhere near the wicket,
as none of these are quick enough or· good throwers enough
for fielding in the country. Briggs might be sent into the
country, but he is so excellent at cover that it would be a pity
to take him from that most important spot. Webbe must then
go into the country, as Attewell and Bowley will be wanted to
bowl; now Webbe is a very safe catch, and a good field anywhere you like to put him; but we must have some really first-
class quick outfield with a good return—the team will not be
complete without such a one. He must also be a good batsman, or else the team will have a passenger on board. Is
there such a man? Yes, our captain thinks there are two
who may do—Gunn of Nottingham, and Ulyett: which of these

should he choose? Gunn is doubtless the best outfield, and a good bat too; but Ulyett is a very good outfield, as good a run-getting bat as Gunn, and at times a dangerous bowler; so let Ulyett have the preference, and be No 10 in our captain's English team. No. 11.—The last man! Now in this place what is wanted is a good all-round cricketer—one who is a good bat,

At wicket after bowling.

a good bowler, a good field and catch, quick on his legs, and a good thrower.

Will Bates do? No, not a good enough thrower, not a safe enough pair of hands, though a good bat and bowler. Peel must be dismissed as not being a sufficiently brilliant field. Flowers ditto. Barlow we don't want: he cannot field in the country, and at sixth wicket, for this is where the eleventh man will have to go in, we want a man to make runs, not to stick. Louis Hall is the same. Lohmann of Surrey is the man, no better—quick field, safe pair of hands, good thrower, a really good bowler, and a correct hard-hitting batsman, who is always likely to make runs.

Our captain has completed his task, and though we should have liked to have seen one or two better throwers in the team, it is still a very good one and a difficult nut for any Australian side to crack :—W. G. Grace, W. W. Read, A. J. Webbe, Shrewsbury, Pilling, Briggs, Barnes, Attewell, Bowley, Ulyett, Lohmann.

In the field all captains should be cheery and bright, and full of encouragement to both fielders and bowlers. A despondent captain, who becomes sad and low when things are going against him, has a most depressing effect on his men. Cricket is a game full of so many chances and surprises that no match is ever lost till the last ball has been bowled, so the bowlers must be cheered and encouraged, and the fielders kept up to the mark till all is over.

Everything that goes on in the game should be noticed by the captain. If a bowler forgets to get behind the stumps when the ball is to be returned to him by a fielder, the captain should at once call his attention to the fact ; if a fielder keeps shifting his position over after over without orders, a gentle reminder must be given ; if a fielder throws unmercifully at the bowler or wicket-keeper when there is no attempt at a run on the part of the batsmen, he must be spoken to. It is a bad fault on the part of a fieldsman to knock the poor wicket-keeper's hands to pieces for no purpose.

If a captain keeps his eye open to all these little things, and does his best to eradicate them and others of the same nature from his men, if he is a keen zealous cricketer gifted with a calm temperament and sound judgment, he may rest assured that before he has led his men very long he will be the captain of a good team.

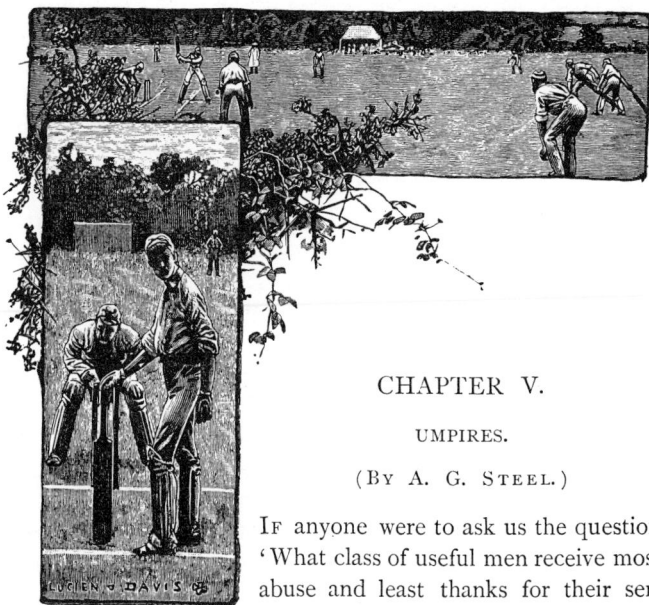

'Guard please, Umpire.'

CHAPTER V.

UMPIRES.

(BY A. G. STEEL.)

IF anyone were to ask us the question 'What class of useful men receive most abuse and least thanks for their service?' we should, without hesitation, reply, 'Cricket umpires.' The duties of an umpire are most laborious and irksome ; they require for their proper performance the exercise of numerous qualifications, and yet it is always the lot of every man who dons the white coat, the present dress of an umpire, to receive, certainly no thanks, and, too frequently, something which is not altogether unlike abuse. Nowhere can any notice be found in the history of cricket of the first appearance of umpires as sole judges of the game ; and from old pictures, and notably the one at Lord's, it is evident that, in the early days of cricket, there were no umpires. The scoring was done by the 'notcher,' who stood by and cut a notch in a stick every time a run was made, and who also most probably would be the one to decide any point of dispute that might arise amongst the players. The earliest copy of the laws of cricket that we have is dated 1774 ; the heading is 'The Laws of Cricket, revised at the Star and Garter, Pall Mall, February 25, 1774, by a committee of noble-men and gentlemen of Kent, Hampshire, Surrey, Sussex, Middlesex, and London.'

These laws are the foundation of those which now govern cricket, and in them rules were laid down with regard to umpires, some of which, with certain modifications, are still in force. Although these laws, promulgated in 1774, are the earliest authenticated, there is still in existence a much older document, though the date is unknown, which contains a few re-marks on the game, entitled 'Ye game of cricket as settled by ye cricket club at ye Star and Garter in Pall Mall,' and then it goes on, 'Laws for ye umpires,' showing that in considerably earlier days than 1774 umpires were recognised institutions in the game.

It has always been the custom, till within the last few years, for each side to choose its own umpire, even in the most im-portant matches, except those played at Lord's and the Oval. The system of each side providing its own umpire existed till 1883. It thus happened that aged and decayed cricketers were rewarded by being chosen as umpires to watch over the interests of their old colleagues.

It was quite impossible for men who were thoroughly im-bued with a strong spirit of partisanship to remain perfectly impartial ; however honest and free from suspicion a man might be, his opinion, at a critical stage of the game, could not fail to be unconsciously biassed in favour of the side with whose name his own had been long associated. Many men became alarmed at the idea of obtaining a reputation for giving partial decisions, and would go to the other extreme, and decide against their own side oftener than the facts justified. There were also men, no doubt—but these were few and far between —who used their important position to unfairly enhance the chances of victory for their own side. This system was a bad one, as it made the position of an umpire so extremely invidious ; but it was not till 1883 that the present practice was introduced. At the beginning of the season each county now sends up the names of two or more umpires to the secretary of the M.C.C. Then from the list of names nominated by the different county committees the secretary has to appoint two umpires for every county match, neither of these two being the nominees of either of the counties that are playing in the match. This system works very well and is a very fair one, as the judges of the game are not now exposed to the charge of partiality, so frequently made under the old rule, their interests being connected with neither side. The list of what may be called the official umpires is almost totally composed of elderly professional cricketers, who, as young men, were themselves famous players, they are consequently men who, having spent many years of their lives in the active pursuit of the game, possess a thorough knowledge of its laws and practice. And our experience of the way in which those arduous duties are performed is that, considering the difficulties of the situation they are placed in, our English umpires, taken as a body, give good and correct decisions. We think that this opinion would be indorsed by most leading cricketers.

The difficulties of an umpire are many, and the nice distinctions he is called upon to draw over and over again during the course of the match may be gathered from the fact that bad decisions in first-class matches are not infrequent. And yet we adhere to the commendation given above. It is an absolute impossibility to find an umpire who will not make mistakes at times. The most likely slip for him to make is, perhaps, when he is appealed to for a 'catch at the wicket.' Let us just glance at some of the difficulties which may, and often do, arise as to this decision. The umpire has to satisfy himself that the bat or the batsman's hand (but not the wrist) has touched the ball before it has lodged in the wicket-keeper's hand. There are often cases where there is no doubt that the bat has touched the ball; the batsman strikes at the ball and hits it so hard that the sound of the 'click' may be heard by every fieldsman on the ground, and even sometimes by the spectators; and then, of course, the umpire has no difficulty. But supposing a batsman in playing forward to a ball just outside the off stump apparently misses it, and the ball turns after the pitch and, without any sound or 'click,' lodges in the wicket-keeper's hand, what has the umpire to say if appealed to? He sees the ball turn after the pitch, and he sees it pass the bat dangerously near, but he hears no sound ; perhaps in this case no one on the field but the wicket-keeper knows for certain what has taken place ; he knows that the ball turned from the pitch, just grazed the shoulder or edge of the bat, and came into his hands. The batsman, perhaps, has in his forward stroke touched the ground with his bat at the very moment the ball grazed the bat. The jar of his bat on the ground has nullified the effect of the touch of the ball, and he doubtless considers that if the appeal is answered against him he has met with injustice. In a case like this the umpire gives, or should give, the batsman the benefit of the doubt that exists, and No. 1 bad decision is chronicled against him by the fielding side. No blame can be attached to the umpire, he has done his very best to give a correct decision, but the circumstances have made it absolutely impossible for him to be certain on the point. Again, it is sometimes next to impossible for an umpire to be sure whether a ball has just grazed the tip of the indiarubber finger of a batsman's glove or not ; for often in such a case no sound can be distinguished. The batsman feels and the wicket-keeper sees it, but none else in the field knows anything at all about what has happened. The umpire can see the ball pass very close to the glove, but whether they have actually touched he cannot at a distance of twenty-four or twenty-five yards decide. An umpire may often be deceived, too, in his vision, if the ball pass the bat quickly and the stroke of the bat towards the ball has been a rapid one ; he may hear an ominous 'click' that sounds like a touch, and yet he may think that he saw daylight between them at the moment the ball passed the bat. We have more than once in a first-class match, in which two good umpires were engaged, struck a ball fairly hard and seen it lodge in the wicket-keeper's hands, and heard in answer to a confident appeal, ' Not out ; he was nowhere near it ! ' and this when everyone in the field heard the sound, and knew it could only have been caused by the ball meeting the bat. And again, supposing a slight noise or ' click ' to be heard just when a ball is passing outside the legs of a batsman, should the ball be taken by the wicket-keeper, it is often a most difficult thing for an umpire to be certain whether the ' click ' has been caused by the bat and the ball, or the batsman's leg or pad-strap and the ball. The click of the ball hitting a strap or hard piece of cane in a pad is very like the sharp sound caused by the bat hitting the ball, and this, added to the impossibility of the umpire actually seeing whether a leg ball passes close to the bat or not, makes appeals for leg-side catches at the wicket extremely hard to answer with any degree of certainty.

These are a few instances of the many very difficult cases which an umpire may be called upon to decide at any moment during a match. Many others will probably occur to the minds of most of the readers of this chapter, at any rate of those who have any practical experience of the game. We do not, however, propose to mention all these cases at present ; some of them we shall have to refer to later on.

We think enough has been said as to the difficult nature of the post to show conclusively that it is an impossibility to find an umpire who will not be liable to give bad verdicts. It is most unfortunate that all umpires, in addition to having to bear the heavy weight of knowing that they may at any minute be called upon to give a decision about which they are uncertain and consequently liable to err, have also too often to suffer from the abuse of those who consider themselves aggrieved by wrong decisions. The chief principle that tends to harmonise the game, and make it the quiet English pastime that it is, is that the umpire's decision shall be final. It would be impossible to play the game if this

were not so ; how would matches ever be finished satisfactorily if every batsman had a right to remain at the wickets
until he himself thought he was fairly out? And yet, though
this principle is universally known as the main one on which
the prosperity of the game depends, we unfortunately find
but too frequently, and even amongst some of the leading
cricketers of the day, a tendency to revile and abuse the unfortunate umpire whenever an appeal has been given against
them. If a batsman considers he has been given out wrong-
fully, he has a perfect right, of course, to give his opinion of
what has taken place privately to anyone ; but he has no right
to stand at his wicket wrangling with and abusing the umpire,
nor has he a right to declare publicly to the pavilion on his
return from the wickets that a wrong decision has been
given. Too often one sees a sulky, bad-tempered-looking face
arrive at the pavilion, and in loud tones declare he was not
within a yard of it, or 'it didn't pitch within a foot of the
wicket.' Such conduct is unsportsmanlike and ungentlemanly,
and, what is more, is unfair, as such a statement is a public
accusation made against the professional capacity of an absent
man who has no opportunity of refuting or contradicting it.

First-class amateur cricketers should remember that it is impossible for them to pay too much deference to the decisions
of umpires, as it is from them that the standard or tone of
morality in the game is taken. They should ask themselves, if
they wrangle and dispute with umpires in first-class matches
when a large assemblage is present, what will happen in smaller
matches, when there is not the same publicity and notoriety to
restrain the rowdiness which has before now been the result of
a wordy warfare with 'the sole judge of fair and unfair play.'
We admit that there is nothing so disappointing and annoying
to a batsman as to be given out by what is really a bad decision.
Take, for instance, a man who cannot for business reasons get
away as much as he would like to indulge in his favourite game.
He has been looking forward for weeks to a particular match,
perhaps one of the greatest importance; he has been practising

hard for the last month in his spare time in the evenings after business hours. The eventful day comes, the time for his innings arrives, and just when he has settled down with ten or fifteen to his score, and has begun to find himself thoroughly at home with the bowling, his hopes are dashed to the ground by a bad decision. He is maddened with anger and disappointment for the moment, and every cricketer will heartily sympathise with him ; but if he allows his feelings to get the better of him, and indulges in an open exhibition of anger against the umpire, that man should never play cricket again until he has satisfied himself that, come what may, he will be able to curb himself sufficiently to prevent such exhibitions, which act so greatly against the true interests of the game.

The majority of cricketers, we are happy to say, are not open abusers of umpires and their decisions, though a considerable number have earned this unenviable notoriety. But by far the greater proportion of batsmen, though not open cavillers at the umpire's verdict, always refuse to allow that his judgment, when adverse to them, is correct, and especially in cases of l.b.w. It is one of the most extraordinary things connected with the game that, no matter how straight the ball may have pitched, how low down it may have hit the leg, and how straight it is going off the pitch to the wicket when stopped by the opposing leg, there is not one batsman in twenty who will allow that he is fairly out. 'The ball pitched off the wicket ;' 'It would have gone over the wicket ;' 'It was twisting like anything and would have missed the wicket ;' and 'How could it be out? I hit it hard,' are the usual excuses that are made to a knot of the crestfallen batsman's friends and sympathisers after his return to the pavilion. Sometimes, no doubt, one or more of these excuses may be perfectly true, and the batsman has been unfortunately dismissed by an error in judgment on the part of the umpire ; but in far the larger number of instances they are simply sham excuses invented by the player to cover his own discomfiture. In some cases a batsman may really believe that the ball would have missed the wicket or did not pitch straight, and if so he has a perfect right, if he thinks fit, to tell his own friends what his opinion is; but as a rule the umpire's judgment is right and the batsman's is wrong. The

A clear case.

mere fact of a ball hitting the leg when it is pitched *so nearly* straight and would have *so nearly* hit the wicket as to justify an appeal to the umpire, shows that the batsman has seriously erred either in his judgment of the pitch of the ball or in his stroke. He has made a mistake—the ball hitting his leg is a proof that he has done so ; and yet, with this proof staring him in the face, he comes out and states positively what practically comes to this : 'The ball must have been very nearly straight and would have very nearly hit the stumps, or else the bowler would not have asked ; I mistook the pace, or the pitch, or the flight of the ball, or all three of them at the same time ; but now that I have had time to think over it, I know for certain the ball was not pitched straight or would not have hit the wicket.' This is the logical conclusion of the vast number of excuses that are made with regard to decisions of l.b.w.

When a batsman says that he has hit the ball, it does not always follow that it is correct, for under certain circumstances he may imagine he has touched it when in fact he has not done so. For instance, if he plays forward with the bat close to his left leg, he may slightly touch his pad or his boot, which may produce in his mind the same impression as if the bat had touched the ball. In a forward stroke a slight touch on a hard ground with the end of the bat will often convey the same idea. There are one or two well-known cricketers, thoroughly keen and honest players of the game, whose habit of finding fault with umpires' decisions adverse to themselves has often provoked great amusement. We remember on one occasion taking part in a match in which one of these critical gentlemen was playing. Shortly after his innings began he missed a perfectly straight ball, and just as it was going to hit the centre of the middle stump it came into contact with a thick well-padded leg. He had to go. Shortly afterwards in the pavilion he was overheard replying in answer to a friend, 'Out? why, it didn't pitch straight by a quarter of an inch !'

One of the worst features connected with the play of the different Australian teams that have visited this country is the tendency they have always shown to dispute the decisions of the umpires. We believe that the chief reason why the Australian cricketers have not achieved that popularity which the excellence of their play would seem to merit is owing to this unfortunate habit. Nothing is so apt to breed bad decisions against a side as public knowledge that the members of it always refuse to abide peaceably by the fiat of the umpire. Men who are continually wrangling and disputing about the decisions of umpires, and who have earned the reputation of so doing, have in the long run more real cause to complain than their more peaceable *confrères*. Umpires are after all but mortal, and if they once realise that a man objects to being 'given out,' when it is palpable and plain that no other verdict can be rightly given, they get what is popularly called 'their backs up,' and are inclined to hesitate before giving that man the benefit of any doubt there may be. This feeling in the minds of umpires is brought about unconsciously, and would certainly be denied if the direct question were asked them, 'Do you treat a man with a wrangling, contentious disposition in exactly the same way as you treat another?' The Australians have always, and especially in the season of 1886, earned for themselves this unenviable notoriety ; and if, as they allege, they have had to fight an uphill battle on English grounds against the bad decisions of our umpires, we firmly believe they have brought this unfortunate result upon their own heads. We wish to say nothing against our Colonial antagonists except in this respect ; they have always proved keen and worthy opponents of our English cricketers. But if the future teams that may visit our shores from the Colonies will accept a hint, and make a firm resolve that the decisions of our umpires shall be accepted without murmurings and disputings, they may rest assured that they themselves will become more popular with our cricket-loving public, and their stay in England will be made more pleasant in every way.

What has been said with regard to the duty of batsmen to abide by umpires' decisions applies equally to bowlers. What can be worse form than a public exhibition of temper on the part of a bowler because an appeal is not answered in his favour? 'Wha-a-a-t?' shouts a bowler at the top of his voice, after a negative answer to an appeal, his eyes glaring at the poor unfortunate umpire as if he wanted to eat him. 'What *is* out, then?' Perhaps in the next ball or two the batsman is palpably out, either bowled or caught. 'How's that, then, sir?' says the bowler in sarcastic glee, as if his success was directly due to the former verdict of the umpire. All this sort of thing is very poor cricket, and not calculated to promote the true spirit of friendliness which should distinguish every match if the game is to be enjoyed.

It is in club cricket that there is always the greatest number of disputes about umpires' decisions. This is owing to the fact that the only way in which umpires can be procured is by each side bringing its own. As a rule the professional bowler of a club stands as umpire in all matches, and this system, as before mentioned, cannot fail occasionally to cause a little wrangling. Supposing, for instance, a side has to get half a dozen more runs to win a match with only one wicket to fall, and the umpire of the fielding side, by giving the last hope out leg before wicket, decides the game in favour of his employers, it must inevitably stir up some angry feelings, especially as a batsman is scarcely ever known to admit the impeachment of being fairly out l.b.w. Considering the keenness and anxiety to win of every cricketer worthy of the name, the fact of serious disputes being almost unknown is a remarkable instance of the generosity and manliness of English players.

But it is in *bonâ fide* country or rustic matches that there is most often good reason for finding fault with the decisions of umpires. We are not speaking of matches between clubs who can boast enough members to enable them to engage a professional bowler, level a good large square piece of turf, and erect a local habitation in the shape of a neat and pretty little pavilion; but of matches between clubs in remote villages, where the village common, rough and uneven as it is, suffices for practice on the week-day evenings and for matches on Saturday afternoons, where the only weapons of the batsmen are the old well-worn and usually desperately heavy club bats, where the village barber is the bowler, the village baker the best batsman, and the umpire, on whom his side relies for victory more than on all the other men in the village, the publican. There are still such clubs in existence, though not nearly so many now as in days gone by. The increased popularity of the game, and the greater facilities for getting about the country, have caused many of these old village clubs to become large and well-to-do. One of the greatest treats that any cricket-lover can have is to take part in a match between two really primitive village clubs. The old fast under-arm bowling, now sixty years at least out of date in first-class cricket, still preserves its pristine efficacy on the rough uneven turf, and against the untutored batsmen. The running and the shouting and the general excitement when the parson misses a catch, or the butcher is bowled, is very pleasing to one accustomed to the stateliness and publicity of a match at Lord's or the Oval. But the village umpire is, perhaps, the most interesting personage on the ground. He is usually a stout elderly man, who, grown too grey on the head and too thick in the girth to give his side any more active help in the field, assists in quite as efficient a manner in his new post. He is generally a genial, jolly sort of fellow ; devoted to the game, he fondly imagines that he is an infallible judge of every point that can arise in it, though really he is wofully ignorant of the whole subject. He is, however, looked up to by the whole village as an authority whose opinion cannot be disputed; probably he has once in his life, many years ago, been to Lord's, and has there, while watching Carpenter, Hayward, and George Parr, laid up a store of information connected with the play of great cricket celebrities which has sufficed ever since to maintain his reputation as a cricket savant.

Before the beginning of a match, he may be seen diligently rolling the stubborn ground with a small hand-roller, in the hopes that some of the numerous adamantine hillocks may be compressed to something like a level with the surrounding dales and valleys.

After this labour of love has been ineffectually bestowed he proceeds to mark the creases. And what marvellous works of art they are when finished! Long crooked lines, some three or four inches in thickness, suggest that straightness and neatness have been sacrificed to the desire of using as much whitening as possible. When it is time for the match to begin, he marches solemnly to the wicket, with a bat over his shoulder, chaffing and joking with the players as he goes. Then, what numerous appeals are made to him! Catches at the wicket, l.b.w., runs out, all follow one another in quick succession. His decisions are always given with deliberation and evident doubt, and often are preceded by questions to the batsman, such as, 'Did yer 'it it, Jack?' or, 'Whereabouts did it touch ye?' Thus the length of a man's innings is often in the same ratio as his moral obliquity in concealing or perverting the truth. However, there is wonderfully little disputing, the good-natured batsmen being quite willing to abide by the fiat of the great authority; and if decisions are given rather more against than for them, they are induced to keep quiet by the knowledge that they have their own village judge at the other end, who, when the time comes, will do his best to equalise matters.

One of the most primitive rustic matches we ever saw was on a village common in Hampshire. We always look back to that match as one which produced more real fun than any we have ever taken part in. The village umpire there, a jolly good-natured old man, but absolutely ignorant of the laws of cricket, caused us the greatest merriment during the whole day. In addition to his official post as umpire, he was the village caterer at all public entertainments, and consequently supplied luncheon at all the matches. It was evident his thoughts in the field were divided between the responsibilities of his two duties—at least we inferred so by his occasionally allowing the bowler to bowl as much as ten or more balls in an over, and giving as his reason, 'If Mr. —— doant have a bit o' exercise, he woant relish my steak pie. O'im vaamous for steak pies, yer know, sir,' he added by way of apology for introducing the subject. This worthy old umpire gave certainly the most astonishing decision we ever saw. A man was batting at one end who was evidently one of the swells of his side. Owing to the roughness and slope of the ground, the slow bowling that he had to play was going about

'You must go, Jack.'

in all directions. Now a ball, pitching nearly a wide to leg, would twist in and pass the wicket on the off side, and then one pitched wide on the off would hit or pass the legs of the batsman, who, after many wild and futile attempts to strike this, to him, peculiar style of bowling, determined, as a last resource, to treat it with supreme contempt. He therefore, whenever the ball pitched wide, got in front of his stumps, turned round, and presented the back portion of his person to the bowler. The umpire watched these proceedings with a somewhat perplexed smile on his broad good-humoured face, but said nothing. Shortly, a ball that pitched a couple of feet on the leg side, twisted in, and struck the batsman on the seat of his trousers. This caused some laughter amongst the lookers-on, and when the mirth had subsided the umpire walked slowly a few yards down the pitch and addressed the batsman thus : ' Why, Jack, that ain't cricket. O'im a pretty favourable umpire as a rule, you know, Jack : but when a man stops the ball with *that*, he must be out. You must go, Jack.' Nothing would induce the injured batsman to remain ; we implored him to stay, but no ; he had been given out and was going out ; and for the rest of the day he enjoyed the importance of being an injured man—an importance enhanced by the opinions of his admirers that, had he not suffered an injustice, the village scorers would have had on that occasion anything but a holiday.

The well-known crack player who now and then plays in village cricket matches usually enjoys perfect immunity from the vagaries of the village umpire ; in fact, he runs only a very slight chance of ever being out at all, unless he is palpably caught or his stumps knocked down. The old style of umpire that we have attempted to describe is immensely delighted at the prospect of seeing what he calls ' real cricket,' and whether the ' swell ' is on his side or against it, he fully makes up his mind that it will be no fault of his if spectators are not treated to an exhibition of the real article. The bowlers may be hoarse with appealing, but the umpire remains obdurate, and it is with real sorrow he at last sees the great man go.

We remember on one occasion coming across a strange umpire in Scotland. It was in a country (very country) match. The writer was batting, and his co-partner at the other end was a well-known sporting baronet. The latter was the continual cause of appeals both from the bowler and wicket-keeper for l.b.w.'s and catches at the wicket. All were answered in the batsman's favour, much to the disgust of the fielders. Thinking that the latter were really being treated rather badly, the writer ventured humbly to ask the umpire whether the last appeal (an enormous thigh right in front of all three stumps to a straight one) had not been a very near thing. 'Lor bless you, sir,' was the reply, 'I have been his valet for fifteen years, and I dussn't give him out ; he gets awful wild at times.'

A little knowledge is a dangerous thing to umpires as well as everyone else. A ball in a country match hit the batsman's leg, skied up in the air, and was caught by point. 'How's that for leg before wicket?' shouted the bowler. 'How's that for a catch?' said point. The bewildered umpire had not an idea what it was, but no doubt he thought such loud appeals meant something, and so said, 'Out.' 'What for?' said the batsman ; 'it didn't pitch anything like straight, wouldn't have hit the wicket, and what's more, never touched it.' 'Out,' said the nonplussed umpire; 'it hit *you below the wrist.*' This story, although told of an ignorant umpire, illustrates a principle which the best umpires should have in mind, but which many of them seem never to have learnt, or else to have forgotten, and that is, never give your reasons for a decision. This is a golden rule for all umpires. An umpire is engaged to say 'Out' or 'Not out' when appealed to, and not to state the reasons which have induced his verdict. When a man adds to his decision, 'It didn't pitch straight,' 'Your toe was up in the air,' 'Your bat was over the crease but not on the ground,' it has a tendency to create useless discussion and waste of time. Besides, an umpire may occasionally be right in his verdict, but may be brought to grief by explaining his reasons. For instance, suppose an appeal for a l.b.w., and the umpire says 'Not out.' The wicket-keeper and the bowler may know that the point for decision is whether the ball pitched straight or not ; the umpire adds, for example, 'The ball would have gone over the wicket.' Well, this may be so, but both the wicket-keeper and the bowler think not ; if the verdict had been a decided ' Not out,' both of these two would have been satisfied—a doubtful point had been given against them, no one was to blame for it, better luck next time, &c. &c. But since the umpire has been guilty of stating reasons, which, according to them, are not satisfactory, he has branded himself with a bad decision in the eyes of the fielding side.

Some umpires—in fact, the majority of them—have a habit of putting their hand and arm in the air and pointing to the skies when they give a man out. A verdict propitious to the batsman is given by a solemn ' Not out,' but one adverse by an annoying silence and a most inappropriate wave of the arm in the air. It would be far more to the purpose if the finger were pointed downwards instead of upwards, as the batsman's hopes are shattered. We never like to leave the wickets till the umpire's voice is heard. The arm may go in the air involuntarily, or the umpire be surprised into a spasmodic upward arm-jerk ; but a good honest ' Out ' can never be doubted.

With regard to the qualifications that a man should possess before he can hope to perform satisfactorily to himself and others the duties of an umpire, the first essential is that he must have been at one time a good cricketer. By good we do not mean first-class, or that he must have had his name amongst the list of the best players of his time ; but he must have been fairly proficient in the game, and must have had a large practical experience. The qualifications of a good judge are, no doubt, of a different nature from those for a good advocate, but before a man can sit on the Bench he must have passed through the wear and tear of the bar, and had, when there, varied experiences in the practice of law. So with an umpire ; it does not absolutely follow that a first-rate player will make a good umpire, but it does follow that a man who has had great practical experience in the game will be better qualified to decide the nice points that arise than one who has only made cricket a theoretical study. Assuming that a man has sufficient knowledge of the game to stand as umpire, he must possess quick and keen sight, a good sense of hearing, powers of rapid decision, and last, but not least, he must be very fond of cricket. The necessity of the first two of these qualifications for good umpiring is apparent. For most decisions a good power of sight only is required, but in appeals for catches at the wicket an umpire has both to be guided by his eyes and his ears. Many cases occur where the ball and the bat pass each other with such rapidity that it is impossible for an umpire to be certain from his eyes alone that they have touched one another, and he must then, to a great extent, be guided by what he has heard. Both sight and sound must help him to come to his conclusion, and he must give no decision if it is inconsistent with the effect of either of these senses on his mind.

No umpire should ever be chosen to stand in first-class matches unless he possesses the perfect use of these two senses. More than once in important matches we have seen an umpire with his ears stuffed full of cotton-wool. This, no doubt, was an excellent preventive against catching cold in the head, but it was a monstrous thing to see the result of a match of some interest depending upon the amount of sound that could penetrate through two or three layers of wadding.

An umpire should possess powers of quick decision, because every time his opinion is asked he has to give it at once, and with firmness. If he shows any signs of doubt or hesitation, he destroys the confidence which it should be his constant endeavour to see reposed in him and his judgment.

An umpire has to concentrate every particle of his attention on the game, every minute of the five or six hours he is in the field has to be devoted to studiously watching every ball that is bowled and every incident in the play. Once let his attention be distracted, or his interest lessened in what is going on around him, and he will make a mistake. The powers of concentration necessary in an umpire are so great, and are required for such a lengthy period, that it is impossible to find them in any man unless he is imbued with a thorough love of cricket. It is this devotion to the game which enables our umpires to fix their attention on it for such long weary hours, in all conditions of weather, and in our most important matches, with such a heavy weight of responsibility upon their shoulders. Firm, free, and unbiassed in their judgment, our English umpires have the satisfaction of knowing that unbounded confidence is placed in them by the players and the public, and that never in the history of modern cricket has there been the faintest whisper of suspicion against their integrity or fair fame.

And now let us discuss the actual duties of an umpire connected with the game. The two umpires before the beginning of the match should be present when the ground is chosen and measured. By rights, it is the duty of the umpires actually to choose the pitch ; but this is seldom done, as so much care and attention is spent on all grounds at the present day by the ground-men, that the wicket intended to be used has been generally prepared with diligence for two or three days previous to the match. They should, however, be present, and see that the ground is the proper measurement, and that the stumps are so fixed in the ground as to satisfy the sixth rule of the game—namely, ' Each wicket shall be eight inches in width, and consist of three stumps. . . . The stumps shall be of equal and sufficient size to prevent the ball from passing through, twenty-seven inches out of the ground. The bails shall be each four inches in length, and when in position on the top of the stumps, shall not project more than half an inch above them. Umpires should be very careful to see that these provisions are complied with both with regard to the width of the wicket and the ball passing between the stumps.' We have often seen stumps in a first-class match so wide apart that the ball would pass between them without dislodging the bails; over and over again have we taken hold of the ball and passed it between them to show the umpire that the stumps were too far apart ; but we have never seen a bowled ball pass between the stumps without removing the bails in a first-class match, though this often happens in smaller matches. Umpires should themselves measure the ground between the wickets ; groundsmen, as a rule, do this, but they occasionally do it in a careless and slovenly fashion, which may result in the distance being a foot too short or too long. The slightest difference in the usual distance of twenty-two yards from wicket to wicket makes a great difference to the bowler, and so it should invariably be checked by the umpires themselves using the chain.

Before the match begins, the umpires should settle what the boundaries are to be. This, of course, will only apply to those places where the boundaries have not been finally settled, as at Lord's and the Oval and other well-known grounds. The usual practice, however, is for the visiting team to accept the boundaries that are customary on the ground; but should there be any dispute on this subject, it must be settled by the umpires. Having arranged all preliminaries connected with the pitch and the boundaries, the umpires should go to the wickets punctually to the very minute agreed upon for beginning play. A vast amount of time is on many grounds lost owing to unpunctuality ; and if the umpires appear on the ground at the appointed time, irrespective of whether the players are ready or not, it has a good effect. The umpire at the bowler's end, when the bowling is over the wicket, should stand as near as he can to the wicket without inconveniencing the bowler in his action ; he should stand sideways fronting the bowler, but with his head looking over his right shoulder down the pitch. The object of this attitude is that as small a surface of his body as possible should be permitted to be in the line of sight of the batsman and the ball. There are some umpires who stand as much as five or six yards from the wicket, no doubt under the impression that so long as they are in a straight line with the two wickets they can see everything; but this is a mistake, as it is evident that the nearer the umpire stands to the wicket the better he can see and judge the points that arise for his decision. Before umpires were required to wear the long white coats which now render them so conspicuous, their dark ones often greatly interfered with the batsman's view of the ball, but now this inconvenience has been done away with, and the batsman can never rightly complain of his sight being obscured by the umpire.

The umpire should stand perfectly still at the moment the ball is delivered; he must not even move his head, as any moving object directly behind the ball, and especially as near to it as the umpire is standing, may distract the batsman's sight from the ball. He must watch the bowler's hindmost foot to see if it touch or cross the bowling crease, in which case it is a ' no ball,' and must almost at the same time watch the bowler's hand and arm to guard against any infringement of the rule against throwing.

The rule with regard to 'no balls' is, 'The bowler shall deliver the ball with one foot on the ground behind the bowling crease, and within the return crease, otherwise the umpire shall call no ball.' The umpire must, therefore, call 'no ball' if the hindmost foot of the bowler is, at the moment of delivery, even touching the bowling or return creases. This rule makes it important that the bowling crease should be neatly and correctly marked. The rule with regard to the bowling crease says that it 'shall be in a line with the stumps, 6 ft. 8 in. in length, &c.,' but says nothing about the width of it. We must, therefore, infer from the words 'in a line' that the bowling crease should not be of greater width than the thickness of the stumps. If it is drawn of this thickness only, it is a very narrow line, but is correct according to a common-sense interpretation of the rules 7 and 11 ; for supposing, as is often the case, the crease is thicker than the width of the stumps, it would then be a manifest injustice to 'no ball' a bowler because his hindmost foot has just touched the edge of it. These two rules evidently mean that the hindmost foot shall be behind the line of the wicket when the ball is delivered. If the crease is too thick, the foot may just touch it and yet not transgress the spirit of the two rules taken together.

With regard to the necessity, laid down in rule 11, for the hindmost foot to be on the ground. . . . when the ball is delivered, we think umpires may take it as settled that it is quite an impossibility for a bowler to deliver a ball with this foot off the ground. Let anyone try to bowl with only the left foot on the ground, and he will at once see the practical impossibility of doing so. A 'no ball' should be called quickly and distinctly directly the ball has been delivered; an umpire must not shout 'No ball' as soon as he sees the foot touch or overlap the crease, but must wait till the ball is actually bowled; otherwise he may land himself in a difficulty should the bowler stop and not deliver the ball. We remember an umpire, who is generally supposed to be about the best in England, making this mistake in 1886; he called a 'no ball' so very prematurely that it gave the bowler time to stop before the ball left his hand.

A wide ball is one that, in the opinion of the umpire, is not within reach of the striker. It therefore does not make the slightest difference where it pitches so long as, in the umpire's opinion, it has *never been* within the batsman's reach. Some people entertain the idea that if a ball has pitched fairly straight but afterwards twisted beyond the batsman's reach, it should not be called wide; but this is wrong, as the rule says positively that 'if it is not within reach of the striker, the umpire shall call "wide ball."' It is often a very nice point as to what is or is not within reach of the striker, and umpires' opinions vary on this head. We think the true reading of the rule is that, on the off side, the batsman's reach should not be limited to what he can only reach when standing still in his original position, but should be extended to what he can conveniently and comfortably reach with either leg across his wicket, say for 'cutting' or 'off driving.' On the leg side we think a ball should be called 'wide' if the batsman in the ordinary swing of the arms and bat for a leg hit could not reach it.[1] It thus follows,

[1] A batsman's reach is further on the off than the leg side, because he has his legs to put across the wicket to help him on the former side.

that a ball may be a 'wide' on the leg side which would not be one if at an equal distance from the batsman on the off side. If the ball passes so high over the batsman as to be out of his reach, it is a 'wide.' This very rarely occurs, but umpires should remember that if the batsman can touch this ball by holding the bat in the air, it is not a 'wide.' It does not follow that it is a 'wide' because the ball goes over the head of the batsman without being played at—most batsmen refuse to strike at such a ball because of the attendant risk—but it must be so high that the batsman cannot reach it when holding the bat in the usual manner.

When the bowler is bowling round the wicket the umpire should stand exactly in the same place as he does for 'over the wicket' bowling, but should of course front the bowler's side of the wicket. He should be watchful to see that the bowler keeps within the limit of the return crease ; if he touches this with his hindmost foot, it is a 'no ball' and should be instantly 'called.' Round-the-wicket bowlers often have a tendency to bowl as far as possible round the wicket, and as this is done with the object of making their bowling more difficult, umpires should be careful to keep them within the prescribed limits. There is rather a slackness in many umpires about calling 'no ball' because the return crease is touched ; but they ought to be quite as particular in this respect as in the case of the bowling crease—in fact, even more so, as a ball delivered an extra inch from the line between wicket and wicket makes more difference to the batsman than one delivered an inch nearer than usual.

The principal duties of the umpire at the bowler's end are those we have discussed—viz. calling 'wides' and 'no balls,' answering decisions for leg before wicket and catches at the wicket—and there are some few other points he may occasionally be called upon to decide. Before mentioning these, let us see what the laws say with regard to the several duties of the two umpires. Law 47 says, 'The umpire at the bowler's wicket shall be appealed to before the other umpire in all cases except in those of stumping, hit wicket, run out at the striker's wicket, or arising out of law 42 (the law relating to any part of the wicket-keeper's person being in front of the wicket, or to his taking the ball before it reaches the wicket); but in any case in which an umpire is unable to give a decision, he shall appeal to the other umpire, whose decision shall be final.' It will thus be seen that the umpire at the bowler's end must be appealed to first in all but the excepted cases ; he therefore has to decide all questions relating to catches ; but if he is uncertain, or from some cause has been prevented from seeing the circumstances of the catch, he may appeal to the other umpire, whose decision shall be final. It is sometimes a very difficult thing for an umpire to be certain whether or not the fielder's hands have got under the ball before it has touched the ground ; if he is at all doubtful, he should at once appeal to the other umpire, whose position may probably have enabled him to get a better view of the 'catch.' A difficulty occasionally arises in connection with what is commonly called a 'bump' ball. A bump ball is one which the batsman, playing hard on to the ground and close to the bat, causes to bound in the air. Should it be caught by a fielder, a question often arises whether it touched the ground after the bat or not. Sometimes these decisions are hard to arrive at with certainty, and especially so if the ground is dry and dusty and the batsman in striking stirs up a cloud of dust, as the actual contact between the bat and the ball is then partially, if not altogether, obscured from the umpire's view. Perhaps the most historical decision on this point is one that was given in the University match of 1881. C. F. H. Leslie, the well-known old Rugbeian, had just begun his innings ; A. F. J. Ford was bowling. Leslie made a half-hit at a well-pitched-up ball, and raised a cloud of dust around him ; the ball came straight back to the bowler, who caught it, and Leslie instantly left his wicket for the pavilion, evidently under the impression that he was fairly out. Before he had reached the entrance of the pavilion circumstances arose which caused the other batsman then at the wickets to appeal to the bowler's umpire for a decision as to whether the catch had been made off a 'bump' ball or not. This umpire, not being able to give a decision, appealed to the other one, who, after some discussion with his colleague, decided in the affirmative, and consequently Leslie resumed his innings.

When an umpire has to decide the question of a 'bump' ball or not, he must be guided by its length, its flight from the bat, and the way in which the latter has been used; the state of the ground sometimes must be considered, as it is unlikely, when the turf is in a soft, spongy state, that a ball will bounce high or far from it.

As will be seen by the latter part of law 47 (just quoted), the bowler's umpire may occasionally be appealed to on matters which are primarily in the discretion of his colleague. If the latter cannot decide, for instance, a question of stumping, which, by the law, must first be referred to him, he may appeal to the bowler's umpire. This power of appealing in cases of stumping is rarely used—in fact, we have never seen or heard of a single case of its exercise, though we once saw a case arise in which an appeal might very rightly have been made. In the University match of 1878, A. H. Evans was batting, he ran out to a slow, hit at it with all his might, missed it, and let the bat slip out of his hands. The ball was taken, and the wicket put down by the Cambridge wicket-keeper, Alfred Lyttelton; but the umpire had seen the bat flying straight at his head, and not wishing to risk a broken crown by sticking to his post, had fallen down with his head averted from the wicket, and was consequently unable to give a decision on a case which he had not seen. Evans was some three or four feet out of his ground when the bails were knocked off, but as no decision was given against him he of course remained at the wickets. This is exactly the case which this part of rule 47 is framed to meet; the other umpire would have been quite able to have given a decision on a plain case like this, and no doubt would have done so had there been an appeal made by him.

Under law 43 many points arise for the decision of the

bowler's umpire, two of which merit discussion here. This law says, '*The umpires are the sole judges of fair and unfair play*, of the fitness of the ground, the weather, and the light for play; all disputes shall be determined by them, and if they disagree the actual state of things shall continue.' But law 46 says, 'They (the umpires) shall not order a batsman out unless appealed to by the other side.' So that no umpire can really decide anything, except wides, no balls, and boundary hits, unless an appeal is made to him. As will be seen from law 43, appeals may be made on the fairness or otherwise of the play. These appeals happily are seldom made, but circumstances may arise in which it is the duty of the umpire to give his opinion under this rule. For instance, should the bowler so cut up the pitch with his feet as to place the batsman at a disadvantage when opposed to the bowling from the other end, it would be the duty of the umpire, if appealed to, to say that such tearing or cutting up was unfair, whether done accidentally or not. When the Hon. Ivo Bligh's team was in Australia in 1882–3, an appeal was made to the umpire by one of this team as to whether the way in which Spofforth was cutting up the wicket was fair or unfair. There was no doubt the wicket was being seriously damaged; the appealing batsman of course made no imputation of intentional unfairness against Spofforth, but only asked for a decision whether such damage was fair to the batting side. The umpire asked to see the soles of Spofforth's shoes; these were held up for public view, and as they only had about one spike each, it was decided that there was nothing unfair. It, is, however, a well-known fact that when ground is cut up, it is done by the force with which the boot is brought on to the ground; the edge of the sole is often answerable for the damage, and the number of spikes that are worn is quite beside the question.

As we have before noted, the umpire at the striker's end has to decide some few points ; his duties, however, are not nearly so onerous as those of his colleague at the other end.

They are decisions on stumping, hitting wicket, running out, and matters arising under law 42. This umpire should stand quite square with the wicket, so near as to enable him to see accurately all that happens without placing himself in any risk from a hard square hit. He should take care that the popping crease is clearly visible to him : if it has got worn out and difficult to see, a pinch of sawdust placed at the end of it will give him its correct line. It is always best, however, when either of the creases has become indistinct to send for the whitening and re-mark it. Stumping rarely gives much difficulty to the umpire ; his position is such that he ought always to be able to see whether the bails are off before the bat or foot are within the line. If the toe of the batsman is on the crease and *no part of his foot within it*, of course the decision must be against the batsman. If the batsman relies on his bat being in his ground when the bails are off, the umpire should recollect that the bat must be *in his hand* according to law 19. We recollect once seeing in a county match a batsman after a tremendous futile swipe fall prostrate outside his ground with the force of the unsuccessful stroke ; he was lying some two feet out of his ground, and his bat was within the crease with the handle resting on his shoulder when the wicket was put down. The umpire wrongly gave him ' not out,' no doubt thinking he was justified in doing so as the bat was connected with a portion of the batsman's body. The bat must, however, be in his hand to prevent a decision against him, unless ' some part of his person be grounded within the line of the popping crease.'

It is generally easy for an umpire to see when a batsman hits his wickets. The ball is usually played by the bat, but the batsman coming further back than usual, either from a mistake in his judgment as to the pitch or from originally standing too near, strikes the wicket. An umpire, however, must keep a sharp look on the wicket-keeper's feet and hands, and see that the fall of the bails is not due to any of these coming in contact with the wicket. It is possible for a wicket-keeper

to dislodge the bails with the tip of his gloves or the point of
his boot, and yet be unconscious that he has done so. An
umpire must also keep his eyes open to guard against any
chance of this being intentionally done. Fortunately there
is now no 'hanky-panky' play in our first-class cricket; but
there have undoubtedly been cases where a smart wicket-
keeper has been unable to resist the temptation of removing
the bail with foot or glove when in the act of taking the ball.
If any part of the batsman's person hits the wicket ' in playing

Stumped.

at the ball,' it is sufficient to justify a decision against him. If
his hat blow off and knock the bails off when he is in the act
of playing, he is out ; several instances are on record of this
unfortunate method of dismissal. In the season of 1886 there
was an instance recorded of a man knocking one of his bails
off with a piece of the string that had been wrapped round
the blade of his bat ; he was, of course, given out. A difficulty
sometimes arises as to whether the bail was knocked off in the
actual stroke at the ball, or whether it was in the action of the
bat preliminary or subsequent to the stroke.

The duties of umpires are so various, and the decisions they are called upon to give are so numerous, that it is an impossibility to discuss them all. Every umpire should remember that when an unforeseen incident occurs in the game he must use his common sense for its solution, and then he will not go far wrong.

CHAPTER VI.

FIELDING.[1]

(BY THE HON. R. H. LYTTELTON.)

'Saving the four.'

CERTAIN natural qualifications are indispensable to enable any cricketer to become a great fieldsman. The highest reputation that can be attained by any painstaking cricketer who is not endowed with these qualifications is that of being a good

[1] We are largely indebted to an article on this subject by the Hon. and Rev. E. Lyttelton, which appeared in *Lillywhite's Annual* for 1881.

safe man. When you hear this epithet, you may take it for granted that reference is made to a man who may cover himself with glory if he has to field a ball within a certain more or less limited space from the spot where he has taken his position, who is generally in the habit of holding a feasible catch, and who will seldom disgrace himself.

In other words, a safe field is generally a slow one, is lacking in electricity and rapidity of movement, and, as batsmen get to know this, the short run is attempted with impunity. Slow fields are earnestly advised to practise throwing; for their defects are less apparent when fielding a long distance from the wicket, and the non-observant spectator does not notice that the ground covered at a distance from the wicket by a slow field is very small compared to that commanded by some space-covering field like Gunn, Maurice Read, and Stoddart.

Again, let safe and slow fields, the roadsters among the thoroughbreds, try and get a respectable knowledge of the game ; for if they obtain this they can in a great measure discount their deficiencies. A good judge of the game gets to know by instinct where a batsman is likely to hit certain balls, and so does the observant fieldsman. He will consequently shift a few yards or so from his original position to the spot towards which his instinct tells him the ball is likely to be hit ; and he will thereby earn the enviable reputation of being a man who is frequently in the right place. It used to be said of the immortal French tennis player, Barre, that he himself did not run after the ball, but the ball ran after him ; his genius told him where his opponent was going to hit the ball, and he planted himself accordingly. In like manner will a fieldsman so plant himself ; and it is important to a slow field to try and acquire this instinct, for if the fieldsman is not on a certain spot of ground before the hit is made, his slowness will prevent his getting there afterwards, especially if the hit is hard and the ground fast.

Directions may now be given on the knotty points, 'Where ought I to stand ?' 'When ought I to back up ?' 'Which end ought I to throw to ?' and a few others ; for this reason,

that many a good fieldsman might be better if he knew where
to place himself and precisely what to do.

First, then, it may be safely asserted that a concentrated
attention on every ball is a *sine quâ non* of even decent fielding. Men often think that if they are simply looking at the
batsman they are doing all that is required. But this is not so.
There is a difference of opinion as to whether the eyes should
be fixed on the batsman, or should follow the ball as it leaves
the bowler's arm ; this is a matter of dispute, our own opinion
being in favour of the former plan. But each man should stand
as if the next ball were sure to come to him, not only as if it

Backing up.

might come to him. One can see a whole eleven doing it now
and then when there are (say) six runs wanted to tie and seven
to win. They are all adopting for a few minutes the position
they ought to adopt always—in short, the position in which great
fieldsmen like Messrs. Royle and G. B. Studd are found invariably. We will first take a few general points, and then the
separate places in the field.

BACKING UP.

This is a matter which demands the earnest consideration
of all who field within thirty yards of the wicket. There
ought always to be two men backing up ; never more.

Nine times out of ten they will be superfluous, but the tenth time they will save a 'four overthrow,' and all the chagrin, demoralisation, and tearing of hair connected with that disaster. No fieldsman can throw his best unless he is confident about the backing up, and the man who ought to be abused when an overthrow occurs is not the fieldsman who throws the ball, but the men who should be backing up and are not. Again— and let young fields take heed to this—there must be ten yards between the two men backing up, and also between the one nearest the wicket and the wicket. This gives them room to stop the wildest throw, but does not give the batsmen time to run if the ball passes the wicket. If the fields stand close together, two are as bad as none, and get in each other's way. Rules for the different fields we give in dealing with them separately.

THROWING.

This is, of course, a gift of nature, not a result of art. Few men can throw far, but everyone can throw quickly, and that is what prevents batsmen from running. There is a moment which decides a batsman whether he can manage to secure another run or not. It is just when a fieldsman, having run some way after the ball, and having his back turned to the wicket, is stooping to pick up preparatory to throwing in. Now any good judge of running, after seeing a man go through this process once, knows exactly how long it will take. Every nerve should be strained to make it as brief as possible: a little extra sign of life and rapid movement will make the batsman hesitate a moment, and the run is lost. The engraving on p. 251 shows what in our opinion is the proper way to pick up a ball going away. The field is not trying to catch the ball up as far as his feet are concerned. He is stretching his hand forward to pick it up, and when he has got it into his hand he will throw it rather over his left shoulder to the wicket. Again, supposing a run is being snatched. The field should then remember that to throw in slowly is of no possible use. The throw may be, in other respects, as perfect and as straight as Robin Hood's arrow, but the batsman will be safe over the crease, and such a throw becomes an example of showy drawing-room cricket, which is sure to be applauded by the spectators, as well as the reporters, but is useless to the side. If every field picked up and threw in as quickly as his knee joints and the state of his arm allowed him, a very considerable percentage of the runs usually scored would be saved. It is commonly asserted by many of those supporters of the game who, having laid down their arms, devote themselves for the rest of their lives to laying down the law, that nobody ought ever to throw down the wicket. This is certainly wrong. We do not mean that everybody ought always to throw at the wicket, but only that some fields, under certain circumstances, ought to do so. These circumstances occur when it is the only chance of running a man out. The ball should be hurled violently at the bails, and if an overthrow occurs, the wise captain will abuse those who ought to be backing up, and not the thrower. But to throw hard at the wicket when there is no chance of running a man out is strongly to be condemned ; it may produce an overthrow, and it is certain to inflict useless concussion on the hands of bowlers and wicket-keepers. No fieldsman is so apt to disregard this advice as the bowler ; at least, it is a fact that many

'Overtaking and picking up.'

bowlers are particularly fond of returning the ball hard to the wicket after they have fielded it. It does not succeed in running a man out once in a thousand times, it often enables a run to be got by an overthrow, and it uselessly troubles the wicket-keeper. A batsman is next door to an idiot who is got out by such means, and we shrewdly suspect that it is often done to secure the applause of an unthinking mob.

DEEP FIELD, OR COUNTRY CATCHING.

This is an art which the above-mentioned critics lament as having died out. It may be suspected that they missed as many catches as the present generation, but still the present generation miss more than they ought. All fine country fields catch the ball close to the body, and rightly so, because the eye is more in a line with the ball, and with the hands in the position shown in fig. 1, not in the way shown in fig. 2. If a young player begins in the wrong way, he will miss one or two and get nervous. It is worth remembering that folios of rules will never make a nervous field keep hold of a country catch. Cold hands are a frequent cause of failure, but loss of confidence and the disorganisation of the nervous system is the commonest reason, and a constant prayer of many a cricketer is to be spared a high catch.

FIG. 1.—The right way to catch.

When a field begins to be uncertain, he should keep wicket to fast bowling for a quarter of an hour a day, and field somewhere close in for a week or so. The wicket-keeping will practise his eye, and the fielding close in will spare his nerves during this educational process. Practice is, of course, useful for long catches, but only up to a certain point. A player may alter from a bad style of catching to a good one by practice, but a very safe catch in practice is frequently a bad performer in a match, simply on account of nervousness. For sharp catches, wicket-keeping is, perhaps, the only thing that will help. The peculiar faculty they demand is, like the spin in bowling, something that cannot be taught, the possession of which is a guarantee of genius.

FIG. 2.—The wrong way to catch.

And now for those who occupy the separate places, first among whom we are surely right in dealing with the

WICKET-KEEPER.

A little thought makes it clear that there are given at least three chances of catching to one of stumping a man out. And so the wicket-keeper must first feel the ball safe and warm in his hands before he attempts to put the wicket down. This advice sounds obvious, but it is so often disregarded that it must be insisted on. The first rule accordingly is, that the

ball must not be snatched at, but received. This snapping is
a very common fault with amateurs, and the great George
Pinder's remark, 'You amateurs snap 'em a bit,' hits on a weak
spot in amateur wicket-keeping. Another reason for not
snapping is one that will certainly strike home, and that is,
that the non-snapper is not nearly so likely to hurt his hands,
as one form of snapping consists in jerking the hands quickly

Wicket-keeper—Sherwin in position.

forward to meet the ball, and thereby resisting a blow instead
of waiting for it. Another danger of snapping is, that you
run the risk of moving your hands in such a way that, instead
of the ball striking the palms of the hand where it does not
hurt, it strikes you on the top of the thumb or fingers, causing
an agony that only wicket-keepers can rightly appreciate.
Hardly any two wicket-keepers stand alike, so take any position
that is natural to you, as was recommended in the chapter on
Batting, only bearing one fact in mind, which is, to avoid

standing so far away as not to be able comfortably to put down the wicket without moving the legs. The postures generally assumed are, it must be confessed, the reverse of graceful ; they are too well known to need description, but the two most common forms are shown in the figures given on pp. 254 and 256. In one figure we recognise the massive proportions of the famous Sherwin. Now comes a most important rule, and that is, *never to move the feet till the ball is hit by the batsman or has passed your hands or is in your hands.* Again, you may not be able to take many leg-balls, but every time you do put the wicket down, not regarding the fact that the batsman may not be out of his ground. If you wait to look, he certainly will not wait to get back, warned as he is by the sound of the ball impinging on the gloves that there is no time for loitering about. We do not say that an appeal ought to be made to the umpire every time that the wicket is put down; that ought only to be done when you think that the batsman was out of his ground; unless this is the case it is an unfair and unsportsmanlike proceeding.

We have before protested against pandering to the vicious tastes of the gallery, and we must protest against it again, and caution wicket-keepers in the following particular. It is supremely difficult to take leg-balls, and the populace applaud accordingly when one is taken. Now we have no objection to a wicket-keeper taking as many leg-balls as possible, but on one condition, and that is, that he does not lay himself out to take leg-balls at the expense of the off balls. It is easy to do this by a different position and a concentration of thought on the leg-balls. The vast majority of catches are given on the off side, and catches, as has been before remarked, out-number stumping chances in the proportion of 3 to 1. We would infinitely sooner have a wicket-keeper on our side who was safe on the off side and did not take one leg-ball in a hundred, limiting leg-balls to those outside the legs of the batsman. Let your first thoughts be concentrated mainly on straight and off-side balls, and pay no regard to the applause of any save those whose knowledge of the game makes their approbation valuable.

A player with no aptitude for wicket-keeping on first going to that position will undergo moments of unspeakable agony. Spectators do not thoroughly realise the position of the wicket-

Wicket-keeper—Another position.

keeper, indeed nobody can who has not attempted the art. In the first place, we will suppose a very fast bowler ; in the second, a fast and possibly a rather bumpy wicket ; in the third place, a batsman with perhaps the bulk of W. G. Grace or Roger Iddison, wielding a bat of the orthodox proportions ; and in the fourth place, three stumps with two bails placed on the top. The body of the batsman in many cases completely obstructs the view the wicket-keeper ought to have of the ball. Even if he can get a good sight of the ball there is that abominable bat being fiddled about, baulking the eyesight in the most tantalising manner, and there are some batsmen who have a provoking habit of waving their bats directly the bowler begins his run, and continuing their antics till the ball is right up to them ; while others seem to be built like windmills, and have a limb always at hand to throw out between the unhappy wicket-keeper and the rapidly-advancing ball. There are several seconds, therefore, when the wicket-keeper is only conjecturing what course the ball is taking, and is certain of but two things —one, that the ball is hard ; the other, that it is advancing in the direction of himself with terrific rapidity. Then, even if you see the ball plainly, it may happen to be, and frequently is, straight, and a straight fast ball raises unutterable emotions in the wicket-keeper's breast ; for who knows what devilish tricks the ball, to say nothing of the bails, will play after the wicket is struck, and the course of the missile diverted, not stopped ? One reads how a bail has been sent a distance of thirty or forty yards by a fast ball, and that bail may take the wicket-keeper in the eye *in transitu.* The writer was once struck by the ball on the eye and by the bail on the mouth at very nearly the same second. The wicket-keeper is grimly told that he must not flinch, and that he never can be really good if he does not keep his legs still. True, most true ; but, like other great people who do great things, he must resist every natural impulse and all his lower nature, and not till he has succeeded will he stand the least chance of reaching to a pinnacle of excellence. Having briefly pointed out these difficulties and dangers, let us beg the field to treat the wicket-keeper as tenderly as possible, to culti-vate a straight throw, either a catch or a long-hop, and not half-volleys or, worse still, short-hops, and never to throw hard when there is no necessity. If the throw is crooked, the wicket-keeper should not leave his position to stop it ; leave that to the men who are backing up. He may be called upon afterwards to put down the wicket, and he ought to be in a position for so doing. Bear in mind also this cardinal rule —namely, to stand behind the wicket to a throw and not in front.

LONG-LEG.

It may be stated first of all in regard to this place, that its importance is very considerably less in the cricket of the present day than it was in former times. The improvement of bowling in mere accuracy, owing to the fact that now compared with twenty years ago five medium pace and slow bowlers exist to one fast bowler, is the reason of this change ; and even when

Hit to square-leg.

a long-leg is used, it is very often because a sort of back-up is required for the wicket-keeper, and the long-leg is consequently placed very sharp, always remembering that there is no long-stop. The man chosen for this grand post ought to know from the way a batsman hits at a ball whether he should stand square or sharp. The old-fashioned long-leg hitting of George Parr is almost a thing of the past; so that long-leg should stand too square rather than too sharp, especially as the right hand will thus get most to do. If the batsman is a weak hitter, alter the position, moving not only nearer the wicket but sharper as well. For a weak hitter's most dangerous stroke will be a snick to leg, and it is rather galling to see a snick score many runs. But a strong square-leg hit is far more dangerous; therefore, leave ample space to cover the ground, and trust to your speed to save two runs. A good runner, after he plays a ball gently to long-leg, makes all haste over the first run, and, as he turns, assumes that there is time for the second if he sees that the long-leg is slackening in the least, or winding up for an ornamental throw, or in any other way wasting time. In such case jump towards the ball the moment you see the batsman turning round to slide it in your direction; run as if a mad bull were behind you, and picking up the ball with one hand (as it is moving slowly enough) hurl it at the wicket-keeper's head—unless he is some distance off, in which case throw so that it goes to the wicket-keeper a long-hop. Occasionally it is useful to throw to the bowler, assuming that he is behind the stumps and that mid-off is backing up, because the batsmen get frightened at this manœuvre, and feel that their second run entails too much of a risk, and this frequently prevents them trying it again. Bear in mind that the aim of good fielding is, not to run men out, but to prevent their trying to run. Remember also that a catch to long-leg has a tendency to curl towards your right hand, so do not rush too violently towards the left directly the ball is hit.

MID-OFF AND MID-ON

have somewhat similar duties to perform, and the latter in one way is the easiest place in the field, for there is less twist on the ball when hit there than is the case with any other hit. When the ground is hard, stand deeper than when it is soft, because on a hard ground a single is easier, a four harder, to save. Again, stand wider when the bowler is bowling your side of the wicket, as he is then responsible for part of the space between you. If the batsman is a timid runner, it is a good plan to tempt him to run by pretending to be slow, and the moment he calls 'run' dash in with unexpected vigour. This artifice, however, can be useful only once in an innings, and must not be attempted by any except quick and good fields. But if by well-ascertained and true report and your own observation you know that either or both of the batsmen are slow or timid runners, stand further back, unless there is any special reason to make you stand in for a catch, for by so doing you cover more ground and can save fourers or threes. Mid-off must back up behind the bowler when the ball is thrown in from long-leg, short-leg, mid-on and long-stop. Mid-on backs up the bowler when it is thrown from mid-off, cover-point, point, and third man. Modern tactics and modern slow bowling have invented an extra field in the shape of an extra mid-off, who stands between cover-point and mid-off, and his duties, when the fashion is to bowl mainly on the off side for catches, are most onerous. Mr. G. B. Studd's fielding here is one of the sights of cricket. The Australians in general, and Boyle in particular, have introduced a new position to bowlers of the Spofforth type—you may call it either an extra short-leg or an extra mid-on. If the wicket is soft and catchy this field stands sometimes only five or six yards from the bat, and makes numerous catches when batsmen are poking forward and the ball is inclined to hang. In short, it is on the on side that which 'silly point'—afterwards described—is on the off side. It will only be seen when bowlers of superlative excellence are bowling, men who can be relied upon to keep a good length, and whose bowling is too fast to allow the batsman to run out for a drive. If the bowler has not these qualities, but bowls a decent average of half-volleys on the leg-stump or a little outside, there will probably be a coroner's inquest required. But Boyle knows that neither Spofforth nor Palmer bowls such balls, and it cramps the batsman unpleasantly to see a field standing there on a tricky wicket. Extreme vigilance is required for this post, and the risk of injury is too great to permit it being made use of when the wicket is fast. It was practically never seen in England till the Australians introduced it in 1878.

COVER-POINT

shares with the three last-mentioned fields a great responsibility connected with throwing and running fast after the ball.
A very common set of strokes are those which send the ball on
either side of cover-point, mid-off, extra mid-off or mid-on, and
realise on a hard ground three runs. Now a really good field
very seldom allows three runs, because he makes the batsmen
suppose that the ball is somehow back at the wicket almost at the
same moment that he is seen picking it up from the ground.
Those who have tried this will testify how very often a sudden turn
and throw-in just checks the third run ; the batsmen feel that
they must watch such a field, and it is this very watching which
prevents them from ever pressing the running. This is a most
important matter and one generally neglected, but it is worth
insisting on, because anybody can act upon this piece of advice.
Anyone can run his fastest and throw his quickest, but the men
who field in these places seldom do their best, though the man
who does not is not a genuine cricketer, and is probably a selfish
animal. Such conscientious fielding as this gets very little recognition, though it saves about one in every ten runs. Spectators
do not observe ; the cricket reporters notice the features of
the game that are obvious to only ignorant spectators, and
they do not waste ink upon it ; but any really judicious captain
estimates it very highly. No doubt a flashy field is very useful at
cover-point ; he cramps all the runs on the off side, and covers
the defects of a third-rate mid-off ; but very often these are
just the men who shirk the burden, heat and hard work of the
day, as we may call these repeated excursions of fifty yards or
so under a strong sun. Cover-point should learn, if possible,
the under-hand throw, practised with such success by Mr. W.
Law. He has to back up behind mid-off when mid-on or the
deep-on fields are throwing in, and behind point when short-
leg and long-leg throw to the wicket-keeper.

POINT.

Success in this place depends almost entirely on natural gifts, and there are two distinctly different methods of first-class fielding in this place. One is the point, who seems nearly to have solved the problem of perpetual motion, and bounds about everywhere, rushing in at one ball and right in front of the wicket to the next, but whose first position is closer in than more stationary fields at the same place. The other variety of point stands a yard or two further from the wicket and is more stationary, and his specialty consists in being a grabber of every ball within his reach. The right way of standing is shown in the figure opposite. There are plenty of good fields at point who stand differently from this, but we are trying to teach those who are not good fields, and we think that this figure is a good position. The important point to observe is that you can move quicker when one foot is drawn a little behind the other, and Carpenter and other good fields used always to stand thus. Some critics would say that point ought to stoop more, and no doubt some good points do. Each must choose his own elevation as far as this goes, but we feel sure that a great many balls go over the point's head when he stoops very much, and that on the whole the figure shows the best stoop. The stationary and the restless both have their merits and both have their characteristics. The tall man with a long reach nearly always adopts the stationary position, and no hit is too hard for him to face. Of course he ought to stand ready to start quickly, but his business consists in covering as much ground as possible from very nearly one position, and he must have a good aptitude for getting his hand in the right place to stop the ball. It is worth noticing that Dr. E. M. Grace, a prominent example of the movable point, always fixes his eye on the batsman and seems to anticipate from his look the kind of stroke that is going to be made. Possibly, after long experience, a look of concern may be detected in the striker's face when a bumper is coming. Anyhow, such a field as Dr. Grace often finds himself in the right place, and gets a perfectly easy catch, where another point would have got none. This is a stroke of genius for which he receives no applause, as it looks so simple.

The position of point ought to be in a line with the wicket, and at a distance depending entirely on the pace of bowler,

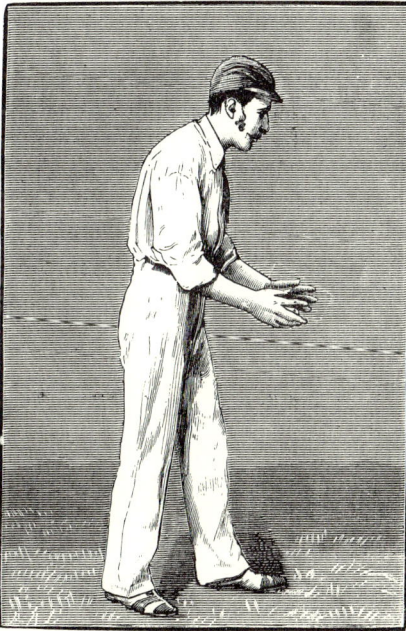

Point.

style of batsman, and condition of ground. The faster the bowler and the ground, the further off the wicket ought point to stand, but in no case ought he to be more than eight yards away. Some points make a great mistake in standing further than this, for a very common catch at point is when a bumping ball rises off the batsman's glove and pitches about four yards from the wicket in the direction of point—a certain catch if point is fielding in his right place, but impossible to get at if he stands too far from the wicket. There is no limit on certain grounds and to certain batsmen to the closeness to the wicket which an active point will stand. The ball has been taken literally almost off the bat. We think, on the whole, that the fieldsman who stands nearly in the same position till the ball is hit, who is quick in starting, and very sure and ready to face and stop a real 'hot-un,' is more valuable than the restless point who runs here and there, and rarely adopts the same position for two consecutive balls. There is, however, much to be said for both styles ; but we feel very sure that the restless point must first acquire a certain faculty of more or less correctly judging where the batsman is likely to hit the ball, or else he will be always rushing to the wrong place.

There is a combination of circumstances which induces modern captains to put their point right forward on the off side about eight yards from the wicket. The circumstances required include a batsman who has got a peculiar forward style, a bowler whose balls are inclined to hang or get up straight from the pitch, and lastly a catchy wicket where the balls are apt to bump and hang. It is a very useful place sometimes, but most dangerous to the field at other times. In the Australian and England match at the Oval in 1880, Morley was bowling, McDonnell was batting. The ball now and then bumped up, and the English captain acceded to W. G. Grace's wish and allowed him to go forward point, or, as it is familiarly called, 'silly' point. Now McDonnell is one of the hardest hitters in the world, and Morley used sometimes to bowl a ball a little over-tossed. A ball of a certain length *might* have been bowled that McDonnell *might* not have smothered at the pitch, and the requisite hang having taken place, W. G. Grace *might* have triumphed. But unfortunately, before this consummation took place, McDonnell got a ball admirably adapted to his extremely powerful off drive. The well-known musical sound of a bat hitting the ball plump was heard, then a second knock higher in its musical pitch and nearly as loud, the ball was seen about twenty yards high in the air, and McDonnell easily scored a run. What really happened was this : McDonnell made a grand hit all along the ground, and long before the burly form of W. G. Grace had unbent itself, the aforesaid ball had struck his toe, which offered a strictly passive, because involuntary resistance, with such violence that the ball ascended into the air like a rocket, and a run was the result. W. G. walked slowly, a wiser man, to his old position on a line with the wicket, and probably in his inmost thought silently adopted the opinion that the position of 'silly point' is only feasible when a batsman of a style directly opposite to that of McDonnell is at the wicket. But this forward point is very useful at times, and should be made use of when circumstances are favourable. The late Mr. R. A. Fitzgerald, in his well-known book 'Jerks in from Short-leg,' says that if there is no good field at point in an eleven, the captain should choose the fattest man, for nature makes it impossible for him to get out of the way of a hard hit. In other words, it sometimes strikes him in the most prominent part of his person and saves four runs. Perhaps Roger Iddison, of Yorkshire fame, can testify to the truth of this remark.

SHORT-SLIP

ought first of all to be as vigilant as if he were keeping wicket. If he is so, and knows where to stand, he will find it the easiest place in the field ; if he is not, it will be the hardest. Wicket-keepers ought always to be able to field short-slip, for it is a post that has all the pleasant moments of wicket-keeping with none of the knocks and bruises and other discomforts of that important place. Stoop as the ball is in the air, and hold the hands ready forward, as shown in figure on p. 266. This position is necessary because many more balls hiss low along the grass than rise into the air from a snick, and if they do rise, short-slip can rise too and be in time for them ; but if he has to stoop he will be too late. So for fast bowling stand finer than most short-slips do, and if the ground is very hard keep a long way off—eight yards is often not too long a distance. But the difficulty in this respect is much greater when the bowling is slow. A late cut adds materially to the speed of a slow ball, though it has scarcely any effect on a fast one. But if, instead

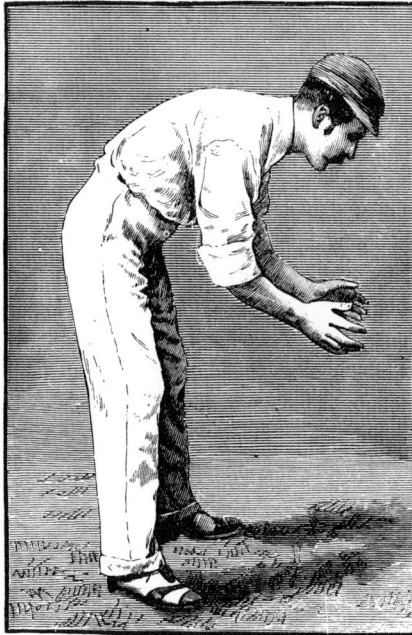

Short-slip.

of cutting, a batsman plays forward and snicks a slow ball, a gentle catch comes at a medium height and drops short. Short-slip must then regulate his position accordingly. When he sees the batsman lean forward he must advance one step ; when the batsman hangs back and the ball is on the off side he should hang back too and hold the hands low; for assuredly if anything comes it will be a hard low catch. He should study the slow bowler's action so as to know when his fast balls are coming, and drop back. He should also ponder on the pace of the ground, and never forget that *wet on the top of a hard ground makes the fastest surface of any* : in these circumstances, there-fore, he should stand finer and deeper. When the rain soaks in, the balls pop, and catches come slower and higher. Short-slip should back up when balls are thrown, not from short-nor from long-leg, but from mid-on and mid-off and cover-point, and should run across, when there is a run to third man, between the wicket-keeper and short-leg. This last is a tiring and often unremunerative process, but if done through a long innings is in the highest degree commendable. Short-slip must also run up to the wicket and take the place of the wicket-keeper when the latter has usurped the functions of an ordinary fieldsman and left his post to pick up and throw in the ball to the wicket.

THIRD MAN.

This is another most scientific post, and one in which a bad fieldsman is very much out of place. First, there is the twist. It is worth knowing respecting a twist from a bat, that if the ground is hard and the cut clean, the ball will not twist till it has lost some of its impetus. Consequently stand straight in the line of a hard cut on a smooth ground, as the ball, though it is *spinning* all the time, will not *curl* till it is some way past third man. But if the turf is soft the ball bites and curls on the second or third bound, seldom on the first unless the stroke is a very slow one. The same holds good with regard to long-leg. The batsman, if he were a genuine judge of a run, would always 'run' to third man when the spin is likely to act at once, since under those conditions the ball wants so much watching that third man cannot well return it in time. But many bats-men do not know these things.

With regard to the distance of third man from the wicket, it is important that he should judge it according as the batsmen are good runners or not. He should estimate this at once from their appearance and demeanour, standing well out if they are men of weight and dignity, and nearer in if they are active and inclined to steal runs. After they have run one run to him he should come a yard nearer in, feeling like a man who has had a personal insult offered him, and is burning to avenge it. Lastly, he has to consider the throw-in. *It is nearly always best to throw to the bowler's wicket* (assuming, of course, that he is ready behind the stumps and mid-on is backing up), for this plain reason: it is generally the non-striker who calls the run, and consequently starts the quickest, runs quickest, as he sees the danger before him, and gets home the quickest. Even if he does not call the run, he is backing up, and starts unshackled by having made a stroke. So leave him alone. The striker, on the contrary, has made a stroke (and one that throws him back a good deal), is not backing up, and does not see the danger. Also, if he runs by the shortest way to the other wicket, he will very likely be cut over. Circumstances, in short, are against him. Above all, he seldom suspects that the ball is coming his way, for very few third men ever throw to the right wicket, very few bowlers are behind the stumps, and very few mid-ons back up. Third man should stand squarer for a strong cutter than for a weak one. He should back up behind short-slip when the ball comes from mid-on, and arrange with cover-point as to the throws from short-leg, himself covering point when the throws come from in front of the wicket, and cover-point taking that place when they come from behind.

SHORT-LEG

is an important place for backing up and saving singles. It is a good plan to put a left-handed man here, as he can better command the strokes between himself and mid-on, which are generally so prolific of runs. Having fielded one of these, he ought not to throw to the wicket-keeper, as he is already facing the bowler's wicket, and the bowler's wicket is facing him, should he wish to throw it down. He should of course previously make a league with mid-off as to the backing up. The late Mr. R. A. Fitzgerald, in the book just mentioned, 'Jerks in from Short-leg,' once urged the importance of putting the 'witty man' short-leg as a convenient spot for cracking jokes. Certainly conversation in the field is often of great service towards keeping the men brisk. Short-leg has to back up all the returns from the off side, dropping well back if short-slip comes across for this purpose, and in any case leaving ten or fifteen yards between himself and the wicket. A captain of an eleven feels himself very often bound by an unwritten tradition to put the notoriously worst field in his eleven short-leg. No doubt it is exceedingly difficult to judge which is the natural position for a bad field, but we unhesitatingly say that several matches have been lost by bad fields at short-leg. In the days of his prime people used to watch W. G. Grace playing ball after ball in the direction of short-leg, especially when left-handed bowlers were on. The late famous J. C. Shaw was not a good field in any sense of the word ; he was consequently often to be seen fielding at short-leg, and we wonder how many times he has missed W. G. Grace in that position ? Missing Grace was, and is still, a most expensive mistake. There are several players who are weak in their play off their legs, and these players are continually sending chances to short-leg, while other players are extremely fond of playing off their legs, and score very heavily by the stroke ; and it is wonderful to see how many runs a quick field will save when such men are batting.

LONG-STOP.

In these days of slow bowling and fine turf captains of elevens do not bother themselves with providing long-stops at all. Wicket-keepers are so good, the bowling is so straight, that, in the present year (1888), it is impossible to say who is the best long-stop in England, for the simple reason that no long-stops are wanted. But in the days of yore, every schoolboy who was fond of cricket could tell you of the prowess of Mortlock, H. M. Marshall, and A. Diver. Mr. Powys was a splendid bowler, and so was Mr. R. Lang. But had not Mr. H. M. Marshall been found to stop Mr. Lang's balls, and Mr. F. Tobin those of Mr. Powys, neither one bowler nor the other could have been put on at all. Such long-stops as these stand rather on the leg side, and if the bowling is very fast, just deep enough to take the ball as it rises after its second pitch. This is not easy to do, and young hands feel tempted to leave more room. But this, when the ball is very swift, scarcely diminishes its speed at all, and the further off long-stop stands, the more chance there is of the ball bounding awkwardly by the time it reaches him. Long-stop, however, would be in an awkward position if the batsmen ran every bye that is possible. To prevent their doing so, he must throw over to the bowler, for the old reason that the striker has the whole distance to run and has his back to the danger. Again, a hard throw, straight down the pitch, places both batsmen in jeopardy, the striker especially, and that is why he so often runs with his hand to the back of his head, of course retarding his speed by so doing. It is a harassing run to steal; and that, combined with the fact that it is not scored to either batsman, is doubtless the reason why it is not oftener stolen. Long-stop should accordingly be a strong thrower, and mid-off a conscientious backer-up. Long-stop should back up (behind short-leg) the returns from cover-point and mid-off.

Before concluding these technical remarks, let us draw attention to one or two circumstances connected with cricket affairs now which are different from what they were formerly. We have said that in these days long-stopping is a lost art, or rather it is not an art that is required in modern elevens. It would appear miraculous to an old cricketer who had seen nothing of the game for the last fifteen years could he watch Spofforth bowling, and Blackham keeping wicket with no long-stop, when the ground was hard. Such a thing would not have been dreamt of twenty years ago. Then a ball used to shoot five or six times in an innings of 135 runs, and the occasional shooter that occurs now always results in four byes if it escapes the bat and the wicket. Hence one important reason why formerly a long-stop was indispensable. Though there are or were, a very few years since, some very fast bowlers, the average pace now-a-days is far slower than twenty-five years ago, and that is another reason for dispensing with long-stop. But the change of tactics in not having a long-stop has had one effect that we regard as pernicious, and that is, that it has spoilt one part of the skill of wicket-keeping, and on the whole worked an enormous change for the worse in the fielding of short-slips generally. The long-stop is not there, both wicket-keeper and short-slip are conscious of this, and they are aware that his place must be filled up by themselves. If a ball goes in the least to leg, even if it only just misses leg-stump, short-slip is usually to be seen backing up the wicket-keeper; for four byes make an appreciable addition to the score. But though the ball is on the leg side, it is quite possible for the batsman to hit it on the on side, and send it straight to short-slip's hands, if he only could have been in his proper place. He is abused if he does not back up the wicket-keeper, and in any case the mere feeling that runs must result from the wicket-keeper not handling the ball makes it impossible for him to give his undivided attention to fielding at short-slip proper. He is continually shifting towards his left hand, and numerous balls that he would have fielded if only there had been a long-stop, now result in runs. The wicket-keeper is also in more danger of being hurt, and as his position is necessarily one attended by extreme responsibility and considerable pain, this further danger ought to be spared him if possible. The risks he runs are from fast balls outside the batsman's legs. He cannot see the ball accurately so that he may judge where to put his hands without moving his feet ; in order, then, to prevent the ball going to the ropes, he has to rush right in front of it, at the risk, if the ball should bump or do anything odd, of getting hit on the face or elsewhere. If a long-stop were behind him, he would try and take the ball for the sake of a possible catch or stump-out, but he would not expose himself to danger by getting in front of it.

Two corollaries must be drawn from what has been already said. The first is that the bowler should be just as prepared to receive a throw-in as the wicket-keeper. When both wickets are menaced, the danger of a short run is doubled, and an overthrow is oftener due to the bowler and backer-up than to the field. But it is said 'This is all very fine, but the bowler cannot get behind his wicket in time.' No assertion could be wider of the mark. Take some genuine cricketer as an example, and no better one could be chosen than Mr. A. W. Ridley, some ten years ago. Lob-bowlers follow their own ball further down the wicket than any other kind of bowler, and of all lob-bowlers Mr. Ridley did this the most. But no one has ever seen a short run got off his bowling, without, at least, at the same moment seeing him dart behind the wicket, and be ready to put down the hardest throw anyone might send to him. He is always there in time, and any bowler in the country might do the same if he were cricketer enough to see what is wanted. The second inference to be drawn is, that it is highly important to pursue a medium hit with all possible speed, and to throw it in as if it burnt the fingers to retain the ball a moment. We do not remember an eleven who neglected this less, as a whole, than the Players eleven of the year 1887, and the number of runs that can be saved by observance of the rule is immense.

These are the two most important directions which can be given to any young cricketer, and especially to any young captain of a side, in order that he may select his men with a view to these requirements of the game. The general fielding capacity of a whole team depends on the attention devoted to such dull points by the eleven minds, not less than on the suppleness of the eleven backbones. No directions, it has already been said, will make a bad field into a good one. But it is equally true that no advice should be offered which cannot be acted upon. Consequently only some duties of a fieldsman have been

described. But it is not too much to say that a careful attention to these points would ultimately turn eleven indifferent
cricket players into a good fielding team.

In a work necessarily somewhat didactic as this is, it may
be advisable to remind youngsters that the finger of scorn is
pointed even more to the very bad field than it is to the very
bad batsman or bowler. A very bad bowler will not be asked
to bowl unless the bowling is hit into a thoroughly entangled
knot—as was the case in an Australian *v.* England match in
1884, when every member of the English team, including
Shrewsbury, had to bowl—and then, if he fails, he has only done
what was expected of him. But it is difficult for anybody to
explain, except on the ground of gross carelessness, how a man
who is a good bat or bowler can be so utterly useless as a field
as some have turned out to be. The cricketer who never
appears to have grasped the rudiments of the laws concerning
twist, who is lazy and will not run after the ball, and who hardly
by accident holds a catch, is an eyesore in cricket. And let us
also assure the young practitioner that an intelligent audience,
though a somewhat rough one, such as you may see at places
like Bramall Lane, Sheffield, will jeer in audible and not too
polite tones at the bad field long before it will do the like at
bad batsmen or bowlers. Every cricketer knows the different
eccentricities of indifferent fields, their wonderful varieties of
error, and the specious appearance of some that fatally delude the
most patient captain. There are some men who are fairly fast
runners, and can throw hard, and yet are fields of a character
to make angels weep. They dash in at the ball like a man
charging at football, with the result that they half stop it, or,
after they stop it, in attempting to pick it up, they kick it
eight or ten yards behind them. They never seem to be
able to judge what sort of length the ball will come into
their hands, and never under any circumstances is the ball
cleanly handled. And yet they go at it so heartily, they
move so quickly, and, at first sight, look so alert and full
of promise, that it is difficult to condemn them until you have

had two or three days' experience of them. This sort belongs to the class we call the specious fieldsman. Then there is the man who might look at a batsman for two hours and yet never discover where his favourite stroke is likely to go, who obeys orders strictly, and when he has taken up the position assigned to him, stands there like a tree, despite the fact that every ball hit in his direction is a little too much on his right or on his left hand. This individual may safely be assumed to be a creature of a low order of intelligence, to whom Providence has probably vouchsafed a natural instinct for bowling, in the absence of which he would never be seen on any cricket-ground again, except as a spectator. He is so stupid that he never can excel in batting. Then there is the man who is very slow and has not acquired the merit of being what may be called an eminently safe field. His position when endeavouring to stop the ball is that illustrated by the figure on the opposite page, which shows what is essentially the wrong position to assume. Probably he will not touch the ball with his hands, and it certainly cannot be stopped by his legs or feet. He can hold a catch sometimes and stop a ball occasionally, but he does not succeed in these two particulars often enough to make one forget or forgive his extraordinary slowness. Another variety is the man who fields tolerably well sometimes, but, when he fails to stop a ball, either runs after it very slowly, which is the sulky form, or else dashes after it and throws it wildly and very hard anywhere, causing overthrows by the dozen, and maiming his comrades' fingers. This is the angry form—an odious type; let every youngster beware of such and develop not into it. Every cricketer ought to try to become as good a field as he can by assiduous practice—for this reason, if for no other : bowlers get disorganised when the fielding is loose.

A natural curiosity is always evinced where a critic shows a tendency to name certain celebrities in any form of game. This is the reason why we now proceed to praise famous men and famous fielding elevens; but let us add that we do not pro-

fess to name every good man who has ever fielded, and can
only beg for forgiveness if we omit to mention some who have
deserved recognition.

The various Australian elevens have earned great fame for
their fielding in England, and it was no doubt very good. At
the same time we think it was not so good as their batting, and
certainly not so good as their bowling. The elevens of 1882
and 1884, which were the best, no doubt won their matches
by all-round play ; but if we had to name a weak point we should
say that, as compared with the batting and bowling, it was
their fielding, although this was very good. The Australians

The wrong position for stopping the ball.

themselves say—at least, so we have heard—that the fielding
in Australia of the Hon. Ivo Bligh's eleven was never surpassed
in the colony; and that must be high praise. Still, judging
by what we know of that team, we think that we can point
out higher standards in England. The finest fielding we have
ever seen was that of the Players in 1887 in their annual
match at Lord's against the Gentlemen, and at the Oval
it was nearly as good. But that was only for two matches.
As is natural, University teams, from their youth and habit
of playing together, have earned great fame as fielding

elevens, and if we had to select four elevens whose fielding reputation ought to be inscribed on the highest pinnacles of fame, we should name the Cambridge representatives of 1861 and 1862 and the Oxford of 1874 and 1875.

The Cambridge celebrities of 1861 and 1862 have faded away into distance, and the present generation know not their names. Both those elevens had several fast bowlers in them, and one—Mr. R. Lang—was superlatively good. It was owing to this fact that Cambridge had to provide itself with a long-stop, and Mr. H. M. Marshall in that capacity has earned undying fame ; for long-stopping on Lord's Ground in 1861 and 1862 was no laughing matter. As general out-field Mr. Marshall also stood very high, and was a perfectly safe catch. Contemporary cricketers of that day are nearly unanimous in their praise of Mr. W. Bury as a fieldsman ; at long-leg he has never been excelled. There were besides these the Hon. C. G. Lyttelton at point, and Mr. R. Lang at short-slip. ' Bell's Life ' of that date mentions as a fact that the fielding of Cambridge in the University match of 1862 was never equalled on Lord's or any other ground. Those were the days when the bowling was mainly fast, the ground rough, and the cautious safe field who got stolidly and fixedly in a certain position was often defeated owing to the ball making unspeakable bounds. It required a touch of genius to be a grand field at Lord's in those times, and several members of those two Cambridge elevens possessed it. The two Oxford elevens of 1874 and 1875 had each only one fast bowler, but they had magnificent fielding teams to support their slow bowlers. When the bowling is generally slow, amateur wicket-keepers can hold their own. This was the case in 1874 and 1875, and in Mr. H. G. Tylecote Oxford possessed a wicket-keeper fully up to the mark for the work he had to do. It used to be, and probably is still, a bone of contention between Messrs. W. Law and A. W. Ridley, the captains respectively of '74 and '75, as to which of the two elevens was the greater in this particular line of fielding. Mr.

Law contended that his eleven in 1874 made no mistake in the inter-University match, whereas the 1875 eleven did. But the Cambridge batting in 1874 was fatuous to a degree, and the Oxford eleven had nothing to stop, whereas Cambridge in 1875 batted very well and kept their opponents hard at it. We are willing to give equal credit to each, and to enshrine the names of Law, Game, Ridley, J. B. Jones, and Royle in the temple of fame.

It is not easy to gauge the merits of the fieldsmen of forty years ago. Some of them have made their names live : Mr. T. A. Anson as wicket-keeper, Mr. R. T. King at point, and the famous W. Pickering at cover-point, for instance. But, though they had rougher ground to field on, still the scoring was nothing like so large, matches were not nearly so numerous, and the wear and tear far from being so great. The first thing that strikes one on reading over old scores and comparing them with those of the present day, is the enormous number of extras that were then given. Bowlers were, no doubt, faster, but they bowled many more wides. Taking one year at random, 1880, we find that for the whole season Yorkshire in all matches only bowled eight wides, five of which were delivered by the famous Tom Emmett, who is, no doubt, a slightly erratic bowler. In the days of Redgate and Mynn the wides were numerous, so were the no-balls, and frequently the extras contributed more to the total than any one batsman. If the bowling was fast and erratic, one cannot wonder that byes became numerous, especially when the rough ground is also considered. In the University match of 1841 Oxford gave Cambridge 56 extras out of a combined total of 223—a very large average. In 1887 Cambridge only gave Oxford 14 extras in a combined total of 461, and Oxford lost but three wickets in the second innings. In the same year Oxford gave Cambridge only 20 extras in a grand total of 459. Though bowling is generally slower now than forty years ago, still in former days they used to have long-stops to bowling that even amateur wicket-keepers would now stop. The long-stopping wicket-keeper—that is, the wicket-keeper that lets nothing pass him—is a marvellous testimony to the excellence of modern grounds, the accuracy of modern bowling, and the skill of the men themselves. The sight of Blackham, standing close up to the wicket, stopping Spofforth and Palmer would have made our forefathers look on aghast. In the well-known print of the Sussex and Kent match in 1840, old Lillywhite is bowling, and he was a slow medium-pace bowler ; yet, though Tom Box was reckoned the best wicket-keeper of the day, he has a long-stop to Lillywhite's bowling.

We may now try to enumerate the greater fields of cricket history. We read of the marvellous feat of Mr. T. A. Anson at the wicket, when he stumped a man off a leg-shooter of Alfred Mynn, one of the fastest bowlers of the period. We yield the place of honour to Mr. Anson for an individual feat, but it is alleged to have taken place a long time ago, and is it certain to be true? The greatest wicket-keepers since 1860 in England have been Lockyer, Pooley, Pilling, and Pinder, and we ask Plumb and Sherwin to forgive us. To discriminate between the first four is impossible ; we merely remark that to genuine slows of the pace of Southerton and Peate, we reckon Pooley to have been the best that ever lived, and to the very fast, Pinder at his prime was unequalled. Still Pooley was relatively not so good to fast, nor Pinder to slow; and, on the whole, we think that these four may be put on an equality. The best wicket-keepers of old days were Mr. Herbert Jenner, Mr. T. A. Anson, Mr. W. Ridding, and Mr. W. Nicholson among amateurs, and E. G. Wenman and Tom Box among professionals. The best English amateur wicket-keeper that ever lived, in our opinion, is Mr. Alfred Lyttelton, and besides him, since 1860, there have been Mr. Leatham, Mr. Bush, Mr. Newton, and Mr. E. F. S. Tylecote.

Perhaps a word would not be out of place here respecting Mr. Blackham, the celebrated Australian wicket-keeper. When the Colonial Eleven came over in 1878, 1880, 1882, and

1884, practically the whole of the wicket-keeping had to be done by Mr. Blackham. In 1880 and 1886 Mr. Jarvis assisted him. Now wicket-keeping is essentially an amusement you can have too much of. In old days, when there was a lot of fast bowling, the cream of the wicket-keeping used to be seen during the first six weeks of the season, because during that time the hands of the wicket-keeper were more or less sound. The famous George Pinder, at the beginning of his career, had faster bowling to keep to consistently than any other cricketer before or since. Freeman, Emmett, and Atkinson were three very fast bowlers, and they all three played for Yorkshire, and after them came Hill and Ulyett. Pinder in consequence very frequently damaged his hands, and no wonder. Blackham, however, during all the four years we have mentioned, had Spofforth and either Garratt or Palmer to stop. Now although these were not so fast as the Yorkshire lot, they bowled a goodish pace ; the Australian season consisted of two matches a week from the beginning to the end of the cricket year, and Blackham did not get very many days off. When his record is examined, therefore, we think that his performances during these four years constitute the greatest wicket-keeping feats on record. Not unless Spofforth bowled his fastest did he ever have a long-stop, and he held his hands closer to the wicket than any other wicket-keeper we ever saw. If the batsman was an inch out of his ground for a second or so, the ball would be put down, and a stump-out resulted, for the hands had no distance to travel, and no time was lost. Of course the bowling he had to stop was very accurate, but when the amount of wicket-keeping that he had to go through and the number of wickets he got are considered, our opinion is that Mr. Blackham is the finest wicket-keeper to bowling of all paces that the world has ever seen.

There have been numerous fieldsmen at point who have made themselves a name, and by universal testimony in his day, Mr. R. T. King, of Cambridge University, was not approached in excellence in this position. The late Mr. John

Walker, who was intimately acquainted with cricket of that period as well as with that of a later date, once told the writer that in his opinion none of the modern points ever came quite up to Mr. King's level. Since 1860 Carpenter, R. C. Tinley, E. M. Grace, and F. W. Wright, have earned high reputations in this position, but a great many excel at point, and in the University Match alone there has been some admirable fielding here ; the Hon, J. W. Mansfield for Cambridge, and Mr. Hildyard for Oxford, both being very good. The place where good fielding is most conspicuous is midway between cover-point and mid-off, and with this post the name of Mr. G. B. Studd is for ever identified. Mr. Royle at cover-point has never been excelled, and the same may be said of Gunn at third man. The celebrated fieldsmen of old were Mr. W. Pickering at cover-point ; John Bickley and Mr. R. Lang at short-slip ; Mr. E. S. E. Hartopp, Mr. H. M. Marshall, W. Pilch, A. Diver, W. Mortlock, and J. Thewlis at long-stop ; while F. Bell, W. Bury, John Smith, and A. Lubbock were excellent at a distance from the wicket. There have been also, and are, many fields who were and are good at any place ; for instance, the renowned Mr. V. E. Walker, and the still more famous Mr. W. G. Grace. We have said before, and we say it again, that the fielding, though probably as good as ever it was, is not so good as it ought to be. The nuisance of the day is the long scoring ; we wonder how many innings of 100 are played where you do not read the well-known remark, 'the batsman gave a chance at 24, another at 62, and a third just before he was out, but none the less he played a fine innings.' The following brief epigram is undoubtedly true—'Good fielding makes weak bowling strong and strong batsmen weak.' An eleven that is really A1 in fielding very rarely has to field out for 300 runs. When we say this we feel inclined to go farther and add that if no feasible catches are dropped this total of 300 runs would not be of anything but the rarest occurrence. This fact ought of itself to be sufficient to make every true cricketer try and become, if not a brilliant field, at any rate one who, when a catch is sent him, does not cause a thrill of agonising anxiety to arise in the minds of the supporters of the side to which he belongs.

An anxious moment.

CHAPTER VII.

COUNTRY CRICKET.

(By F. Gale.)

I can remember the first cricket match I ever saw as well as if it happened yesterday ; and moreover I can give the names and description of many of the players.

The *locus in quo* was the meadow opposite the Green Lion at Rainham, in Kent, which is situated halfway between London and Dover. The cricket field is now built over. It adjoined the vicarage garden, in which a stand was erected for my brother and myself, and from which we, as little boys, saw the first game of cricket we ever witnessed, in the summer of 1830, as we had come into Kent from a Wiltshire village where cricket was not known.

Our grand stand was immediately behind the wicket. Farmer Miles, a fine-set-up man, was the best bowler, and he bowled under-arm, rather a quick medium pace, and pitched a good length and bowled very straight, his balls curling in from the leg ; for be it remembered that but two years had elapsed since it was allowable to turn the hand, knuckles uppermost, in delivery. I was seven years old at the time, and was perfectly fascinated at the sight ; and as the gardener, an old cricketer, stood by me all day and explained the game, before the sun had set I had mastered most of the main points in it. One thing I am certain of, which is that there was an on-break from Farmer Miles' bowling ; for I watched the balls pitch and curl.

The dress of the cricketers was white duck trousers and flannel jackets, and some wore tall black hats and some large

MITCHAM COMMON

straw hats. A few old fogies, veterans who played, had a silk
pocket-handkerchief tied round the left knee so that they could
drop down on it without soiling their white trousers ; for in
the rough out-fielding when the balls jumped about anyhow
old-fashioned fieldsmen would drop on one knee, so that if
the ball went through their hands by a false bound their body
was in the way. Josiah Taylor, the brazier, was long-stop, and
played in black leather slippers with one spike in the heel
which he claimed as his own invention, as cricket-shoes were
little known. The umpire was Ost, the barber, who appeared in
a long blue frock-coat like Logic's, the Oxonian, in ' Tom and
Jerry,' and who volunteered ' hout ' to a fieldsman who stopped
a bump-ball ; and when remonstrated with by men of both
sides remarked, ' Surely first " bounce " is " hout " at cricket
and trap.' This occasioned a change of umpire. There were
two very hard hitters, Charles Smart, a tall young fellow, son
of a rich farmer, and ' Billy Wakley,' a very stout tall young
farmer ; there were many hits to the long-field off and on, which
were well held ; and Charles Watson, a promising lad of about
sixteen, the butcher's son, who played for the first time in a
man's match, immortalised himself by making a long catch close
to the vicarage hedge. The batting mostly consisted of hard-
hitting, and the catching was good. The booth was made up of
rick-cloths strained over a standing skeleton woodwork frame ;
and on the right of it was a round table with six or eight arm-
chairs placed on either side ; a large brass square tobacco-box
out of which those who sat round the privileged table could
help themselves by putting a halfpenny into a slit which caused
the box to open (on the same principle as the chocolate and
sweet-stuff automatic pillars seen now at railway stations), kept
company with a stack of clay-pipes. The arm-chairs were for
the accommodation of the principal farmers and magnates of the
parish who subscribed to the matches and who sat in state and
smoked their pipes—as cigars were little known—and drank
their grog out of rummers—large glasses which stood on one
gouty leg each and held a shilling's worth of brandy and

water; and for the accommodation of the smokers, the ostler, who always appeared in his Sunday best costume, which consisted of a 'Sam Weller' waistcoat with black calico sleeves, brown drab breeches, and top-boots, provided a stable horn lanthorn, the candle in which he lit with the aid of the flint and steel tinder box, and brimstone matches; for lucifers were not yet invented.

Another honour belonged to the knights of the round table : as the cricket ground was bounded on the southern side by the high road, and as coaches were passing all day, the drivers never forgot the 'Coachman's Salute' with whip and elbow and nod of the head as they drove by, and this was always returned by a cheery wave of the hand from the cricket ground. The patriarchs of the village had a form to themselves on the left hand of the booth ; and old Billy Coppin, the half-pay naval purser, who had a snug little house on the bank of the roadside, sat outside his door waving his pipe and crying out, ' Make sail, my lads, make sail,' whenever a good hit was made.

When the match was over, one of the villagers, an ill-tempered thatcher, who was always ready for a set-to, picked a quarrel with someone from a neighbouring parish, and they adjourned to a quiet corner close to our grand stand behind the booth, pulled off their shirts and had a pretty stiff rough and tumble fight, which I described, in my innocence, at supper when I went in, and thereby got the gardener into a scrape for allowing me to see it. A very serious relative told me that she was 'cock sure' of the future fate of the two men who fought, quoting cases out of Dr. Watts's hymns. Let us hope that some of the Doctor's tips have proved wrong.

'Would you be surprised to hear,' as Lord Coleridge was always saying, that, with the exception that cricket has much improved as regards grounds and some of the implements in general use, old-fashioned village cricket in its true and pure spirit still flourishes in many rural districts, and not very far from London even, now? You will find this happy state of things mostly where village greens exist in a real cricketing county ;

and having formerly devoted much of my leisure, during very many years, to country cricket, I can speak from actual experience, down to present date.

In the first place, every village green has a history of its own, and the people are proud of their old traditions. On many of these greens some of the best-known cricketers in England have from time to time appeared during a century past, and some come there occasionally now during every summer; so the cricketers of all classes have always had good models to work from. The green is common to all, and all have a common interest in the honour of the parish. This charming home feeling is admirably described by Miss Mitford in the 'Tales of our Village;' and she has not exaggerated it. The consequence is that by one consent the centre of the green is always left for good matches, and as every village boy learns the management of turf, you would be surprised to see what an admirable pitch youngsters of fourteen or fifteen years of age will make for themselves on somewhat rough ground with the aid of a five-pronged fork, a watering-pot and a hand-roller; and you would be surprised to see what *real* good cricket many of them play. Of course there is always a sprinkling of sons of good cricketers who have been well taught, and they have the opportunity of instruction from old players.

The training of village boys is very analogous to cricket fagging at school, and anyone who takes an interest in village cricket will do well, when he and a few friends practise, to have any little boys of twelve or thirteen who show any proficiency to field out for them, and to encourage them with a few coppers, making them understand that the honorarium is dependent on their trying to do their best. The next step is to take a lively interest in the boys' eleven, which consists of boys under fourteen or fifteen, to promote their matches in every way, and to inculcate the value of fair play. It does them a great deal of good if an old cricketer will spare half an hour, when the boys are practising, to criticise their play, pointing out any faults, such as running over the crease, bowling no balls, not backing up for a run, explaining to them the principles of running, and calling their partner (secrets which some really good batsmen never *have* learned and never *will* learn), and so on. The grand thing is to try and make cricket *real*, and to make youngsters understand that playing the strict game is the secret of true enjoyment. We all know how all pleasure depends on observance of simple rules, and on doing in practice all things as carefully as if we are engaged in a match, or any other friendly strife. Even if I play at 'beggar your neighbour' with a child I insist on the rigour of the game. Many of us must know as cricketers, too, that long after we had given up playing in matches, there was immense pleasure in having a first-rate professional, on a real good wicket, to bowl, with sixpence on the wicket.

The very mention of single wicket now is like the mention of jalap and rhubarb and calomel and bleeding, those terrible remedies of the past, to a modern doctor ; but single wicket with seven or eight in the field is the finest practice for training, and we found it so on our village green, a very few years ago, played thus. Every man's hand was against his neighbours in turn, and there were no sides. Of course, with six or seven in the field, byes and hits behind wicket counted, and this fact made the youngsters try to cover as much ground as possible. The batsman went out if he got ten runs ; and as in these games there was, at least, one good professional bowler, it took a good man to score ten runs. The professional and any amateur who had any pretence of being a bowler changed about. These games were very good for putting a youngster into ; and I have seen three or four hundred people on the green watching one of these trials. It was also a good thing, in the event of a substitute being wanted in a good match, to try one of them, as it accustomed an aspirant to accept responsibility and to play before a crowd. It is a wholesome state of things when young cricketers are at hand anxious to fill a vacancy ; it shows zeal.

Anyone who has charge of village cricket falls very short of his duty if he does not arrange at least one real practice afternoon a day or two before a match. He must have a good wicket made, and all who are going to play in the match must come for some part of the play. And this is a good opportunity for letting young bowlers come and try their hand, with sixpence on the wicket. I have much faith in that sixpence on the wicket. It is useless to waste any trouble on a boy who has not got cricket at heart, but it is a great deal of use training one who has. The difficult stage is when a boy's strength is growing and he is old enough to be taught strict cricket as regards defence, and in trying to steady him down you must be sure to steer clear of the evil of cramping his hitting power. We know from experience that sometimes matches are lost or draws made owing to the want of a man who will go in and hit. In my boyhood days there used generally to be one, or perhaps two, in every eleven who could field splendidly, and who made no pretence to scientific batting, but who, aided by a strong nerve and quick eye and a heavy driving bat, could sometimes make a terrible example of the bowling and help the score. Mr. Absolom, of Cambridge, and afterwards of the Kent eleven, was one of this class. He was worth playing in any eleven in England for his bowling, fielding and hard work, and if he never made his runs, his share towards success was as great as those who made a score. The thing to 'burn' into a young player's mind is, that unless he can concentrate all his thoughts on the match in which he is playing he will never be an English cricketer. He may, perhaps, by long practice acquire the knack of getting a lot of runs, and building up an average, but if that is all that he is worth, he had much better never have been in the eleven at all. Amongst eleven men, some are sure to get a lot of runs generally, but the men who win matches are those who prevent the other side getting them. Take one of the best samples of cricket in the season of 1887, as a proof of what saving runs means. I think that anyone who knows the game can hardly help coming to the conclusion that Gunn, in the long field, saved more runs in 1887 than the best man made, and saved a good many more too. The Australians put their main trust in their field, and they taught us a good lesson when they came first, and it has done us good. Gunn's batting is often equal to his fielding, to say nothing of his bowling.

Now we come to a more serious matter—management and finance ; and, unless the world has very much changed in the last few years, anyone who takes a new lead in country cricket will find himself surrounded by hosts of friends (?) who are worth nothing. They will all want to come on the committee, and make all kind of wild suggestions about a stock of club bats, pads and gloves, &c. There is only one antidote to this, which is to stand firm on one point—that no public subscriptions shall be asked for for any purpose other than keeping the green in order, paying for balls for matches, match-stumps, hire of tents, umpires, scorers, and other inevitable expenses ; the simple inducement for subscriptions being the having a few good matches during the season, and keeping up a ground for the use of those who cannot pay for themselves. Unless you keep up a good parish eleven, everyone will do as he thinks best, and the whole green will be cut to pieces and will never be repaired.

In these days you cannot get an eleven who will make a good stand in a match without some professional training. Many places are fortunate enough to have an old professional or two amongst its inmates, men who have given up grand public matches, but who are worth their weight in gold as practice bowlers, trainers, and members of the village eleven. Men of this class, who will play in a match for ten shillings or will come in the evening after work for a crown or so, and who are always on the spot, are the best aids towards keeping together a good set of young players and forming an eleven. They know the young players and take a pride in them, and will find out their failings and good points ; and nothing cheers a captain more than an invitation from a local professional to come and see Bill Smith or Tom Brown bat. When such an invitation is given, you may be sure that the professional has found a recruit who can play a length ball with a straight bat and confidence, and who can punish a loose ball. You will find numberless cricketers who can get runs—if they once get set ; but, like precious stones, many get spoilt in the setting. What you want is batsmen who, in wet or fine weather, on rough or smooth ground, will go in with nerve to have a good try. If you want a few runs to-day from A, and he breaks down through that cricket malady called 'funk,' it is no consolation to hear from his *claqueur* B that ' A got seventy, not out, last week.'

You must try and raise the standard of a village eleven by letting them play when you have the chance against teams who are stronger than themselves. A licking is good medicine for them sometimes ; and if, on the other hand, they win by the chances of the game, a victory of this kind 'sets their tails up.' The worst thing for them is playing against weak teams, making a tremendous score, and knocking their opponents' wickets over for a few runs. It is astonishing how a captain, by working steadily on, can ' educate his party,' as the late Lord Beaconsfield said ; and if by quiet persuasion he can influence some of the rougher element to abandon their horse-play and ' flowery ' language, and to assist in keeping good order—at the same time warning them that ladies and gentlemen are kept away from the green for fear of their ears being contaminated by rough language—he will find that visitors who come prepared for a noisy rude crowd will be surprised to find perfect order ; and if some one trangresses the bounds of good manners, he will hear a cry of ' Better language there ! ' This kind of thing *can* be and *has* been done ; and the result was that, in a place where the possibility of such a thing as a ladies' tent on the green was laughed at, not only was the ladies' tent a great success, but subscriptions flowed in in a wonderful manner. One dear old lady—an Exeter Hall-er who took omnibuses full of people to hear Sankey and Moody—sent ' two guineas for the green, which is now, I believe, a place of innocent amusement and happiness,' as she stated in her letter. She *was* a good Christian, as her house stood deep long-leg, and many a time has a ' four ' been scored for a hit through her window—and this is fact.

With the enormous number of large schools in England where cricket is played, it will seldom happen that any cricket neighbourhood has not some young fellows from school, or possibly a few from either University, close by ; and if they happen to be of the right sort they are a great boon.   At the same time it should be a golden rule never to put out of the eleven a good one, who has worked for and earned his place, for a 'swell.'   The rule must be kept hard and fast, that the eleven is open only to those who have proved themselves good enough, and if that rule is observed, in the event of a real first-rate amateur turning up, you will generally find that more than one volunteer will offer to stand out for him.

Captaining a village team is not all a bed of roses ; but if you are really a cricketer at heart, you will soon acquire the absolute confidence of people of all classes, especially of the humbler order.   It is not an unpleasant thing, as you walk across the green on your way to the train, to hear a pack of little boys on their way to school, who look on you as a kind of big dog that won't bite, all chattering about the match the day before.   'Ah ! Sir, I heerd my father say that he won a pot over the match,' says one.   'That boy, Sir, got the stick for playing truant yesterday morning,' says another. 'Well! if I *did*,' replies the culprit, 'I *see* the beginning of the match, and *you* did not—there!'   That boy may be another Fuller Pilch some day.

And if you are sitting in the tent when your side is in, revolving many things in your mind, and you feel that the whites of the eyes of Mr. Chummy the sweep, a good cricketer formerly, who sits on a form just outside the tent, behind a very short pipe, are glancing round on you, what a comfort it is, if you turn round, to see an almost imperceptible nod of Mr. Chummy's head—for he never speaks during a match— which says, 'Going on all right—we shall win !'   That nod of the head is only intelligible to a cricketer, just as a very 'shy' rise of a trout is only perceptible to a genuine fisherman.   Those, too only who have known some celebrated cricketer from childhood, and have watched his career and promotion from the little boys' to the big boys' eleven, and eventually to the parish eleven, and have seen his cricket talent developed from year to year until he appears in his county team, can imagine how painful is the excitement to those who are interested in his success. It has been my fate to go through—I had almost said the agony of—that state of suspense many times, and I must relate one instance. A young player, twenty years old, after my earnest entreaty, was allotted a place in the county eleven. He broke ground in London against Notts, and at his *début* had to stand the fire of Alfred Shaw and J. C. Shaw. Directly I saw him play the first ball my mind was quite at rest, as he showed that he had not the stage sickness. He got twelve runs in an hour and a quarter. His next public appearance in London was a 'caution,' as he scored 20 not out, in his first innings against Cambridge University; and, going in first, scored 82 in his second innings. This occurred nearly twenty years ago, when cricketers played with their bats and not with their pads, and boundary hits, except against the pavilion, were unknown ; so fifty runs was a grand score. I never shall forget my feelings when the colt had made 47, within 3 of his 50; I could look no more ; when, all of a sudden, I heard a roar from the crowd which told me that our village boy had done it. The secretary of the club said, 'He must have his sovereign for fifty runs,' and he promised me that if he made thirty more, which would make a total of 100, including his 20 not out, he would give him two sovereigns, if I would give him one for his first fifty. I undertook to raise that capital ; whereupon, a stranger, a very tall, handsome, gentlemanly man, said, 'And I will give him a sovereign too ; for ' (turning to myself) 'your excitement, which I found was only occasioned by interest in a village boy, and not heavy betting as I imagined, has done me real good. I have been for thirty years in India and am going back again in a month, and nothing pleased me more than to find this keen love of sport still existing.' He would not give his name, and I could never find out who he was ; possibly he is alive and may read this, and may let us know who he was, for I am sure he has not forgotten it. Richard Humphrey was the colt, and I sent for him into the Pavilion, and the 'illustrious stranger' shook hands with him and gave him the sovereign.

The foregoing remarks about clubs apply to a country place with some pretensions to first-rate cricket and a village green. In a rural out-of-the-way place where the population consists of a class which cockney writers call ' Hodge,' and which we call ' chaw-bacons,' bats and balls and stumps and all implements must be provided by subscription. In all other cases those who want to play cricket must pay for their own cricket things. If a good ground is provided the cricket ought to grow of itself. ' And this country cricket must cost a good deal of money,' perhaps you will remark. Of course it does ; so does fishing, or shooting, or hunting, or any other sport. There are many men who want to skim the cream of the cricket and to play in a good home match who will not play in an out match because 'they have not time,' really because they are too stingy. If you mean cricket you must back it everywhere with all your heart and all your strength. Whatever you do, never forget the wind-up match and supper at the end of the season, and get some good cricketers from amongst your foes to join, and above all a parson or two if possible. In these days, I need not say ' abolish all ribald songs and drunkenness,' as cricketers have good manners now.

As a last word, I must say something for country umpires. When changes in the game are proposed, a lot of outsiders who try their hardest to prevent penal laws being made intelligible, on the ground that ' the change will put too much on the umpires' shoulders—especially country umpires,' are talking nonsense. In the days of Caldecourt, John Bayley, Tom Barker, and Good at Lord's, umpires did their duty without fear or favour, and did not let men ' cheat, and the same stamp of umpires still exists in counties and on many a village green ; and if there are any umpires on public grounds who cannot administer the law fearlessly, they had better be supplanted by those who can. If batsmen in the past had shamelessly stopped the ball with their pads without ' offering ' at the ball with their bat, country umpires would have given them out for unfair play, on the same principle as wilfully obstructing the field. I suppose they would call it l.b.w; and the crowd would have given the retiring batsman (?) a *very* cold reception ; or perhaps a very hot one : neither extreme of heat or cold is pleasant. The late Chief Justice Cockburn said of county magistrates : 'They may sometimes administer bad law, but generally good justice ;' and the remark applies to village-green umpires.

CHAPTER VIII.

BORDER CRICKET.

(BY ANDREW LANG.)

MR. GALE has been saying his very pleasant say on country cricket in England. A Border player, in his declining age, may be allowed to make a few remarks on the game as it used to be played in 'pleasant Teviotdale,' and generally from Berwick all along the Tweed. The first time I ever saw ball and bat must have been about 1850. The gardener's boy and his friends were playing with home-made bats, made out of firwood with the bark on, and with a gutta-percha ball. The game instantly fascinated me, and when I once understood why the players ran after making a hit, the essential difficulties of comprehension were overcome. Already the border towns, Hawick, Kelso, Selkirk, Galashiels, had their elevens. To a small boy the spectacle of the various red and blue caps and shirts was very delightful. The grounds were, as a rule, very rough and bad. Generally the play was on *haughs*, level pieces of town-land beside the rivers. Then the manufacturers would encroach on the cricket-field, and build a mill on it, and cricket would have to seek new settlements. This was not the case at Hawick, where the Duke of Buccleuch gave the town a capital ground, which is kept in very good order.

In these early days, when one was only a small spectator, ay, and in later days too, the great difficulty of cricket was that excellent thing in itself, too much patriotism. Almost the whole population of a town would come to the ground and

take such a keen interest in the fortunes of their side, that the
other side, if it won, was in some danger of rough handling.
Probably no one was ever much hurt ; indeed, the squabbles
were rather a sham fight than otherwise ; but still, bad feeling
was caused by umpires' decisions. Then relations would be
broken off between the clubs of different towns, and sometimes
this tedious hostility endured for years. The causes were the
excess of local feeling, and perhaps the too great patriotism of
umpires. 'Not out,' one of them said, when a member of the
Oxford eleven, playing for his town-club, was most emphatically
infringing some rule. 'I can *not* give Maister Tom out first
ball,' the umpire added, and his case was common enough.
Professional umpires, if they could be got, might be expected
to prove more satisfactory than excited amateurs who forgot
to look after no balls, or to count the number of balls in an
over. But even professionals, if they were attached to the club
or school, were not always the embodiment of justice.

The most exciting match, I think, in which I ever took part
was for Loretto against another school. In those days we were
very weak indeed. When our last man went in, second innings,
we were still four runs behind our opponent's first score. This
last man was extremely short-sighted, and the game seemed
over. But his partner, a very steady player, kept the bowling,
and put on some thirty-eight more. We put our adversaries
in to get this, and had lowered eight wickets for twenty-eight.
I was bowling, and appealed to the umpire of our opponents
for a palpable catch at wicket. 'Not out !' Next ball the
batsman was caught at long-stop, and a fielder triumphantly
shouted, 'Well, how's *that ?*'

'Not out,' replied the professional again, and we lost the
match by two wickets.

If this had happened on the Border there would have
been trouble, and perhaps the two clubs would not have met
again for years. I have no doubt that a more equable feeling
has come in among those clubs which retained a good deal
of the sentiments of rival clans. The Borderers played too

much as if we were still in the days of Scotts and Carrs, and as if it were still our purpose

> To tame the Unicorn's pride,
> Exalt the Crescent and the Star.

Sir Walter Scott encouraged this ardour at football when he caused to be unfurled, for the first time since 1633, the ancient banner of Buccleuch, with its broidered motto 'Bellendaine.' The dalesmen, the people from the waters of Yarrow, Ettrick, and Teviot, played against the souters of Selkirk, all across country, the goals being Ettrick and Yarrow. The townsmen scored the first goal, when the Galashiels folk came in as allies of the shepherds, and helped them to win a goal. 'Then began a murder grim and great,' and Scott himself was mobbed in the evening. But he knew how to turn wrath into laughter.

''Tis sixty years since,' and more, but this perfervid ardour, while it makes Border cricket very exciting, is perhaps even now a trifle too warm. The great idea, perhaps, in all country cricket is not so much to have a pleasant day's sport, win or lose, but to win merely. Men play for victory, as Dr. Johnson talked, rather than for cricket. This has its advantages ; it conduces to earnestness. But it does not invariably promote the friendliness of a friendly game.

Border cricket is very pleasant, because it is played in such a pleasant country. You see the angler going to Tweedside, or Teviot, and pausing to watch the game as he strolls by the cricket-ground. The hills lie all around, these old, unmoved, unchangeable spectators of man's tragedy and sport. The broken towers of Melrose or Jedburgh or Kelso look down on you. They used to 'look down,' as well they might, on very bad wickets. Thanks to this circumstance, the present writer, for the first and only time in his existence, once did the 'hat trick' at Jedburgh, and took three wickets with three consecutive balls. Now the grounds are better, and the scores longer, but not too long. You seldom hear of 300 in one innings on the Border.

In my time the bowling was roundhand, and pretty straight and to a length, as a general rule. Perhaps, or rather certainly, the proudest day of my existence was when I was at home for the holidays, and was chosen to play, and bowl, for the town eleven against Hawick. I have the score still, and it appears that I made havoc among Elliots, Leydens, and Drydens. But they were too strong for our Scotts, Johnstons, and Douglasses : it is a pleasure to write the old names of the Border clans in connection with cricket. The batting was not nearly so good then as it is now; professional instruction was almost unknown. Men blocked timidly, and we had only one great hitter, Mr. John Douglas; but how gallantly he lifted the soaring ball by the banks of Ettrick ! At that time we had a kind of family team, composed of brothers and other boys, so small that we called ourselves *Les Enfants Perdus*. The name was appropriate enough. I think we only once won a match, and that victory was achieved over Melrose. But we kept the game going on and played in all weathers, and on any kind of wickets. Very small children would occasionally toddle up and bowl when the elder members of the family were knocked off. Finally, as they grew in stature, the team developed into 'The Eccentric Flamingoes,' then the only wandering Border club. We wore black and red curiously disposed, and had a good many Oxford members. The Flamingoes, coming down from Oxford, full of pride, had once a dreadful day on the Edinburgh Academy Ground. We were playing the School, which made a portentous score, and I particularly remember that Mr. T. R. Marshall, probably the best Scotch bat who ever played, and then a boy, hit two sixes and a five off three consecutive balls. It is a very great pity that this Border bat is so seldom seen at Lords ;' his average for M.C.C. in 1886 was 85. The Flamingoes lasted for some years, and played all Teviotdale and Tweedside.

In those days we heard little of Dumfries and Galloway cricket, into which Steels, Tylecotes, and Studds have lately infused much life. In recent years, Lord Dalkeith, Lord

George Scott, and Mr. Maxwell Scott, of Abbotsford, have contributed very much to the growth of Border cricket. Money has never been very plentiful north of Tweed, and when scarcely any but artisans played, the clubs could not afford good grounds, or much professional instruction. In these respects there has been improvement. Perhaps the boys' cricket was not sufficiently watched and encouraged. Veterans used to linger on the stage with a mythical halo round them of their great deeds in the Sixties. Perhaps the rising generation is now more quickly promoted, and better coached than of old. I feel a hesitation in offering any criticism because I had only one quality of a cricketer, enthusiasm, combined for a year or two with some twist from leg. But, if I never was anything of an expert, my heart hath always been with those old happy scenes and happy days of struggling cricket. What jolly journeys we had, driving under the triple crest of Eildon to Kelso, or down Tweed to Galashiels, or over the windy moor to Hawick! How keen we were, and how carried beyond ourselves with joy in the success of a sturdy slogger, or a brilliant field! There were sudden and astonishing developments of genius. Does J. J. A., among his savages on the other side of the globe, remember how he once took to witching the world by making incredible and almost impossible catches? *Audisne, Amphiarae?* Michael Russell Wyer, I am sure, among Parsee cricketers, has not forgotten his swashing blow. But one of whom the poet declared that he would

> Push into Indus, into Ganges' flood,
> While all Calcutta sings the praise of Budd,[1]

will no more 'push leg balls among the slips.'

> No longer make a wild and wondrous score,
> And poke where never mortal poked before.

This is the melancholy of mortal things.

[1] The maker of a formidable bat.

As Mr. Prowse sang

> The game we have not strength to play
> Seems somehow better than before.

Our wickets keep falling in this life. One after the other goes down. They are becoming few who joined in those Border matches where there was but one lady spectator, when we made such infrequent runs, and often dropped a catch, but never lost heart, never lost pleasure in the game. Some of them may read this, and remember old friends gone, old games played, old pewters drained, old pipes smoked, old stories told, remember the leg-hitting of Jack Grey, the bowling of Bill Dryden and of Clement Glassford, the sturdy defence of William Forman. And he who writes, recalling that simple delight and good fellowship, recalling those kind faces and merry days in the old land of Walter Scott, may make his confession, and may say that such years were worth living for, and that neither study, nor praise, nor any other pleasure has equalled, or can equal, the joy of having been young and a cricketer, where

> The oak, and the ash, and the bonny ivy tree,
> They flourish best at home in the North Countrie.

CHAPTER IX.

HOW TO SCORE.

(By W. G. Grace.)

Ask any player who has scored over a hundred in an innings if he felt any particular influence at work on the morning of the match, and he will probably answer in the negative ; but press him, and he will admit that he felt fit and well, and that the feeling was owing to a good night's rest, together with the careful training of days and weeks. I am aware that there are exceptions to this rule, and that players have been known to score largely after a night of high feasting and dancing ; but in my own experience, whilst admitting that occasional freaks of this kind have been followed by moderately large scores, I cannot recollect many of my big innings that were not the results of strict obedience to the rules which govern the training for all important athletic contests. Temperance in food and drink, regular sleep and exercise, I have laid down as the golden rule from my earliest cricketing days. I have carefully adhered to this rule, and to it in a great degree I attribute the scores that stand to my name in cricket history, and the measure of health and strength I still enjoy.

Early in the season every cricketer knows the difficulty of getting his eye in, but though he may be disappointed at the small score attached to his name match after match, he plays steadily on, trusting that by constant practice the coveted hundred will come. If he hopes to score largely he must be careful in his manner of living and moderate in all things, even though nature may have blessed him with exceptional wrist power and sight.

The capacity for making long scores is not a thing of a day's growth, and it may be years before strength and skill come and enable the young cricketer to bear the fatigue of a long innings. He cannot begin too early to play carefully and earnestly, and in all club and school practice the lad should play as if he were engaged in an important match, and the result depended upon his individual efforts. In my own case, thanks to careful guidance, I was early taught to keep my wicket up, never to hit recklessly, always to play straight or good-length balls with force, and if possible away from the fielders. Habits of that kind thoughtfully cultivated will not desert you in first-class cricket. Great scores at cricket, like great work of any kind, are, as a rule, the results of years of careful and judicious training and not accidental occurrences.

If you have occasion to travel a considerable distance to play, make an effort to get to your destination the night before, or at least some time before, the match begins. There is nothing so fatiguing to the eyesight as a long railway journey, and going straight from the railway station to the wicket is often fatal to long scoring.

I have tried hard, especially of late years, to arrange so that I could reach the ground in good time and save everything in the shape of hurry or bustle. There are but few cricket grounds within a hundred miles of each other where the light and conditions are alike, and it takes some time for eye and mind to accommodate themselves to new surroundings. You will find it just as trying to play in a blaze of sunshine, after three days of smoke and leaden skies, as you will in a change from the sunny south to the bleak, sunless north.

You must also not only bear in mind the vast importance of reaching the ground in good time, but the greater importance of getting five or ten minutes' batting practice before the innings begins. Very few grounds are the same as regards the way in which the ball rises off the pitch, even if the light be similar to that you have been playing in for days, and it requires nothing short of a genius for the game to change from a fast to a slow wicket, and play with the same ease and confidence.

I shall not readily forget an experience that came to me in 1871, when I travelled from London to Brighton to play for the Gentlemen against the Players for the benefit of John Lillywhite. Being very much younger than I am now, I was blessed with clearness of vision and quickness of action that suited themselves very readily to most conditions of light and ground. Perhaps it was the inexperience of youth that led me to put off reaching the old Brunswick ground at Hove until the moment of beginning my innings. This I know, I felt as fit as ever I did in my life, walked to the wicket with confidence, and took my guard carefully to the bowling of J. C. Shaw. He was on at the sea-shore end, and there was a glare on the water, delighting the artistic eye I have no doubt, but to me shifting and dancing like a will o' the wisp. There is no need to deny the fact, I was all abroad to his first ball, and knew it had beaten me before it came within two yards of me. I tried hard to play it, but the ominous rattle told me I had failed, and I returned to the pavilion and made the mental note. The dazzling light, the railway journey, and want of five minutes' practice did it. I had no desire to re-peat the performance in the second innings, and had little fear of doing so. I took care to have some practice, and scored 217, my brother G. F. made 98, and we increased the total by 240 runs in two and a half hours.

There is this also to be said in favour of five or ten minutes' batting practice before a match, that it enables you to test pads, gloves, and shoes. To have the fastening of a glove or pad break off when you are well set is a disagreeable and annoying interruption. It takes some time to put things right, and when you return to the wicket, the confidence you felt has very likely to a great extent deserted you. And how often have you placed your boots in your bag, all the spikes seemingly firm, to find one or two missing after you have been batting for a few minutes ! One has gone out of the toe of your boot, and you play forward to a ball, miss your footing and get stumped; or one has vanished from the heel, and you are called by your partner for a short run, sent back again, slip, and get run out. Inattention to these apparently small points causes annoyance, and may prevent you from getting a long score.

You are now ready to go in, and if you are first on the list you may do it leisurely ; but if you follow first wicket down, or later, impress strongly upon your mind that it is your duty to get to the wicket within the limit of time the law allows, and as quickly as possible, particularly if your partner has got his eye in and looks like making a large score. You will expect a like consideration when your turn comes to wait, and nothing upsets a player so much as having to loiter three or four minutes when he is warm and at home with the bowling, especially when he knows there is no need for delay. There will be a lack of confidence between you for some time at least, and indifferent judging of runs.

You will doubtless please yourself as to the guard to be taken ; but whether you take it to cover the middle and leg stumps, or middle or leg only, be sure to keep your legs clear of the wicket. A good umpire notes at the first glance if your leg is covering any part of it, registers it against you, and remembers it when called upon for a decision. If you stand clear of the wicket, he realises that you are taking every precaution, will not decide without thinking, and will give you the benefit of every doubt.

Be sure you have your right foot firmly planted behind the popping crease, or you may play a little too far forward and be stumped. You may as well remove any small piece of grass or loose bit of turf that catches your eye as you look along the wicket. After you have taken guard, and marked it clearly, look all around and note the position of the fieldsmen. It is something to know you may hit out to certain parts of the ground without the risk of being caught.

It is not very many years since, if you had asked the question how you were to begin an innings, you would have been told to play quietly for an over or two, and hit at nothing straight until you got your eye in. With all my heart I say, do not be in a hurry to hit; keep up your wicket and runs will come; but do not think that this means that you are not to punish a loose ball if you get one, whether it be your first or your twentieth. I understand it to mean that you are not to hit at a good or doubtful ball for the sake of a start, or to shake off the nervousness that affects a great number of players until they have scored the first run. No; begin as you mean to go on, playing good balls carefully, hitting loose ones, and bearing in mind that a large score is not made in half-a-dozen hits or overs. Do not be surprised and disappointed if the first few overs are maidens, or ruffled that the score-sheet is still clean so far as you are concerned. Possibly your partner has been placing balls that you could not get away, and you grow impatient. That is foolishness, and fatal to your chance of scoring. Remember he had been batting before you came in, and had obtained the confidence and mastery over the bowling that is now coming slowly but surely to you. Runs will come if you stay in, and few bowlers can go on bowling over after over for half an hour or more without giving you a loose ball or two.

It is bad judgment to attempt sharp runs early in your innings. Inclination that way is sure to be encouraged by the bowler, and when you least expect it he will in some way unknown to you communicate with the wicket-keeper and fielders, and the next attempt may end in you or your partner being run out. A deal of harm has been done even if you just saved it by an inch or two, and you will be in a most unhappy state of mind for some time afterwards. It dawns upon you that there was a degree of stupidity in the attempt, and it does not improve your temper to have words of caution showered upon you from the pavilion. The state of the game, the condition of the score did not demand it, and you will be very lucky if you realise the fact, and recover your usual coolness and confidence before resuming your innings.

Exercise judgment when running out big hits. If you find the fielders a little careless in throwing in, you may make a five out of what looked like a four ; but remember that to do this you will have to make an exceptional effort that will try your wind. And now you have the opportunity to show if your head is of the thoughtful kind. The bowler will be delighted if he can tempt you to play the next ball before you have got rid of the flurry and excitement, and you will be looked upon as very obliging and thoughtless if you do. Very likely you have resumed your position in front of the wicket with no intention of playing for a second or two; perhaps the bowler is aware of the fact, but that does not prevent him from bowling at you in the hope that you may change your mind. Do not blame him if you play and are bowled. He was not supposed to know that you were not ready, and you had no right to be there recovering your breath ; it will come back as freely to you a yard or two away from the wicket as in front of it, and neither bowler nor fielders ought to blame you for waiting for that purpose. You are playing the game for your side as well as your individual reputation, and ought to take all needful precautions.

Be careful what you take to drink during a long innings. If you are not accustomed to large scoring you are sure to feel thirsty, and your mouth will become very dry before you have made many runs. A big drink at this or any other time when you are in is a great mistake. For the moment you feel as if you must quench your thirst, or you cannot go on ; you must, however, refrain, for there is nothing so insidious and infectious as indulgence in drinks of any kind. In half an hour you will want another, and the fieldsmen generally will sympathise and lean to your way of thinking. Then there will be five minutes' break, you will probably lose sight of the ball, and very likely get out immediately after. If you must have something, call for a little water : it will answer the purpose perfectly. Rinse your mouth with it, swallow as little as possible, and the thirst will quickly pass away.

It is the first long innings that requires nerve and judgment. The hopes and fears that spring up in the young player's breast when he has scored something between fifty and a hundred make it a severe trial ; and I daresay if you and I could read his thoughts we should find that every run of the last ten was made in mental fear accompanied by a thumping heart. But when the hundred is reached, who can describe the joy that thrills him as he hears the hand-clapping and shouting !

I will not say, be modest in the hour of victory, but rather be modest after it. It is after the victory, as we listen to outside praise, that conceit and its enervating influence steal in. Turn a deaf ear, and remember it was in fear and trembling that you reached the much-desired score. Quiet confidence is a widely different thing from conceit. The former will help you to a run of big scores, the latter will cripple every effort to sustain your hardly earned reputation.

So far I have not touched upon the different wickets that are met with during the season. There have been years, such as 1887, when the weather has continued dry and fine for weeks, and the change from ground to ground was hardly perceptible ; but I have known the wicket to change in a single match from dry, fast and true, to wet and soft, and then to have finished sticky and unplayable. Anyone who can score heavily through changes of that kind will be exceptionally fortunate. I venture to think it may be of some use to young cricketers if I tell them how they should play under these different conditions of ground. I will begin with what is known as a fast, dry and true wicket.

This is the wicket which all good cricketers like to play on, and, if it does not crumble before the match is finished, long scores may be expected. Never hesitate to play forward on a wicket of this kind, for the bowler can get little or no work on the ball, and, what is more, the further it is pitched up and the faster it comes along, the easier it is to play it forward and the more difficult to play it back. On such a wicket as this do not go in for lofty and 'gallery' hitting, or you will very likely throw away your chance of making a long score. If the bowler gives you a ball well up, instead of hitting very hard at it, I should advise you to drive it along the ground; although you may not score so many runs for it, still you do not incur the risk of being caught out, and you will get the applause of those who know what scientific batting means. Cuts and leg-hits travel at a rare pace on a good fast ground, and timing and placing are of more importance than strength. A snick to long-leg may bring more runs than a hard hit straight, and a tap past long-slip goes flying to the boundary with a very small expenditure of strength. Most long scores have been made on a wicket of this description, and you do not tire half so much as you would if the wicket were wet and heavy.

In the season 1876—one of my best years—I remember playing in three matches following each other when the ground was fast, dry and true. The first match was at Canterbury, for Marylebone C.C. *v.* Kent. Kent made the long score of 473, chiefly owing to the magnificent batting of Lord Harris, who made 154. We responded with the comparatively small total of 144. To follow on with so large a deficit was not encouraging; but the wicket was still everything to be desired in pace and quality, and I made up my mind to play a fast game, knowing that the bowler could get little or no work on the ball, and that any attempt to play carefully for a draw would be useless. It is now a matter of history that we scored the first 100 in forty-five minutes, 217 well under the two hours, and finished up with a total of 557 for nine wickets, converting what appeared to be inevitable defeat into a creditable draw. It took me a little over six hours to make my 344; but so good and fast was the wicket that I played forward to most of the good balls.

Two days after, on a similar wicket against Notts, playing for Gloucestershire at Clifton, I made 177, and the same week 318 not out, against Yorkshire at Cheltenham. The last wicket was one of the very best I ever played on, and right through the innings I could play forward without danger to nearly every ball bowled. Remember, then, on a wicket of this kind to play forward as much as possible.

I come now to a fast, good, wet wicket. It may surprise a great many players when I say, play almost the same way as upon a fast dry wicket. The bowler has still as much difficulty in getting work on the ball, as it cuts through the ground and he cannot hold it owing to its wet and slippery state, and you will find playing forward the better way. You will have to be a little more watchful, for some balls will keep low and travel at a terrific rate after they pitch, and should you get a shooter it will come to you even faster than on a dry wicket. Batsmen on our perfect wickets of to-day think a ball that keeps low is a shooter ; but I wish they could come across the shooters we used to have at Lord's ground twenty years ago. They seemed completely to baffle some players, and gave them the impression that the ball, instead of travelling all along the ground, went under it and came up again at the bottom of the wickets.

Of course you will distinguish between a fast wet wicket and one that is not thoroughly saturated. The latter, though perhaps quite as true, will not be so fast, nor will runs come so quickly. A wicket of this kind was formerly considered much in favour of the bowler ; but that opinion has been upset, and a good punishing batsman, who takes no liberties, has the bowler pretty much at his mercy. In 1873, on a wicket of this kind, I made 160 not out for Gloucestershire *v.* Surrey at Clifton. In the early part of the innings the wicket was fast and wet, and the ball travelled at a rare pace ; but later on it became softer, and the ball did not travel so well.

A slow, good, dry wicket. You will occasionally meet with this kind of wicket after rain, when the ground has not had time to dry sufficiently to make it fast. The bowler can get more break on than he can on a good fast wicket, but the ball rises slowly off the pitch and you have plenty of time to watch it. You will rarely get a ball higher than the bails, and you can play forward or back as the pitch admits. When playing forward, you must not play too quickly, as the ball sometimes hangs a bit and you may play it back to the bowler. It was on a wicket of this kind at Clifton College ground that I scored a hundred in each innings for Gloucestershire *v.* Kent in 1887. The first day the wicket was perfect of its kind, every ball coming easy and with very little break, travelling quickly when hit, as the outside ground was much harder than the pitch, which had been watered. I made 101 in less than three hours. Rain stopped play for some time on the second afternoon, Friday, but by Saturday afternoon the wicket recovered, and I scored 103 not out in two hours and twenty minutes. Years ago, when youth was more on my side, I preferred a very fast dry wicket ; but now I confess to a leaning for a good, slow, and dry one.

The three wickets I have described must be considered easy, and attention to the points I touched upon at the beginning should help the batsman to score largely. I now come to two of a very different nature, on which, as a rule, the bowler has a high time of it, and where special nerve, skill, judgment, and luck on the part of the batsman are required before he can make a large score.

First, a bumpy wicket. By a bumpy wicket I do not mean a fast fiery wicket where the ball only goes over the top of the stumps and raps the knuckles occasionally, but a wicket upon which you may get a shooter one over and a blow on the chest the next, as a pleasing variety to those that come frequently right over your head the first bound and straight into the hands of the long-stop without again touching the ground. I can assure all young players that there is a new and curious sensation in facing balls of this kind. Skill, patience, a quick eye and ready arm are useful for the occasion, but dogged pluck is worth the whole of them. Do not let thoughts of hard knocks trouble you, or your chance of scoring even a double figure will be remote. Take your position at the wicket in your usual

way, stand up to the bowling pluckily, and do not have it said
of you that you are only a good wicket player.　On a ground
of this kind every run is valuable, and you may risk stealing a
sharp run or two now and then.　One of your side may make
fifty or more runs, but the average score is sure to be small,
and you must face the possibility of hard knocks and play as
if you expected every ball to come true and a large score depended upon you.　I am glad to be able to say that, owing to
the general improvement that has taken place in the principal
grounds, you rarely now meet with a bumpy wicket.　When
the Yorkshire County Eleven made their first appearance at
Lord's in 1870 to play against the M.C.C. and Ground, the
wicket was as bumpy as a wicket could be, and very few players
on either side escaped knocks of some kind.　It was the first
match in which the alteration in law 9 came into operation, by
which a bowler could change ends twice in the same innings
but not bowl more than two overs in succession ; and Alfred
Shaw and Wootton availed themselves of it in the second
innings of Yorkshire.　The M.C.C. went in first to the bowling
of Freeman and Emmett, and were all out for 73.　Yorkshire
made 91, George Pinder, the well-known Yorkshire wicket-
keeper, who was playing for the first time at Lord's, contribut-
ing 31.　The prospect in our second innings was not encouraging, and the wicket anything but good, when that accomplished
Essex sportsman, Mr. C. E. Green, joined me ; but if ever a
good and sterling cricketer played pluckily under adverse
circumstances, Mr. Green did that day, and in seventy minutes
we scored 99 runs.　Freeman bowled a terrific pace, and Emmett was in his glory, his bowling bumping and kicking up as
I have never seen it since.　We were hit all over the body, Mr.
Green twice painfully hard on the chest ; but he was cool and
cheerful, and made 51 in his best style—and that is saying a
great deal considering the number of balls he had to dodge
with his head.　Just before I was out, last man, Emmett
bowled a ball which hit me very hard on the point of the left
elbow, the ball flew into the air, and we ran a run before it

LUCIEN DAVIS

M.C.C. AND GROUND V. AUSTRALIANS, LORD'S, MAY 22, 1884

W. G. GRACE, L.B.W. BOWLED PALMER—101

came down into short-leg's hands ; but I could not hold the bat properly afterwards, and was glad when the innings was over. I made 66, and our total was 161. Freeman, Iddison, Pinder and Wootton were all badly knocked about. Yorkshire won by one wicket ; thanks to the plucky hitting of Luke Greenwood and the steady batting of Emmett.

Now I come to a drying, sticky wicket. This is about the worst you can play upon, and he who scores largely on it deserves to be praised indeed. If the bowling be indifferent the player who can pull or hit a long hop to leg has a decided advantage, as the ball hangs a great deal at times and favours that kind of play. If the bowler be on the spot, then tall scoring is an impossibility. The work to be got on the ball is astounding ; I have seen balls break a foot or more.

This kind of wicket is oftener seen at Lord's after a good deal of rain and a drying sun than anywhere else. We all remember that great match when the Australians made their first appearance there in 1878. I had a fair conception of what might happen, and after hitting the first ball of the match to the boundary was not surprised at being caught out from the fourth. One ball of Spofforth's was enough for me the second innings. The best advice I can give is to watch every ball on a wicket of that kind, and score when you can.

In conclusion, never treat a straight ball with contempt, however badly bowled. I have met with a ball that bounded twice or thrice before it came to me, varying every bound and at the finish twisting or shooting, and becoming a very difficult ball indeed. I have made it a rule all my life to hit a straight long hop or full-pitch with a straight or nearly straight bat, so that when a ball of this kind was bowled to me I had the full length of my bat to play it with, whereas if I had tried to pull or hit across at it, I should only have had the width of my bat, and should have been more likely to miss it.

When an indifferent bowler is put on, you cannot be too careful. He is put on to tempt you to hit, and does not mind how many runs you score off him ; but presently you will get a good ball, and if you are not careful, especially if you are trying to bring off a favourite stroke, you will hit at it and very likely lose your wicket.

After you have made a boundary hit do not make up your mind to hit another off the next ball.

Keep your eye on the bowler, watch how he holds the ball and runs up to the wicket before delivering it ; that will help you considerably to detect alteration in length and pace.

It is a mistake to hit at the pitch of slow, round, or underhand bowling. The twist is sure to beat you, and if you do not miss the ball altogether, you will most likely get caught at cover-point. In my younger days I always ran out to underhand bowling and hit it before it bounded, or waited and got it long hop. When a first-class bowler tries to bowl a slow ball with an extra amount of break, look out for a bad ball, and when it comes, as it will sooner or later, punish it, and you will upset him a bit, and very likely prevent him from bowling good balls afterwards.

I think I have touched upon nearly everything that might help a young player to a long score, and with just a word about playing against odds I have done. Whether against eighteen or twenty-two in the field, play the same game that you would against an eleven. I have very often found that the fieldsmen in the outfield are placed too deep, and a second run can be stolen after the ball passes the men close in. Do not hit to leg, but rather place or snick the ball ; you will get just as many runs without the risk of being caught. It was when playing against odds that fine placing to leg was first cultivated, and now it has to a great extent superseded leg hitting.

I need not say how delighted I am to watch the progress of every young and rising cricketer. My heart is in the game I love above all others, with a love that is as strong to-day as it was when I made my first large score, and when eye, hand, and foot were much quicker than they are now. I do not believe that there are no days like the good old days of cricket, but I do strongly believe that the prospects of the game are as bright and hopeful to-day as they have been at any time in its history, and that in future years as great if not greater things will be done with both bat and ball. I ask every young cricketer to study the points I have submitted, and it will be sufficient reward to me if they in some way help him to make a big score.

CHAPTER X.

THE AUSTRALIANS.

(By A. G. Steel.)

Not until Monday, May 27, 1878, did the English public take any interest in Australian cricket. Prior to this date four English teams had visited Australia, but their doings, though recorded in the press, did not interest the cricket community at home. The Australian players met with in the Colonies were no doubt learning from the English teams they had seen and played against, but the idea that they were up to the standard of English first-class cricket seemed absurd; and to a certain extent this estimate was justified by the records of the English visitors. In 1862 H. H. Stephenson, Surrey player and huntsman, took out twelve professional players to the Colonies under the auspices of Messrs. Spiers and Pond. They played twelve matches against eighteens and twenty-twos, won six, lost two, and drew four. In 1864, two years later, George Parr took out a team, which played sixteen matches against twenty-twos and was not beaten at all. In 1873 Mr. W. G. Grace visited the antipodes at the request of the Melbourne Cricket Club; his eleven played fifteen matches, all against odds, won ten, lost three, and drew two. In 1876 James Lillywhite followed, and it was during this tour that the Australians first won a match on equal terms. Lillywhite's team played Australia on March 15, 16 and 17, 1877, with the result that Australia won by 45 runs. This match was noteworthy for another reason. C. Bannerman made 165 for Australia, and was the first amongst Australian batsmen to score a hundred against English bowlers. Now, though English cricketers had been beaten on even terms as recently as 1877, the fact seemed to have been lost sight of at home in 1878, and when the first Australian eleven that ever visited England arrived early in the latter year, it never occurred to anyone that it could have any chance of actually storming the citadel of English cricket with success. On May 27, 1878, English cricket and its lovers received a serious shock, as on that day, in the extraordinarily short space of four and a half hours, a very fair team of the M.C.C. were beaten by nine wickets. The famous English club was certainly well represented, seeing that W. G. Grace, A. W. Ridley, A. J. Webbe, A. N. Hornby, Shaw, and Morley did battle for it. Gregory's team, as the Australians were called, had a very successful season, beating, in addition to M.C.C., Yorkshire, Surrey, Middlesex, Leicestershire, Sussex, Gloucestershire, and a bad eleven of the 'Players,' and being beaten by Nottingham, the Gentlemen of England, Yorkshire, and Cambridge, the latter the most decisive defeat of all.

The British public were surprised at these results, especially as it had expected so little from the visitors. Many of the lower classes were so ignorant of Australia itself, to say nothing of the cricket capabilities of its inhabitants, that they fully expected to find the members of Gregory's team black as the Aborigines. We remember the late Rev. Arthur Ward 'putting his foot into it' on this subject before some of the Australians. One day in the pavilion at Lord's, the writer, who had been chosen to represent the Gentlemen of England against the visitors in a forthcoming match, was sitting beside Spofforth watching a game, in which neither was taking part. Mr. Ward coming up, accosted the writer, 'Well, Mr. Steel, so I hear you are going to play against the niggers on Monday?' His face was a picture when Spofforth was introduced to him as the 'demon nigger bowler.' Gregory's team, in the writer's opinion, contained four really good bowlers: Spofforth, Boyle, Allan, and Garrett, and two fair changes in

Midwinter and Horan, but as batsmen they were poor when compared with England's best.

Charles Bannerman was a most dashing player, his off-driving being magnificent, and Horan and Murdoch were fairish batsmen. Murdoch then was very different to the Murdoch of 1882 and 1884 ; but the rest were rough, untutored, and more like country cricketers than correct players. Had this team come to England in a dry instead of a wet season, it would probably have had a very different record at the end of its visit. Spofforth, Boyle and Garrett were most deadly to the best batsmen on the soft, caked wickets they so often had to assist them ; and the Australian batsmen, with the rough crossbat style which distinguished the majority, were just as likely to knock up fifteen to twenty runs on a bad wicket as on a good one. Nothing brings good and bad batsmen so close together as bad wet seasons. When Cambridge University met them the match was played on a hard true wicket, the Australian bowling was thoroughly collared, and none of the eleven, except Murdoch, C. Bannerman, and perhaps Horan, showed any signs of being able to play correct cricket on a hard ground.

Gregory's team, however, had a wonderfully stimulating effect on English cricket. Their record taught us that the Australians could produce men to beat most of the counties, and who *might*, after a year or two of experience, play a very good game with a picked team of England.

In 1880 W. L. Murdoch brought over a Colonial team to England. The close of the season showed that in the eleven-a-side matches, Derbyshire, Yorkshire, Gloucestershire, and a good eleven of the Players of England had been beaten, while only two matches had been lost : Nottingham succeeded in winning by one wicket, and England by five wickets. This latter match was the first in which a picked team of England did battle against the Australians, and the excitement was intense. It was most interesting, and will be ever memorable for the splendid innings of W. G. Grace and W. L. Murdoch, who made 152 and 153 respectively, the latter being not out.

England's first innings was 420, Australia's 149 ; the latter followed on, and when the last man, W. H. Moule, came in there were still wanting 32 runs to save the innings defeat. Moule played a stubborn game with his captain, and put on 88 for the last wicket. How England lost five wickets on a goodish wicket in getting 57 runs will never be forgotten. The writer had taken off his cricket clothes at the end of the Australians' second innings, thinking all would soon be over ; but cricket is a strange game, and he soon had to put them on again. The result of the first pitched battle between England and Australia, though a win of five wickets for the former, was a marvellous performance on the part of the Australians ; indeed, seeing how far they were left behind on the first innings, it was one of the best things ever done at cricket to get so near the victors at the finish, especially as the wicket on the last innings was not to be found fault with. It should also be mentioned in fairness to the Australians that their best bowler, Spofforth, was prevented by an accident from taking part in this match.

The next team that visited England was in 1882, and was again under the captaincy of W. L. Murdoch. On this occasion G. Giffen, S. P. Jones, and H. H. Massie were introduced to the British public for the first time. As this eleven succeeded in defeating England, and was perhaps the best that ever represented the Colonies, we record the names :—A. C. Bannerman, J. M. Blackham, G. J. Bonnor, H. F. Boyle, P. S. McDonnell, W. L. Murdoch, G. E. Palmer, F. R. Spofforth, T. W. Garrett, T. Horan, and the three new players above mentioned. The result at the end of the season was : Matches played, 38 : won, 23 ; lost, 4 ; drawn, 11 ; Nottingham beaten once, Lancashire once, Yorkshire three times, the Gentlemen of England once, and Oxford University once. The four defeats were by Cambridge University, the Players of England, Cambridge Past and Present, and the North of England. This team played the second pitched battle between Australia and England on Monday, August 28, and after the close finish and creditable display made in

1880 against England by worse players, the match created the most intense excitement. The Australians went first to the wickets, which were very sticky, and were all disposed of for 63. England topped this by 38. Prior to the beginning of Australia's second innings, a heavy shower deluged the ground. Going in on the wet cutting-through wicket, Massie hit the incapacitated bowlers all over the field, and when the first wicket fell for 66 had scored 55 out of that number. With the exception of Murdoch and Bannerman, nobody else troubled the English bowlers, and the ground rapidly drying and caking, the whole side were disposed of for 122. The Englishmen wanted 85 to win, and when the score was at 51 for one wicket, it seemed as if the game were over. Spofforth, however, was bowling splendidly, and the wicket had become most difficult. He was bowling over medium pace, coming back many inches, and often getting up to an uncomfortable height. The English batsmen could do nothing with him, and after the keenest excitement, the game ended in a well-won victory for the Australians by 7 runs. Though this defeat was a great blow to the English representatives, there were none who grudged Australia her success, which was obtained by sound and sterling cricket. This is the only occasion on which Australians have ever defeated England. We think there is no doubt that the 1882 team was better than the one that visited us in 1884. In 1882 they had as bowlers, Boyle, Spofforth, Palmer, Garrett, and Giffen ; in 1884 they had Spofforth, Palmer, Boyle, Giffen, and Midwinter, but they had lost Garrett. The '82 team contained two excellent batsmen in Horan and Massie, whose absence was not sufficiently compensated for by Scott and Midwinter. Murdoch, Horan, Giffen, Blackham, were all likely to make runs, while Massie, Bonnor, and McDonnell often succeeded on the worst wicket in making mincemeat of any bowling.

In 1884 W. L. Murdoch again brought over an Australian team to England, and played thirty-two matches, winning eight and losing seven. This time it was decided by the English

authorities not to allow the fame of English cricket to depend
on the result of one match only, but on the best of three, and
accordingly three matches were arranged to be played between
England and Australia, one at Manchester, the second at
Lord's, and the third at the Oval. The first, at Manchester, was
seriously interfered with by the weather. Rain prevented any
play on the first day. England began to bat on a sodden
wicket and made 95, and Murdoch's team responded with 182.
England had now a difficult task to prevent being beaten, but
at the end of the match were 92 runs on, and one wicket to
fall. This was doubtless a draw in favour of the Australians,
but still a hundred runs on a bad wicket against the flower of
English bowling take a lot of getting, and it must be remembered that a month before the Australian team were all disposed
of for 60 on a sticky wicket by Peate and Emmett. The second
match was at Lord's, and was the only one of the three that
was finished. England won easily by an innings and 5 runs.
The Australians never appear to have relished Lord's ; the pace
of the ground always seems to have beaten them. The third
match at the Oval was a memorable one. The Australians
won the toss, went in on a perfect wicket, and made the
terrific score of 551 : McDonnell 103, Murdoch 211, Scott 102.
This was a truly great performance, and it was remarkable that
every member of the English team tried his hand with the ball,
by far the most successful having been the Honourable A.
Lyttelton with the analysis of four wickets for 19 runs. England made 346 first innings, in which was a magnificent display
from W. W. Read of 117. In the second innings England
made 85 for two wickets, and thus required 120 runs on a true
wicket with seven good batsmen to save the single innings
defeat.

The next and last team that visited England was in 1886,
H. J. H. Scott being the captain. This is memorable as the
first Australian team in England that did not contain W. L.
Murdoch. Several unknown men now made their appearance,
W. Bruce, E. Evans, J. McIlwraith, and J. W. Trumble, but

this was undoubtedly the least successful of all the Australian elevens. Their season's record showed : Matches played, 38 ; won, 9 ; lost, 7 ; drawn, 22. Here again, as in 1884, England *v.* Australia was to be played at Manchester, Lord's, and the Oval ; but it is unnecessary to give an account of these three matches. It will suffice to say that at Manchester England won by four wickets, at Lord's by an innings and 106 runs, and at the Oval by an innings and 217 runs. It will thus be seen that eight matches have now been played between England and Australia. England has won five, Australia has won one, and two have been drawn. We hardly think, in face of these facts, anyone can say that the Australians have succeeded in establishing their superiority over English cricketers.

An opportunity has lately been offered of comparing the individual performances, both in bowling and batting, of the leading English and Australian cricketers, in the carefully compiled statistics contained in a recent work entitled ' England *v.* Australia,' by Messrs. Brummfitt and Kirby. We there find that, in all the matches played since 1878 between the Australians and the various English teams, both in this country and in Australia, of the eleven batsmen who have the best averages the first four are Englishmen, followed by two Australians, then come three Englishmen, then one Australian, with an Englishman in the last place. The averages are as follows :—

Batsmen			Number of innings	Times not out	Total runs	Average
W. G. Grace	.	.	57	3	1,955	36·2
A. G. Steel	.	.	53	4	1,637	33·4
A. Shrewsbury	.	.	85	13	2,221	30·8
W. W. Read	.	.	46	2	1,338	30·4
W. L. Murdoch	.	.	187	21	4,574	27·5
Charles Bannerman	.	.	47	3	1,156	26·2
W. Barnes	.	.	76	5	1,832	25·8
C. T. Studd	.	.	28	2	663	25·5
R. G. Barlow	.	.	93	13	1,987	24·8
H. H. Massie	.	.	85	5	1,906	23·8
Lord Harris	.	.	30	1	688	23·7

It may be of interest here to give a short extract from this book : —

It may be urged, with some show of reason, that it is not fair to draw a comparison between the English and Australian averages because the Australians have played so many more innings than the English. It might be replied that most of the leading English-men have played quite sufficiently often to have their capabilities fairly tested ; but in order to put the Englishmen through as severe a test as the Australians, the pages of 'Lillywhite' have been consulted, and accepting the accuracy of the figures there given, a calculation has been made of the averages obtained by the eleven leading English batsmen on page 280 in all the first class matches played in England, since the advent of the first Australian team. The result arrived at is as follows :—

	In the Australian matches		In the English first-class matches	
	Completed innings	Average	Completed innings	Average
W. G. Grace . . .	54	36·2	315	34·7
A. G. Steel . . .	49	33·4	167	29·43
A. Shrewsbury . .	72	30·8	224	29·45
W. W. Read . . .	44	30·4	254	35·6
W. Barnes . . .	71	25·8	318	25·03
C. T. Studd . . .	26	25·5	132	31·08
R. G. Barlow . . .	80	24·8	302	20·7
Lord Harris . . .	29	23·7	190	30·2
E. F. S. Tylecote . .	22	23·45	77	22·2
J. M. Read . . .	57	23	238	25·1
G. Ulyett	91	22·2	408	27·2

Although in these two tables there is such a great disparity in the number of innings played, the *general standard* of averages remains much the same. In some individual cases is lower, in others higher, and on the whole there is a slight increase. The general accuracy of the averages obtained by the English batsmen against Australians is thus fully confirmed, and to any unprejudiced person the superiority of the Englishmen is apparent.

With regard to the merits of the English and Australian bowlers, we think there are few English cricketers who would deny that Spofforth is the best bowler ever seen on English grounds, at any rate in modern times, and yet these statistics show that he is not at the head of the average list.

The following is the list of the first eleven bowlers :—

				Overs	Runs	Wickets	Average
Attewell .	.	.	.	855	762	64	11
Shaw	.	.	.	1,319	1,136	88	12
Emmett .	.	.	.	1,213	1,535	117	13
Spofforth	.	.	.	5,866	9,551	715	13
Boyle	.	.	.	3,316	4,624	329	14
Peate	.	.	.	1,789	2,305	163	14
Morley .	.	.	.	736	863	58	14
Barnes .	.	.	.	1,494	1,843	122	15
Palmer .	.	.	.	5,713	8,748	548	15
Barrett .	.	.	.	475	824	51	16
Garrett .	.	.	.	3,993	5,657	345	16

The English averages against English batsmen during the same period are very nearly the same as the above. The best all-round cricketer the Australians have brought to this country in our opinion is G. Giffen. He was a thoroughly sound and hard-hitting batsman ; his bowling was at times most deadly even to the very highest class of batsmen. He had a big sure pair of hands, was a good field and fine thrower. It would be a difficult task to find any man (the English champion excepted) either in Australia or at home who has done in the last six years better all-round service to his side.

It will seem strange to all English cricketers that Spofforth should be surpassed by three English bowlers. His power of pace, command over the ball, loose shoulders, long arms and fingers, made him far and away the best bowler of the day. How is it, then, that he does not come out at the top of the averages ? There are two reasons. First : because of bad captaincy—that is to say, he used to be kept on far too long when not taking wickets ; and, secondly, because he never bowled to keep down the runs. His object was to get men out, and he tried every artifice with this in view, quite irrespective of how many runs were being scored off him. This was one thing, apart from his skill, which raised him head and shoulders above maiden-over bowling English professionals. Spofforth bowled five thousand eight hundred and sixty-six overs for seven hundred and fifteen wickets ; he consequently got a wicket once every eight overs (roughly speaking). Attewell got a wicket once every thirteen overs ; Shaw once every fourteen overs ; and Emmett once every ten overs. Spofforth was consequently, on the figures themselves, a far more deadly bowler than Shaw, Attewell, or Emmett.

In addition to Spofforth, the Australians have had a wonderfully good lot of bowlers : Palmer, Garrett, Boyle, Allan, Evans, Giffen, all being most admirable. It appears extraordinary at first sight that a country whose whole population does not exceed that of London should in the course of a few years have been able to develop such exceptional talent. We believe, however, that Australia will always possess excellent bowlers, for the following reason. In Melbourne, Sydney and Adelaide, the chief nurseries of Australian cricket, the grounds are so excellent, and usually so hard and fast, that no bowler can possibly expect the slightest amount of success unless he possesses some peculiarity of style or action, pace or power, over the ball. These, or some of them, the young Australian assiduously cultivates. In England the conditions are different, as, by reason of our variable climate, naturally weak bowling often becomes most effective. Young Australian bowlers have also ample opportunity for gaining experience and developing their skill, as there is in the colonies a very great dearth of the professional element. Members of the same club have to rely for their batting practice on the bowling of one another, and their bowlers come to acquire some of the peculiarities abovementioned that will strike terror into the hearts of their opponents in the next tie of the cup contests. These cup contests in Australia are an excellent institution, as professionalism is barred. They produce the greatest interest and excitement, and each club does its utmost to secure the much-coveted distinction of being premier club for the season. The Australian climate is a great aid to bowling and fielding. Its warmth and mildness prevent the rheumatic affections that so often attack the arms and shoulders of our players, and the Australians consequently retain their suppleness of limb and activity of youth longer than their English cousins. Nothing illustrates this better than the prevalence of good throwing amongst Australian fieldsmen. The every-day sight on our own grounds of a man who has thrown his arm out and can do nothing but jerk is almost unknown in Australia ; even Colonials who have passed their cricket prime and have reached the age of thirty-eight or forty can still throw with much the same dash as of old. In our county teams we find a woeful deficiency in this essential to good fielding ; the cold and damp of our northern climate having penetrated into the bones and created a chronic and incurable stiffness.

Unfortunately we hear that at the present time cricket in the big towns of Australia is not so popular as it was a few years back, and that the best matches do not attract more than a sprinkling of spectators. This is greatly to be regretted. A sudden change must certainly have come over the Australian cricket-loving public of six or seven years ago. In 1882, when the writer was out with the Hon. Ivo Bligh's team, the beautiful grounds of Sydney and Melbourne were simply crammed at every match. The excitement over the representative matches was intense ; in many cases public holidays were given, shops were shut, and the whole place went mad about cricket for about three days. The writer—in common with everyone who has had the good fortune to visit the Colonies with a team —has very pleasing recollections of his trip. The people are generous and hospitable to a degree.

One occasionally hears a really good cricket story in Australia. The following was vouched for as a fact by several leading members of Australian cricket, and was told me as illustrative of the skill and dash of some great fieldsman whom I have never had the good fortune to meet. This man was standing

THE CRITICS

coverpoint one day—his usual place in the field. He was marvellously quick, sometimes indeed his returns were so smart that none could tell whether he had used his right or left arm. He was, however, apt at times to be sleepy and inattentive to the game. On one occasion he was in this state, and just as the bowler started to bowl he noticed his sleepy coverpoint standing looking on the ground with his back to the wickets. 'Hulloa, there, wake up !' shouted he. Quick as lightning turned the coverpoint, and seeing something dark dashing past him made a dart, and caught, not the ball as he had thought, but a swallow. Talk of Royle or Briggs after that !

It is indeed deplorable that cricket in Australia has diminished in popularity, but we have not to go far to find the reasons for it. In the first place, we believe it is owing to the fact of international cricket having been overdone in the last few years, and secondly to the dull slow sticky style of play that has become so common in first-class cricket both here and in the colonies. We trust that this summer will be the last time we shall have the Australians over with us for certainly the next five years. Their first few teams encouraged and gave a fillip to English cricket, and our return visits were of equal service to them. But the thing has been too much laboured, and we in England are now weary of these continued invasions, not because the Australian players are unpopular with us at home, but because we want some rest and time to turn our attention to domestic cricket affairs. After the present season an Australian team will not be really welcomed by our English players, till the Spofforths, Palmers, Graces, and Shrewsburys are no longer on the war-path, and a new generation of cricketers has arisen to engage in the friendly rivalry of the Lion and Kangaroo.

CHAPTER XI.

THE UNIVERSITY CRICKET MATCH.

(BY THE HON. R. H. LYTTELTON.)

IF to play drawn matches be a constant reproach against certain elevens, neither University eleven can be blamed on this score. Fifty-three matches have been begun between these old rivals, and no fewer than fifty-one have been finished. Of the two drawn matches, one, the first ever played, was confined to one day only ; the second was so long ago as 1844, and that was confined to two days. All the rest have been fought out to the end, and of the fifty-one completed matches Cambridge has won twenty-six times and Oxford twenty-five ; thus Cambridge has a proud balance of one in its favour. All the matches except five have been played at Lord's ; the remaining five were played at Oxford, three on the Magdalen ground, one on Cowley Marsh, and one on Bullingdon Green. The dark blues appear to have been slightly favoured in this respect—for presumably they knew their way about Oxford grounds better than their rivals—and out of the five matches played at Oxford, Cambridge only succeeded in winning one. The rules of qualification to play in this match are now strict only in one particular, and that is that nobody is allowed to play more than four times. Several players have played five matches, and their names are : C. H. Ridding, A. Ridding, C. D. Marsham, and R. D. Walker, all Oxford men. The fact that some players play on a side for five years may constitute a slight reason for causing the side they assist to lose matches and not win them ; but during the last three years that Mr. R. D. Walker helped his University he also helped the Gentlemen of England in their annual matches against the Players both at Lord's and at the Oval; and C. D. Marsham was certainly not excelled by any gentleman bowler for accuracy and general efficiency during all the years he played for Oxford. Oxford were strong all the five years he played, and won four out of the five matches; the other match resulted in a victory for Cambridge, mainly owing to the performances, both in batting and bowling, of the famous Mr. J. Makinson. Not since 1865, however, when Mr. R. D. Walker last played for Oxford, has any cricketer played more than four times, and since that time the rule has been well established, limiting the period to four years. But there is considerable elasticity allowed in permitting players to represent their University within those four years. A residence for a week is apparently sufficient, provided that the man's name is kept on the books of some College or Hall. Mr. O'Brien, who represented Oxford in 1884 and 1885, resided for one summer at New Inn Hall and never went near his University again, but if he had chosen and had been selected he might have played for the full term of four years. Mr. Leslie, after residing at Oxford for one year, went into business in London, but played three years for Oxford, and till his last year performed yeoman's service. In 1856, Makinson's year, Mr. T. W. Wills, with the concurrence and sanction of Oxford, played for Cambridge without ever having resided at Cambridge for one single day, though his name was entered on the College books. However, his part in the match consisted of getting five runs in one innings and bowling nine overs for one wicket. It appears very clear, then, that Oxford have profited very much by having five matches played on their own ground and making use, for five years, of Mr. C. D. Marsham, the best bowler they ever possessed, to say nothing of Mr. R. D. Walker.

Of course the characteristics of University cricket have changed very much, following the example of cricket generally. About the first match of all the Bishop of St. Andrews, who played in it, has very kindly written the following note :—

The First Inter-University Cricket Match.—1827.

In the newly published Life of my younger brother Christopher, the late Bishop of Lincoln, the following words are to be found, quoted from his private journal :—' Friday' (no date—but early in June, 1826). ' Heard from Charles. He wishes that Oxford and Cambridge should play a match at cricket' (p. 46). And as I have been asked to put upon paper what I can remember concerning the first Inter-University Cricket Match, with a view to its insertion in the present volume, I venture to take those words for my text. Yes ; I was then in my Freshman's year at Christ Church, and both my brother and I—he at Winchester, and I at Harrow—had been in our respective school elevens. But more than this, as captain of the Harrow Eleven I had enjoyed what was then a novel experience in carrying on correspondence with brother captains at other public schools—Eton, Winchester, Rugby and even Charter House ; and I well remember how the last amused us at Harrow, by the pompous and, as we presumed to think, bumptious style of his letter, proposing ' to determine the superiority at cricket which has been so long undecided.' Having played against Eton for four years, from the first match in 1822 to 1825, and in the first match against Winchester in the last-named year, I had a large acquaintance among cricketers who had gone off from those schools and from Harrow to both Universities. My brother, as I have said, was one of these, but though successful in the Wykehamist Eleven at Lord's in 1825 (when he got 35 runs in his second innings, and ' caught' our friend Henry Manning—the future cardinal—of which he was wont to boast in after years), he did not keep up his cricket at Cambridge, whereas I continued to keep up mine at Oxford and was in the University Eleven during the whole time of my undergraduate course. Nothing came of my ' wish' to bring about a match between the Universities in 1826. But in 1827 the proposal was carried into effect. Though an Oxford man, my home was at Cambridge, my father being Master of Trinity ; and this gave me opportunities for communicating with men of that University, many of whom remained up for the vacations, or for part of the vacations, especially at Easter. I remember calling upon Barnard of King's, who had been captain of an Eton Eleven against whom I had played, and who was now one of the foremost Cambridge cricketers, and he gave me reason to fear that no King's man would be able to play at the time proposed (early in June), though that time would be within the Cambridge vacation and not within ours, because their men, at King's, were kept up longer than at the other Colleges. And this, I believe, proved actually the case ; and if so, some allowance should be made for it. But the fact is, there were similar difficulties on both sides, and I am not sure they were not as great or greater upon ours. In those ante-railway days it was necessary to get permission from the College authorities to go up to London in term time, and the permission was not readily granted. To take my own case :—My conscience still rather smites me when I remember that in order to gain my end, I had to present myself to the Dean and tell him that I wished to be allowed to go to London —not to play a game of cricket (that would not have been listened to)—but to consult a dentist ; a piece of Jesuitry which was *understood,* I believe, equally well on both sides ; at all events my tutor, Longley—afterwards Archbishop of Canterbury—was privy to it.

Thus, though not without difficulties, the match came on, but unhappily, the weather presenting a fresh difficulty, it did not fully go off. We could only play a single innings ; with the result which the score shows. The precise day in June on which it was played has been disputed. One report gives the 4th ; another states that 'the match did not take place on the 4th as intended, but was deferred for a few days.' I can only say that I do not remember any postponement, as I think I should do had such been the case ; and what is more, 'a few days' later would have brought it within our vacation, and so would have rendered my piece of Jesuitism unnecessary. The players on the Cambridge side were mostly Etonians, though there was, I think, no King's man among them; and on the Oxford side, mostly Wykehamists. We scored 258 runs to our opponents' 92, but it cannot be said we were a strong eleven. The bowling was divided between Bayley and me ; and the state of the ground being in my favour, I was singularly successful with my left-hand twist from the off, bringing down no less than seven wickets in the one innings for only 25 runs. Jenner, famous as a wicket-keeper, and well known afterwards as Sir Herbert Jenner Fust, was the only batsman who made any stand against it. He had learnt by painful experience how to deal with it. We had been antagonists in the Eton and Harrow match of 1822 ; and I can well remember even now, though it is 66 years ago, his look of ineffable disgust and dismay when I had pitched a ball some four or five inches wide to the off, and he had shouldered his bat meaning to punish it as it rose by a smart cut to point, the tortuous creature shot in obliquely and took his middle stump, when he had only got two runs. Precisely the same happened again in his second innings, only then he got no runs at all. Again in Eton v. Harrow 1823 I had bowled him at 7. And yet he was considered the best bat on the Eton side next to Barnard. He now made 47 runs, while no one else on the Cambridge side scored more than 8. He was also successful as a bowler, taking five wickets, mine included (against which he had a very strong claim), though I do not remember that he had much reputation in that line ; and certainly upon the whole the Cambridge bowling must have been very indifferent to allow some of our men to run up the scores which stand to their names.

Though often successful as a bowler (left-handed, under-hand), batting (right-handed) was, if I may be bold to say so, my *forte*. In 1828, the next year after this match, my average, upwards of 40, was higher than that of any other in the Oxford eleven. I mention this with the less compunction because in the second Inter-University match my name appears without a run in either innings, and I wish to state how the failure is to be accounted for. In that year, 1829, the first Inter-University boatrace took place at Henley, and I was one of the eight. As boating and cricket were then carried on in the same (summer) term, and the race and the match were both to come off in the same week, I wished to resign my place in the eleven. But this was not allowed. I had therefore no alternative but to make my appearance and do my best, though I had not played once before during the season, and though I was suffering from the effects of my rowing in a way which made it almost impossible for me to hold a bat. However, though I got no runs, I was so far of use that I bowled two, and caught two of our opponents ; and we won the match, not quite so triumphantly as in 1827 (if a ' drawn ' match can be so described), but quite easily enough, as we had won the boatrace quite ' easily ' two days before, Wednesday, June 10th.

Of the players in the two elevens, who contended at Lord's more than 60 years ago, five—if not six—I believe, are still living. Who shall say how much the lengthening of their days beyond the ordinary span of our existence here is to be attributed to ' Cricket's manly toil ' ?

I have now done the best I could to comply with the request

made to me as an old cricketer, and if I have been garrulous, and if I have been egotistical, I can fairly plead, that this is no more than was to be expected when an ultra-octogenarian was applied to for his reminiscences.

CHARLES WORDSWORTH.

ST. ANDREWS : *May* 16, 1888.

In the match of 1827, Oxford, strange to relate, got a total of 258 runs, and exactly realised 200 runs in the third match in 1836, while Cambridge got 287 runs in the fifth match in 1839 ; but from 1839 to 1851, when Cambridge scored 266 runs, there was no innings played by either side which resulted in 200 runs, and this notwithstanding the gigantic number of extras that were sometimes given. Cambridge in 1841 won by 8 runs, but scored in the two innings 56 by extras. In 1842 Cambridge again won by 162 runs, and scored 81 by extras ; while Oxford in 1843 gained 65 by extras, losing the match, however, by 54 runs. After 1851 scores of 200 runs and over became more frequent, and still extras formed a formidable item in the various totals. Cambridge gave 34 extras out of a total of 273 in 1852, or 1 run in every 8 ; and Oxford in the same year gave Cambridge 40 extras out of a total of 196, or an average of a little under 1 in every 5. We have made a careful comparison showing the different totals and the percentage of extras, and have found the following remarkable fact : in the first twenty-six matches the total of runs scored came to 11,192, the number of extras amounted to 1,767, making the percentage of extras to runs amount to a little over 1 to 6. In the last twenty-seven matches 16,457 runs were scored and 988 extras, reducing the proportion to 1 to 16. In other words, for the first twenty-six matches extras constituted 16 per cent. of the total amount scored, while during the last twenty-seven years they only amount to 6 per cent.

Most earnestly is it to be hoped that some improvement will soon be visible in the bowling at both Universities, for the scoring is getting very tediously large. Since 1880 Cambridge has had Messrs. A. G. Steel, C. T. Studd, and C. W. Rock, who were good bowlers, and Messrs. P. H. Morton, A. F. J. Ford, and C. A. Smith, who may be called fair bowlers. Oxford during the same period has turned out, in our judgment, only one really good bowler—Mr. A. H. Evans ; but she has produced more fair bowlers than Cambridge—Messrs. Peake, Bastard, Whitby, Cochrane, Buckland, Forster, and Nepean, having all claims to be included under this head. These fair bowlers could be relied on to get men out on difficult wickets, but more can hardly be said of them. The four good bowlers, Messrs. Steel, Studd, Rock, and Evans, had great merit, and were worthy to be compared with C. D. Marsham, W. F. Traill, W. F. Maitland, E. L. Fellowes, and E. M. Kenney of Oxford, and R. Lang, H. W. Salter, H. M. Plowden, Hon. F. G. Pelham and W. N. Powys of Cambridge. These last were all fast, with the exception of Messrs. Maitland, Pelham and Plowden, while the four later bowlers were all slow, except Mr. Evans.

No fewer than sixty-nine men have played four matches ; and it is curious to notice that out of these sixty-nine there are only one Oxford man and three Cambridge men who have played in four winning elevens. The three Cambridge men are Messrs. T. A. Anson, W. Mills, and W. de St. Croix ; and the one Oxford man is Mr. S. C. Voules. Mr. Voules played in the four winning elevens of 1863, '64, '65, and '66, Messrs. T. A. Anson and W. de St. Croix played in the four winning elevens of 1839, '40, '41, and '42, and Mr. W. Mills played in 1840, '41, '42, and '43. Two unfortunate Cambridge men had the bad luck to play four losing matches—namely, Messrs. R. D. Balfour and G. H. Tuck, in the years 1863, '64, '65, and '66. So far no Oxford man has had this fate. Cambridge once won five consecutive matches, and on two occasions they have won four, while Oxford has twice won four consecutive matches. As may be expected, the runs scored by the more recent batsmen altogether exceed the earlier players' efforts. Up to 1870, when Mr. Yardley made the first hundred, Mr. Bullock's 78 for Oxford, obtained in 1858, was the highest individual score, and the highest individual aggregates in any one match are 92 in 1849 by Mr. R. T. King, 95 by Mr. Makinson in 1856, 90 by Mr. Mitchell in 1862, and 92 by the same gentleman in 1865. One of Mr. King's innings was not completed. So Mr. Yardley in 1870 beat the record of any two aggregates by his one innings. Since 1870 the individual scores of 100 have come fast and furious, and altogether thirteen hundreds have been played, seven by Cambridge to six by Oxford. Mr. Yardley is still in the proud position of being the only batsman who has twice got into three figures, and nobody who saw either of his great performances will ever forget it. Unless, however, there is a change for the better in bowling or an alteration in the laws, it is certain that hundreds will come with comparative frequency, and we cannot help pining for a return to the old state of things when 200 was reckoned a very large total. The highest aggregate in any one match is Lord George Scott's 166 in 1887, and the highest individual score is Mr. Key's 143 in 1886. No performances, however, are entitled to more credit than Mr. Makinson's aggregate of 95 in 1856, and Mr. Mitchell's 90 in 1862, and the fewer long scores made in former days made a far larger proportion of the total runs obtained by the whole side. Mr. Makinson's runs in 1855 were obtained against perhaps the best bowling eleven that Oxford ever possessed, containing Messrs. C. D. Marsham, A. Payne, W. Fellowes, and W. Fiennes, while Mr. Mitchell's score in 1862 was not much less than half of the total score of his side. Against him are to be found the names of Plowden, Lang, Salter, and Lyttelton, and never in any match, except in the previous year when they had the same quartet, has Cambridge been so strong in bowling as they were in 1862. The highest average has been secured by Mr. Key of Oxford, and this amounts to no less than 49. Close behind him comes Mr. Wright of Cambridge, with an average of 48·4 ; then Mr. Mitchell with 42·4, and Mr. Yardley with 39·5. Mr. Mitchell's average is remarkable, as his highest score was 57, though he was once not out. Mr. Wright was twice not out, Mr. Key and

Mr. Mitchell once each ; Mr. Yardley, however, was always got out in the end.

The earlier bowlers, as far as analysis is a guide, carry all before them. Not till the twentieth match, played in 1854—Mr. C. D. Marsham's first year—was any analysis kept. To judge, however, by the standard of wickets, Mr. G. E. Yonge of Oxford, who in four years obtained thirty-nine wickets, Mr. E. W. Blore and Mr. Sayres, both of Cambridge, who in the same time got thirty-two, are entitled to the highest place.

Naturally enough, as Mr. Marsham played five years and was also the best bowler on the whole that Oxford ever turned out, most wickets fell to his share. He got forty wickets at a cost of 361 runs—that is to say, of only 9 runs a wicket—a great performance under any circumstances. Two wides only were scored against Mr. Marsham, and there is no record of a 'no ball.' He bowled a strictly orthodox round-arm of fast medium pace, and generally round the wicket.

Mr. E. M. Kenney was a very fast and dangerous left-hand bowler, most terrifying to a nervous batsman, for he delivered that unpleasant sort of ball which pursues the batsman, and is apt, to adopt a pugilistic metaphor, to get in heavily on the ribs. During the three years that Mr. Makinson played for Cambridge he took twenty-one wickets at a cost of 194 runs, or just 9 runs a wicket ; and when it is remembered that he was also distinctly the best bat in the two elevens each of the three years he played, it may be safely assumed that, as an all-round man, he has never had a superior, with the exception of Mr. A. G. Steel. At the same time it must be admitted that in bowling he was quite as successful against Oxford as his merits justified.

The famous Cambridge fast bowler, Mr. R. Lang, played three years and got fifteen wickets at a cost of only 84 runs, or a fraction over 5 runs per wicket—an analysis that has never been surpassed, and deserves to be quoted as an example for young players to emulate. In 1860 he bowled in the two innings twenty-one overs for 19 runs and six wickets. In 1861

he lost his pace owing to an injured arm and was unsuccessful, bowling twenty-six overs for 30 runs and no wicket. In
1862, in the two innings, he bowled twenty-nine overs for
35 runs and nine wickets ; and, to take the first innings alone,
we find he bowled only thirty-four balls for 4 runs and five
wickets all clean bowled. Considering his pace he was very
straight, and only bowled 6 wides in all three matches. H. W.
Salter of Cambridge played two years, and obtained fourteen
wickets for 74 runs, or a fraction over 5 runs a wicket, another
extraordinary performance. Mr. H. M. Plowden, who played
four years from 1860, lowered nineteen wickets for 153 runs,
or an average of 8 runs a wicket. In no previous or subsequent
years has either University been so amply provided with bowling
strength as was Cambridge during these three years, as, besides
Salter, Lang, and Plowden, in 1860 she had Messrs. E. B.
Fawcett and D. R. Onslow, and in 1861 and '62 the Hon.
C. G. Lyttelton, who bowled for the Gentlemen.

The greatest bowling feat in the whole history of University
cricket belongs to Mr. S. E. Butler, of Eton and Oxford renown, and took place in 1871. Cambridge had some good
bats in her eleven—Messrs. Money, Tobin, Fryer, Scott,
Yardley and Thornton, a rough and ready hitter in the person
of Mr. Cobden, and a fair batsman in Mr. Stedman. But
Mr. Butler found an old-fashioned Lord's wicket, and he
bowled a terrific pace and got on a spot which shot and made
his balls break considerably down the hill. He got the whole
ten wickets in one innings and in the match he lowered fifteen
wickets for 95 runs. His bowling was unplayable on the first
day ; eight of the ten wickets in the first innings were clean
bowled, and twelve out of the whole fifteen.

It will interest and comfort young cricketers to remind
them how many great batsmen have failed in these matches.
We feel sure that these latter will excuse us for pointing out
their shortcomings ; for they will know that we do so only to
sustain their weaker brethren and illustrate the glorious uncer-
tainty of the game. The late Mr. John Walker, who for several

years represented the Gentlemen, got 19 runs in six innings, or a proud average of 3. His younger brother, Mr. R. D. Walker, the silver-haired veteran of five inter-University contests, gallantly led off with an innings of 42 ; but the result of his five years' batting against Cambridge was 84 runs in ten innings, his first innings in fact amounting to one-half of the total runs he scored in five years. Yet he played for the Gentlemen in 1863, 1864, and 1865, and these were the last three years he played for Oxford. Mr. A. W. Ridley played for four years, and his runs for seven innings came to a total of 61, or an average of 10 runs per innings, as once he carried his bat. The present Lord Lyttelton, who played for the Gentlemen of England his first year at Cambridge, batted exactly on a par with Mr. Ridley, as he also made 61 runs in six innings, and was once not out. Cambridge men of his date will tell you that on Fenner's nobody was ever more dangerous, and his scores for those days were enormous. Mr. C. G. Lane—of whom the poet wrote

> You may join with me in wishing that the Oval once again
> May resound with hearty plaudits to the praise of Mr. Lane—

played seven innings for a total of 35 runs. Take courage then, young cricketer, and know that if you fail, you fail in good company !

Most extraordinary have been the vicissitudes of fortune in several of these matches. Oxford in 1871 had a fine eleven, which easily defeated Cambridge by eight wickets ; and in 1872 they played no fewer than eight of their old eleven. Cambridge played seven, and the four new men were the famous pair of young Etonians, Messrs. Longman and Tabor, the Harrovian, Mr. Baily, and the Wykehamist, Mr. Raynor. The odds on Oxford at the start were about 2 to 1. Yet Cambridge on winning the toss put together the largest total yet realised by either side in any one innings, namely 388 runs. The two Etonian freshmen were on the whole entitled to the chief honours on this occasion, as for the first time they

made over 100 runs before the fall of a wicket. Mr. Longman was badly run out by Mr. Yardley after batting for about
two and a half hours, or else another 100 runs might have been
put on. When the Oxford eleven went in to bat, not one of
them could look at Mr. Powys, the fastest bowler of the day,
except Messrs. Ottaway and Tylecote, who both played remark-
ably well in the second innings. Mr. Powys secured thirteen
wickets at a cost of 75 runs, or a trifle under 6 runs a wicket.

Everybody has heard of the 2-run success of Cambridge in
1870, and the 6-run victory of Oxford in 1875. The difference
between the two matches consisted in the fact that in 1870 not
till the last wicket was actually bowled down did it appear
possible for Oxford to lose ; in 1875 the issue was quite doubtful till Mr. A. F. Smith made that fatal stroke to a plain lob.
Cambridge in 1870 were on the whole the favourites ; not
that there was much to choose between the two elevens, but
because they had won the three previous years. In batting,
Cambridge had Messrs. Dale, Money, and Yardley ; and
Oxford, Messrs. Ottaway, Pauncefote, and Tylecote—quite a
case of six of one and half a dozen of the other, though Yardley
was far the most dangerous man. In bowling Oxford were
handicapped by Mr. Butler's strained arm, which prevented him
from bowling more than a few overs ; but they possessed Messrs.
Belcher and Francis, two good fast bowlers. Cambridge had
Cobden for a fast bowler, Harrison Ward for a medium pace,
and Bourne for slow round. So while Mr. Francis was some
way the best fast bowler of the two elevens, Oxford were deficient in variety, while Cambridge possessed all paces and
also Mr. Money's lobs. Cambridge won the toss and put together 147 runs, the good bats all failing, and only Mr. Scott
doing credit to himself by an innings of 45. Oxford scored
more equally, though neither Ottaway nor Pauncefote contributed more than modest double figures ; the total, nevertheless,
came to 175, or a majority of 28. The next hour's play apparently saw Cambridge utterly routed. Mr. Dale stopped all
that time, but nobody stopped with him. The total at the fall of

the fifth wicket was 40, or only 12 on. 'We are going to win a match at last !' said one of the Oxonians to another who had been educated at Rugby. 'Wait a bit,' said the Rugbeian, who turned his head and saw Yardley advancing to the wicket ; 'I have seen this man get 100 before now.' The companion of the last speaker possibly had not seen Yardley perform this feat, but he had not long to wait. There are several batsmen whose play baffles criticism, and Yardley was one of them. He certainly played some balls in a manner that purists found fault with, but good judges of the game could see that there was genius in his method ; and genius, as we all know, rises above canons and criticism. If Mr. Yardley had not touched a bat for six months, still he might walk to the wickets and play a magnificent innings ; for genius requires little or no practice. Those familiar with his play knew that they might look out for squalls if he was allowed to get set. Mr. Dale was at the other end, playing every ball with a perfectly straight bat and in the most correct style. In the minds of both of them it was a crisis ; for each knew that unless they put on a lot of runs the match was lost, as five of their side were out. One mistake and Cambridge would have to retire beaten. But no mistake was made. Yardley got set ; the bowling was fast and so was the ground, and the former was hit into a complete knot. There seemed to be no prospect of getting either of them out, when Mr. Yardley sent a ball hard back to the bowler, who made a fine catch off a fine hit, and the Cambridge man retired with the first Inter-University 100. Mr. Dale made a leg hit, and was splendidly caught by Mr. Ottaway with one hand over the ropes.

In a short time the innings was over, and Oxford had to face a total of 178 to win the match. In these days on a hard wicket this is regarded as a comparatively easy feat ; but runs were not so easy to accumulate eighteen years ago, and the betting was now even, Cambridge for choice. One Oxford wicket was soon got, and then a long stand was made by

Messrs. Fortescue and Ottaway, both of whom played excellent cricket. The total was brought up to 72 for only one wicket, the betting veered round to 2 to 1 on Oxford, and Mr. Ward was put on to bowl. This change was the turning point of the game. Mr. Fortescue was soon bowled, so was Mr. Pauncefote, and with the total at 86 the betting was again evens, Oxford for choice. Mr. Ward had found his spot and was bowling with deadly precision when Mr. Tylecote came in. Both Ottaway and Tylecote now batted cautiously and well, and Mr. Ward went off for a time. Mr. Tylecote was a very good bat, but compared to Ottaway only mortal; how on earth Ottaway was to be got out was a problem that seemed well-nigh insoluble. The total went up to 153, or only 25 runs to win and seven wickets to go down; the betting 6 to 1 on Oxford. A yell was heard, and Mr. Tylecote was bowled by Mr. Ward, Mr. Townshend came in only to go out for a single, and then appeared Mr. F. H. Hill.

Again did the match seem over, for Mr. Ottaway's defence appeared perfectly impregnable, and the new comer batted with the greatest confidence. The Cambridge fielding had not been tiptop at any part of the innings, and few of them were up to the mark now—in fact, if the match had finished against them, they would have deserved their fate for their slovenliness in the field. Mr. Ward was bowling to Mr. Ottaway, who made a characteristic hit, not hard but low, in the direction of short-leg. Mr. Fryer was not a good field, but he rose to the occasion and made a good catch close to the ground, so close that Mr. Ottaway appealed, but the decision was given against him. Oxford only wanted 18 runs, Mr. Hill was batting well, and there were four more wickets to go down. Mr. Francis came in, made a single, and was out l.b.w., amid Cambridge yells; when over was called by the umpire the betting was 3 to 1 on Oxford. The Oxford eleven might have been seen sitting in the pavilion quite happy in the anticipation of a victory, for only 3 runs were wanted to tie and 4 to win. For three long years the Cambridge eleven had been blessed by victories; the turn seemed to have come at last; and Mr. Charles Marsham's face wore a look that his friends knew well, the best description of which is that it bore the greatest contrast to his expression when Oxford's star was not in the ascendent. Mr. Butler now walked to the wicket. Mr. Butler this year of grace was not a bad bat; he had greatly improved since the previous year, and had made 18 runs the first innings. He had not now to receive the ball, for Mr. Hill, who was bustling the field a good deal, stood at his place ready to play, and amidst dead silence the ball was tossed to Mr. Cobden.

We say with confidence that never can one over bowled by any bowler at any future time surpass the over that Cobden was about to deliver then, and it deserves a minute description. Cobden took a long run and bowled very fast, and on the whole was for his pace a straight bowler. But he bowled with little or no break, had not got a puzzling delivery, and though effective against inferior bats, would never have succeeded in bowling out a man like Mr. Ottaway if he had sent a thousand balls to him. However, on the present occasion Ottaway was out, those he had to bowl to were not first-rate batsmen, and Cobden could bowl a good yorker.

You might almost have heard a pin drop as Cobden began his run and the ball whizzed from his hand. Crack! was heard as Mr. Hill's bat met the ball plumb and hard, and a yell that beat Donnybrook burst from several thousand Oxford throats. The Oxford eleven still sat at the threshold of the pavilion ready to welcome their comrades after the winning hit was made, and they yelled louder than the rest. The ball was hit hard and low in the direction of long-off, where stood Mr. Bourne, a safe fieldsman; but that he could save this ball from going to the ropes and winning the match by three wickets nobody dreamt. However, the yell of Oxford subdued to a gentler tone, and it was seen that Mr. Bourne had got his left hand in the way and converted a fourer into a single; as the match stood, Oxford wanted 2 to tie and 3 to win and three wickets to go down : Mr. Butler to receive the ball. The second ball that

Cobden bowled was very similar to the first, straight and well up on the off stump. Mr. Butler did what anybody else except Louis Hall or Shrewsbury would have done, namely, let drive vigorously. Unfortunately he did not keep the ball down, and it went straight and hard a catch to Mr. Bourne, to whom everlasting credit is due, for he held it, and away went Mr. Butler—amidst Cambridge shouts this time. The position was getting serious, for neither Mr. Stewart nor Mr. Belcher was renowned as a batsman. Rather pale, but with a jaunty air that cricketers are well aware frequently conceals a sickly feeling of nervousness, Mr. Belcher walked to the wicket and took his guard. He felt that if only he could stop one ball and be bowled out the next, still Mr. Hill would get another chance of a knock and the match would probably be won. Cobden had bowled two balls, and two more wickets had to be got ; if therefore a wicket was got each ball the match would be won by Cambridge, and Mr. Hill would have no further opportunity of distinguishing himself. In a dead silence Cobden again took the ball. Everybody knows that the sight of a yorker raises hope in a batsman's breast that either a full pitch or a half-volley is coming. To play either of these balls ninety-nine players out of a hundred raise their bat off the ground as a first preliminary. If you are not a quick player the raising of the bat sometimes means nothing less than opening the door of defence, and the ball getting underneath. This is precisely what happened on the present occasion, and Cobden shot in a very fast yorker. A vision of the winning hit flashed across Mr. Belcher's brain, and he raised his bat preparatory to performing great things. He had not seen till too late that neither a full pitch nor a half-volley had been bowled ; he could not get his bat down again in time, the ball went under, and his wicket was shattered. There was still one more ball wanted to complete, and Mr. Belcher, a sad man, walked away amid an uproarious storm of cheers.

Matters were becoming distinctly grave, and very irritating must it have been to Mr. Hill, who was like a billiard-player watching his rival in the middle of a big break ; he could say a good deal and think a lot, but he could do nothing. Mr. Stewart, *spes ultima* of Oxford, with feelings that are utterly impossible to describe, padded and gloved, nervously took off his coat in the pavilion. If ever a man deserved pity, Mr. Stewart deserved it on that occasion. He did not profess to be a good bat, and his friends did not claim so much for him ; he was an excellent wicket-keeper, but he had to go in at a crisis that the best bat in England would not like to face. Mr. Pauncefote, the Oxford captain, was seen addressing a few words of earnest exhortation to him, and with a rather sick feeling Mr. Stewart went to the wicket. Mr. Hill looked at him cheerfully, but very earnestly did Mr. Stewart wish the next ball well over. He took his guard and held his hands low on the bat handle, which was fixed fast as a tree on the block-hole ; for Mr. Pauncefote, having seen that Mr. Belcher lost his wicket by raising his bat and letting the ball get under it, had earnestly entreated Mr. Stewart to put the bat straight in the block-hole and keep it there without moving it. This was not by any means bad advice, for the bat covers a great deal of the wicket, and though it is a piece of counsel not likely to be offered to W. G. Grace or Daft, it might not have been inexpedient to offer it to Mr. Stewart. Here, then, was the situation—Mr. Stewart standing manfully up to the wicket, Mr. Cobden beginning his run, and a perfectly dead silence in the crowd. Whiz went the ball, Stewart received the same on his right thigh, fly went the bails, the batsman was bowled off his legs, and Cambridge had won the match by 2 runs ! The situation was bewildering. Nobody could quite realise what had happened for a second or so, but then—— Up went Mr. Absalom's hat, down the pavilion steps with miraculous rapidity flew the Rev. A. R. Ward, and smash went Mr. Charles Marsham's umbrella against the pavilion brickwork.

One word more about this never-to-be-forgotten match. The unique performance of Cobden has unduly cast in the shade Mr. Ward's performance in the second innings. It was a good wicket, and Oxford had certainly on the whole a good batting eleven. Yet Mr. Ward bowled thirty-two overs for 29 runs and got six wickets, and of those six wickets five were certainly the best batsmen on the side. He clean bowled Messrs. Fortescue, Pauncefote, and Tylecote, and got out in other ways Messrs. Ottaway, Townshend, and Francis. It is hardly too much to say that in this innings Mr. Ward got the six best wickets and Mr. Cobden the four worst. In the whole match Mr. Ward got nine wickets for 62 runs, and this again, let it be said, on an excellent ground. Comparisons are odious, however, and the four Cambridge men, Yardley, Dale, Ward, and Cobden, have no reason to be jealous of each other, and every reason to be satisfied with themselves.

Oxford have got a victory to set off against this Cambridge triumph in 1870. It took place five years later, and though Mr. Ridley's bowling at the finish was not condensed into one sensational over like Cobden's, still the greatest credit is due to him for putting himself on at the right moment, fully realising an undoubted truth, that lobs are most terrifying to very nervous players at a crisis.

Comparing the two elevens, on paper it would appear that Oxford were the better bowling eleven, and were considerably superior in fielding. In 1870 Cambridge deserved to have lost the match on account of their bad fielding; in 1875 they succeeded in doing so. Messrs. Webbe and Lang started by making 86 for the first wicket, and Mr. Webbe was twice badly missed at short-slip. Mr. Lang ought to have been easily stumped. In Oxford's second innings four Oxford wickets, including Ridley and Webbe, were down for 34. Mr. Briggs came in and was badly missed at short-slip directly, and disaster was averted for some time; and Mr. Game, who scored 22, was missed shortly after he went to the wicket. The Oxford fielding was very fine all through, though one member missed two easy catches. The bowling was more evenly divided; Oxford had more bowlers than Cambridge, though Messrs. Sharpe and Patterson were as good as, or better than, Messrs.

Lang and Buckland. But besides these two Oxford had Mr. Royle and Mr. Ridley and Mr. Kelcey, while the two Cambridge bowlers had to do most of the work.

In batting the position was somewhat similar. Ridley and Webbe were superior to Longman and the second best Cantab, but on the other hand Cambridge were stronger all through. On the whole the sides were very even.

Oxford made a good start, thanks to the politeness of the Cambridge field, though both Webbe and Lang played well, and fair scores were made by Ridley, Pulman and Buckland, but at no time during the match did Mr. Ridley appear at home to Mr. Patterson's bowling. The total reached 200, and there were 20 extras, of which 15 were byes ; and the Cambridge wicket-keeping was not up to the mark. Cambridge batted on the whole disappointingly in the first innings ; the captain, Mr. G. H. Longman, played a very good innings of 40, but the other scores were below what was expected, and again did extras prove of great value, for Cambridge realised 17 thereby. But, on the whole, the Oxford fielding was very fine, and both Messrs. Longman and Blacker, who played good steady cricket, found great difficulty in getting the ball away.

At the close of the Cambridge innings Oxford had a valuable balance of 37 in their favour, and most thoroughly did they deserve this advantage on account of their very superior fielding. It is always consoling to an eleven who are beginning their second innings to feel that every hit adds to the total that the other side must get before they can win, and that their energy is not to be applied towards wiping off a deficit. Oxford had this balance of 37 in their favour, and very sorely was it needed, for their wickets fell with depressing rapidity. Both Sharpe and Patterson bowled admirably ; the former had both Lang and Campbell with the score at 5 only. Ridley again fell to Patterson, with the total at 16, and at 34 Webbe was out to a good running catch from short-slip to short-leg.

The match now looked well for Cambridge, as Ridley and Webbe were far superior to their comrades. Mr. Webbe had

THE INTERVAL

scored most consistently all through the year ; this second innings of 21 contained no mistake, and nobody ever could have looked more firmly set for a large score. Four wickets for 34 was a very bad start, but again did the Cambridge eleven show great politeness to their opponents ; for directly Mr. Briggs came in he was badly missed at short-slip off Mr. Sharpe, and Messrs. Briggs and Pulman raised the score to 64, when the former was clean bowled by a lob. Mr. Pulman stayed till the total reached 74, when he was stumped off Mr. Sharpe for an admirable innings of 30. He had played very well in his first innings, but his second stopped an undeniable rot, was quite chanceless, and no innings under the circumstances could have been more useful. Mr. Game then came in, and again did Cambridge rise to the occasion and miss him off an easy chance when he had made 3 only ; and he showed his gratitude by hitting up 22 before he was well caught, the total being 109. Mr. Buckland was clean bowled by Mr. Patterson first ball, and nine runs later Mr. Royle was stumped, having played a most useful innings of 21. Both Messrs. Tylecote and Kelcey smacked up small double figures, and the total of the innings was 137—a very much better score than at one time seemed probable. If the chances had been taken the total might not have reached 100, and if a list could be made of the matches lost by bad catching, angels would weep.

Oxford's second innings was not over till a quarter to seven, but Mr. Ridley rightly insisted on the letter of the law being kept, and five minutes before the drawing of the stumps Oxford were in the field and two nervous Cambridge batsmen in a fading light were walking slowly to the wickets. Only one over was bowled, and a leg-hit for four was the only result.

We have said that the Oxford captain rightly insisted on Cambridge going in, and we contend that Mr. Ridley acted wisely and not unfairly in so doing. He had the law on his side, and if the law is not to be enforced in the University match, when is it ever likely to be ? Mr. Ridley also probably anticipated the fact that the Cambridge captain would be unwilling to run the chance of sacrificing one of his good wickets, and that the order of going in would be altered. This may be a considerable disadvantage to the side ; it is not certain that it was in the present case ; but Mr. Macan, who went in fifth wicket down in the first innings, had to go in considerably later in the second innings, and thus a good batsman was wasted.

Messrs. Sharpe and Hamilton went in first ; at the beginning of the third day Cambridge wanted 171 runs to win, and had all their wickets standing. Both Sharpe and Hamilton played well at the start, and brought the score up to 21, when the latter put his leg in front and departed. Mr. Lucas came in, but was clean bowled for 5 runs : two wickets for 26. Mr. Longman, the captain, came in, and played steadily and well, and the bowling for the first time in the innings seemed to be collared ; Lang went off, Ridley bowled three overs for 11 runs, and Mr. Royle took the ball. Mr. Royle's bowling proved the turning point of the game. He was not by any means an accurate bowler, but at times his balls broke fast and were most difficult to play. He bowled three maidens, and with the fifteenth ball clean bowled Mr. Sharpe, who had played an excellent innings of 29. He had stepped into the breach overnight and gone in when twilight was coming on ; having passed through that ordeal safely, he completed a most useful innings next day. Messrs. Longman and Sharpe had brought the score from 26 to 65, but Royle made Blacker play a ball on at 67, and clean bowled Longman at 76 for a second very good innings. The ball that bowled Mr. Longman was a dead shooter of the old sort, which came back also considerably. Messrs. Greenfield and Lyttelton were now in together, and the score again steadily rose, though Mr. Lyttelton was manifestly uneasy with Royle's bowling. However, the total came to 97 when Lyttelton was badly missed, and a snick put 100 on the board ; but at 101 Greenfield made a bad hit and was caught at mid-off, and in walked Mr.

Sims.   Sims this year was a powerful and dangerous bat—in fact, he was the most determined hitter in the two elevens, and on the present occasion he made a great bid for victory.   He possessed a bulldog courage in whatever he undertook, and his contemporaries at Cambridge could scarcely believe that so strong a man could have caught a chill and died so quickly as he did some few years later while in full work as an energetic clergyman in the North of England.   Shortly after Sims had gone in, Lyttelton was a second time missed, though fortunately for Oxford the mistake mattered little, for from a fine leg-hit he was grandly caught by Webbe close to the ropes while running at full speed.   It was not a high hit, but it would have hit a spectator on the nose if the fieldsman had not caught it. There was no finer bit of fielding in the match than this, and it was hard to be got out in such a way, though the batsman was lucky to have made 20 runs.   The score was 114 when Lyttelton was out, or 60 to win and 3 wickets to go down, and the betting 7 to 4 on Oxford.   Messrs. Sims and Patterson played well, and brought the score to 128, or 46 to win, when down came the rain and play was stopped for an hour and a half.   It rained hard for a time, and Oxford had to turn out to bowl with a wet ball and field on slippery ground.   Mr. Patterson played well, and Sims shut his teeth and went to work with savage determination.   The runs came fast ; in 20 minutes the score had been raised from 128 to 161, when Ridley went on to bowl and with his first ball clean bowled Patterson. Macan then came in and made a single (13 to win), and a mighty whack did one of Ridley's balls then get from Sims, who sent the ball over the bowler's head to the ropes like a cannon shot, and Lang took the ball from Royle, 9 runs being wanted to win the match for Cambridge.   A leg-bye was got from Lang's first ball and a no ball followed, making 7 to win.   It appeared good odds on Cambridge, for Sims did not look like getting out, and his hits had a way of going to the boundary.   Be it remembered that the ball was wet and heavy, and forgetfulness of this fact on the part of

Sims at this stage cost him his wicket and Cambridge the match. Mr. Game was fielding deep square-leg close to the ropes by the tennis court, and Pulman was on the on side close to the left-hand corner of the enclosure that stands on the left facing the pavilion. There was a considerable space between these two fields, and off the full pitch on his legs which Sims now received from Lang the ball might have been swept safely under the ropes anywhere between the two men. But Sims no doubt felt as strong and as lusty as an eagle, and forgetting that the ball was wet and heavy, got under it and tried to lift it over the ropes. The sodden ball refused to go so far, and Pulman, running some distance, made what with the ball dry and of a normal weight would have been an ordinary country catch. With the ball wet and heavy, however, his success was the more commendable, and back to the pavilion, crestfallen and sad, went Sims. Returning for a moment to the 2-run match, the two men for whom sympathy may be felt because the game did not result in favour of their side were Ottaway in 1870 and Sims in 1875. Ottaway got out when his side wanted 18 runs to win and had four wickets to go down, and Sims when only 7 runs were wanted and there were two wickets to fall. Both are now dead, but as long as any matches in England are remembered these two innings will be borne in the memory of those who witnessed them.

Mr. Smith had to face a crisis he had long been dreading, and he walked apprehensively to the wicket. Mr. Macan, who was in, had only received two or three balls, so both had to feel their way cautiously. It is, perhaps, true to say that at the extreme moments of nervousness climatic surroundings have no effect on the constitution ; be this as it may, the air was chilly, the ground was wet, and the sun invisible. Probably Mr. Smith felt as cold as if he had been in a damp cellar. A well-known Harrovian told the writer at this stage that he had seen Mr. Smith get over 25 runs against the famous George Freeman's bowling. What did that matter if he was unable to get 6 runs against Ridley's lobs? He somehow or other stopped two balls in a doubtful sort of style, and played slowly forward to the third, thinking that after the manner of lobs it would twist. The wet ground prevented this ; it went on and hit the middle stump, and Oxford won the match by 6 runs.

We regard this match as a model of what a cricket match should be ; the runs were not too numerous, the interest was kept up to the very end. It would have been hard lines perhaps for Oxford to have lost the match, for the rain that fell in Cambridge's last innings was unlucky for the dark blue ; it is impossible to bowl or field well with a wet ball, and it happened that Sims was just the man to take advantage of this state of things. The bowling was managed with great skill by Mr. Ridley, and, as we have said before, he realised an undoubted truth that lobs are often fatal to a batsman who is paralysed by nervousness.

The Universities are on the whole going off in bowling, though there have been former years when the bowling was as weak, but the roughness of Lord's prevented very long scoring. This was the case in 1864. Oxford were led by the famous Mr. Mitchell, and were a strong batting eleven. Cambridge were fairly strong in batting, but they deliberately chose to meet Oxford with only two bowlers, Messrs. Curteis and Pelham. So well did these two gentlemen perform that almost to the very end the result was doubtful. Messrs. Fowler and Booth each succeeded in getting a wicket in the first innings, and Mr. Booth one in the second innings, but between them they only bowled twenty-two overs in the whole match, while Mr. Curteis bowled seventy-five overs for eight wickets, and Mr. Pelham fifty-six overs for five wickets. This was a fine match, won at the finish by a grand innings of Mr. Mitchell's. No man ever went in at a more critical time than he did this second innings, neither did anybody ever bat with better nerve. Out of 125 required to win the match, no fewer than 55 (not out) fell to his share, and Oxford won by four

wickets.   The Cambridge eleven of 1878 had a most extraordinary run of success, never, as far as we know, equalled by
any University eleven.   They won no fewer than eight matches,
and not a defeat or a draw is found against them.   They beat
Oxford by 238 runs, and the Australians in one innings.   There
is no doubt that during that year, if a representative English
eleven had been chosen to play Australia or any other eleven,
no fewer than four out of the Cambridge eleven would have been
found in the English team.   They were not all good, but the
superlative excellence of those four made the eleven one of the
best that has yet played in these matches ; and that of 1879
was almost as good.

It may interest some of our readers if we make a few remarks as to the standing of the various public schools in regard to the composition of the University elevens.   We have
analysed the elevens from 1860 to 1887 inclusive, and, as is
perhaps natural, Eton comes first, having had during that period
forty of her alumni representing one or other of the Universities.
We are not reckoning the number of years that each played,
but forty different Etonians have in the last twenty-seven years
played in the University match : twenty-three for Cambridge,
seventeen for Oxford.   Harrow is represented by thirty-six
players : eighteen at Oxford, and eighteen at Cambridge.
Rugby comes next with twenty-two : fourteen for Oxford and
eight for Cambridge.   At one time Rugby was almost on a level
with Eton and Harrow, for from the years 1861 to 1873 inclusive there were always two Rugby men playing in the match,
and sometimes more ; since that time, however, more than two
Rugbeians have never played, two have played only twice, and
from 1884 downwards not one has played.   Mr. Leslie was the
last good cricketer Rugby sent out, and her prowess seems
much diminished as compared with the days of Pauncefote,
Yardley, Francis, Kenney, and Case.   Winchester and Marlborough have each been represented by thirteen.   No fewer
than eleven of the thirteen Marlborough men have played for
Oxford, but Cambridge men will ever gratefully tender their

thanks to Marlborough for the services of Mr. A. G. Steel, by far the greatest player ever turned out by that school, and perhaps the best all-round cricketer that has yet played for either University. Oxford have had more than the due proportion of Wykehamists, for eleven out of the thirteen have played for Oxford. Eleven Cliftonians have played for Oxford, and none for Cambridge ; but seven out of eight Uppingham boys have represented Cambridge. Tonbridge, Cheltenham, Charterhouse, and Westminster have each had five players representing them, and on the whole the proportion between Oxford and Cambridge has been about equal.

Of all-round players both Universities have had their full share in numbers, but Oxford has never produced three to equal the famous trio, Makinson, A. G. Steel, and C. T. Studd of Cambridge. When we say this we take as our basis the performances of the three in the University matches, and we do not consider the men who played before 1854, for it is difficult to make fair comparisons over so long a distance of time. The above-mentioned three will be found in the first half-dozen of batsmen and in the first half-dozen of bowlers. Messrs. Makinson, Yardley, Lucas, A. Lyttelton, and A. G. Steel are the best batsmen from Cambridge, and Messrs. Mitchell, Ottaway, Key, and Pauncefote the four best from Oxford. In bowling, the champions from Oxford are Messrs. Marsham, Traill, and Kenney ; from Cambridge, Messrs. Plowden, Lang, and A. G. Steel. This is an opinion only, and would have to be considerably altered if we were to take another basis than the Inter-University match to draw our conclusions from. Mr. Kenney never played for the Gentlemen against the Players, and neither he nor Mr. Plowden could be compared as a bowler to Mr. Kempson, whose performance against the Players is historical. But he failed against Oxford. In the same way Lord Lyttelton, Mr. Ridley and Mr. Lane were each as good as Mr. Pauncefote, but they failed in the Inter-University match and consequently are out of our list.

Neither University can claim a superiority up to the present date, and both may derive a legitimate pride from the feeling that their rivalry is of a healthy and vigorous nature. If ever the University match should cease to be played, a great blow will be struck at amateur cricket, for these matches are a model of what all matches ought to be.

CHAPTER XII.

GENTLEMEN AND PLAYERS.

(BY THE HON. R. H. LYTTELTON.)

AT first sight it appears impossible that amateurs—men who play when they chance to find it convenient—should be able to hold their own against professional cricketers who make the game the business of their lives. Cricket, however, is the one game where the two classes contend more or less on an equality, unless football be also an exception. Many amateur cricketers are not bound to work for their daily bread, and they can consequently find time to play as much as a 'professional,' if the accepted slang in which the adjective is employed as a substantive be permissible. Such was the state of things a few years ago when the Walkers, the Graces, Mr. Buchanan, and others could always be depended on to take part in the annual matches against the Players.

But there are other reasons besides; and here we tread on rather delicate ground. Suffice it to say that at one time, and that was when the Gentlemen used heavily to defeat the Players, there was such a very thin border-line between the status of the amateur and professional, that a definition of 'amateur' was often asked for and never obtained. The position was getting acute when finally the Marylebone Club, which is not in the habit of moving except when very strong pressure is exerted, was obliged to discuss and legislate on the matter. Broadly speaking, the rule stands that amateurs may take expenses, and a difficult and delicate point is now set at rest.

It is a striking illustration of the great popularity of the game that a large and increasing number of men annually give themselves up to the profession of cricket, and it is only in cricket that amateurs and professionals regularly compete against each other. We have heard that from the county of Nottingham alone several hundred professional bowlers emerge every year, and go to fulfil cricket engagements in various parts of the kingdom. The limits of cricket seem likely to be extended, and we know of several English professionals who have accepted offers from America and elsewhere. So long ago as 1864 the famous Wm. Caffyn was engaged in Australia ; later on, Jesse Hide, of Sussex, was in South Australia, and several other players have been in America. All professionals, or nearly all, first come into notice as bowlers. A club with a ground wants a man who can bowl to its members for an evening's practice, and he has to be there to attend on any member who may happen to come. As a rule also, he is required to play for the club in the Saturday matches, and he may earn by way of fixed salary, together with what he makes by bowling at a shilling for half an hour, 3*l.* or 4*l.* per week.

If the club is situated in a county which possesses a county club, the professional may have inducements held out to him to take up a permanent residence and become a naturalised resident. The county of Nottingham, for instance, has only one county eleven, but she has hundreds of professionals. These men get engagements in all directions, and if they are good enough to be asked to play for their adopted county, it would be hard to deprive them of a livelihood ; though no doubt it is provoking to Nottingham to see the success of Lancashire largely owing to the play of Briggs, a Notts man of whose virtues Lancashire became aware before his own county. Nor is Briggs a solitary specimen, for Walter Wright, Mills, Bean, Brown, and Wheeler play respectively for Kent, Surrey, Sussex, Cheshire, and Leicestershire.

The congestion of professional ability in certain favoured districts is hard to explain. Every cricketer has heard of Lascelles Hall, the famous village near Huddersfield, to which Bates, the Lockwoods, the Thewlises and Allan Hill belong. There are several villages and small towns near Nottingham where cricketers appear indigenous to the soil, just as primroses are in certain localities. There have always been cricketers in these parts, and so sure is this constant supply that some scientific society ought really to go down and inspect the spot, make a theory to explain the phenomenon, and read a paper about it. Nottingham itself raised and reared Daft, Shrewsbury, Gunn, Scotton, and Selby ; the famous Sutton-in-Ashfield nursed Morley, J. C. Shaw, Barnes and Briggs in their infancy. There are several large towns in Yorkshire, such as Sheffield, Leeds, and other manufacturing centres, where the traditions of the place are in favour of cricket ; but it is curious to observe that, though it was not so in the days of Noah Mann, David Harris, and the Hambledon Club, the modern professional now springs entirely from populous centres. The only reason we can give for this is that for young players between the ages of eight and eighteen practice is everything, and of this youngsters can generally make sure in populous places. In a rural district the same chances may seldom occur. In Nottingham and the West Riding towns, hundreds of boys may be seen playing almost at the mouth of coal-pits, and the practice they get enables them to become professional players.

Amateurs are not by any means in the same situation. Apart from the natural qualifications any lad may chance to possess, he is largely benefited or the reverse by the atmosphere of the schools to which he is sent. About the age of thirteen he is sent to a large public school, where cricket is regularly taught, and he has a great deal of experience if he can manage to get into his school eleven. After that he may go to Oxford or Cambridge, and if he is fond of the game, he may play an unlimited quantity of cricket. Many amateurs after they leave the university disappear for ever from first-class cricket, as their time then ceases to be their own.

When we examine the M.C.C. cricket 'Scores and Bio-

graphies,' we find the same story over and over again : 'This
year the Gentlemen had to regret the absence of Messrs. Hankey
and Kempson.' 'Mr. Felix did not play for the Gentlemen,
they as usual losing one of their best men.' In a footnote
attached to the score of the 1847 match at Lord's, the editor
gives a list of no fewer than sixteen gentlemen who had to
abandon the game when in their prime. It was in consequence
of this that in 1862 a match was tried between Gentlemen and
Players all under thirty, but with no better success for the
Gentlemen.

The first Gentlemen and Players' match took place in 1806
on the old Lord's ground, so the contest between these teams is
not so old by one year as the Eton and Harrow. It is true that
in 'The Cricket Field' Mr. Pycroft says that Lord F. Beauclerk
and the Hons. H. and T. Tufton had previously made an attempt to get a Gentlemen and Players' match, and the Players
won, giving the services of T. Walker, Beldham, and Hammond.
These three men were nearly the best in England, and to call
the Players a representative eleven without them was absurd.
The same objection may be mentioned in discussing the next
match in 1806, when the Gentlemen were helped by two of the
foremost players : this made a more equal match, but apparently
rather too much was given, for the amateurs beat the Players in
an innings and 14 runs. Beldham and Lambert were the two
given men, and at that time Lambert was unquestionably the
finest player of the day. A second match was played a fort-
night later, when the amateurs were a second time victorious,
and in this case Lambert alone was given. After this match
there was a considerable hiatus, for the rival teams did not
meet again till 1819, when a match was played on even terms,
the players winning by six wickets. Mr. Budd scored 56 for
the Gentlemen, and Tom Beagley 75 for the Players—

> . . . Worthy Beagley,
> Who is quite at the top ;
> With the bat he's first rate, a brick wall at long-stop.

Mr. Budd in this match stumped six of the Players, and only one bye was recorded against him and the long-stop. In 1820 T. C. Howard, who had bowled for the Players, was transferred to the Gentlemen, and they won by 70 runs. In 1821 the Gentlemen scored 60 and the Players 278 for six wickets, at which stage the Gentlemen succumbed and gave up the match. Beagley, who appeared to be partial to amateur bowling, made 113 not out, and began the long list of hundreds that have since been obtained in this match. In 1822 Lord F. Beauclerk bowled finely, Mr. Vigne stumped four and caught two at the wicket, Mr. Budd made 69 runs, and the Gentlemen won by six wickets. Elated by this victory, in 1823 the amateurs again threw down the gauntlet on even terms and were defeated heavily by 345 runs.

This knock-down blow must have cowed the Gentlemen, for in the next four matches they played fourteen, sixteen with Mathews, and seventeen in the two matches of 1827 ; and each side won two. In 1828 there was no match, and in 1829 and 1830 they stole two players to help them. This was a period when the superiority of the professionals was very marked, for in 1831, '32, and '33 odds were given on each occasion, but still victory refused to crown the efforts of the amateurs. In 1832 the Gentlemen defended smaller wickets than those of their opponents, but the game was admitted to be a failure. The extraordinary result of all the matches between 1824 and 1833 in which the Gentlemen had odds, was that out of eight matches the Players won six. The bowling of W. Lillywhite, Cobbett, and others was far too good for the amateurs, and the records of the Players were wonderful.

In 1833, however, for the first time the famous Alfred Mynn appeared on the scene. This crack amateur was the idol of Kent and the terror of his opponents. Very tall in stature and heavy in weight, he was at that time and for many years subsequently one of the fastest bowlers in England. His physique was enormous, and he could bowl a great number of balls without any sacrifice of pace or precision. When asked how

many balls he should like the over to consist of, he said as far
as he was concerned he should like a hundred. He was a hard
hitter, fond of driving the ball in front of the wicket, and was
probably the champion at the then frequently played single-
wicket matches. It must have been a fine sight to see Alfred
Mynn advance and deliver the ball ; he took a short run and
held himself up to nearly his full height as the ball left his
hand. He was of unfailing good humour, and is immortalised in
by far the best cricket poem yet published, which may be found
in the 'Scores and Biographies,' vol. ii. p. 200. Altogether he
was one of the leading players of his day, and his arrival gave a
strength to the amateurs that was sorely needed,

Proudly, sadly we will name him—to forget him were a sin ;
Lightly lie the turf upon thee, kind and manly Alfred Mynn.

In 1834 the match was played on even terms, but again
the result was disastrous to the amateurs, for they were beaten
in an innings and 21 runs ; nor did the assistance of Cobbett
and Redgate, two of the crack bowlers of the day, save them
from defeat in 1835, though Alfred Mynn scored 53 and bowled
down four wickets. In 1836 eighteen Gentlemen won by 35
runs, and again was Alfred Mynn to the fore, for he scored 29
and 30 and got eight wickets. In the following year was played
a match, when the Gentlemen defended three wickets, 27 inches
by 8, and the Players four, 36 inches by 12. The match was
the famous 'Barn Door Match,' or 'Ward's Folly,' but again
the impotence of the amateurs' batting caused them to be defeated in one innings and 10 runs. Thirteen was the highest
amateur score and the only double figure, and Lillywhite and
Redgate apparently did what they liked in the way of bowling.
In 1838 Alfred Mynn was away, so the amateurs helped themselves to Pilch, Cobbett, and Wenman, three good men from
the professional ranks ; they lost the match, however, by 40 runs.
This was the last match in which odds have been given. A
drawn game was played in 1839, and twice the Players were
victorious in 1840 and 1841. In 1842 and 1843 the Gentle-

men gained two victories, the match in 1842 being their first win on even terms since 1822. Mynn and Sir F. Bathurst got all the wickets for the Gentlemen ; the former scored 21 and 46, and Mr. Felix played a fine innings of 88, having been missed badly at short-slip before he scored. In 1843 the Gentlemen actually won in one innings on even terms, for the first time on record. Again Alfred Mynn did excellent service, for he made 47 runs and lowered eight wickets. Mr. C. G. Taylor scored 89 runs and then his hat fell on the wicket, or rather it was knocked off, which showed that Lord's had a way of testing the bravery as well as the skill of batsmen. In 1844 the Gentlemen lost the services of Mr. Felix, perhaps their best bat, and Sir F. Bathurst, their second best bowler, and were defeated by 38 runs. The famous William Lillywhite, who 'handled the ball as he would do a brick,' and Hillyer were the crack professional bowlers at this time, and sad havoc they made of amateur wickets. Lillywhite was fifty-two years old in 1844, five years older than the well-known Tom Emmett, who in the year 1888 is *par excellence* the veteran cricketer. The era of Alfred Mynn and Sir F. Bathurst was the golden age of amateur bowling, for Mynn was at the top of the tree in this department of the game for a far longer period than any amateur has been since. He played twenty matches for the Gentlemen against the Players, and though he was generally on the losing side, did great things both with bat and ball, especially with the latter. In 1845 the Players again won, old Lillywhite, aged fifty-three, taking twelve wickets for 96 runs—a remarkable performance.

The match for the year 1846 is an historical one for one or two reasons. It was the first time that George Parr, aged 20, and William Clarke, aged 47, represented the Players. Both were Nottingham men ; the younger was very nearly the best bat in England, and the elder, if not the best bowler all round, certainly by far the most successful bowler of lobs that has ever appeared. Clarke had played for thirty seasons before he was chosen to represent the Players. He died in 1856 at the age of 57, played cricket during the last year of his life, and took a wicket with the last ball he ever bowled. He was head and captain of the 'All England Eleven' which used to tour about the country. Very amusing work it must have been for old Clarke, bowling on rough provincial grounds to provincial batsmen ; and who can wonder that he, with several other bowling captains, had a great dislike to taking himself off? He was one-eyed, having lost his right eye while indulging in the manly game of fives. He certainly got a lot of wickets in the best of matches, but there is nothing to guide speculation as to how Clarke and Lillywhite would have fared if they had bowled to W. G. Grace and McDonnell. Round old Clarke's head, as round the heads of Fuller Pilch, Alfred Mynn, and William Lillywhite, an aureole has gathered ; they are the great lights of that epoch of cricket, and during his career old Clarke must have been one of those few bowlers who generally made fools of batsmen.

To return to this year of 1846, as it was Parr and Clarke's first Gentlemen and Players, so it was C. G. Taylor's last. This great player at all games was an Eton and Cambridge man ; and, like many old cricketers, formed the theme of poets. 'Taylor the most graceful of all,' one writes, and again he is represented as being

> Unlike our common sons, whose gradual ray
> Expands from twilight into purer day,
> His blaze broke forth at once in full meridian sway.

Mr. C. G. Taylor was evidently born with an eye ; he often ran out to bowling to drive, could field splendidly either at point, coverpoint, or mid-wicket, and bowled slow round-arm, we are told, both well and gracefully. We suspect that, as may be inferred from the description of his style of play, there was a weak place in his defence, and he used to have long bouts of small scores. But so graceful and altogether fascinating was his style, that all his great innings were indelibly stamped on the memory of those who witnessed them. In this his last Gentlemen and Players match he got 23 and 44. It was a great match, won by the Gentlemen by one wicket, and the credit was due to Messrs R. P. Long and Taylor for batting, and to Alfred Mynn and Sir F. Bathurst for bowling.

In the following year, 1847, the Players again won, but at this period the sides were far more even than they had been before for any long time together. The redoubtable bowlers Mynn and Bathurst were helped by Harvey Fellows, the celebrated Etonian, and George Yonge the Oxonian; and we doubt if the Gentlemen have ever been so strong in this line since. These two bowled out the Players in 1848 for 79 and 77 runs, Mynn getting eight wickets in the second innings and hitting up 66 runs. In this year, in fact, it is a question if the amateurs were not stronger in bowling than batting.

In the next year, 1849, further triumph awaited the amateurs, for winning the toss they scored 192 runs, compelled the Players to follow on, and won the match in one innings and 40 runs. Alfred Mynn did not get a wicket, but Harvey Fellows bowled his fastest, first hurt his opponents, and then got them out. Old Wm. Lillywhite played his last Gentlemen and Players match this year, and we read that he refused to bat in his second innings because he was hurt by Mr. Fellows. He was 57 years old, so may be excused if he felt a little nervous on old Lord's ground at standing up to one who used to make the ball hum like a top.

The famous 'Nonpareil bowler,' as old Lillywhite was called, was the king of bowlers in the days when he flourished. Mr. Robert Grimston, who remembered him well, said that though a slow bowler he was quicker off the ground than Alfred Shaw. He lived in the days when wides were common, but it is recorded that during his whole career he did not deliver half a dozen. He was born in Sussex in 1792, and played as a given man for the Gentlemen in 1829 and 1830; after that began his long career as principal bowler for the Players. He was, therefore, no less than 39 years of age when he played his first match for the Players. If to other cricketers may be given the credit of inventing round-arm bowling, still to Lillywhite and Broadbridge all honour is due for having been the first really good round-arm bowlers. Lillywhite bowled in seventeen matches against the Gentlemen and got 132 wickets, or close upon eight wickets per match. He was occasionally useful as a bat, and though he refused to go in, as just recorded, he had plenty of pluck when younger, for in a single wicket match he stood up for 278 balls to George Brown, to whose bowling Little Dench of Brighton used to long-stop with a sack stuffed full of straw to protect his chest. Batting gloves were not used in those days, and Lillywhite had his fingers broken three times before they were invented. Fuller Pilch played his last Gentlemen and Players match this year, which is famous for witnessing the farewell of such great cricketers as himself and William Lillywhite. Pilch was born in 1803, and was therefore 46 years old in 1849.

> Another young tailor, as fine a young man
> As e'er hit a ball and then afterwards ran.

Pilch was undoubtedly the champion of his day, and his mantle fell on George Parr. He was the originator of what we call in modern times ' forward play,' and his object was the sound one of smothering the ball at the pitch. He was the worst enemy of William Clarke, for he left his ground to balls that were well up and ran him down with a straight bat. He was one of the dauntless five that carried Kent into a unique position among cricket counties.

> And with five such mighty cricketers 'twas but natural to win,
> As Felix, Wenman, Hillyer, Fuller Pilch, and Alfred Mynn.

In 1850 the famous Johnny Wisden came to the front and the Players grew stronger, and George Parr made 65 runs not out. Wisden and Clarke bowled unchanged, and got rid of their rivals for 42 and 58, winning the match in one innings and 48 runs in 1850, and in 1851 they also won in a single innings. Wisden, Grundy, and Caffyn were three fine all-round men, and Joe Guy of Nottingham was apparently quite at home to amateur bowling. Both Mynn and Fellows had lost their devil, or perhaps it might be more correct to say that the latter had lost his straightness and accuracy. In 1852 the Players won by five wickets, and the great Alfred Mynn retires from the scene as far as this match is concerned.

In 1853 fine bowling won the Gentlemen a match by 60 runs. Both Sir F. Bathurst and Mr. Kempson bowled unchanged all through the two innings of the Players, and got rid of them for 42 and 69. Martingell got seven wickets for 19 runs in the second innings of the Gentlemen, so this was essentially a bowlers' match; and though it is an historical fact that it was the first time the Gentlemen never had to change their bowling, in 1846 Mynn and Sir F. Bathurst got all the wickets, and Mr. Taylor was only on for a few overs. Sir F. Bathurst might therefore have bowled one end all the time if Mr. Taylor had relieved Mynn. At any rate, to Sir F. Bathurst is due the credit of being one of the main causes of two defeats of the Players. He was a fast bowler with a low delivery, but very straight.

In 1854 both sides played weak, four Players refusing to come forward because of a dispute between Clarke and the M.C.C., and the Gentlemen losing Messrs. Hankey and Kempson. An uneventful match was the result, and the Players again won. From 1853 to 1865 the match was played on even terms, but the Players had a run of victory, and not once during that time did the Gentlemen prove successful. There is no doubt that the batting strength of the Players during these years was very considerable, and, though George Parr, Hayward, and Carpenter did not score their hundreds as the men of modern times so often have done, they made their fifties and sixties with nearly the same consistency. Parr was a most regular scorer during the decade between 1853 and 1863, and his average for the whole series of these matches must have been very high.

In 1855 the Players won easily by seven wickets, though the Gentlemen began well; but in their second innings Dean and

John Lillywhite got them out for 43, five consecutive wickets falling without a run. In 1857 the Gentlemen lost several of their best men, but the famous Oxonians, Messrs. Marsham and Payne, bowled finely, and though the Players had only 70 to get to win, they only pulled through by two wickets. Willsher played this year for the first time, and he and Wisden were too much for the Gentlemen. The year 1857 was an historical one for two reasons. In the first place at Lord's was played one of the closest matches of the series, a game also famous for one of those great batting feats the recollection of which lingers long ; and in the second place because a second match was played for the first time at the Oval. The historical innings was that of Mr. Reginald Hankey, whom George Parr considers the finest bat he ever saw. This is the proverbial effort quoted by all who saw it as the masterpiece of its day, and Mr. Grace himself has never played an innings that made more sensation. Mr. Hankey got 70 runs in an hour and three-quarters, and hit the fast bowling of Willsher, Wisden, Jackson, and Stephenson all over the ground. Messrs. Hankey, Haygarth, Drake and Lane amassed 224 runs, the other seven only 58 between them, and in the end the players won by 13 runs. Mr. Drake played his hardest to win, making a score of 58 out of 114.

At the Oval the Players won easily by ten wickets, and on this ground the Gentlemen lost every match till 1866. In those days the Oval was what we should call a better ground than Lord's—that is to say, it was more in favour of the batsmen and long scores ; and consequently the weak amateur bowling was at a considerable discount. In 1858 at the Oval the Players won by three wickets, and R. Daft played for the Gentlemen for the first and only time. At Lord's in the same year the Gentlemen collapsed in batting and lost by 285 runs, the bowling of Jackson being at this period an object of dread among the amateurs. In 1859 the Players won both matches easily, and the famous Robert Carpenter made his first appearance, scoring 44 runs at the Oval.

In 1860, at the Oval, the Players won by eight wickets ;

Mr. T. E. Bagge made two scores of 62 and 60, and the scoring altogether was very large for those days. Carpenter made 119 in his one innings. At Lord's the other great Cambridgeshire player, Tom Hayward, came on the scene with a vengeance, scoring 132 runs, and the Players won in one innings and 181 runs, though George Parr could not play. At this time the tremendous bowling of Jackson and Willsher was at its best, and Hayward, Carpenter, Parr, and Daft were too good for amateur bowling. In 1861 the Players won in one innings and 60 runs at Lord's, and in one innings and 68 runs at the Oval ; Carpenter for the second time making a hundred.

In 1862 a famous drawn match was played at the Oval. Over 200 runs were made in each innings, and there was curious equality of scoring, the highest figures on each side being 108, made by Mr. John Walker for the Gentlemen, and by Hayward for the Players. The match was drawn, the Players having lost eight wickets and still wanting 33 runs. Mr. Walker was bowling lobs a good deal in this match, and whilst Anderson and Stephenson were batting just before stumps were drawn at the end of the day, each having made 33, the famous Tom Lockyer, who could not endure lobs, was continually to be seen nervously looking at the clock ; to go in against these dreaded balls was a privilege he did not covet. Willsher, Parr, and Daft could not play for the Players, nor Messrs. Makinson and Mitchell for the Gentlemen. At Lord's a match was played between the elevens, all the engaged being under thirty, and the Players won by 157 runs. Mr. C. D. Marsham, the steadiest of all Gentlemen bowlers, played his last Gentlemen and Players match this year. He had taken part in ten matches, but never had the good luck to be on the winning side.

In 1863 the great Hayward made 112 runs in his only innings, and nobody else except Mr. Walker got 30 runs in the match, which the Players won by eight wickets, Jackson and Tarrant being quite unplayable on the rough Lord's wicket. Mr. R. A. H. Mitchell played for the first time, and, with the exception of Mr. Grace, no greater batsman has appeared for the Gentlemen, though he did not play for many years. At the Oval in the same year Mr. Mitchell scored 76 and 6 ; but the Gentlemen were weak in bowling, and the Players won by nine wickets. At Lord's in 1864 Tarrant and Willsher bowled unchanged during the match, and the Gentlemen scored 119 in the two innings; but at the Oval there were a lot of runs made, Stephenson putting together 117, and Messrs. C. G. Lyttelton and Makinson playing two fine innings for the Gentlemen.

In 1865 began what brought about a revolution in cricket, for W. G. Grace played his first match, and at once began to score. Originally more famous as a bowler, he has since made runs in a manner and to an extent altogether unparalleled in the history of cricket, and soon after his appearance the almost dull monotony of professional victory was changed for the almost equally dull monotony of professional defeat. When he first began to play there was a schism in the professional ranks which lasted several years ; between 1863 and 1871, many of the crack Northern players refused to play at the Oval, and soon afterwards at Lord's also. It is a curious fact that at Lord's in 1865 the amateurs won by eight wickets, scoring a victory for the first time since 1853, after losing nineteen matches in succession. This was W. G. Grace's first match and George Parr's last, the latter having scored sixty runs in his actual last innings. Grace was sixteen years old, and Parr, who first played in 1846, was 39. Parr's average for these matches was no less than twenty-eight, and his was altogether one of the best and longest careers ever seen.

Up to 1886 Mr. Grace had played 78 innings in these matches, and averaged 45 runs an innings ; and he is still the best amateur bat. The cricket schism weakened the Players very much for several years after he played, and the matches were in consequence not so interesting. At the Oval, in 1866, the Gentlemen followed their innings but won the match by 98 runs, and this was the first time they were successful at the Kennington ground ; but no Northern players appeared except

Grundy, Wootton, Luke Greenwood and Alfred Shaw. It was the same story in 1867 and in every match till 1872, and the amateurs were generally successful. Since that period, however, it has always been considered a special honour to be asked to represent either eleven, and the Committees at both Lord's and the Oval now offer higher terms to the professionals for this than for any other match. For some reason which we are totally unable to explain, between the years 1867 and 1877 there was a blight on the Players. Their batting fell off to an extraordinary extent, nor was their fast bowling at all up to the level of what it used to be. Of course W. G. Grace was the main cause of the apparent weakness of the bowling, but this could not account for the great batting deterioration. The Players won at the Oval in 1865 and did not win again till 1880, though one match was drawn considerably in their favour. Up to 1874, including the Oval matches and omitting three unfinished, the Players lost twelve matches in succession, mainly owing to Mr. Grace.

If we take the best of the innings of 100 played in these matches, we find that there have been 36 individual innings of over 100 runs played, and Mr. Grace has played eleven himself, or nearly a third of the whole ; and when we remember that he has had a great deal of bowling to do as well, it may be said with confidence that no such performances for so many years have ever been seen in the history of cricket. In 1873 he got 163 runs at Lord's, and 158 at the Oval, and in the latter match secured seven wickets in the Players' second innings. In 1874 the Gentlemen won by seven wickets, having to go in for 226 runs to win. Mr. Grace had got 77 runs in his first innings, went in first in the second innings, stayed in till 152 runs were scored, and was then out for 112. The match was won by seven wickets.

The most exciting match that has occurred in recent years was in 1877. The Players made 192, and the Gentlemen 198 in the first innings, and the Players 148 in the second. Consequently, to win the match 143 runs were wanted by the

Gentlemen. The wicket was not quite a first-rate one, and good judges anticipated a close finish. Grace made 41, and Alfred Lyttelton 20 ; but Watson, Ulyett, and Morley bowled well, and the Gentlemen wanted 46 runs to win when nine wickets had fallen. Mr. W. S. Patterson and G. F. Grace were in, and gradually, by excellent play, the runs were secured.

In 1883 a tie match was played at the Oval, for the first and only time. The wicket was difficult on the third day, and the Gentlemen, who lost the services of Mr. W. G. Grace for the first time since 1867, were 31 runs ahead on the first innings. Bates did well for the Players in the second innings and scored 76 runs, making his last 30 runs in eight hits. Rain fell in the night, and Flowers found a spot. Mr. Lucas, who scored 47 not out, was really caught at point when he had got 8, but the catch was a low one, and neither umpire would give a decision when appealed to. So he continued his innings, which was hard for the Players. Fourteen were wanted when Mr. Rotherham joined Mr. Lucas, and when 8 runs were wanted Bates badly missed Rotherham. When the match was a tie, Peate was put on, and clean bowled Rotherham with his second ball. The Players had rather hard lines in Lucas's case, but they lost the match through the bad miss of Bates.

In 1879, following the good example set by Sir F. Bathurst and Kempson, the Gentlemen won the Oval match without once having to change their bowlers. Messrs. Steel and Evans were the heroes ; Evans got ten wickets, and Steel nine. The wicket was difficult, but the batting was feeble, and only realised totals of 73 and 48.

For the last few years the Players have gradually recovered their lost prestige, and reached the high-water mark of excellence in 1887, when, for the first time since 1861, they won both matches in one innings each. At the date of writing (1888) they possess not only perhaps the most consistent scorer of the day in Shrewsbury, but they have many all-round men, famous for bowling and batting. The names of Barnes, Flowers, Bates, Ulyett, Barlow, Briggs, Lohmann, and Peel will at once suggest themselves, and at no previous time have they been so good all through in fielding as they proved themselves in 1887. Mr. Grace, whose experience has been gained in the course of twenty-three years, has publicly stated that they never had such a good eleven in his time as they possessed in 1887, and the Gentlemen show symptoms of decline. In batting the amateurs are still fairly strong, but in bowling—let us draw a veil.

A survey of the whole series of matches points to the fact that, as is natural, the Gentlemen have been, and probably will be, beaten as a general rule. Every cricketer knows what it is to play in an eleven with a comrade, either a batsman or bowler, of commanding superiority. Such a man makes an eleven. He does this by giving confidence to the other ten members of the team. They feel that the match does not depend on them, that if they fail he will pull them through, and consequently they go in boldly and score. The two notable instances of one man making an eleven are W. G. Grace and Spofforth. Of course there were good players amongst the Australians and amongst the Gentlemen, but the presence of Grace and Spofforth was an incalculable benefit. The Australians began a match feeling sure that, even if they did not run up large scores, Spofforth would get rid of their opponents for less. It is probably the absence of this feeling that partly accounts for the apparent falling off in Australian play.

In conclusion, let us express a hope that the Gentlemen and Players match will never fall through ; for, having been played off and on since 1806, it has a notable history, and it ought to be the summit of ambition in every cricketer, be he amateur or professional, to appear in these great classic contests.

CHAPTER XIII.

THE ART OF TRAINING YOUNG CRICKETERS.

(By R. A. H. Mitchell.)

A six-year old.

IF you want to play cricket you must begin as a boy, is a true, if not an original, remark. We remember asking a member of a well-known cricketing fraternity what promise a younger brother gave of future excellence, and his reply was, 'He's no good—but then he hasn't had a chance, for he was so delicate he couldn't begin till he was six years old.' We do not ourselves presume to say that the game must necessarily be learnt whilst a child is under his nurse's care ; but nevertheless we know of no instance, unless Mr. A. E. Stoddart forms an exception to the rule, of anyone attaining to the first rank who has not received his early lessons in the noble game while still a boy. If this be so, it is of interest to all cricketers to consider what training a boy ought to have. Is he to be left merely to the light of nature and his own powers of observation, or is he to be systematically coached, and taught daily how each stroke is to be made and each ball bowled ? Many think that a training of this kind can hardly be begun too soon or carried out with too great care and rigour. This may be so ; but we are by no means inclined to agree with such a Spartan discipline. We believe that in games, as in life, if a thing is worth doing at all, it is worth doing well ; but, although we claim to be second to none in our keenness to see good boy cricketers, we differ in the method we advocate from those who support so severe a system of coaching young boys.

Let us give some reasons in support of our view. In the first place, success in cricket, and not in cricket alone, depends on the enjoyment and interest taken in the game, and we believe that there is great danger of destroying this enjoyment and interest by incessant coaching and teaching at too early an age. In the second place, all coaching has a tendency at first to eradicate individual peculiarities and to cramp a natural style. Mr. W. G. Grace, Mr. A. G. Steel, Shrewsbury, and many other well-known batsmen have peculiarities of their own, which could not have been taught in early boyhood, but which might very easily have been cramped, and perhaps entirely obliterated, much to their detriment, in the hands of even a skilful coach. We do not deprecate all advice even to very young boys, but we dislike anything that tends to interfere with the powers of nature ; and although we shall be told that a good teacher merely directs them in the best possible way, we do not think that the advantage likely to be gained will at all compensate for a cramped style or loss of enjoyment. What should be taught, and when, we will endeavour to suggest as we proceed.

First, however, one word to anxious parents and teachers of the art. It is quite hopeless to expect that every boy can be made into a cricketer. Countless are the excuses we hear to cover the feebleness and incapacity of would-be players, made sometimes by their parents, sometimes by themselves. They have never been coached, or they have been badly coached ; they have been made to play too much, or they can't play often enough ; the ground they play on is so rough, or it is so easy that they can't play on more difficult ground. They used to bowl very well ; but they were overbowled, or they were never put on ; or they are always put on at the wrong end, or the catches are always missed off their bowling. These and many other excuses are urged on their behalf ; but those who have watched cricket for but a few years will soon learn to take such futile pleas for what they are worth. No boy can become a good cricketer who has not a natural capacity for the game. The batsman must have a good eye and is all the better for a good nerve ; the fieldsman must be active; the bowler—ah! what must he have? *Nascitur non fit*; we will not commit ourselves at present to his requirements.

In saying this do not let it be supposed that we wish those only to play cricket who are likely to become good cricketers—far from it; but we are concerned with the game as an art and not as an exercise, and do not wish to raise vain hopes of success where success is impossible.

Now let us consider the three great departments of the game in detail; for, although they are necessarily and closely connected, we cannot treat of batting, bowling, and fielding in the same paragraph.

The batsman then first demands our attention, not because he is more useful to his side than the bowler, but because it is here that more may be taught than in any other department of

OUR NATIONAL GAME

LUCIEN DAVIS

the game. Take a boy ten years old—we start with double figures, let it be an omen for his future!—what can we tell him? Very little, we think, but certainly this: never to move his right foot, but to plant it firmly just inside the crease, with the toe barely clear of the leg-stump.

The left foot should also be placed in the same line, but it must be moved into the position which is found to be the easiest for playing or hitting any given ball. The batsman must learn to stand perfectly still with his eye fixed on the bowler's hand, and he must try to think of the ball, and the ball alone; any fidgeting about is apt to interfere with an accurate habit of sight. A boy should also be told to drive the ball in front of the wicket and along the ground. We do not approve of the cut for young boys; it is the batsman's most finished stroke, but it is absolutely fatal when attempted at an unsuitable ball. This is all we think it necessary to teach our juvenile batsman, though occasional hints beyond this may sometimes be useful. Do not, however, cramp a boy who is disposed to hit, but tell him to hit straight; it is easier at a later age to stop hitting than to teach it. For this reason single-wicket matches among small boys are not without their use, as they naturally encourage hard hitting in front of the wicket.

A danger which is not sufficiently guarded against at some private schools is the habit of allowing young boys to play to fast bowling; masters and others take part in the games and the practice, and bowl at a pace which would be called medium in a man's match, but which is very fast for boys under fourteen years of age. The result of this is that boys learn to be afraid of the ball; and if they once show fear they will never become good players. It seems all but impossible to restore confidence even at a much later age, and we know of many instances—we will not be so unkind as to mention names—in which boys with great natural powers have never overcome their fear of the ball, which they had acquired before coming to a public school. For the same reason the growing custom of small boys playing in men's matches is to be strongly deprecated.

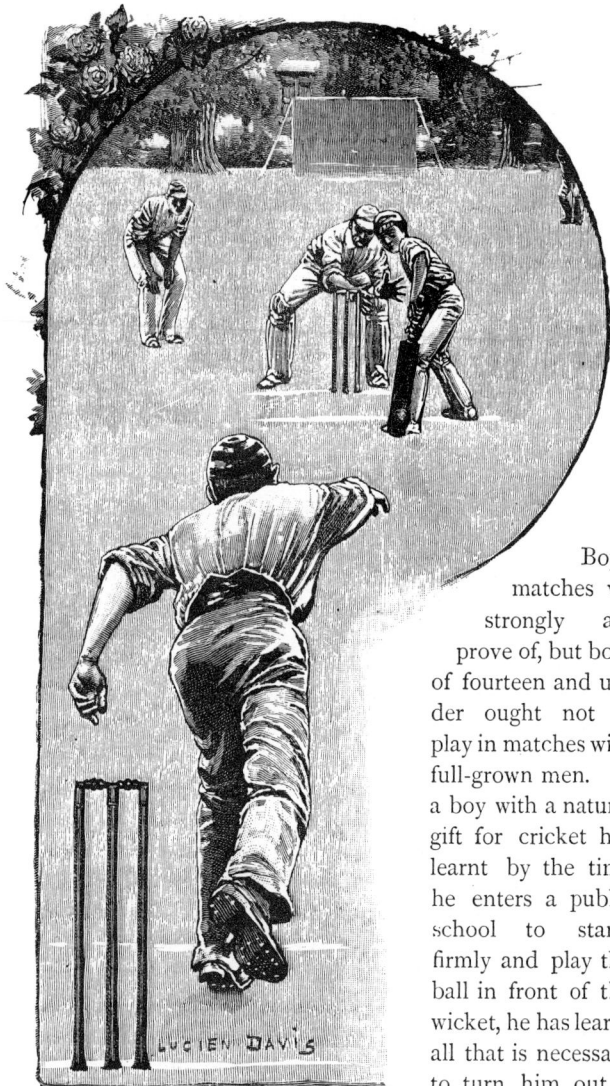

Drawing away from the wicket.

Boys' matches we strongly approve of, but boys of fourteen and under ought not to play in matches with full-grown men. If a boy with a natural gift for cricket has learnt by the time he enters a public school to stand firmly and play the ball in front of the wicket, he has learnt all that is necessary to turn him out a good batsman later on ; but if fast bowling has taught him to fear the ball, we have but little hope of ever seeing him attain to the first class.

A few years have elapsed, and our young batsman at the age of thirteen or fourteen is passing into the larger sphere of a public school. What ought to be his training there ?

It cannot be expected that he will receive the same attention that will be given at a later age, when he is a candidate for his school eleven, nor do we think that he need be subjected to any rigorous system of coaching. On the other hand, he ought to have some one of experience to give him occasional hints and instil into him the true principles of the game. Above everything else, he should have good ground to play upon, so that, if his confidence has not been previously shaken, he will not now learn to shrink from the ball. The question of ground must always be a great difficulty ; for, although it may be easy to get an extent sufficient to satisfy the requirements of a large public school, it is no easy matter to keep it in proper order and provide good match and practice wickets throughout the summer for a large number of boys, especially as the ground is generally required for football or other purposes during the winter. However, the better the ground the better the batsmen ; and if this be true, a good ground is one of the most important requirements in the training of our cricketers.

As a boy grows in years he will require, and will probably get, more instruction, and if he meets with a coach of good judgment and experience he will soon learn all that can be taught. His success will depend on his own natural powers, his temper, and his perseverance. We do not propose to deal in detail with all the duties of a coach, but perhaps a few hints may not be altogether out of place.

First of all, then, we would say, do not coach a boy too often. Once a week is all that is either necessary or desirable. A boy who is anxious to learn will lay to heart the hints and instructions he has received, and he will find it easier to carry them out when he is practising with his schoolfellows than when he is actually receiving instruction from a coach. A new attitude or a new stroke always presents great difficulty, easy as it may seem in itself; and a boy who is trying something new will not at first play better, and will become nervous and disheartened if he is being too constantly pressed by an ardent teacher.

Do not let a boy practise for more than half an hour at a time, or he will become careless and lose interest. During that time he should play to both fast and slow bowling, but never to more than two bowlers ; and it would be well if he could play for a quarter of an hour to two slow bowlers, and another quarter to two fast. It is confusing to some boys to receive fast and slow balls alternately, particularly when they are trying to alter or improve some point of style under the direction of a coach.

Do not allow boys to play to fast bowling on bad wickets : slow bowling on a bad wicket is a good lesson occasionally, as it necessitates careful watching of the ball and accurate timing; but fast bowling on bumpy ground can only do harm. Never allow throwing instead of bowling,—it does infinite mischief.

A coach will naturally have to give instruction on numerous points, and try to get his pupil to carry out what he teaches; but there is one warning which must be impressed on the lad more strongly than anything else. It is this : when you go to the wicket in a match don't be thinking of this or that position, or this or that stroke, but fix your eye on the bowler's hand as he comes up to bowl. Think of and watch the ball only ; if you learn correct habits in practice, your instinct will throw you into the right position and enable you to make the right stroke, provided that your eye does not fail you with the ball.

We do not purpose to describe how each stroke should be made or to enumerate all the instructions that should be given to the youthful batsman ; for such details would be long and wearisome, and entirely unnecessary for the guidance of anyone who understands the true principles of the game ; and certainly no one ought to try and teach until he has (at all events theoretically) mastered these, though it is by no means necessary for a good coach to be himself a first-rate exponent of the batsman's art. We would point out, however, that, apart from natural gifts, over which the coach has no control, the most important point to teach the batsman is first to watch the ball; secondly, to throw himself at the right moment into the right position—if he can do this, it is an easy matter to hit or play almost any given ball; thirdly, to meet the ball either in playing back or forward, and not to play in front of the left foot when playing forward or behind the right when playing back.

And now what are we to say of the bowler's art? How are we to teach our boys the most unteachable department of the game? This part of our subject we approach with many misgivings, and though we wish to limit our advice to what is strictly practical, we feel that this very limit will make many think that our hints are but meagre and uninteresting.

We must again 'put back the clock' (oh that some of us decrepit cricketers could do so in reality!) to the age of ten. Again we ask for some natural power of propelling a ball with ease, strength proportioned to age, perseverance, and a real love of the game. Given these materials to work upon, how are we to begin? First of all, let the distance be short, certainly not more than eighteen yards at the age of ten; let the ball be smaller and lighter than the regulation size, and let a boy be taught at first to aim only at one length; as he becomes fairly master of straightness and pitch, let him try to vary the length a little, but not too often, or he may sacrifice regularity and injure his delivery. Change of pace can hardly be looked for at this age; but great care should be taken to prevent a boy from bowling fast, and he should not bowl for long together. In practice it is a good plan to take alternate overs with another boy, as it is easier to bowl four or five balls well and then rest than to go on bowling a greater number. A boy should be taught to measure the distance he runs before delivering the ball, and he should learn to bowl on both sides of the wicket. Great care should be taken to prevent a boy from bowling too much; and if his bowling seems to be getting worse rather than better, let him leave off for some days. We offer no advice on the more abstruse arts of bowling, as the subject has been exhaustively treated in a previous chapter.

Supposing that our boy bowler has by the age of fourteen acquired straightness and pitch, with some power of variation, will he have a fair chance of improving his bowling and distinguishing himself when at a public school? We fear that this will be a trying time—indeed must be so, even if he is taken in hand by some one who understands and takes an interest in the game. In the first place, batting is more attractive to most boys; in the second, the young bowler will probably have a very indifferent field, and the missing of catches tempts the youthful player to abandon the slower pace for the faster, with disastrous results to himself. Almost all young boys wish to bowl as fast as they can, and this ends frequently in ruining a good action and a good arm which had at one time threatened the fall of many a good wicket.

At this point, then, in a bowler's career, public schools, we think, have something to answer for; but we do not agree with those who say that subsequently, when a boy is old enough to be a candidate for his school eleven, there is any great lack of system or careful training. Rather, if a short digression may be pardoned, we think that the Universities, or the laziness of University men, may chiefly be blamed for the dearth of gentlemen bowlers. Our argument shortly stated is this. If we compare gentlemen bowlers of the age of nineteen with professionals of the same age, we shall find that the former have nothing to fear from the comparison. But pass on for five or six years, and the gentlemen are seen to be behind in the race for pre·eminence. Can this be the fault of public schools? Is it not rather that after leaving school few, scarcely any, systematically practise bowling, although they are just at the right age to improve, having stronger muscles and more experience, to say nothing of leisure hours and increased opportunities? If University men would practise their bowling both at nets and in matches with the same assiduity that boys do at a public school, we think that it would approach more nearly to the professional standard than it now does.

We do not propose to offer our readers any special advice as to the method of attack, which will naturally vary with different batsmen. Experience and observation will suggest what may be done, if we can only teach our young bowler to bowl straight, to vary his length, and as he gets older his pace, and if nature has given him strength, and a happy genius enables him to make the ball turn more or less at will. Let us leave the bowler himself, and see if we can offer any hints on providing him with a good field.

It is a common fallacy to suppose that anyone can field well if he takes the trouble to do so. With this we cannot agree; but we feel strongly that most cricketers might improve themselves very much in this department if they took the same pains they do to improve their batting.

But we must return to our small boys. First of all, let us teach them to catch by throwing the ball from one to another, and let the ball be small, proportioned to the size of their hands. Teach them to take the catch opposite the upper part of the chest, when they can get to it in that position, and to draw their hands back as the ball comes into them. Do not keep them too long at this, or they will find it irksome. Vary with a little ground fielding, but do not let them throw too often or too far, or their arms will soon go, and you will ruin your bowlers and your throwers as well. It is not, however, at this early age that the most special attention ought to be given to fielding. It is rather at our public schools that we here look for improvement; this is the time at which we think most may be done. As a boy gains strength and activity he gains two of the qualities most necessary for a good fieldsman, and if nature has given him a good big pair of hands and the power of throwing, it will be owing to his laziness if he does not become a valuable aid to any bowler. We might dwell on the necessity of keenness, watchfulness in the field, position for starting, and many other essentials, but we have said enough for practical purposes ; all else will be easily learnt by a boy who has the energy and determination to train himself into a good field.

It will be noticed that in our suggestions to the batsman we have not advised him to make that use of his legs in defending his wicket which now finds such favour with our leading players. We confess to regarding this as an ignoble art; but we admit that if the l.b.w. rule is to continue as at present, the art, ignoble as it is, must be taught in self-defence, or our pupils will necessarily be handicapped in being expected to stop balls which break and turn with their bat instead of with their legs. Fortunately age will relieve us personally of teaching how this may best be done. It is for the rising generation either to alter the law or to learn the art of getting in front of the wicket when the ball does not pitch straight.

It is in vain to lament over long scores and unfinished matches, over dearth of bowlers and slackness in the field, whilst all the time we are doing everything we can to make matters easier and easier for the batsman, giving him perfect wickets, on which he can score 100 runs without getting out of breath, devoting his legs to the new purpose of systematically intercepting the more difficult balls. How different this from having honestly to run out every hit, and from being compelled to play a real 'snorter' before the breath is fairly recovered after the effort of running several fourers in succession !

CHAPTER XIV.

SINGLE WICKET.

(BY THE HON. R. H. LYTTELTON.)

IT is necessary in any work which professes to treat of cricket generally, that the laws and regulations of single wicket should be discussed, though the subject is not of much importance in these days; for, as far as first-class cricket is concerned, the game played with only one wicket has vanished altogether. Some few years ago, if an ordinary three-day match were over early, a scratch single-wicket match was sometimes improvised ; but the effect was generally depressing.

Few people now take the trouble to read through the rules which govern single-wicket matches, and the almost total disappearance of such games may be mainly attributed to two circumstances : (1) The great increase in the number of three-day matches ; (2) the diminution in the number of fast bowlers.

In the days of Alfred Mynn and Fuller Pilch matches practically never took more than two days, and first-class contests were in number about one-half what they are at present. A professional of the front rank, such as Lohmann or Barnes, now has to play two matches a week, and if a match is over on the second day, he is only too glad to have a rest before beginning again elsewhere, it may be more than a hundred miles away. The public also have the opportunity of seeing such a quantity of first-class play, that there is no demand for single-wicket matches.

In the second place, the rules of single-wicket cricket make it essential that driving in front of the wicket must be the staple stroke of the batsman, and for this reason, because the second rule provides that, to entitle the striker to a run, the ball must be hit before the bounds. Now the bounds are placed twenty-two yards each in a line from the off and leg stump, and there must be bounds unless there are more than four players on each side. The third rule compels the striker at the moment of hitting the ball to have one of his feet behind the popping crease and on the ground. These two laws contain the essence of the game of cricket as played with a single wicket. It is not sound cricket to play any bowling that may be called slow in the widest sense of the term with your right foot absolutely fixed. In the chapter on Batting the young player is advised to go out of his ground to slow bowling of a certain length and drive. But at single wicket the batsman may not move even an inch in front of the popping crease, to get a lob, for instance, on the full pitch. So the effect of bowling slows in a single-wicket match is that a batsman must abandon what may be called the orthodox and correct method of play, and merely wait till he gets a ball far enough up for him to drive it without getting out of his ground.

No correct player can ever drive slows, unless they are right up, without going out of his ground, and a great many would be so cramped that they would be at a disadvantage altogether, and obliged to play an ugly pokey game. If a slow bowler with perhaps two or three fields were bowling to Mr. Webbe, who plays slows as well as anybody in England, that gentleman would find himself obliged to abandon his natural game, stand still, watch the ball carefully, and play it gently, till he got a real half-volley or outrageous long-hop, off which he could score. But if certain skilful bowlers were on, the batsman would very likely have to wait the best part of an hour before such a ball came ; and it would be sadly dull to watch such a game.

If five play on a side bounds are abolished, the slow bowling may get hit behind the wicket, and so the game becomes considerably livelier. The run consists of touching the bowler's stump with the bat and getting back to the popping crease. Thus one run at single wicket is exactly equivalent to two at double wicket. To get three runs in one hit if there are two fields is almost an impossibility, though it has been done. There is no wicket-keeper, and nothing can be scored by byes, leg-byes, or overthrows. To run a man out, it is necessary that the bowler run to the wicket and put it down, unless of course it is thrown down. The fieldsman must return the ball so that it shall cross the ground between the wicket and the bowling stump, or between the bowling stump and the bounds ; and three are scored for a lost ball.

In very ancient times five players a side used often to contend at single wicket, and in this sort of match there are no bounds, though the batsman must have his right or left foot on the ground behind the popping crease when the ball is hit.

Single-wicket matches were once very common. Indeed, during the last century they were played nearly as often as double-wicket games, and we will briefly notice some of the most famous.

In the year 1772 five of Kent with Minshull beat five of the famous Hambledon Club by one wicket, but in 1773 the same five men of Hambledon vanquished five men of England. Happy village of Hambledon that could thus defeat All England, a deed that at double wicket no county could accomplish now ! With the redoubtable Lumpy given, the same village in 1781 beat England by 78 runs, five players on a side. In the following year six of Hambledon beat six of Kent, and the Duke of Dorset, Privy Councillor, Knight of the Garter, and Lord Steward of the King's Household, played for the village against his own county, for what reason history telleth not. John Nyren says that this nobleman 'had the peculiar habit, when unemployed, of standing with his head on one side.' He is also celebrated in verse :

> Equalled by few he plays with glee,
> Nor peevish seeks for victory.

His Grace for bowling cannot yield
To none but Lumpy in the field.
And far unlike the modern way
Of blocking every ball at play,
He firmly stands with bat upright
And strikes with his athletic might,
Sends forth the ball across the mead,
And scores six notches for the deed.

The Duke must have been the first who conceived the idea of international cricket; for while ambassador in France he wrote to Golden, of Chertsey, to form an eleven to play at Paris. Unfortunately, when they had got as far as Dover, they met his Grace, who had to flee the faithless Frenchmen in consesequence of a revolution, and the match was abandoned.

Six of Hambledon again beat six of England in 1783, but six of Kent defeated the village in 1786. This was a famous match, though seeing T. Walker batting for nearly five hours for 26 runs must have been a trifle monotonous. A Kent player named Ring went in when 59 runs were wanted to win and two more wickets to go down. He made 15 overnight, and Sir Horace Mann promised him a pension if he carried out his bat, and, we presume, won the match. He failed to do so, but got out when 2 runs were wanted. Aylward then went in and played 94 balls before he made the winning hit. We hope Sir Horace Mann gave the pension to Ring, for he must have deserved it.

Six of Hampshire twice beat England in 1788, and in 1789 a drawn match was played between six of Kent and six of Hants. In this match betting at the start was 5 to 4 on Hants, but David Harris was seized with the gout, and the betting, therefore, stood at 5 to 4 on Kent. David Harris used sometimes to walk to the ground on crutches, but bowled splendidly, we are told, when he got warm.

In 1806, three of Surrey—William Lambert, Robinson, and William Beldham—beat three of England—Bennett, Fennex, and Lord F. Beauclerk—by 20 runs. This was the famous match when Beldham, father of thirty-nine children—none, so far as we know, cricketers—took a lump of wet dirt and saw-dust, and stuck it on to the ball, which developed an extra-ordinary twist and bowled Lord Frederick out. His lordship was of an irritable disposition, and must have been very angry at this, for he had made 30 runs and was well set.

In 1814, Osbaldeston, Budd, and Lord F. Beauclerk beat three of England—Sherman, T. C. Howard, and Lambert. The famous Squire Osbaldeston clean bowled all his rivals in each innings for 19 runs only. The Squire, whose reputation as an all-round sportsman still survives, was the fastest bowler of his day. In 1818, so great was his fame and that of Lambert, that they challenged Budd, Humewood, T. C. Howard, and George Brown; but the four won in one innings, which so pro-voked the Squire that he withdrew from the M.C.C.—another irritable man.

The celebrated William Lambert alone beat two accom-plished cricketers, Lord F. Beauclerk and Howard, by 15 runs. The Squire was too ill to play, so Lambert played them both, and drew the stakes, 100*l.* Up to 1827, wides counted for nothing, and Lambert bowled wides on purpose to Lord F. Beauclerk to put him out of temper. They were a choleric race in those days. The fame of Lambert is tarnished for selling a match at Nottingham, and he was warned off the ground at Lord's for ever.

Mr. Budd in 1820 played a fast bowler called Brand, the match ending most disastrously for the latter. Mr. Budd went in first, got 70 runs, knocked his wicket down on purpose, and bowled his opponent out for 0. Budd then got 31, again knocked his wicket down, and again bowled his rival out for nothing. Mr. Brand ended his days in a lunatic asylum ; we hope the malady was not brought on by this match, which was got up by Mr. Ward, who backed Mr. Brand.

The two brothers Broadbridge, one of whom was called 'our Jem,' beat George Brown and Tom Marsden of Sheffield in 1827, but were beaten in the return match. In 1832 Alfred

Mynn played his first important single-wicket match against Thomas Hills, Mynn winning with his wicket standing. Hills said that Mynn bowled at least 50 wides, which seems to prove that the chief bowlers of that day must have been slightly deficient in accuracy. Why in this match the wides were not reckoned is not clear, the rule scoring against the bowler having been put in force some few years before. A return match was played, and Mynn again won, this time in one innings, and Hills retired, satisfied, we suppose, that in Mynn he had found his master.

In 1833 Mynn and Pilch were perhaps the two greatest all-round players, and Marsden of Sheffield in this year challenged the immortal Pilch, who won in one innings and 70 runs. Pilch was not a great bowler, neither was he fast, but Marsden's style was fast underhand, and Pilch's bat was too straight for such bowling. In the return Pilch got 78 runs in the first innings and 100 in the second, and won the match by 127 runs. The supremacy of Pilch over Marsden was fully asserted by these two matches, and Marsden must have returned to Sheffield somewhat crestfallen.

> Next Marsden may come, though it here must be stated
> That his skill down at Sheffield is oft overrated.

But the Yorkshiremen, we know, are always proud of their countrymen. Pilch was a great batsman, and we do not feel surprised that he scored so largely against fast underhand bowling.

The ground ought to have been now cleared for a match between Mynn and Pilch, and great would have been the interest if such a game had been played — Voltigeur and The Flying Dutchman would have been nothing to it. The two men belonged to the same county, so probably there was wanting a sufficient motive ; but together they would probably have beaten any three other cricketers.

Mr. Mynn next heavily defeated James Dearman of Sheffield twice, in the first match by 112 runs, and again in one innings and 36 runs. Mynn scored 46 in the last innings off 46 hits, which sounds strange, but then, as is recorded naïvely in the 'Scores and Biographies,' Mynn was always a great punisher.

Mr. Felix next challenged Mr. Mynn, and he must have been of a sanguine temperament to have done so ; for, though perhaps a better bat than Mynn, he was a left-handed lob bowler, a delivery not suited for single-wicket matches. The first game Mynn won in one innings and 1 run, only 9 runs being made in the whole match. In Felix's second innings Mynn bowled 247 balls for 3 runs. Single-wicket matches had already begun to get out of favour ; this was the most important that had taken place for some time, and Squire Osbaldeston was a spectator. In the return Mynn won by one wicket, and this was a small scoring match. Mynn now was left unchallenged, having won all the single-wicket matches in which he was engaged alone. In 1847 Wisden beat Sherman twice. Thomas Hunt of Chesterfield was a great single-wicket matchplayer, and beat Chatterton, Dakin, Charley Brown, and R. C. Tinley.

Single-wicket playing has been practically dead since 1850, though Hayward, Carpenter, and Tarrant played two matches about the year 1862. The subject possesses only an historical interest now, but in old times it created enormous excitement, and no doubt the pride of the men of Kent in Alfred Mynn was largely owing to his single-wicket prowess. If such matches were played on the smooth wickets of modern times, the fortunate man who won the toss might never be got out all day, and the game would become a burlesque on cricket. Eleven fieldsmen, and not one bowler merely, are now required to get out Mr. Grace and Shrewsbury, and but few wickets are bowled down as compared with the days of fast bowling and rough grounds. When the All England elevens used to tour about the country under the management first of William Clarke and then of George Parr, some of the best bowlers in England were to be found in their ranks. Jackson, Willsher, Furley, Tarrant, and others used often to play, and occasionally when the regular match was over one of them would earn a cheap sort of notoriety by challenging eleven of the natives at single wicket. Eleven straight balls were sometimes found sufficient to get the eleven out, and one run by the England player gave him the victory. Such matches are absurd, and it is not a matter of regret that they are played no longer.

However, it seems right that a notice of the famous contests of old should have been written, on account of the interest they formerly excited, and on village greens, where eccentricities of ground are to be met with, they may still perhaps be played. But they are a relic of the past.

CHAPTER XV.

OUTFIT.

(By W. G. Grace.)

Amongst cricketers generally opinions are many and divided as to this or that particular style of batting and bowling, but sound them upon the materials necessary for the outfit of a player, and you will find as a rule that perfect unanimity prevails. They will tell you that these must be of the best quality, that too much care cannot be taken in their selection, and that badly fitting boots or trousers may mean all the difference between a small score and a large one, not to speak of the discomfort they cause when bowling and fielding. I have very seldom met with a cricketer of eminence who did not take the greatest care in the choice of a bat, pads, or gloves, or who did not impress upon his tailor the momentous importance of comfortably fitting clothes.

I propose to say something about everything that is needful in the outfit of a cricketer, beginning with his personal clothing. It is advisable for the sake of health and comfort that he should wear flannel or woollen material next his skin. It was no unusual sight ten or twenty years ago to find an eleven or county twenty-two dressed in all the colours of the rainbow. White is now usually worn, and it certainly looks better and cooler than any other colour. Shirts should be made to fit easily at the shoulders, but not too loosely. They should also be made large at the neck, as nothing is more disagreeable on a hot day than a shirt which is too small round the throat.

The best material for trousers is white flannel or cloth manufactured for the purpose; I like cloth the best, and nearly always have my trousers made of it, as it does not shrink so much in washing, and that is a very important consideration if you play right through the season, from May to September. Braces are not worn when playing cricket, so there is no need to have buttons for them on your trousers; a strap and buckle at the back should be used instead. The straps should be made so that the buckle can be removed when washing is necessary, as the buckle is very likely to stain and cut the trousers if left on. Do not forget loops at the side for scarf or belt to go through. Many of the old cricketers used to wear belts to keep their trousers from slipping down; I prefer a scarf, as it looks better and will grip quite as firmly, and you will not run the risk of being given out caught at the wickets through the handle of the bat coming in contact with the buckle of the belt and the noise being mistaken by the umpire for a snick off the bat. I once saw a man given out for this very thing. It certainly was very hard lines; the ball passed so close to the bat that the umpire, hearing a snick, thought the ball must have touched it, and, on being appealed to, gave the batsman out.

Nothing can look much worse in the cricket field than to see fieldsmen with their hands in their pockets, and it is certainly not conducive to quick, smart fielding. I have observed that nearly all good fielders keep their hands hanging loosely by their sides, and are ready to dash after the ball immediately it is hit anywhere in their direction. Be sure to try on every new pair of trousers when sent home from the tailor's, or you may find out when too late to rectify the mistake that they are either too small or too large, and are completely useless. A revelation of this kind when you arrive on the cricket field and are getting ready to go in is destructive alike to high scoring and sweetness of temper.

Caps I think indispensable and preferable to any kind of hats, unless in very hot weather under a broiling sun, when some protection to the neck and back of the head is necessary.

1887 was one of the hottest seasons I ever played through, but only once did I change my cap for a hat with a large brim. Hats are very apt to fall off; caps rarely do so if they are made to fit properly. Many cricketers never wear any covering on their heads. Mr. A. N. Hornby and Mr. Frank Townsend have always played bare-headed, and seem to revel in it whatever may be the state of the weather. Most of the leading clubs and counties have a distinguishing colour of their own, and cricketers generally wear caps made of this colour.

Jackets and jerseys, or 'sweaters,' as they are commonly called, have their place in the outfit of a cricketer. A jacket on a hot day is useful when one is not actually engaged in the game; special attention should be given to its colour and pattern—very often it is made of the same flannel and shade as the cap, and when well chosen forms a very pleasing contrast to the white of the trousers. It can be used when fielding, but certainly not when batting or bowling. A jersey or sweater is preferable; it fits closer to the body, is much pleasanter, and in the field on a very cold day it helps to keep you warm, which is necessary for smartness and comfort. It is bad enough at times to watch a series of maiden overs and only get the crossing over between them for exercise, but when you add to that the sensation of shivering from insufficient clothing, then you have a very unhappy situation indeed. You must exercise judgment in the use of a jersey when batting or bowling, for the warmth it affords will be more than counterbalanced by the hindrance to freedom of arms and wrists. I have worn one in very cold weather when first going in to bat or going on to bowl, but have discarded it after an over or two. Always carry it in your bag, for a hot and fine morning may be followed by a cold or wet afternoon.

Experienced cricketers know that the most trying thing during the season is to keep the feet from getting sore and blistered; if they become so, much of the pleasure of the game is gone; therefore everyone who wishes to be comfortable should wear thick woollen socks, and always have an extra pair or two in the bag when travelling about. They are better made plain, not ribbed, and in natural colours they are more comfortable and do not mark the feet.

Cricket boots or shoes must be worn. I prefer lace-up boots, and think most cricketers who play a good deal do the same. Have them made of brown or white leather. It is rather difficult to say what is the best thickness for the sole ; for while a heavy man must wear very thick ones when the ground is as hard as a brickbat to prevent the feet being hurt by the spikes or bruised by the ground, a thinner pair would be sufficient under different conditions. I always wear thick-soled boots with low flat heels ; by having the heels low and flat you are not nearly so likely to sprain or twist your ankle as you would be with high and narrow ones. To prevent slipping, it is necessary to wear spikes or nails in your boots or shoes. Be careful what sort of spikes or nails you use ; I prefer short spikes, which are made in different sizes and can be screwed into the boots in a very short time. These spikes are very convenient, as when they wear down short they can be taken out and new ones easily put in. Nails are used by some cricketers ; they are of different sizes and shapes, but large square-headed ones hold best. I should advise all cricketers who play often to have two pairs of boots, one with short spikes or nails which will hold and prevent slipping on a hard dry ground, and the other with longer spikes for a soft wet spongy ground.

Pads were not worn in the early days of cricket, and although I have seen a few first-class cricketers who never use them, at the present time I cannot call to mind anyone who plays without them. It is much safer to wear them, and when they are properly made and fit well they but slightly affect the freedom of the legs. The sense of confidence that comes from wearing them more than makes up for the slight loss of freedom. No doubt the old players of whom we hear so much from certain old fogies did not like being hit on the shin any more than we do at the present time, so some one invented pads or shin-protectors, which consisted of two pieces of wood so placed as to guard the legs. The next kind we can trace consisted of several pieces of wood fastened together, and since then they have been gradually improved until the present pads were invented, which consist of rows of wadding or stuffing of some kind with layers of cork and a piece of cane for each row, the whole being covered with leather. At first they were fastened with pieces of tape wound round the leg and tied ; then came india-rubber or elastic straps with hooks, and finally the present arrangement of buckle and strap, which meets with general approval. Some makers of the present day have them fastened by loops and a long strap lacing up the back of the leg.

When choosing pads see that they are exactly your size and fit well, for large, heavy, and uncomfortable pads will do as much to tire you out in a long innings as hard hitting. As soon as you begin to feel them loose and shifting, strap them tight again, or they may cause you to be run out.

Batting gloves are of the highest importance, and players should accustom themselves to wear them as soon as they begin to play regular cricket, or very possibly they may have to use them on some important occasion and will feel all abroad when wearing them for the first time. There are some grounds where the pitch is so easy that you rarely find a ball rising higher than the top of the stumps, and you could almost dispense with gloves altogether ; but occasionally a ball comes which rises and catches you a whack on the hand, causing a damaged finger which may spoil your cricket and comfort for the rest of the day, or perhaps season. At Lord's and some other grounds not so many years ago fast bumping balls had to be watched very carefully, and knocks on the fingers and body were very frequent. Players then had to use gloves, who at other times went in without them. I am sure it is a mistake not to wear them constantly, and calling for gloves as some players do after getting a nasty knock on the hand or knuckles is like locking the stable-door after the horse has been stolen. I think prevention is better than cure, and know of nothing more disappointing in cricket than to be compelled to decline an invitation to play in a first-class match owing to a damaged finger, which might have been prevented by simply wearing a glove. Gloves are generally made of leather, with strips of thick fluted india-rubber sewn on the back to protect the fingers and hand. When purchasing gloves be careful to see that the rubber is stout enough to resist the blow when the ball hits your hand or fingers, or you might just as well do without gloves altogether. See that the rubber on the fingers of the right-hand glove comes down slightly over the tops of the fingers, and on the side of the thumb instead of the back. Just remember that the side of the thumb, and not the back of it, is towards the bowler when you are batting. I have seen many a bruised and smashed thumb from want of care in this apparently small point. We first hear of batting gloves about the year 1825, when round-arm bowling came into force; but of course they were then clumsily made, and lacked the comfort which characterises the gloves of the present time. They had more the look of our present wicket-keeping gloves, were much heavier, and only the backs of the hands and part of the fingers were protected, cork, cane, or rubber being used for this purpose. The improvement in the make of them has been of steady growth. It is not many years since they were made with leather on the inside, which covered the palm of the hand, preventing, as everyone knows, a firm grip of the bat; however, that is a thing of the past, and now a good number of players not only wear gloves without anything covering the palm of the hand, but go so far as to cut out pieces of the inside covering to the fingers; the idea being that the more you can get of the natural hand to grip the bat, the greater your command and power over it.

Look to the fastening of your glove even more carefully than to the fastening of your pads. Carelessness in this respect will make the hand feel uncomfortable, and a loose flapping glove may very probably be the cause of your losing your wicket, as the ball is more likely to hit a glove of this description than a firm well-fastened one.

Gloves are generally fastened at the wrist by a band of elastic sewn on the top and buttoned. You can fasten them by a band of elastic without a button, or have the thumb separated from the body of the glove and sewn on to a piece of elastic, the other end of which is fastened to the back of the glove, and long enough to pass once round the wrist ; this contrivance will keep the glove well in its place. Although I have never used a glove of this description, I consider the idea a good one and well worthy of a trial.

And now that the cricketer is fully equipped, so far as dress and safety to limbs are concerned, it is time to refer to those indispensable requisites of the game—bat, ball, and wickets. I have no doubt a number of young enthusiasts will say that they ought to have come first, and that what I have touched upon are small matters in comparison. I know it is the ambition of all youngsters to possess a bat long before they are able to play or to take part in club practice and matches; only give them that, and they think they are fit to do battle with the finest exponents of the game. Whilst ready to admit its primary importance in cricket, I should be sorry indeed if what I have said should appear to them of no importance. Believe me, and I speak earnestly, it is careful attention to the apparently small things that commands success so far as the playing of the game is concerned. I do not believe in elaborate dress, or being over-particular as to the look of your trousers or shirt, but I cannot too strongly impress upon the young player the importance of being able to walk to the wicket with everything about him fitting comfortably; and that can only be brought about by careful consideration of the matters indicated. When you have attended to them, you have done all that you are able to do as far as preparation for the struggle is concerned; you have determined to leave nothing to chance, and now you are at the wicket, and it is simply a matter of skill and luck whether you are going to perform brilliantly or indifferently. With all good cricketers, as with all good soldiers, drill and attention to little things have become a doctrine, and a doctrine that is worthy of attention.

The bat used by our forefathers was more like a crooked club, and in their time there were not any rules or restrictions as to its length and width. An old cricketer named Small is said to have been the first man known to have made and played with a straight bat, and from that time bats have gradually become more like those at present in use. White of Reigate, another of the old school, had a bat made wider than the wicket, and this led to the first rule as to the width and size of the bat. Eventually the present law came into force, that the bat must not exceed 38 inches in length and $4\frac{1}{4}$ in width. The length is more than enough ; I have never seen a cricketer play with a bat 38 inches in length. The ordinary and best length is $34\frac{1}{2}$ inches, the blade 22 and the handle $12\frac{1}{2}$; anything longer would be unwieldy, the blade would be likely to dig into the ground and the handle into the stomach when playing. The weight and balance of a bat are the chief points, and make more difference in a cricketer's play than is generally known.

I believe that if a bat is well balanced, it is not of much importance if it is a little heavy ; a good player can play nearly as well forward or back, and drive as well as he could with a lighter one; but of one thing I am certain, and that is, if he wants to cut and hit to leg well, he must play with a light bat ; if he plays with a heavy one, he will not only miss a good many balls he ought to cut effectively, but others he will just touch, and if he is not in luck will be caught at the wicket or in the slips. A bat should weigh from two pounds to two pounds five ounces. Many young cricketers play with bats far too heavy and long for their strength and height. The length of a boy's bat should vary according to his height. A tall boy might play with a full-size bat if not very heavy, but small boys should play with shorter bats ; the blade and handle should be made shorter but not narrower. Some cricketers prefer thick handles and others like thin ones; this point must be determined by the size and length of the hand. Naturally a man with a large hand, especially if the fingers are long, will need a thicker handle than a cricketer who has a small hand and short fingers. The shape and size of the handle is a matter of opinion and suitability. I myself use a thick handle which is not too round, but must advise a cricketer to use whichever suits him best. Occasionally one comes across a man the handle of whose bat is two or three inches longer than usual, but I do not think he gains anything by it, unless he is very tall, and makes up his mind for sensational hitting; for it is certain that a tall man with a long-handled bat, if he times the ball properly, will hit it further than he could with a short-handled one, as 'the longer the lever the greater the power.' Most cricketers try to keep up their wickets as long as they can, knowing it is only a matter of time until runs come. If you try and play a series of maiden overs with a bat with a handle longer than you are accustomed to, you will find how difficult it is, and recognise the impossibility of playing as well as you could with one of ordinary length.

Some cricketers cover the handle with chamois leather, or india-rubber cases made for that purpose. I can say very little about such devices, as I have not tried them sufficiently to give a decided opinion, favourably or otherwise. I am sure if the leather or rubber case is at all loose, as I have seen it on some bats, you will not get a firm grip of the handle; what is more, it will turn in your hand, and a dangerous hit in the air may be the result. Years ago there were only a few bat-makers, now the times are altered and their name is legion. Many of them are trying to invent some new handle or blade that will make the bats drive more than they do already. What will the poor bowlers do then? I find the present bat drives quite enough, and have sometimes thought it drove too much; but then I was bowling, not batting. I have tried many of these new inventions, and have no doubt some of them will answer very well when the makers have succeeded in producing handles with the proper amount of spring and yet strong enough to withstand the strain put upon them. It is very annoying to have the handle of your bat breaking in the middle of a long innings, for you do not feel at home with a new one for an over or two. I am repeatedly asked whose bats are the best, and what maker's I play with. My answer is I play with any good bat I can get hold of, never minding who is the maker, as long as the bat is not too heavy and is well balanced, and suits me as to handle. In the season 1887 I made most of my long scores with a bat made by a maker comparatively unknown. When you get hold of a good bat take care of it, oil it now and then, and when the season is over, put it away in a dry place; during the winter months oil it occasionally, or it may get too dry to drive properly when the next season comes.

The ball used when cricket was first played was much smaller than the one employed at the present time, and was more like our 'rounder' ball. The rule says the present ball must not weigh less than five ounces and a half, nor more than five ounces and three-quarters, and it must not measure less than nine inches nor more than nine inches and one-quarter in circumference.

It requires much knowledge and experience to tell a good ball from an indifferent one. They are all pretty much the same in appearance, size and weight, and it is only after a hard knock or two that a bad one begins to show its real nature. I have seen an apparently good ball knocked out of shape after half an hour's play, while a real good one will last and keep its shape and firmness throughout a long innings.

Ball-makers like bat-makers are very numerous, and as cricketers must trust them to supply a good article, I would say buy only from those who have earned the right to be classed amongst the best makers. A badly made ball is dear at any price.

And now, having described the materials necessary to complete a cricketer's outfit, the only thing required is a suitable bag in which to put them. One made of good leather is preferable to any other sort. Mind you have it large enough to hold everything you can possibly require. Have a strong lock and key for it, and straps as well. Have your name inscribed on the brass round the lock, and your initials painted in plain bold letters on the side. In the hurry of hand-shaking and bustle to catch a train the wrong bag has been often taken for want of this simple precaution.

CHAPTER XVI.

CRICKET REFORM.

(By the Hon. R. H. Lyttelton.)

A GREAT enthusiast on behalf of any game or sport is sometimes a little apt to argue that the game in which he delights is a perfect one, that nothing ought to be reformed, and that any change must be for the worst.

We yield to nobody in our enthusiasm for the game of cricket, but we are certainly in favour of judicious reform in the laws which govern the game ; and we can scarcely help supposing that the opponents of all change are either oblivious of the enormous alteration that has taken place in cricket in consequence of the improvement of grounds, or else their attention is principally devoted to batting, and this causes them to think a little too much of the joys of hitting. No doubt they revel in the hot days, perfect wickets, and loose bowling that bring about the supremacy of batting.

We feel confident that our younger critics fail to recognise the gigantic change that has taken place simply on account of the invention of the mowing-machine alone. That is only one of the many causes of the superiority and billiard-table aspect of modern grounds, as compared with the same grounds in former days. The champion operator with the old-fashioned scythe was bound to leave some long blades of grass, and anybody can see the difference between a lawn mown by the scythe and the lawn shaved close by a machine. It is this machine, and the knowledge that comes from experience of the proper sorts of soil and seeds, that has caused the beautiful wickets of the present day, and the corresponding increase in the number of runs scored. The gigantic scoring is an evil. Everything is made easy for the batsman. In no respect, save that of allowing overhand bowling, has the poor bowler had any consideration shown him, and the results are batting made easy and drawn games. The scoring during the season of 1887 reached a pitch that, for the sake of cricket, we hope will never be seen again ; but it will be repeated when the next dry season comes round, unless in the interval some changes are made in the laws of the game to help the bowler and fieldsman this time and not the batsman. The unlearned and unlettered spectator, it is true, seems to regard a match as interesting according to the number of runs scored, but this is a perverted view. Such a one likes to see a good finish if he can, but he feels slightly disappointed every time a wicket falls, unless indeed it happens to be the wicket of a proverbial stick. His ideal day's amusement requires a hot day and a hard and perfectly true wicket—W. G. Grace, at the head of a strong side, batting for five hours and scoring over 200 runs ; other batsmen piling up fifties and sixties—and when the stumps are drawn at seven he loves to see on the telegraph the follow-

ing sort of figures : $\dfrac{\frac{573}{8}}{101}$.

We have no wish to be hard on our unintelligent friend, but we must point out to him that his conception of the game is based on an altogether wrong principle. If he tries to understand and appreciate the skill of bowling, and the beauty and grace of fine fielding and wicket-keeping, he will keep a tender spot in his heart for professors of these branches of the game, and not like to see them utterly defeated by the skill of modern batsmen, largely helped by the modern wickets. Where the score is in such a ridiculous state as the above, there will ensue one of two results : either the match will be drawn, or else W. G. Grace and his comrades will win an absurdly easy victory. The ideal match is a match that does not last more than two days, where the wicket has got a bit of devil in it, where no individual innings realises more than 80 runs, no one complete innings exceeds 200 runs, where the side that have to go in for the fourth innings must get about 180 runs to win, and win the match by two or three wickets or lose it by 15 or 20 runs. This is genuine cricket, and far better worth seeing than the type of matches so often played in 1887.

We will first consider a few points that are not changes in the law, but only consist of a strict observance of the laws as they now stand. Rule 45 is one of a set of rules that are supposed to inform an umpire of his duties, and runs thus : 'They (umpires) shall allow two minutes for each striker to come in, and ten minutes between each innings. When they shall call play, the side refusing to play shall lose the match.' Here is a perfectly straightforward rule that we do not hesitate to say is ignored as completely as if it was not a rule at all. No doubt it was not required in former days, when individual scores of 50 did not occur oftener than hundreds do now. There was no hurry then. Even in fine weather very few matches lasted into the third day, and no doubt a certain laxity crept into the system. But the rule was in existence, nevertheless, and is still ; and surely now is the time for putting it into force.

A few statistical facts may prove how important a feature a tolerable observance of time is in considering how to stop this endless succession of drawn games. Elsewhere it has been pointed out that there has been no drawn match played between Oxford and Cambridge since 1849. There have been plenty of runs got and to spare, but on Lord's a far stricter jurisdiction has been kept in the matter of time than on any other ground.

But even here nobody can affirm that a strict ten minutes is never exceeded for the interval between the innings. It may be taken as a general truth that thirty minutes is frequently allowed to elapse on other grounds ; and let us see how many hours' play takes place on a fine August day.

Play is advertised to begin at 12. As a rule it does not begin till 12.15. Luncheon is at 2, and there is always three-quarters of an hour consumed by the meal and dawdling about afterwards. A side is got out say at 4.30 ; this means another interval of half-an-hour between the innings, and stumps are drawn at 6.30. This makes the actual time spent in playing cricket on a grand summer's day exactly five hours. On a second and third day play usually begins at 11.30, so an additional half-hour is gained, making sixteen hours' play for the three days. Who can wonder that this state of things causes so many drawn matches ? Yet the remedy is simple. What possible objection can there be against beginning at eleven after the first day, and thus getting three hours' uninterrupted play before luncheon ? Again, why not make a rule of the ground that spectators are not allowed to break into the ring when the innings is over, and that the game shall recommence after the wicket has been properly swept and rolled ? That to prevent the spectators from walking into the ring is feasible is proved by the example shown both by the Yorkshire Committee at Sheffield, where the rule is in strict force on the Bramall Lane Ground, and by the Lancashire Committee at Old Trafford.

If this regulation of the ground is in force, the players will all be in the pavilion two minutes after the close of the innings, and the rolling of the wicket will have begun. Let there be a five minutes bell rung at the expiration of that time, and let the umpires then take up their position at the wickets. The rolling and sweeping need not occupy more than ten minutes, and directly the roller is moved off the wicket the two batsmen and the field ought to be in their places. The rule is perfectly easy to work, and there can be no reasonable argument against adopting it. After it had been in force for a month people would wonder that the old-fashioned waste of time had ever been permitted. The alteration, or rather the systematic carrying out of this one rule alone, will do as much to enable matches to be played out as anything in reason can ; and that some rule is necessary seems to be evident from the following statistics. In the Australian tour of 1886 thirty-nine matches were begun, and no less than twenty-two left unfinished. During the same season Notts played fourteen matches, and no fewer than seven—or exactly one-half—were drawn.

The same rule which provides ten minutes between each innings allows two minutes for the incoming batsman to succeed the outgoing. It is unfortunate that no mention is made of any penalty for the infringement of this; there should be one, and it ought to be rigidly exacted if the rule be not observed. The strict enforcement of this law would go far to stop the existing evil of drawn games.

We will now discuss what we consider to be a hardship to bowlers and field, and an undue favouring of the batsman—a point about which there is no rule. Twenty years ago, England was not so densely crowded, the average number of spectators was not nearly so large as it is now, and it was not the custom to have an all-round boundary. Every hit was run out, and the fieldsman in pursuit of the ball plunged right into the middle of carriages, spectators, and horses' legs, and picked it up, the batsman in the meanwhile running out the full value of the hit. Now the case is altogether altered. There is a strong cord running all round the ground, every decently hard hit is certain to reach the ropes if the ball once passes the fieldsman, and the batsman stands coolly in his ground, being altogether spared the trouble of running and the loss of breath which naturally follows the exertion. There is another reason why the batsman is favoured by this system of boundaries, and that is, the chance of a run-out is materially diminished. The position we take up in all these matters is, that in these days runs are too easily accumulated, that the perfection of modern wickets has so affected the bowling that the reform of the future ought to be in the direction of favouring the bowlers and fieldsmen, and not the batsman. Those who were spectators of cricket matches in former days can call to mind many a run-out owing to a batsman attempting a fourth or fifth run. The fieldsman had hold of the ball at a distance say of 100 yards from the wicket; just a second or so before the batsman started for a fifth run the ball had been thrown, a hard low and straight throw pitching about 15 yards from the wicket ; the ball was handled by the wicket-keeper, and the batsman was run out by a few inches. If the thing is done with real skill there is no prettier sight in cricket ; but the boundary has practically stopped all this. A spectator picks the ball up, chucks it to the expectant field, who dribbles it along the ground to the bowler, while the batsman, having had his smack, saunters about in the most unconcerned way and prepares for the next ball. Cricketers well understand that this saving of breath to a batsman is an enormous advantage ; he is enabled to stand quite cool and collected in his ground, and hit away without, as a rule, having to run more than two runs, while the bowlers and field are perspiring away in their efforts to get the side out. The remedy we propose is a very simple one, and in our judgment would meet the case perfectly. It consists of running a net, two feet high, round the ground along the same circumference that the boundary ropes now go, and unless the ball goes over this net, let the hit be run out. The batsman will frequently get three runs for a hit of equal value to that for which he now gets four, he will be compelled to run them out, and the fine thrower will have opportunities of distinguishing himself. The net must be like a common rabbit net, and fixed down so as to prevent the ball going under. We feel certain that this system will, if adopted, insure that the batsman will not be the only player on the ground who is in full possession of his breath.

We have heard it maintained that in a run-getting match where there are no boundaries the field gets tired before the batsmen, and that therefore the rabbit net would benefit the side it is desired to handicap. Now, in the first place, we do not agree with this statement, and in the second place the circumstances on a ground like Chatham lines or Woolwich Common must be different from what they are on Lord's or the Oval, where 10,000 spectators are looking on. The two batsmen run out every hit, and these two batsmen for the moment constitute the whole of one side. But when a hit is made the whole eleven of the fielding side have not to run after the ball; only one of them does so ; it follows, therefore, that the work to these two individual batsmen must be harder than that of any one field. No doubt the batsman feels pride and pleasure in the getting of runs ; but if he is much of a hitter he must be in wondrous training if, after having had to run 80 runs in 45 minutes or thereabouts, he does not feel just a bit fagged ; and everybody knows that a real fine ball is likely to get out a man in this condition. What we complain of now is that a batsman may be four hours at the wicket and never once feel even out of breath. What makes the rotund Quidnunc and the festive Zingaro feel a little queer is the chase after a ball to a Medway stroke at Chatham, where the ball runs in front of the perspiring fieldsman down a hill and with a wind behind it, as Mr. Pickwick's hat did in an historical scene.

The introduction of round-arm bowling has been described, and it may safely be said that no change which has ever taken place in cricket has caused so great a revolution. Immediately prior to the introduction of this style of bowling the scoring got so high that it became a nuisance, as is the case now, though no doubt it is far higher at present. The batsman had learnt the art of successfully dealing with underhand bowling even though the paces and twists were of a most varied character, and so the existing problem of how to keep down runs at that time also presented itself. There was this important difference in the circumstances, however, that the modern grounds have reached a perfection which has never been attained before, and it is probable that the old-fashioned underhand bowling was more difficult to play on the average wicket of sixty years ago than the modern round and over-hand bowling is on the wicket of to-day. If, then, there was sufficient reason in 1827 for permitting the introduction of some reform to stop the run-getting, there must be more reason now, for there is no doubt runs are more easily obtained at the present time than they were at any former period. The excellence of modern grounds, so often referred to in this book for reasons that have been described, is a matter the importance of which cannot be exaggerated, and it appears to us useless to shut our eyes to the fact that, in consequence of these improved wickets, some steps must be taken to check run-getting, or at any rate prevent as far as possible drawn matches.

Since 1827 the only noteworthy revolution which has taken place is in the concession to the bowler of permission to deliver the ball with his arm above the shoulder, a change only made after a fierce opposition. The bowling of Spofforth at his fastest, Ulyett, Mr. Rotherham and others on the old-fashioned wickets, before the introduction of the mowing-machine and heavy roller, would have prevented heavy run-getting by the simple expedient of severely injuring the batsman —not a desirable method by any means. But the new rule for a time somewhat diminished scores, and only ceased to be more efficacious as the grounds improved. As far as bowl-ing is concerned things have not been altered since, and it is impossible that any further change can take place, as public opinion has spoken out strongly in regard to throwing, which, owing to the weakness of umpires and to the great laxity of cricket committees, crept into vogue a few years ago. Now comes the question, What can be done to check the run-getting? Note first, that a great and important change took place about 1835 by means of a quiet decision of the umpires, reminding lawyers of the method whereby entails were abolished by the judges in a celebrated suit called 'Taltarum's case.' This deci-sion affected the interpretation of the law of leg before wicket. There was a difference of opinion between two celebrated um-pires of that period, Dark and Caldecourt, as to how the rule was to be applied. Dark thought that the rule ought to be interpreted in the way that it is now ; Caldecourt, on the other hand, maintained that if the ball left the bowler's hand and was proceeding in a straight line from hand to wicket, the batsman was out if he let the ball hit his leg. In other words, whereas now the ball must go straight from wicket to wicket, Caldecourt's idea was that it was sufficient if it went from hand to wicket. It may be mentioned, as showing that these two authorities were interested in the question, that Dark bowled with a low action *over* the wicket, and Caldecourt with a low action *round* the wicket. Before 1835 the rule ran thus : ' Rule 25. Or if with any part of his person he stop the ball, which in the opinion of the umpire at the bowler's wicket shall have been delivered in a straight line *from it* to the striker's wicket and would have hit it.'

In consequence of the dispute between Dark and Caldecourt the matter was referred to the M.C.C. Committee, and the result of their deliberation was that the two words ' from it ' were inserted and Dark triumphed—unfortunately, as we think.

While this book was being written the sub-committee of the Marylebone Cricket Club determined not to make any change in the existing law of l.b.w., but framed a sort of homily to the effect that systematically stopping the ball with the leg is a reprehensible practice, and ought to be discouraged. The whole question of l.b.w. has been discussed largely during the last twelve months, and it is impossible to refrain from expressing an opinion one way or the other ; we trust, therefore, that we shall be excused if we differ from the M.C.C. authorities.

Let us see, in the first place, what the opponents of change regard as objections. Some say that runs are not too numerous, large scores are not an evil in themselves, and they perceive no necessity for any change which would tend to diminish scoring. To these we only say that if they really think so we agree with them that the rule had better stand as it is. We feel sure, however, that the majority of cricket judges do not agree with this opinion, and the tiresome number of drawn matches is one reason for altering the law ; another being that batting as an art is being spoilt, notwithstanding the larger scoring.

Besides this, the sight, which is now common, of bowlers

and field utterly demoralised owing to the splendid condition
of the modern wickets, and runs coming like a flood, is discouraging to the lover of genuine cricket. Here we suspect we
reach·a truth, and that is, the people who do not think runs
are too numerous are the batsmen themselves ; and we should
like to hear what the bowlers think ? It is also said that the
people who pay the gate money and come and look on at
matches like to see long scores made, and if these are diminished in number they will come no longer, and the clubs will
suffer in consequence. Even if this be true, should the authorities legislate from the standpoint of ignorance — in other words,
are the people who do not profess to thoroughly understand
the game to determine the direction of future legislation ?
This is a democratic age, but we cannot think that such a contention is admissible.

Then there are others who protest that any change will give
too much power to umpires. Again we respectfully say we
cannot agree with this view. We suppose that this class of
objectors mean that any change would make it more difficult
for umpires to determine whether a batsman is out l.b.w. or
not. This cannot be so, as we feel sure that proper consideration would show. Every umpire will admit that the hard thing
to determine now is whether the ball pitched straight or not.
Under an altered law this would not have to be considered at
all, so a change certainly would not make the umpire's task a
harder one, but rather, on the contrary, easier. The umpires
now have enormous powers entrusted to them, and if the rule
were made more stringent it would very soon be found that
batsmen would alter their style of play, and the appeals for
l.b.w. would gradually become fewer. The modern teachers of
batting instruct the young cricketer to play forward with his
left leg right up to his bat, so as to leave no space between the
bat and his leg. Under the present rule this is correct ; but
twenty-five years ago this method was neither taught nor practised, and cricket was all the better for it. In like manner in
back play the youngster puts his right leg up to his· bat, and

this is an innovation about which it may be said that cricket would be improved if it was no longer the fashion. In fact, the modern idea is that, failing the bat, the legs must protect the wicket ; and we say most emphatically that this is against the spirit of the rules and practice of cricket. One hears a batsman who has been given out l.b.w. come away from the wicket and talk as if he were the victim of the greatest hardship. And why? Because he maintains that the ball pitched perhaps an inch off the off stump. But where is the hardship? He does not go to the wicket to play with any other weapon except his bat, and if he is in front of his wicket and the ball hits his legs, the real hardship is suffered by the bowler unless the umpire gives him out. The famous Robert Grimston used to say that it was bad play to be hit on the leg at all ; and he was right, if the legs happened to be in front of the wicket. Small sympathy did anyone get from this sound old sportsman if hurt under these circumstances. ' Hurt? I hope he is hurt. I hope he will feel it in the night if he wakes up ; his leg was before all three stumps, and he ought to have been out, and would have been out under the old law. He put his leg in front purposely, and it isn't fair cricket; it is cheating !'

There was a proposal made, we think by Mr. Webbe, to the effect that the umpires shall give a man out who wilfully stops a ball with his legs. We would earnestly ask Mr. Webbe and his supporters to tell us how this change can ever work? One class of objectors to any change allege that too much power would be given to the umpires. Mr. Webbe's proposition would not only entail on an umpire a thorough knowledge of cricket as a game, but would also require him to be a judge of morals. How can one decide on the wilfulness of an act? A batsman puts his leg in front of the wicket and hangs his bat in front of his leg. The ball misses his bat and hits his leg. He is given out, and he will stoutly maintain that there was no wilful act at all ; that he never played such a ball in any other way in his life, and it was bad luck that it missed his bat. Who can settle this question?

A word now on behalf of the unhappy bowlers. The wondrous excellence of modern grounds has driven the bowler to adopt all sorts of devices to get wickets, and the great increase in the number of curling and breaking bowlers is owing to this. To acquire a curl or a break back is most difficult, and the highest amount of credit is due to bowlers who have gained this skill.

Heavily handicapped as the bowler is by the smooth wicket, is he not entitled to a little consideration when all his efforts to bowl a man by a breaking ball are neutralised by the leg and not the bat? It may be reckoned a certainty that neither Dark nor Caldecourt could have foreseen the prevalence of modern leg play; if Dark had done so he would have supported Caldecourt. Now surely it is no small reason why the law should be altered if a state of things has arisen, altogether unsportsmanlike and utterly unforeseen, in consequence of the interpretation of a certain rule which in old times was by certain umpires treated differently? We can only hope that the force of public opinion will cause the Marylebone Club to reconsider their judgment. Before we leave this subject we cannot help expressing an opinion that, impartial as the M.C.C. sub-committee may be, it was a pity so little of the bowling element was represented on it. It is the bowlers who have most cause to grumble at the modern leg play; but with the exception of Mr. Ridley and Mr. V. E. Walker, both lob bowlers, the committee consisted of past or present batsmen entirely, or at any rate of members whose chief *forte* was batting and not bowling. However, the homily which was finally adopted has been preached, and it may have effect. We hope it will.

Some good results, however, followed the conference of the M.C.C., which was held just prior to the writing of these remarks. The position of affairs about 4 o'clock on the third day of a match, stumps having to be drawn at 7, until lately very often was that the in side were two or three hundred runs on and only five wickets down. The captain of the side, seeing that if his men played their natural game the match must be drawn, instructed them to get out. What followed was merely a burlesque of cricket. The batsmen knocked down their wickets or ran themselves out, while the out side, knowing that they could not win, and not wanting to be defeated, as they would have been if they had gone in to bat, wasted time by actually bowling no-balls, and refusing to put the wicket down or hold catches.

The captain of the in side, by the new rule of the M.C.C., now has the power at any stage he likes of the second innings of his side to declare that the innings is over. Say that his side is 250 ahead and the time is 4 o'clock. The other side have consequently to go in for nearly three hours' batting, and of course in that time they may get out, and the match instead of being drawn may be finished. The runs may not be so numerous, the captain may make a mistake, and the out side may go in and win the match. That is a risk which the captain has to run, but he runs a certain risk now when he tells his men to get out on purpose, and he saves cricket from becoming ridiculous. Besides, it is hard on the young professional to be obliged to get out on purpose ; cricket is his business, and a low average might handicap him in his profession.

A small reform that the Australians advocated has also been suggested. The M.C.C. committee have recommended an increase in the number of balls in an over from four to five, and herein we think that they have acted wisely.

The conclusion we arrive at as an upshot of the whole matter is that the recommendations already made are wise and will improve the game, and that still further improvements will ensue if the following regulations become the law of each ground:—(1.) Stricter observance of the rules of time both between the innings and between the fall of each wicket. (2.) A new rule ordaining that matches begin at 11.30 or 12 on the first day, and at 11 sharp on the second and third days. On the leg before wicket question we hold that a change in the law would be better than the little sermon of the M.C.C., but the latter may nevertheless do good, and we sincerely hope it will.

INDEX.

———◆◇◆———

E E